Bath University Library

THE
SUBNORMAL MIND

UNIVERSITY OF LONDON
HEATH CLARK LECTURES, 1933
delivered at
The London School of Hygiene and Tropical Medicine

The
Subnormal Mind

By

SIR CYRIL BURT

THIRD EDITION

OXFORD UNIVERSITY PRESS

Oxford University Press, Walton Street, Oxford OX2 6DP

OXFORD LONDON GLASGOW NEW YORK
TORONTO MELBOURNE WELLINGTON CAPE TOWN
IBADAN NAIROBI DAR ES SALAAM LUSAKA ADDIS ABABA
KUALA LUMPUR SINGAPORE JAKARTA HONG KONG TOKYO
DELHI BOMBAY CALCUTTA MADRAS KARACHI

ISBN 0 19 261130 5

© OXFORD UNIVERSITY PRESS 1977

FIRST EDITION 1935
SECOND EDITION 1937
THIRD EDITION 1955
RE-ISSUED WITH A NEW FOREWORD 1977

PRINTED IN GREAT BRITAIN
BY BILLING & SONS LIMITED
GUILDFORD, LONDON AND WORCESTER

FOREWORD

PROFESSOR H. J. EYSENCK

Professor of Psychology
Institute of Psychiatry, London

SIR Cyril Burt was probably Great Britain's most outstanding psychologist in the years between the wars; and his influence has been tremendous, not only in academic psychology but also in various applied fields, ranging from educational to abnormal, and from criminological to industrial. He showed certain qualities which are rarely combined in one and the same person. In the first place, he was obviously a brilliantly *original* person who introduced new methods, new theories, and new ways of looking at psychological phenomena. His early work on psychometrics and statistics, particularly his contributions to factor analysis, have been absolutely fundamental, and later on his work on the statistical analysis of human behavioural genetics provided an essential link between the early work of Sir Ronald Fisher, and the methods which are now current.

Burt's second most outstanding quality, and it is one which is seldom combined with originality, was *balance*. The measured rhythm of his sentences, consciously imitating Macaulay, was matched by his habit of never over-emphasizing one side or the other, but carefully putting the case for both and assigning the correct weighting to all the competing causal factors suggested by different authors. The debate concerning the influence of heredity and environment (or nature and nurture as he preferred to call it) on intelligence provides a good example, in which there had been an endless see-saw battle between extremists. Locke and his school preached a total environmentalism, in which the mind was simply a *tabula rasa* on which the environment could inscribe anything it wished; in the nineteenth century, on the other hand, there arose a strong hereditarian school which tried to account for all human differences entirely in genetic terms. Burt went out of his way to look at both genetic and environmental causes, to try and measure the importance of each, and to arrive at a balanced conclusion which would once and for all stop this absurd swing of the pendulum from one over-emphasis to an opposing one.

When Burt wrote *The Subnormal Mind*, which was originally delivered as a series of lectures at the London School of Hygiene and Tropical Medicine (the Heath Clark Lectures in 1933), he brought the qualities of originality and of balance to bear on a very unwieldy and complex topic. He treated subnormality not only as a lack of intelligence, as many modern writers would tend to do, and he did indeed deal with dullness and backwardness, but he also dealt with other aspects of behaviour which might be called 'subnormal'—delinquency and neurosis, for instance, are as disabling and as 'subnormal' as is simple intellectual backwardness. For anyone interested in children and their development, he painted a masterful picture of what was known about these conditions, based very largely on his own rich experience as educational psychologist to the London County Council. The book was meant to be popular rather than a report of original research work, and it can be read quite easily by the intelligent man in the street; Burt never submitted to the American habit of regarding a book as academic and scientific only if it indulged in the ugly jargon of the sociologist or the social psychologist. He always wrote clearly, intelligibly, and with a respect for the English language born of his love of literature and poetry. Much of what the book said was novel when it was published, and is commonplace now; how does the message contained in it stand up to modern scrutiny?

Let us look first of all at the question of mental defect. Burt clearly differentiated between two major causes of mental defects. One of these is environmental, in the widest sense, and Burt gives a typically detailed and balanced account of the many possible environmental causes for low intelligence and backwardness in school. But the other and much more important cause is genetic. Burt was among the first to stress the influence of heredity on individual differences in intelligence, and although he also collected data to support this, the case for the importance of heredity in this field is not of course based entirely or even mainly on his work; it rests much more broadly on literally hundreds of studies carried out all over the world, using many different experimental paradigms.

At the time Burt was delivering these lectures it was taken for granted by all competent geneticists and psychologists that the case had been made for the genetic determination of IQ, with a relatively less important environmental contribution; Burt uses data to illustrate the point, and he also uses these data didactically to demonstrate new methods of analysis. He never intended his work to be used as the main or solitary proof for these conclusions. The whole conception of genetic determination of IQ has come under strong attack recently, and some individuals, not necessarily known for their scientific contributions in this field, have come forward to deny completely the influence of genetic factors. It may be useful to summarize briefly the many directions which the search in this field has taken, all leading to very much the same conclusion, namely that of the total variance in IQ, something like 80 per cent is due to genetic factors, and something like 20 per cent due to environmental factors.

It would of course be wrong to imagine that the search for heritability is the only or even the major purpose of empirical work in this field. This is quite untrue. What the geneticist is trying to do is to construct a model containing all the major factors active in a given field, and to assign some quantitative estimates to the importance each of the different factors has in that field. Thus a modern model lists additive genetic factors as one item, and additive environmental factors as another. These however are far from being the only parts of the model. The geneticist also posits several different types of *interaction* between environmental and genetic factors; he posits non-additive genetic factors, such as assortative mating (the tendency of bright men to marry bright women and vice versa) and dominance or recessiveness (high intelligence is dominant over low intelligence). It would be too technical an exercise to describe here the model in all its detail, or to go into a discussion of the differences between within-family and between-family environmental and genetic factors; let it merely be said that the exercise is a highly complex one demanding great statistical ingenuity, and no one lacking in a strong background in genetic theory, and without specialized training in the statistical methods involved, can understand the intricacy of the results of all this work.

Let me illustrate how we can determine some of the factors involved. Assortative mating of course is relatively easy; all we have to do is to measure the IQ of large numbers of married men and women, and then correlate their IQs. Usually this amounts to something like 0·6 or thereabouts, indicating a considerable degree of congruence between spouses. This is true of intelligence, but is not true, oddly enough, of temperament or personality, where the correlations are nearly always around zero.

How can we determine the presence of dominance? It is well known in genetics that whenever a character is inherited in the dominant fashion then we find a phenomenon called 'inbreeding depression'. What this means is simply that when people who have some form of familial relationship marry (e.g. cousin marriages), their children have a lower IQ than would the children of equally intelligent parents not familially related. This effect is of course due to the undue number of recessive alleles in related people which lead to the emergence of the recessively inherited traits i.e., in this case, low intelligence. This inbreeding depression has been found both in Japan and in Arab countries, where cousin marriages are fairly frequent, and it has of course also been found in the rather rare instances of brother–sister marriages. This is just one example of the many that could be given indicating the way in which the geneticist looks for specific types of information in rather unusual groups of people.

One major source of evidence for the influence of heredity is the study of identical and fraternal twins. Identical twins brought up in separation provide interesting evidence for the importance of heredity; it is usually found that identical twins brought up in separation from each other are almost if not quite as similar in intelligence as are identical twins brought up together. Identical twins brought up together, or apart from each other, are certainly much more alike than are fraternal twins brought up together. This is very powerful evidence for the importance of heredity, in view of the fact that identical twins share identical heredity, whereas fraternal twins share only 50 per cent heredity on the average, i.e. are no more alike genetically than siblings born at different times.

Another powerful source of evidence is the study of familial relations. One knows from genetic theory the average amount of genetic concordance between parents and children, uncles and nieces, siblings, and various other types of relatives; on a genetic basis this should correspond with different degrees of similarity in intelligence, and many studies have shown that there is very good correspondence between these two lines of evidence. Familial studies comprise probably the most widely used method of genetic analysis, and have been carried out in many different countries, with very positive results.

The geneticist can also make use of certain genetic phenomena little known to the man in the street. Let me illustrate this by referring to regression and pleiotropy. By regression is meant the well-known effect that very tall parents have tall children, but that these tend to be less tall than the parents—they regress to the mean of the whole population. Similarly parents who are very short have children who are also shorter than the average, but tend to be taller than their parents; in other words they, too, regress towards the mean. This has been found equally true of intelligence, and as regression is predicted by genetic theory, and as the degree of regression is a good measure of heritability, this phenomenon has been a very useful one in determining the amount of heritability. Pleiotropy is the genetic term used to refer to the fact that one single gene can sometimes influence two totally different and disparate characters. As an example consider the shape of the mandibular symphysis (the jaw bone). This can be measured very accurately by means of X-rays, and has been found to be quite highly correlated with intelligence! No environmental influences are known to affect the shape of the mandibular symphysis, and the fairly high correlation between it and intelligence can hardly be explained on other than genetic grounds.

Adopted children provide a quite different type of evidence again for the importance of genetic factors. Adopted children are very much more like their true parents than their adopted parents as far as intelligence is concerned, although the adopted parents in fact provide their environment, in many cases almost from the day of birth. This is very powerful evidence, and is very difficult to argue against. Altogether adopted children are a rich source of information. It is possible to correlate their intelligence with certain environmental properties of the adopted home, such as socio-economic status of the parents, their educational level, the drive for educational achievement in the home, the number of books, nutrition, and many other factors of the same kind. When these are all separately measured and then combined to give the maximum correlation between the adopted child's IQ and environmental facilitation, the outcome is that the environment as so measured accounts for less than 20 per cent of the total IQ differences observed in the children.

It would be possible to go on and give a more detailed account of these and other methods that have been used to verify the hypotheses which Burt outlined in this book, but this would be a task of supererogation. Few theories have been more strongly supported, and have a wider factual basis, than the one linking intellectual achievement with genetic factors. Burt drew many practical consequences from this theory, and in spite of what many left-wing politicians assert nowadays it seems that he was essentially right in his prescriptions for educational and other social policies. The disastrous consequences of deviating from these prescriptions are now becoming apparent, even to those who enthusiastically welcomed the doctrines of total egalitarianism. Burt's balanced view on all these matters has been replaced by fanatical and factually unsupported enthusiasm for instant solutions which in the nature of the case cannot exist. Policies based on these enthusiasms rather than on fact can only have consequences which we all shall rue.

Some doubts have recently been thrown on Burt's own work on the heritability of IQ, and a few words may be said about this episode, and the suggestion that Burt faked his data.

This accusation of fraud originated with the London newspaper, the *Sunday Times*. Its medical correspondent, Oliver Gillie, had just published a popular book on what he called 'the genetic controversy', and apparently considered the opportunity ripe for launching an all-out attack on the man who was probably Britain's outstanding psychologist for many years, who had been knighted for his services to education, and who had achieved world fame for his contributions to psychometrics, to social psychology, and to behavioural genetics. Basically, it was alleged (1) that Burt had published articles in collaboration with two ladies whose very existence Gillie doubted; he suggested that, in spite of consulting people close to Burt, looking at registers at University College, where Burt was Professor for many years, and even advertising in the papers, he had been unable to find any trace of these mysterious ladies. (2) A second allegation was that Burt had guessed rather than measured the IQs of many of his subjects, and (3) the third major accusation was that he had on some 20 occasions published data in which the numbers of subjects varied, but not certain statistics, such as the correlation between the twins constituting the samples. On these grounds Gillie accused Burt of forgery, and suggested that this might be one of the great scientific frauds of the century. He found support in a well-orchestrated chorus of condemnation of Burt by various psychologists, none of whom had actually worked in the behavioural genetics field, and the '*affaire* Burt' soon became an international scandal. Gillie and his followers also suggested that the facts disclosed would inevitably lead to a complete reconsideration of the whole argument about the influence of genetics on IQ, the IQ and race debate, and various other important issues.

On the face of it, there seemed to be some substance in what Gillie alleged; looking closer, however, one gets a whiff of McCarthyism, of deliberate smear campaigns, and of character assassination. Let us first of all assume that what Gillie suggested is in fact true. He did not even begin to suggest that Burt actually *forged* his data, or dealt with them fraudulently. The *possibility* that he did cannot *a priori* be ruled out, but unless we abandon completely the principle that a man must be considered innocent until proved guilty the insistence on fraud, on faking, on intentional misdemeanour seems a little premature. What Gillie might justifiably have said might have been that there were certain inconsistencies in Burt's data which called in question the interpretation which might be

put upon them; to go further than that can hardly be considered
a fair deduction, simple decency, or even justifiable criticism.
If Burt had indeed been careless, then his scientific reputation
would inevitably suffer; that is the low of scientific endeavour.
With this it is impossible to argue; if there is any question at all
about a set of data or calculations, then that set must be
eliminated from serious discussion.

Let us look at the accusations. The first relates to the alleged
non-existence of two female co-authors of Burt's, both associated with him in the authorship of papers published in the
British Journal of Statistical Psychology, edited at the time by
Sir Cyril. Professor J. Cohen, of Manchester University, has
since written to say that he was acquainted with one of the
two when he was at University College, as a student of Burt's;
this rather weakens the force of this particular charge. One
also wonders how seriously Dr. Gillie took his task of investigation when he failed to contact Professor Cohen, known as one
of Burt's most eminent pupils, or myself, also one of Burt's
pupils at the same time. I think one must conclude that this
first charge is not only false, but possibly malicious and founded
on carelessness and imperfect investigative procedure.

We must next turn, after this comic interlude of the missing
ladies, to the much more serious accusation of errors in calculation. Here the situation is rather different. Some four or five
years ago, Professor Arthur Jensen went through all the
published articles of Sir Cyril (as well as much other material)
to bring together and re-analyse evidence concerning the
inheritance of intelligence. He discovered 20 cases where Sir
Cyril had re-analysed twin data several times, adding new
cases each time; thus the number of cases in the analyses
differed. However, some of the results, such as the correlations
between twins, were identical from analysis to analysis, even
to the third decimal. This is so unlikely as to be practically
impossible, and as Jensen says: 'Any particular instance of an
invariant r despite a changed N can be rationalised as being
not too improbable. But 20 such instances unduly strain the
laws of chance and can only mean error, at least in some cases.
But error there surely must be.' Jensen concluded that Burt's
data could no longer be relied upon for further analysis and

theory-testing, and had to be rejected as useless, a conclusion which it is difficult to find fault with. Note that it does not contain any suggestion of fraud, but simply of error, possibly of carelessness. These are serious accusations to bring against a scientist, but they do not carry the implications of Gillie's unjustified attacks.

What are the reasons for these errors? Here again I must side with Jensen, who writes: 'The reporting of kinship correlations at times with and at times without noting the sample size, the rather inconsistent reporting of sample sizes, the higher than ordinary rate of misprints in Burt's published tables . . ., and the quite casual description of the tests and the exact procedures and methods of data analysis all stand in quite strange and marked contrast to the theoretical aspects of Burt's writings in this field, which were elegantly and meticulously composed, with profound erudition and impressive technical sophistication. It is almost as if Burt regarded the actual data as merely an incidental backdrop for the illustration of the theoretical issues in quantitative genetics, which, to him, seemed always to hold the centre of the stage.' This is well said, and from personal knowledge of Burt's attitude I think almost certainly true. One must bear in mind that at the time of data collection and calculation, standards of evidence were less strict than today, and it would be wrong to judge anyone whose work in this field was begun before his critics had been born, by today's standards. We shall just have to collect our own data, paying attention to the more rigorous standards of today, and make use of the advances in data analysis and model building which we owe to Sir Cyril, without hysterical accusations of fraudulence and fake. We should also pay attention, I think, to the fact that the errors were discovered by Arthur Jensen, several years ago, and published by him in the journal *Behavior Genetics*; the sensationalized version published by Dr. Gillie does not even mention this fact, and suggests that his investigative zeal was responsible for amassing the evidence which led to Sir Cyril's 'unmasking'.

We still have to consider the third accusation, namely that Burt did not measure IQs, but in part at least attributed them on a purely subjective basis. Here again we must take an historical point of view. When Sir Cyril began his work, there were no standardized tests of intelligence in existence; he was the first to introduce such tests into England. Hence for some time he was working with tests he was standardizing, and with novel test problems he was trying out. This made it impossible for him to list the tests used, as would be done today. But there is an additional point, relevant to his use of 'final assessments' instead of raw IQ scores. As Burt used to argue, the IQ is an imperfect measure of the wholly innate 'intelligence' which we are trying to measure. The IQ is an imperfect measure because the genetic part is disturbed by environmental effects, such as poor upbringing, bad schooling, etc. If we could get evidence on these 'perturbations', then we could correct the observed values of the IQ, and thus come nearer to the 'true' values of the child's (or adult's) intelligence. Thus two children might both have an IQ of 120; yet he would argue that if one of these came from a poor, badly educated, and generally deprived home, while the other came from a typical upper middle-class home, then the former child clearly was born with a superior intelligence, and his IQ should be corrected upwards, and that of the other child should be corrected downwards. This is the origin of his 'adjusted scores', and with someone of his unrivalled expertise and experience in this field the method would almost certainly produce results nearer to the genotype (i.e. the inherited degree of intelligence) than would the uncorrected IQ. This method does not amount to any attempt at fraudulence, but is a reasonable, although unfortunately highly subjective, effort to derive the best available assessment of a child's inherited ability. We would nowadays prefer to do this by giving numerical values to the various environmental elements entering into the calculation, and combining them for the purpose of correction in a proper regression formula. This in effect was what Sir Cyril did, but unfortunately he never published the details, and to that extent he was culpable by our present-day standards. This again is a far cry from complaints of faking or arbitary invention of data. Note also that Dr. Gillie was far from having 'discovered' these possible aberrations; Jensen published a detailed account of the criticisms to be made of Burt's methods of work in 1974, and anticipated all later complaints. Thus Gillie is merely sensationalizing, in a particularly nasty and suggestive form, facts brought out in a dignified and reasonable way by Jensen.

One further point should be noted. For an experienced psychologist to interview a child, or an adult, and suggest a reasonable IQ estimate is far from black magic or fraud. It is well known what children of different IQ can achieve in the way of reading, writing, general knowledge, etc. at different ages, and obtaining information on these points from parents, teachers, and others enables the experienced child psychologist to give a tentative estimate which is unlikely to be far out. Catherine Cox Miles, a collaborator of Terman's in his famous studies of genius, published a most interesting book in which she took hundreds of historical figures, such as Napoleon, Goethe, Macaulay, Mill, etc., and estimated their IQs on the basis of such material as was available about their childhood performances. We would nowadays have some methodological and other objections to this kind of analysis, but at the time it was accepted as perfectly valid, and to criticize Sir Cyril in terms of our present-day more critical standards for what at the time of his work was considered perfectly admissible seems a trifle hypercritical.

In addition to his studies of intelligence, Burt's work on delinquency is rightly famous. In this book he devotes one chapter to the delinquent, and in doing so again displays his usual balance of judgment. Dealing with 'moral deficiency' for instance he points out that this was a phrase introduced to denote an innate defect in an innate moral faculty. He goes on to say, 'This conception we have already examined. We found no evidence for it whatever. The phrase, in short, is wholly misleading, and should be dropped in favour of some other form of words, such as "temperamental deficiency". This would accurately describe a mental state which, though far rarer than so-called moral deficiency is assumed to be, undoubtedly exists. The temperamentally defective are not necessarily immoral, but they may easily become so.' In these words Burt has anticipated much modern research which has indicated a strong correlation between personality and anti-social conduct; and indeed it seems very likely that the genetic determination of criminal behaviour, for which there is also much evidence, is largely mediated by these temperamental factors.

Burt was also right in his assessment of the possibility of rectifying the temperamental defects from which delinquents suffer. As he points out, 'when certified and sent to a specially organized institution, they often gain sufficient stability to be allowed out on licence, and may eventually prove capable of maintaining themselves satisfactorily by regular employment, and give no further grounds for anxiety on account of bad conduct. Experience, indeed, shows that, while intellectual deficiency is almost impossible to cure, so-called moral deficiency—granted favourable conditions, and judicious treatment starting from an early age—can very often be remedied. Character is as amenable to training as intellectual disabilities are resistant. That is a point which practical psychology continually verifies: a man's intelligence is limited from birth; his character is far more plastic, and can be developed for evil or for good. The innate presence of certain temperamental disabilities, like the innate lack of intelligence, may no doubt render that training far more difficult. But it should not lead us to abandon all hope of treatment, and imagine that the only course to take with such cases is to condemn them forever to an institutional life.' This quotation is of interest because Burt has been accused of 'therapeutic nihilism', i.e. of attributing all behaviour to genetic causes and allowing no room for environmental intervention. Nothing could be further from the truth, as this passage clearly indicates.

In his treatment of the neuroses, too, Burt has shown his uncanny anticipation of future developments in the field. He divides neuroses into the asthenic neuroses, embracing such forms as anxiety states, 'neurasthenia', and quite generally the 'fatigue-neuroses'. These he contrasts with the 'sthenic' neuroses, i.e. 'those forms of neurosis that seem to arise chiefly in temperaments of an aggressive rather than of an inhibited type'. As he goes on to say, 'it is not generally realised that these are instances of neurotic disorder quite as much as those that are marked by worry, depression, or fatigue. To the teacher and the parent children of this type may seem naughty rather than nervous. Unlike the former group, they usually look healthy, happy, and strong; and accordingly no suspicion of a morbid disturbance may ever be aroused.' These sthenic neuroses often shade into criminal behaviour, and the distinction between the asthenic and the sthenic neuroses corresponds closely to modern conceptions of introversion and extroversion. To the reader interested in the young or older child suffering from some form of neurotic disability, what Burt had to say 40 years ago is still of much greater value than all the volumes of psychoanalytic and psychotherapeutic writings that have been accumulating in the meantime. He was a great observer and was able in a unique manner to link his observational faculties with his scientific knowledge. That indeed was his great forte, and few psychologists before or since have equalled him in that.

Altogether then, although there have been great developments and much research done since the balmy pre-war years when Burt wrote his book, there has been no real change in the general way in which we look at the subnormal mind. Many details have been added to the picture, and much supporting evidence has been brought forward in one direction or the other, but the broad outline is still very much as Burt painted it. Scientific books usually have a fairly short lifetime; as new knowledge develops so older books fall by the wayside. This one is an exception. If an interested layman were to ask me what book to read in order to get a good introduction to the subnormal mind, I would be hard put to suggest anything better than Burt's book, now happily available again. Even for the psychologically sophisticated reader the book may still be of value. In re-reading it for the purpose of writing this foreword I was constantly amazed at the way in which Burt had anticipated later discoveries and developments. When I read the book as a student, I was of course unable to realize the direction research would take, or the developments that would be taking place; I simply accepted what he had to say as the summary of the present position. It is only in retrospect that one can see how far beyond the then present position Burt went, and how his extrapolations from knowledge then available have been justified by more recent studies. Few scientists can wish for a better testimonial!

PREFACE TO THE THIRD EDITION

THE primary aim of these lectures was to describe, in a form intelligible to those having no special knowledge of psychology, the various types of mental subnormality encountered among children, and to discuss their causes, diagnosis, and practical treatment. At the same time I hoped that results already achieved in a field where the problems were comparatively simple and the scientific methods firmly established, might indicate how the various psychological techniques, developed during recent years, could be adopted with some prospect of success for the study of the obscurer and far more controversial problems of mental disorder among adults. Since this book was first published, the interest in clinical psychology, particularly as applied to school children, has rapidly expanded, and spread to a far wider public. Accordingly, in preparing this revised edition, I have tried to make it useful, not only to the school medical officer and the general practitioner, but also to teachers, education officials, clinical psychologists, and indeed all who are concerned with the welfare of the child.

Contrary to current opinion, child psychology is itself a plant of native origin, not an exotic imported from beyond the Atlantic. The first to attempt a scientific study of the subject were the founders of the British evolutionary school —Darwin, Spencer, Galton, and their immediate disciples. Then, towards the close of the nineteenth century, stimulated by Galton's novel proposals, James Sully, Professor of Mind and Logic at University College, London, established a psychological laboratory in connexion with his education department, and founded an Association for Child Study. 'Child Guidance' was his term (a literal translation of the Greek παιδαγωγία) for the practical application of scientific methods to the treatment and training of young children, particularly those who are mentally subnormal. In 1913 the London Education Authority resolved to introduce what was the first—and for long the only—official scheme of child guidance in this country, and appointed its own psychologist. The facts reported in the following pages and the conclusions deduced were drawn mainly from work which I carried out in that capacity with the aid of London teachers, social workers, and school doctors.

In undertaking our preliminary surveys the procedure which we gradually worked out has proved a most useful instrument of research. It was based on a combination of the method of case-study with the methods of statistical analysis. The intensive study of individual cases was used chiefly to suggest hypotheses. In every inquiry the group of cases which formed the central problem—the dull, the defective, the delinquent, or the neurotic—was examined side by side with a parallel group of normal children. The mass of data so obtained was then subjected to a rigorous statistical analysis in order to confirm or to confute the various tentative hypotheses that had been put forward by others or seemed to issue from the facts themselves.

During the twenty years that have elapsed since the results were first collated and published, numerous child guidance centres have been established in London and elsewhere, and knowledge of the subject has greatly increased. In the main, however, this further experience has ratified rather than modified the general views advanced in this book; and the few changes or additions that have seemed necessary consist mainly of added evidence and fuller references. Most of these have been incorporated in notes inserted at the end of each chapter.

The passing of the Education Act in 1944, with its revolutionary provisions regarding the instruction and treatment of what it describes as 'mentally handicapped children', has placed new responsibilities upon the educational and medical services, and thus fostered a growing interest in the scientific approach to such problems. The old improvised procedures, based on common sense or personal experience, will no longer suffice. And there is a widespread desire that they should be replaced by more objective modes of investigation and treatment, whose value has been checked by systematic research.

The changes introduced by the Act, and by the Regulations issued by the Ministry, have entailed a few minor emendations in the pages that follow. The most important relate to the treatment of the mentally deficient. In the chapter on this subject I had ventured to urge that, during the school period at any rate, 'the dull and defective should be treated as forming one broad problem'. This the new Act now proposes to do. Quite rightly, it has abolished the certification of what used to be called 'educable defectives'; and it groups together the dull, the backward, and the mentally deficient under the comprehensive heading of 'educationally subnormal'. Nevertheless, from the standpoint of practical treatment, it is still convenient for both doctor and teacher to distinguish the various grades and types of mental retardation included within that wider term.

It is encouraging to find that most of the views which were put forward in the following pages, and which were regarded at the time as either new or controversial, have since gained increasing acceptance. The criticisms urged by those who were good enough to review the first and second editions rested, I fancy, more on misunderstanding than on any real disagreement with what I briefly stated or took implicitly for granted. To them I owe at least some brief reply. In particular there are two basic principles running through the whole of the book that appear to call for a slightly fuller defence. For each of them much additional evidence has accumulated during the last two decades.

The most fundamental was the view that the medical practitioner is concerned, not with a series of clinical entities called diseases, each with its specific material cause, but with individual patients, every one of whom is a living psychophysical organism, reacting as a unique and complex whole to environmental disturbances. As I argued in discussing the general nature of nervous disorder (p. 199), the cardinal error in the traditional notion of mental illness springs from the fact that it was based, not necessarily on a materialistic conception, but on a mechanistic conception, of the mind. Freud's theory of neurotic disorders is not materialistic, like the theories of Maudsley or Mercier; but it is certainly mechanistic. Now organisms are something more than mere machines; they are alive. Hence for the older oversimplified notions we have to substitute a biological conception of the working of the mind and of the causes of its disorders.

Adaptation or adjustment is essentially a biological process. The 'maladjustments' on which Sully and other evolutionary psychologists laid so much stress are not the maladjustments of a mechanism, whose parts have got out of gear, but the maladjustments of a living creature to an environment which is packed with other creatures like itself.[1]

This view carried with it a protest against three common mistakes which even today hamper much of the study and treatment of mental disorders. First, the physician must treat his patient, not as a mere physico-chemical apparatus, with some specific structure deranged or impaired: he must regard him as a more or less integrated biological unit. Secondly, he must not regard the mind as one part and the body as another part (or collection of parts); he must think of his patient as a complex psychophysical whole, to be examined, no matter whether his illness be 'mental or physical', 'functional or organic', from *both* a psychological *and* a physical standpoint. But thirdly, the physician must not be content with a mere 'clinical' examination of the patient and nothing but the patient, seeing him, as it were, stripped in bed, as though he were just looking for a broken rib or an inflamed appendix; he must picture him in his everyday

[1] Among recent medical writers, Dr. J. L. Halliday and Dr. R. R. Bomford have accepted and emphasized a very similar point of view. Dr. Halliday sums it up with exceptional lucidity. The old view of aetiology, he says, was 'mechanismic': it held that 'the human organism is a machine composed of mutually adjusted parts; illness corresponds to a breakdown in the machine'. The newer 'biological' aetiology regards illness 'not as a fault in the parts but as a reaction or mode of behaviour; the cause is therefore twofold, and is to be sought in the nature of the individual and the nature of the environment' ('Principles of Aetiology', *Brit. J. Med. Psychol.* xix, 1943, pp. 368 f.). Dr. Bomford preaches the same doctrine, and draws a practical corollary which cannot be too strongly affirmed. 'Medical action should be designed (*a*) to alter the characteristics of the person known to be causal, and (*b*) to alleviate or remove factors of the environment known to be causal' ('Changing Concepts of Health and Disease, with Particular Reference to Psychosomatic Medicine', *Brit. Med. Journ.*, 1953, pp. 633-9).

life, reacting to the stresses and demands of his own peculiar environment. It is not so much the individual that he must investigate as the interaction between the individual and his surroundings.

This standpoint is tacitly recognized in provisions laid down in the recent Education Act. For the first time in any statutory enactment 'the maladjusted' are named as a group of children requiring official recognition and special consideration and provision. Where the sole or primary cause for the maladjustment lies in the child's environment, the problem in the main is social or administrative, and will concern us only indirectly here. In this book I have dealt chiefly with those cases in which the personal factor is also influential; so that the maladjustment really springs (as it does in the vast majority of cases) from a twofold source.[1]

Much has been written during recent years about what is sometimes called the 'psychosomatic hypothesis'. But the phrase is used in two different senses. Properly interpreted, the 'psychosomatic hypothesis' implies an unqualified rejection of the old Cartesian dualism which depicted man as a body *plus* a mind, or (as I put it in my opening chapter) 'a corpse coupled with a ghost'. Ψυχάριον εἶ βαστάζον νεκρόν, said the old Stoic slave.[2] Yet the antithesis may be most misleading. Nor is the contrary view—which holds that each human being, and every individual organism that shows signs of conscious life, must be thought of as a 'psychophysical unity'—by any means a recent innovation. It was one of the main contributions of the evolutionary school of psychology, endorsed even by philosophical writers like Ward and Broad. But, since the term 'psychophysical' had itself been used in a rather specialized sense, they sometimes substituted the name 'psychosomatic' to avoid confusion.

More recently, however, many medical writers have borrowed the word as the slogan for a somewhat narrower doctrine. The earlier materialists had laid great stress on

[1] For the history of the concept of 'maladjustment' and for the main types to be encountered, see C. Burt and M. Howard, 'The Nature and Causes of Maladjustment among Children of School Age', *Brit. J. Psychol. Stat. Sect.*, v, 1952, pp. 39–58.
[2] Epictetus, quoted by Marcus Aurelius, *Meditations*, v, p. 4.

the fact that mental symptoms might often be produced—indeed some alleged that they were always produced—by physical disturbances; and the phrase 'psychosomatic medicine' was coined to stress the complementary fact that in certain so-called 'functional' disorders physical symptoms may be produced by mental disturbances.[1] Unfortunately those psychiatrists who limit their study to this latter group are still apt to treat body and mind as two distinct entities, and overlook the fact that *all* illnesses are really psychosomatic disorders. Their accounts sometimes recall the story of the automaton that played chess and draughts: the doll was operated by a legless youngster hidden in the base, and more than once, when defeated in a hard-fought game, he lost his temper and began to wreak his vengeance by breaking the box. In much the same fashion the mind is supposed to work most of the time like a purely physical mechanism, but in cases of stress or disorder to be capable of acting in some mysterious fashion directly on the body and to produce startling effects of its own.

The second of the two important assumptions on which my discussion was based evoked more vigorous criticism at the time, but has, I think, been amply justified by later work. This was the contention that the human mind—or, to avoid dualistic terminology, let us say the human personality—has a definite underlying structure. The theory was strenuously contested by psychological critics on the ground that it implied a discredited doctrine of mental faculties, and was just a 'refurbished version of the notions popularized by nineteenth-century phrenologists'. The later associationists, like their modern representatives, the behaviourists, had argued that all concrete mental processes could be adequately explained in terms of one fundamental law, that of association. The 'law of association' still forms

---

[1] The interest in 'psychosomatic medicine' in this narrower sense begins with Dr. Helen Dunbar's book (published just after these lectures were given) on *Emotions and Bodily Changes.* It was followed a year or two later by an American journal specifically devoted to *Psychosomatic Medicine* (1943), and by Dr. Dunbar's larger volume on *Psychosomatic Diagnosis* (1943). For an excellent criticism of the narrower interpretation, see R. R. Bomford, *loc. cit. sup.*

the main stand-by of most physiological and medical writers. The materialists, from Huxley and Maudsley to Pawlow and his American disciples, assume that every phenomenon of the mind, conscious or unconscious, can be accounted for by the physiological linking or 'conditioning' of reflexes. The psycho-analysts, Freud, Jung, Adler, and their followers, tacitly rely on much the same principle. Even among more orthodox psychologists, most of whom would repudiate associationism in its cruder forms, many still find it difficult to accept the view that the mental endowment of every human being is based upon the same general ground plan. 'The mind', says Sir Godfrey Thomson, 'has hardly any structure. . . . Compared with the body it is Protean and plastic, lacking in separate or specialized organs.' Spearman similarly rejects the notion of specialized abilities or specialized instincts, and holds that what seems to be a coherent structure is imposed by training, experience, and individual interests. Thurstone, who admits the existence of special abilities, treats them as an entirely unsystematic and miscellaneous collection—a haphazard set of handy tools, not an orderly equipment of biological functions: he gives us, not a mind, but the *disjecta membra* of a mind.

This noncommittal doctrine has brought with it two practical disadvantages. First, the enterprising amateur is left free to fill the vacuum with his own improvised ideas about the make-up of the human personality. The result has been innumerable fanciful pictures based on the passing interests or the unverified conjectures of the inventor, with the most dramatic versions securing widest attention. Secondly, the more conscientious investigator is deprived of any systematic scheme to guide his examinations or provide a basis for his reports. Consider what might happen had the medical inspection of school children been handed over to persons who knew nothing of anatomy and who were therefore at liberty either to fabricate their own conceptions of the inner structure of the body or even to suppose that it had no structure at all.

The view put forward in this book, and reinforced by an

abundance of empirical evidence, is that the mind has a definite constitution, and that its structure is, to borrow a term popularized by Hughlings Jackson and Sherrington, hierarchical. It maintains that in the course of evolution mental life has become increasingly differentiated. As a result the human mind exhibits three distinguishable aspects —cognitive, affective, and conative—and four main levels— sensory, perceptual, associative, and relational. Each aspect and each level is characterized by its own generic factor; and each generic factor in turn becomes differentiated into a succession of subordinate factors, each characterizing certain species and subspecies of mental activity. To determine what precisely are the more important components is the essential task of what is sometimes termed factor analysis. Tentative hypotheses as to their nature and manifestations are derived from various fields of investigation—observation, introspection, biology, neurology, pathology, and the application of tests or questionnaires. But the verification or refutation of the various hypotheses must be the outcome of carefully planned statistical research; and factor analysis is simply an adaptation for such purposes of the stock procedure of ordinary dynamics—the resolution of tendencies or 'forces' into their hypothetical components. The conclusions so reached, in addition to their fruitful contributions to our knowledge of the mind, provide a valuable working scheme for taking case-histories.

The idea of introducing quantitative methods, and particularly statistical techniques, into the study of the human mind encountered vehement opposition both from physiologists of the behaviourist school and from psychiatrists of the Freudian and Jungian schools. Many of their objections were due to a misunderstanding of what the statistical psychologist is attempting to do. He does not for one moment suggest that the experimental methods of the laboratory or the observational methods of the clinic should be abandoned in favour of a mathematical juggling with test-measurements. Tests are desirable to ensure standardization; but they provide only a modicum of the psychologist's data. Statistical analysis is not an alternative, but an adjunct, to other methods of inquiry: it is not a substitute, but a supplement; and its purpose is not so much to discover as to verify and check.

Thanks largely to the advocacy of Major Greenwood and Bradford Hill, medical readers have become more reconciled to the use of statistical procedures than they were when this volume was first published. But many still doubt the need for the somewhat elaborate devices on which the psychologist so constantly relies. Why, says one of my reviewers, cannot the psychologist rest satisfied with 'the maxim of all scientific research—vary one causal factor at a time'? The reason is plain. In the simpler sciences, like physics and chemistry, and in the simpler problems of the more complex sciences, like physiology and medicine, the traditional rule of research can as a rule be adopted; but in the more concrete problems of psychology such a policy is no longer practicable. To investigate the inheritance of mental deficiency we cannot deliberately breed from a pair of feeble-minded parents, and then bring up the offspring in an institution where all outer circumstances are kept uniform and constant. And similarly in studying every other problem of mental subnormality, it is impossible to control all the variable agencies except one.

Hence, as I have said elsewhere, 'the equations we have to solve must inevitably be stated in terms not of one but of many unknown variables'.[1] Factor analysis is merely a specialized method for solving simultaneous equations involving several unknowns, subject to certain limiting conditions; and, although throughout this volume I have abstained from entering into technical details, it is on factorial verification that most of the conclusions formulated were originally based. Perhaps the best vindication for the use

[1] Cf. *Brit. J. Psychol. Stat. Sect.* iv, 1951, pp. 31. The medical reader will find it instructive to note that the experimental study of the brain has led to a very similar formulation of the technical problem. 'Classical physiology', says Dr. Grey Walter, 'tolerated only one unknown quantity in its equations: in its experiments there could be only one thing at a time under investigation'; in the modern study of brain-processes, by the electroencephalograph, for example, 'not one but many observations must be made at once and compared. . . . This is analogous to the solution of simultaneous equations' *The Living Brain*, p. 42; cf. pp. 118 f.).

of such expedients is their rapid and fruitful extension
into numerous fields of inquiry during the past twenty
years.

Instead of encumbering the account here given with
erudite discussions of the detailed evidence, I fancy the best
way to satisfy those critics who have asked for fuller information will be to print a selected list of references for
readers who may desire to pursue some particular problem
a little further. This I have attempted to do by adding
a fresh appendix. Here I need only say that those who
care to dip into the more recent publications there cited
will find that nearly all the guiding generalizations put
forward in the first edition have been fully confirmed by
later studies among normal and abnormal adults as well as
children. As regards normal adults, Professor Vernon,
founding his conclusions on a vast array of data obtained
from testing normal men and women in the forces, declares
that 'results obtained from analyses among recruits during
the 1939–45 war confirmed the hierarchical theory, to
which', as he says, his own book 'is committed'.[1] Professor
Cattell and Professor Allport uphold very much the same
view. Moreover, there is an increasing agreement that the
general structure of the mind in the abnormal is not fundamentally different from what it is in the normal: some,
indeed, have gone so far as to maintain that even in psychotics the aberrations are similar in kind to those found in the
healthy, though carried to a more extravagant degree.

At the Institute of Psychiatry, one of my former pupils,
Dr. Eysenck, has been lately able to carry out extensive
inquiries, in collaboration with other members of the staff,
on neurotic and psychotic patients. And here again the
result is a scheme of factors, physical as well as mental,
very similar to that outlined here. 'A hierarchical view of
personality structure', he concludes, 'akin to Burt's conception of "factors" and McDougall's theory of sentiments,

[1] P. E. Vernon, *The Structure of Human Abilities* (1950), p. 11. Professor
Vernon adds that 'Thurstone, Guilford, and other factorists in America from
1938 on, opposed the notion of a general factor and hierarchy. However,
more recent work suggests a *rapprochement* between the hierarchical and the
Thurstonian viewpoint'.

would appear to account for the facts better than any other.'[1]

Finally, let me insist on a point of more practical interest. In discussing methods of treatment I ventured to suggest that the physician should approach his problem quite as much from the standpoint of the teacher or social worker as in the spirit of a doctor who has some illness to cure. With the young most of the remediable forms of mental subnormality resemble faults in development rather than pathological disorders. Hence the principles to be followed in treating such cases should largely resemble those we adopt in our attempts to ensure the healthy development of the normal youngster. Often the basic trouble is mal-adjustment; and we may seek to relieve the situation, not only (as is usually done) by trying to adjust the child to his environment, but also—and perhaps with greater hope of success—by seeking to adjust the environment to the child. As regards treatment of the child himself, the essential measure, though not the only measure, will be an individual training specifically adapted to his individual needs. Back-wardness may be remedied, and many of the disadvantages of sheer incurable dullness alleviated, by improved methods of teaching; and to make appropriate suggestions will require specialized knowledge and familiarity with the techniques of school instruction. Where the disability is cognitive, this is so obvious that it scarcely needs statement. But precisely the same holds good in dealing with emotional and moral difficulties. Character can be trained as well as intellect.

In this direction much that is of direct practical utility has been discovered by recent investigations on the psychological nature of learning and habit formation. As a result the psychologist who trains is often more successful than the psychiatrist who treats. Yet we are still deplorably ignorant of the reasons why the methods of training and re-education that are so effective in some cases seem sheer waste of time in others. Here our only hope of better results lies in further scientific research. What are the most frequent forms of mental subnormality, and how each

[1] H. J. Eysenck, *Dimensions of Personality* (1947), p. 16.

is most commonly caused, are points on which our knowledge is now tolerably complete. But in regard to the value and efficacy of different modes of treatment we are still forced to trust chiefly to hunches and guesswork. Here, indeed, is a most urgent field of inquiry. The study of basic principles must of course be left to the psychologist, experimenting in the laboratory, the school, or the residential institution. But towards the collection of observational data every trained practitioner can make welcome contributions. Hitherto the psychiatrist, unlike his medical colleagues in other spheres of work, has relied too exclusively on the description of a few striking case-histories; the psychologist perhaps has been tempted to rely too much on statistical analysis. Neither by itself is sufficient. Nowadays in most mental hospitals and child guidance centres the psychiatrist can usually find a psychological colleague who will be ready to co-operate and assist with more technical devices. Intensive case studies are indispensable if we are to secure adequate material; but statistical comparisons, needing as a rule only an elementary application of arithmetic, are an indispensable supplement if we are to make our evidence convincing. May I hope that one outcome of this book will be to stimulate research on what are some of the most important problems of the day?

C. B.

June, 1953

PREFACE TO THE FIRST EDITION

THE chapters that make up this volume consist of the third series of lectures given under the terms of Mr. Charles Heath Clark's bequest to the University of London. Certain portions have been slightly expanded; and the whole has been revised for publication.

The two previous courses dealt with the rise and the teaching of preventive medicine; and were delivered by Sir George Newman, Chief Medical Officer of the Ministry of Health, and by Dr. Carl Prausnitz, Professor of Hygiene in the University of Breslau. It was, therefore, a new and significant step when the authorities of the London School of Hygiene decided that the third series of lectures should be undertaken by a psychologist. In the past psychology has owed much to the profession of medicine. The older psychologists, from Plato and Aristotle to Hume and Herbart, were, it is true, chiefly philosophers; but they had given much time to the study of medicine as it was understood in their day. As early as the days of Galen, and with increasing frequency from Fechner down to Freud, some of the most fertile and productive ideas have been contributed to psychology by those who, first and foremost, were medical men. It is time, therefore, that the psychologist should seek in some measure to repay his debt.

The particular subjects which I was invited to discuss comprise a group of connected problems in social and psychological medicine—the problems of the subnormal mind. More especially it was proposed that I might deal with that branch in which my own work has chiefly lain, namely the diagnosis and treatment of school children who are mentally subnormal. This, indeed, is a sphere of work which has lately become of growing importance to teachers, medical officers, educational administrators, and all who are concerned for the future welfare of the community. To investigate such defects or disorders as they first manifest themselves in early years forms the most hopeful line of approach. Children are far more accessible than adults to prolonged and systematic study, and to experimental methods of treatment. Moreover, at these younger ages the nature of the difficulties, and of the causes that produce them, is presented in a simpler and more transparent form. Finally, as with all other ailments, it is wiser to detect and deal with such difficulties on their first appearance than to wait until the mischief has become firmly established and the constitution of the sufferer less pliable and plastic. By such preventive methods far graver consequences may be forestalled, and the mental health of the whole community effectively improved; for the future of every civilized society depends, first and foremost, on the health and mental development of its children.

My first duty is to acknowledge the honour conferred on me by the Senate of the University and the Board of Management of the London School of Hygiene by inviting me to deliver such a course; and, in doing so, I should like to express my gratitude for the faith which such an action implies. It marks a recognition that the time has now come for psychology to play a larger and more helpful part both in the curriculum of the medical student and in the regular work of the consultant, the medical officer, and, indeed, of every practitioner.

At the same time I should like to place on record my personal indebtedness to many workers in the field of medicine, whether teachers, colleagues, or friends. Of these I owe most to Dr. William McDougall, who first introduced me to modern psychology when I studied in his laboratory at the University of Oxford, and to Sir Charles Sherrington, who so generously accepted me, when my undergraduate days were over, as his assistant in the Physiological Laboratory at Liverpool. Among my colleagues under the London County Council I may be permitted to mention more especially Dr. James Kerr and Dr. F. C. Shrubsall: much of what I have written is the fruit of early discussions over cases and problems that we shared in common. But, first and last, my greatest obligations are to my father, Dr. C. Barrow Burt, who gave me a practical introduction to the problems and methods of medicine at the early age of ten, and to my sister, Dr. Marion Burt, who has always been ready to assist me with advice on special topics, and in addition has been good enough to read these chapters both in manuscript and in proof.

Finally, I must express my thanks to the Dean of the London School of Hygiene, Professor W. W. Jameson, for his personal help and kindness at so many points during the preparation of these lectures and the publication of this book.

C. B.

UNIVERSITY COLLEGE, LONDON

April, 1935

CONTENTS

I

THE NORMAL MIND

I

THE NORMAL MIND

BETWEEN the normal and the subnormal there is no sharp line of cleavage. Hence it is hardly possible to understand the various forms of mental subnormality without first knowing something of the normal mind. In the past the practice of medicine has been apt to regard the healthy and the sick as forming completely separate groups, and to recognize no link between the two. Sane or insane, guilty or not guilty, whole or diseased—to one category or the other every human being is supposed to belong. The assumption is natural. But it easily leads to what the logician would call a confusion of opposites with contradictories.

Nowhere is this love of sorting people into sharply contrasted types more prevalent and more misleading than in psychology. We shall meet it again and again. If, at the very outset, we insist that all men must be either normal or abnormal, we are bound to ask—Is any one perfectly normal? There is wisdom in Stevenson's *Fable of the Goat-Sheep*: ' "Whoever", said the old goat-sheep, "divided all living things into sheep and goats, was ignorant that we neutrals and nondescripts outnumber all the rest, and that your sheep and your goat are merely freak-specimens of ourselves, chiefly remarkable for their rarity." '

Even in physical medicine it has proved highly precarious to class the population under two mutually exclusive headings—the healthy and the diseased. Certainly, in his medical text-book the student may discover a tabulated list of six hundred definite diseases, all duly labelled, with the symptoms differentially described, as though each was a well-defined entity. And he finds his first impression confirmed by his early experiences in the hospital and the sick room; for there he sees illness chiefly in its fully developed form. He has, therefore, to be warned that his task in every case will be to deal not so much with a definable malady as with an individual patient. The research worker has long ago discovered that the conventional classification of diseases, and even of disease as such, assumes hard and fast lines of division that are seldom encountered in nature.

If this is true of physical medicine, it holds still more strongly of psychological medicine. Here by far the most important contributions during recent years have been concerned precisely with those intermediate conditions that hover between ordinary soundness of mind and definite insanity or deficiency. Little by little we are coming to realize that the vast majority of abnormal mental states consist simply of exaggerations of natural peculiarities or impulses common to all mankind.

But there is a second reason why a knowledge of the normal mind is needed. Practical medicine is no longer restricted to the diagnosis and treatment of disease. The medical officer has to deal quite as much with the health-problems of normal individuals—with questions and difficulties that arise when ordinary men, women, and children are collected together in houses, in factories, in schools, in cities or towns at home, in tropical colonies abroad, and, indeed, wherever a civilized community has sprung up. Medicine has thus become one of the most far-reaching and essential of all our social services; and, since social life is largely mental life, the psychological aspect of these complex problems is becoming more and more insistent.

This convergence of the two sciences is comparatively new. Until quite recent years psychological medicine remained almost wholly out of touch with other branches of psychology. Psychiatry, as it was more commonly called, was chiefly engrossed with the severer forms of mental aberration—with mental defects and diseases that were thought to have a definable organic basis, such as downright insanity or imbecility. No doubt, when contrasted with the normal man in full command of his intellectual functions, the imbecile and the lunatic seemed at first to stand entirely apart. Yet, even by the end of the nineteenth century, a few isolated workers on the Continent, such as Janet, Binet, and Freud, had already drawn attention to the existence of borderline states, and to their supreme significance for psychology; and in our own country Galton and his followers had shown that individual differences were not a matter of mysterious idiosyncrasy or inscrutable caprice, but followed statistical laws of variation.

It was perhaps the First World War that most effectively brought home to the medical world the artificiality of the distinction between the normal mind on the one hand and its abnormal conditions on the other. The application of intelligence tests to nearly two million American recruits led to the startling conclusion that nearly 40 per cent. of the population had a mental age below the level then currently accepted as marking off the mentally defective. In the military hospitals the study of so-called shell-shock revealed that symptoms quite as serious as those of the well-defined psychoses might arise from simple stress or strain, and yet prove quickly curable by psycho-therapeutic methods.[1] And thus it became gradually apparent that much of what had been held abnormal might be discovered in the mind of the average man.

The medical investigator was quicker to recognize this than the psychologist; for, if the medical man based his notions of the abnormal on his experience of advanced disease, the psychologist had derived his picture of the normal from samples high above the average. Indeed, he tended to identify the normal with the perfect; and, since all human beings are more or less imperfect, the most ordinary persons were liable to be assessed as falling short of the appropriate standard of normality.

This attitude, however, was largely an accidental outcome of the history of his subject. Psychology, though the youngest of the sciences, is one of the most ancient of human interests. It is older than Aristotle, who first christened it; and from his day onwards it remained, for nearly ten

[1] The work of Myers, Rivers, McDougall, Elliot Smith, and others deserves special mention: it was largely their efforts and their writings that first aroused medical interest in the 'new psychiatry' of Freud. See also *Report of Southborough Committee on Shell Shock* (1922). For the work of American psychologists in the First World War see *Memoirs of the U.S. National Academy*, xv (1921). For psychological work during the Second, see P. E. Vernon and J. B. Parry, *Personnel Selection in the British Forces* (1949).

centuries, a department of philosophy rather than a branch of science. The early psychologist sought to describe the mind in general, and so bequeathed to us a useful terminology and a working classification of mental functions. But he took his own mind as the most accessible sample; and his sole method of inquiry was that of introspection. Such an approach has serious limitations. To this day the materialist, and those trained in the more materialistic sciences, are inclined to complain, with Dr. John Watson and the behaviouristic school, that psychology is still 'too metaphysical'—'trammelled with outworn legacies from mediaeval days, like the concepts of consciousness and the soul'.

With the opening of the nineteenth century the beginnings of a fresh approach were evident. Stimulated by the new discoveries of physics and physiology, trained himself very often in the field of medicine, the psychologist at last thought of applying to his time-honoured problems a different and a more objective method—the method of experiment. And the revolution was completed when he added to the experimental methods of the physicist the evolutionary theories of the biologist. A year before Fechner published his great work on psychophysical experiments, Darwin had published his *Origin of Species*; and a few years later his *Descent of Man* proclaimed that the primary explanation of man's mental processes was to be sought in their biological utility.

It is often asserted that psychology is nothing but a branch of physiology; indeed, psychology has quite recently been criticized as 'an indirect and inexact substitute for the study of the brain and its functions'. Actually, as I shall try to show, we know far more about the working of the mind than we do about the working of the brain and nervous system; and the medical student, who knows by heart his cerebral topography, is nevertheless disposed, from the very nature of his training, to be blind to all that is most characteristic in the psychology of man. He assumes that mental processes are but physiological processes viewed from a subjective and a vaguer aspect; and thus he is tempted to ignore the most distinctive thing about them, namely, that they are conscious, or at any rate can be described only in words appropriate to conscious states. He forgets that the reduction of conscious processes to material processes means begging an unsolved metaphysical question, and that those who maintain that mental phenomena must in the last resort be interpreted in physical terms are committing themselves to a hypothesis that the physicist of to-day would be the first to discountenance.

Psychology, therefore, is to be considered not so much a branch of physiology as *a branch of biology*: for, if biology is the science of life, psychology is the science of mind; and mind, so far as we know it, is found only among living organisms. It follows that the materialistic approach of the nineteenth century and the mechanistic approach of the earlier psychoanalytic schools, although valuable advances in their day, are bound in the end to remain inadequate. It is the biological interpretation of mental and social phenomena that throws most light upon the behaviour of both normal and abnormal persons.

No doubt, with the progress of physiology and biochemistry, the workings of the mind will be found subject to physical and chemical influences, in ways that at present we can but dimly guess; and new forms of treatment will in consequence become available. But the final upshot of our mental processes will still defy description except in psychological language. To describe visual and auditory sensations, or even visual and auditory illusions, in terms solely of the underlying nerve-processes, to reduce wishes to conditioned reflexes, and pleasure and pain to the flow of nerve-currents, is plainly as absurd as to reduce *Hamlet* to permutations and combinations of twenty-six letters, or the *Fifth Symphony* to complex vibrations of the air. Or if the reader still maintains that science may ultimately achieve such feats, it is incontestable that science has not done so yet. Hence, for the present at any rate, descriptions, diagnoses, and even treatment within this field must remain psychological rather than physiological.

Meanwhile, therefore, it cannot be too strongly insisted

that psychology is, and will long continue, a relatively
independent science with a special technique of its own.
In some respects, indeed, it demands a point of view quite
opposed to that which is induced by the ordinary medical
and surgical training. No one has urged this point more
convincingly than medical writers themselves, particularly
those whose study has been devoted to minor mental disorders, like the commoner psycho-neuroses; and it is, if I
am not mistaken, the conclusion of the foremost investigators who have studied the functions of the brain from
physiological and psychological aspects.[1]

In what follows I shall restrict myself to those forms of
subnormality which seem to be chiefly mental in their
origin. Defects and diseases of the mind that have an obvious organic basis I shall almost entirely pass by. I must
repeat, however, that the line of division is artificial. A man
is not to be regarded as a potential corpse loosely coupled
with a potential ghost. Each individual is a unique psychophysical whole; and the mental aspect and the material are,
in the last resort, inseparable.

In passing, let me note that this is true even of those
ailments and injuries that have, not only a purely physical
origin, but exclusively physical symptoms. Hence, I would
add that, even in dealing with bodily disease, physician
and surgeon alike might profitably give an eye to the mental condition of each patient. Those whose training and
interest have been concentrated chiefly on physical conditions hardly realize how intimately interlinked are the
physical and mental factors in almost every form of illness.
The value of a good bedside manner, of tactfully arousing
the patient's faith and sustaining the patient's confidence,
is, of course, already a commonplace; but the psychological issues are far more intricate than this. In a creature
with a consciousness so sensitive as man's, burdened, too,
with a mind whose inner working is always to some extent
irrational if not unconscious, the mere occurrence of physical
disability is bound to precipitate an abnormal mental state.

[1] See, for example, Sir Charles Sherrington, *Integrative Action of the
Nervous System*, especially pp. 377 et seq.

Every patient, just because he is a patient, inevitably becomes more or less neurotic. Accordingly, even the general practitioner needs to keep in view the mental aspect of his daily work.

The teaching embodied in the medical curriculum at present gives little help towards understanding these intercurrent factors or appreciating these subtler problems. The existing courses on psychological medicine are concerned with mental disease rather than with mental disorder—with definite psychoses, such as are met with at mental hospitals. The lectures deal mainly with the well-marked organic forms; the demonstrations with cases of a grave or advanced type. Numerous as they may be in absolute figures, such cases are exceedingly rare in comparison with the everyday occurrence of minor and curable disorders. They are, after all, the concern of the specialist rather than of the general practitioner; and, though a precise diagnosis and treatment may be difficult, the mere detection of such major abnormalities is comparatively easy. It is now over sixty years since this branch of the subject was added to the medical curriculum, and the teaching has undergone little or no extension. Meanwhile, psychology has been making fresh discoveries in every direction, and has added new fields to medicine, quite as important as those of bacteriology or radiography. It is time, therefore, that its results should be incorporated into the instruction now given.

The chief question is—what kind of psychology will prove most useful? What does the doctor need most—a broad acquaintance with the general foundations, or a specialized study of the most relevant branches? For every medical man some knowledge of general psychology is desirable; for the mental specialist it is as essential as a knowledge of anatomy to the surgeon. But the branch which concerns the practising physician most of all is that of individual psychology—the branch that deals with the mental peculiarities of individual persons. Were I asked, therefore, what addition was most urgent in the overcrowded curriculum of the medical student, individual psychology is the subject I should name. The specialist and the general

practitioner alike are engaged in the examination and treatment of individuals: each of these individuals has a mind,
and some seek professional help because their minds are
out of order. Hence every medical student should learn
something of the methods which modern psychology pur-
sues in examining the individual mind, just as he is taught
how to examine the various systems of the body. In
the ward, for example, he is constantly asked: 'Will you
examine this patient's chest?' or 'What do you make of that
patient's heart?' Seldom is the question put: 'What do
you make of this man's temperament?' or 'How would you
test such a patient's mental functions?' Indeed, the student
scarcely realizes that there *is* a method for these problems:
he attacks them, if he attacks them at all, either by the light
of popular common sense, or by falling back on a routine
physical inspection, believing his task to be done when he
has demonstrated some slight physical derangement or no
physical derangement at all.

A definite technique has now been worked out for such
purposes. In some directions, for example in testing the
innate intelligence of children and young persons, it has
proved singularly accurate; in other directions, for example
diagnosing minor nervous disorders, it is more cumbersome and uncertain, but, considering the complexity of the
problem, far more trustworthy than the criteria of unaided
common sense; in all directions it is subject to constant
modification and improvement. Much of it demands first-
hand experience, with demonstration, training, and instruction at the hand of experts. But in its general outlines it
can be summarized and described.

The methods themselves are neither startling nor occult.
The psychologist attempts no snapshot diagnosis, such as
the layman commonly expects. His general procedure is
simply that of the conscientious physician. He takes a full
case-history; but the case-history is based upon a systematic
scheme. Just as our bodies show the same general structure,
so the mind in every one of us is built up on the same general
ground-plan. Men's minds are like their faces: each seems
at first unique; yet analysis reveals that in all instances the

component features are the same. All have two eyes, two ears, a mouth, a forehead, and a nose; but the length, the width, and the prominence of each part vary within certain limits from one man to another. So with the mind: all inherit the same fundamental tendencies and capacities; and the psychologist's main task is to estimate the extent to which each known potentiality is developed or arrested, much as a surveyor marks down, at given stations on his map, the eminences and depressions of the land.

It is, therefore, the first business of individual psychology to define the various tendencies that can be usefully assessed, and then to devise a method for the quantitative measurement of each. This sounds an ambitious project. Where are we to find a precise and exhaustive inventory of mental qualities or powers? Different lines of research have been attempted. The biological investigator tries to sort out the unit-characters of the mind; the statistical investigator seeks to discover what processes, if any, depend on general functions, and what processes are restricted or specific. And these theoretical inquiries serve to confirm and extend the results of the practical worker. The latter, moving largely on empirical lines, has endeavoured to work out a scheme for himself; and the scheme proves to be much the same in cases of the most varied types. Terman dealing with the supernormal, Healy dealing with the delinquent, Huey with the dull, the backward, and the defective, the industrial psychologist dealing with problems of vocational guidance, have each of them, often it would appear in relative independence of the others, reached very much the same general plan of case-analysis. Their work has led to a classification of types and characteristics very similar to that of the statistical psychologist. According to the nature of the problem, greater time or emphasis may be given to different details: with the neurotic or delinquent, temperament may require study at greater length; intelligence or social efficiency with the borderline defective. But the broad outline is similar throughout; and it is tempting to suggest that it offers a fairly accurate reflection of the structure of the human mind.

Take, then, almost any psychologist's case-study, and you will find that it is usually divided into three main stages: first of all, a retrospective inquiry, tracing back the causes of the disorder to their origins in the past; secondly, a conspective survey of the conditions as they obtain at the present moment; and thirdly, a set of prospective conclusions, indicating treatment and prognosis for the future. With a given patient or child, these points are not necessarily taken up in this particular order: sometimes it proves more convenient to start with present symptoms and work back to the past; sometimes it is imperative to recommend forthwith some tentative line of treatment, and the subsequent analysis may be largely governed by its failure or success. Here, however, if only for the sake of logical sequence, let us begin with the retrospective survey, and take up the other aspects later.

I. Past History

First of all, then, what points are of psychological significance in the previous history of the case?

The historical retrospect should embrace both personal history and family history. The personal history should review, in greater or lesser detail according to the nature of the case, the whole mental development of the patient. It will start from the very beginning—namely the conditions of pregnancy and birth; it will note the chief land-marks of physical and mental growth—the date of talking, walking, first and second dentition, entrance to school, puberty, and the like; it will include any event that might hinder physical and mental growth—accidents, illnesses, operations, changes or defects of family life, of parental control, of social environment generally; it will take special note of early emotional manifestations; and will, in short, cover the chief stages of the patient's intellectual and moral progress at home, at school, and during later years.

The data will be obtained partly from the patient's parents, teachers, and medical attendants, partly from the patient himself. What information can be extracted from the patient must depend on his age, his intelligence, his reliability, and on the time that can be spent with him. For simple external facts, direct questions will suffice: nearly every psychologist compiles, either mentally or on paper, a series of points that he finds it useful to put in the greater number of his cases.[1] For the internal history of the mind, particularly in its more emotional and less conscious aspects, an indirect approach is more effective, and, indeed, almost indispensable. In some respects the whole procedure of the psycho-analyst might be truly described as a special technique for eliciting a mental case-history from the patient himself.

But a personal history is not enough. Pre-natal conditions may be as significant as post-natal. And the inquiring psychologist goes back farther still. He passes behind birth to ancestry, and endeavours to procure a family history as well. The family history may shed some light on the patient's heredity, and possibly supply some hints for the prognosis. In treating a backward child, it is essential to know whether the backwardness rests on some inborn or inherited deficiency, or whether it springs mainly from some accidental circumstance. In dealing with the delinquent or the neurotic, it is always wise to consider whether the instability is part of the patient's inherent mental constitution, or whether it arises from some transitory maladjustment to his present or his previous environment.

Here, in these preliminary questions, it will be observed how modern psychology, adopting a biological standpoint, lays stress upon the genetic approach: it views the individual as the product of his past development. What special weight should be attached to each of the two main factors—the innate and the environmental—is a point about which current belief has constantly changed. From the time of Locke down to that of Bentham, English psychology tended to regard the new-born mind as a piece of unformed wax, moulded entirely by conditions acting after birth. With

[1] I have published such a schedule in *The Young Delinquent* (University of London Press, 1925), together with a brief note of other questionnaires that have been compiled for this purpose. The detailed methods of examining a psychological patient are described in full in that volume, and, with obvious modifications, are applicable to cases of all types, not to delinquents only.

the inquiries of Darwin and Galton, opinion began to veer towards the opposite extreme. Some investigators even declared that 'nature is ten times as powerful as nurture'. Since the advent of the behaviourist and psycho-analyst, the pendulum has swung back once more; and heredity is held to be of smaller influence, at any rate in functional disorders. Biologists themselves would now probably agree that the psychologist's ideas of heredity have always been too crude and simple, and would be disposed to argue that any sure answer to such questions must await the conclusions of more exact research.

The practising psychologist, therefore, must be chary of any bias in one direction or the other. In this case heredity, in that case environment, may appear to be preponderant; and in most cases, probably in all, both factors have their share—combining no doubt in different proportions, but combining so closely that it may be hopeless to attempt to dissever the two.

II. Present Conditions

Viewing, then, the individual's whole life-story as a growing tree with ramifying roots and branches, we begin, as it were, with a longitudinal section, piercing down to the ground, and seeking, wherever possible, to delve below the surface. The next step is to take what may be called a cross-section of the main trunk. We proceed to analyse the existing situation.

The conditions to be studied will not consist exclusively of the conditions to be discerned within the patient himself: we must investigate his outer circumstances first. Here is another peculiarity of the psychological approach. Physical illness is largely a reaction to some trouble within the organism—to poisons or bacteria that have somehow found their way inside the man's system: mental disorders are largely a reaction to conditions operating from without. That is what the mind is for. The stomach has to digest the food that lodges inside it; the brain has to react to stimuli that come from outside. At this point the attitude of the behaviouristic school may prove extremely helpful. The behaviourists emphasize the fact that the nervous system is built up on the basis of the reflex arc: they even contend that our whole mental life may be depicted as a set of conditioned reflexes. Stimulus and response, tit for tat—that, as behaviourism rightly insists, is the essential principle on which the mind acts.

The practical import of this standpoint comes home to us most strongly in dealing with juvenile cases. When prescribing for the so-called 'problem child', the psychologist is forced to recognize that rarely, if ever, is it the child alone that constitutes the problem: it is the relation between the child and the forces outside him—his parents, his teachers, his companions at work or at play. It is the child's reaction towards the various difficulties or duties that confront him in his day-to-day existence that has primarily to be analysed and understood. What we are called upon to study and treat is always the total situation, not the isolated personality.

The mind is essentially an organ for making adaptations or adjustments. And accordingly, before he can follow the workings of an individual mind, the psychologist or psychologizing doctor must first explore the detailed circumstances to which that mind is trying to adjust itself. He cannot understand a neurotic patient without knowing something of the stresses and strains which that patient is called upon to meet. He cannot understand a delinquent or a criminal unless he knows something of the temptations and the restraining influences that surround him. To study a mind without knowing its milieu is like studying a fish without seeing water.

A. The Patient's Environment.

In accordance with this standpoint, the modern psychological clinic is giving a larger and larger place to what it is the fashion to call the psychiatric social worker—the trained investigator who inquires into the particular social conditions in which the child or grown-up patient is living. She investigates the patient's environment, and reports her findings to the doctor or psychologist. Such reports are indispensable in the case of children and younger patients;

and it is essential that the worker herself should have some psychological experience and training, so that she may know precisely what to look for.

Of all the various social influences that affect the individual mind, the most important are those obtaining within the patient's home. Recent studies have made this abundantly clear. In dealing with the backward child, for example, teacher, doctor, and inspector alike have been far too prone to lay sole stress on influences exerted within the school walls. Nowadays, however, the larger education authorities have begun to institute throughout their areas a system of local care committees, with organizers, visitors, or nurses, who can supplement the work carried on within the classroom by work outside.

In the earlier days social investigators were inclined to look mainly at material conditions. Their reports on home circumstances were confined principally to such points as income, rent, expenditure, number of rooms, number of children in the rooms, and the sanitary state of the dwelling. Gradually, however, they have been led to recognize that mental conditions are more potent than economic. The cultural status of the home, its moral character, and—most important of all—its general emotional atmosphere, these constitute the crucial factors in nearly every case. Here both social workers and psycho-analysts have been brought independently to much the same conclusion: it is the child's reaction to the members of his family, and their reaction to him, that count for most in his mental and moral life.

B. The Patient Himself.

1. *Physical Condition.*

Having glanced first at the patient's heredity and then secondly at his environment, it is time to turn to the patient himself.

Here our scheme of inquiry may be conveniently divided into two broad sub-headings—physical conditions and mental conditions respectively. Neither can be overlooked. The doctor, whose scientific training has been concerned mainly with the body, is apt to search almost exclusively for bodily causes: having found adenoids in the dull child, worms in the bad-tempered, or an irritable heart in the adult neurotic, he is too often satisfied that he has hit upon the real root of the trouble.

Outside the medical profession the popular notion of mental diagnosis and treatment still runs along crudely physical lines. Schoolmasters who send pupils to the psychologist constantly suggest that the child must be suffering from 'a kink in the brain'; and many even suppose that this kink can be located by means of X-rays, and that the cure will consist of a surgical operation on the tissue of the brain itself. After all, it is not so long ago that surgeons of the first rank, like Horsley and Lannelongue, were performing craniectomy on microcephalics to relieve a premature synostosis of the skull, in the hope of allowing the small brain to expand and so improve the defective's mentality.

It seems as difficult for the non-psychological to avoid thinking of the mind as a material system as it was for the early physicists to avoid thinking of heat as a substance or of electricity as a fluid. The brain is held to be the organ of the mind; and any mental disturbance, it is inferred, must therefore be traceable to some concrete change in the brain itself. The brain is pictured on quasi-phrenological lines as a collection of localized centres for separate faculties or propensities: and, since the brain is lodged in the skull, an over-development of some one propensity or faculty is expected to reveal itself in some peculiar formation of the head. Not long ago an education authority invited a phrenologist to take part in the examination of children for the award of junior county scholarships; and, until quite recently, many school medical officers still based their diagnoses of mental deficiency on measurements of the circumference or the cubic capacity of the skull. Even to-day much of the terminology used by psychiatric writers to describe mental characteristics and processes is largely derived from the vocabulary of Edinburgh phrenologists of the early nineteenth century, and so from the old Scottish faculty school from which so many of their concepts were borrowed.

It cannot, of course, be denied that anatomical peculiarities, especially about the head, are often observable in marked cases of intellectual deficiency and of temperamental abnormality; and recent research has done something to confirm the old notion of a correlation between certain physical diatheses and certain temperamental types. The diagnostic value of these various symptoms we shall have to examine as we consider each mental state in turn. Broadly speaking, however, it may be said that what is psychologically significant is not so much the structure of the head, or face, or body as a whole, but rather the functions and movements of the body and its parts, as expressing the stability and adjustability of the mind: facial expression is more suggestive than facial shape; posture, gait, and general demeanour than the proportions or build of the physique. All such points should naturally be noted during a physical inspection; but, in the main, the tendency of statistical work is to show that such indications are far less trustworthy than has hitherto been imagined, and their causation is far less simple and direct than popular theories have assumed.

The main purpose of the physical examination, therefore, will be to ascertain the state of the patient's general health, and in particular to detect any bodily ailment or defect which may have an influence, direct or indirect, upon his mental state. Disease or disturbance of the nervous and glandular systems may act as a direct and immediate cause; but, as we shall learn later on, there is hardly any bodily disorder which may not hamper intellectual progress and upset the moral or emotional balance. A routine examination of all the systems of the body in turn is therefore essential; and it must be remembered that a deviation from the normal, which from a physical standpoint may seem trivial in itself, may nevertheless have a decisive influence on the patient's mind.

2. *Mental Condition.*

We now at length reach the central part of the psychologist's task—the direct examination of the mind itself. The examination must be complete, and conducted according to a systematic plan. In no branch of medicine is this more essential; and in no branch is it more frequently ignored. To test every capacity, and note every propensity that the human mind contains, may at first sight appear an unending project. But here a recent series of researches has greatly simplified the tangle. These inquiries have been directed to a question of great practical importance: What mental qualities, if any, are usually found together? To determine the concomitance the investigators have adopted a special statistical device—the method of correlation.

The introduction of mathematics may sound pedantic. It is, however, essential in all biological inquiries. Biological characteristics, unlike physical qualities, hardly ever obey simple rules that hold good without exceptions. In physical science it is always safe to assume that lead is heavier than iron, or that the volume of a gas varies inversely with its pressure, if the temperature remains constant. But in the biological sciences there are so many 'ifs', and the 'ifs' are so frequently unknown, that it is safe to speak only of tendencies, hardly ever of laws; and to measure such tendencies becomes a problem of the first importance.

If one lump of lead is 5 per cent. larger than another, we may fairly infer that it will be 5 per cent. heavier. But if one man is 5 per cent. taller than another, we cannot infer that he will be 5 per cent. heavier, much less that his children will be 5 per cent. taller than the children of the other man. He will *probably* be heavier; and his children will *probably* be taller. But before we can use such generalizations as a basis for safe inference we must measure the probability in quantitative terms. This is done by means of a 'coefficient of correlation' and a 'probable error'. For height of fathers and sons, the correlation is about 0·5. Thus, if a father is 2 inches taller than the general average, his sons will be, on the average, 0·5 × 2 inches (= 1 inch) taller than the average; but their individual heights may easily vary $1\frac{1}{2}$ inches on either side of that figure.

Similarly, in psychology it would be quite unsafe to

assume that no adult with a skull less than 20 inches in circumference can possess a normal mentality, that no defective can have a good memory, or that no one can have a perfectly healthy mind unless he also has a perfectly healthy body. Such generalizations were constantly uttered by writers forty or fifty years ago; and it would be difficult either to accept or to deny them in that form. The fact is that, if a man's intelligence is defective, his memory *tends* to be weak more or less; if his head is extremely small, his intelligence *tends* to be more or less below average; if his body is unhealthy, his mind *tends* to be more or less abnormal as well. Indeed, it proves to be a general rule that unfavourable qualities of whatever nature *tend* to go together, and the same is true of favourable. Thus, a child who is above the average for general intelligence will probably be above the average in height, in weight, in physical health, in length and strength of limb, in size of skull, in quickness of perception and movement, in attention, memory, and reasoning, in emotional stability, and even in moral character as well. The essential point is, however, to measure the *degree* of these several tendencies. When this is done, it is found that the correlations vary widely. If, for example, a child's height is above the average, it would be fairly safe to wager that he had long legs; not quite so safe to wager that his weight was above the average; still more precarious to wager that his intelligence was not below normal; and exceedingly rash to infer that his moral character was excellent.

When the degree of concomitance is expressed as a fractional coefficient, it appears that the correlation between stature and length of leg-bones is about 0·9; between stature and weight, about 0·6; between intelligence and memory, about 0·5; between intelligence and the size of head, about 0·3; between intelligence and moral stability, about 0·2 only. Medical writers constantly speak of this or that characteristic as a sign or symptom; but, before we can use such characteristics for diagnosis, it is imperative to know their diagnostic value. Thus, when we know that the results of an intelligence-test correlate with intelligence to the extent of 0·7, it becomes comparatively futile to rely predominantly on head-measurements for the diagnosis of deficiency. And if a new test is put forward, the first question to ask is: How closely does it correlate with the quality it is supposed to measure?

However, a single correlation for a single test or symptom is not enough. A simple correlation will tell us how far the test will improve on a purely *random* judgement. But what the practical physician wants to know is how far it will improve on *antecedent or concurrent* information. And that entails the more refined techniques of partial and multiple correlation.

The method of correlation has been applied to almost every mental quality that can be tested, measured, or assessed. The results are of immediate practical significance. It appears, for example, that many characteristics go together in groups. The correlations can be explained by supposing that each characteristic within a single group depends upon an underlying 'group-factor'—a 'general factor', as it is sometimes termed. It follows that if we can devise efficient tests for the more general factors, we need not stop to measure all the dependent characteristics in turn: we can infer them with a reasonable amount of certainty—a certainty which will vary with their several correlations.

There are, therefore, what may be termed 'key-factors' governing the detailed make-up of each individual mind. Hence, in studying any particular person, the main points to examine are the several key-factors, which seem to be the same for all.

What general factors, then, have been established, and how may they be assessed? To begin with, it appears that nearly all intellectual qualities go hand in hand, but are relatively independent of the emotional: at the same time, the emotional qualities are also linked together, and constitute a second group relatively independent of the intellectual. Within these two broader groups there are many smaller sub-groups: so that the mind may be pictured as a system or *hierarchy of group-factors*, of a wider or a narrower range.[1]

[1] The view that mental abilities and impulses form a hierarchical system is fully in accord with the notion of a 'neural hierarchy' developed by neuro-

In many instances it has been shown that these group-factors may be inherited. This can be demonstrated by the same statistical device. As we have just seen, the resemblance between parents and their children can be measured by means of a coefficient of correlation. If the figures can be trusted, it would appear that mental inheritance is of much the same order as physical: in both cases the coefficients range between 0·3 and 0·5. But correlation alone will not suffice to solve the problems of mental heredity. The facts of inheritance, either physical or mental, can never be properly explained until we have discovered what qualities are transmitted in the form of alternative units. This is a line of research that human biology has only just begun to take up. Nevertheless, for practical purposes we may provisionally try to keep apart those ingredients in a man's mental make-up that appear to be hereditary and therefore innate, and those that are acquired or post-natal.

We thus reach a trio of important distinctions: we can distinguish (1) intellectual and emotional characteristics, (2) inborn and acquired characteristics, and (3) general and specific factors. On this threefold classification of mental qualities we can found a systematic plan for the study of each individual: we can draw up in outline what has sometimes been called a 'psychographic scheme'.

Let me insist upon one important reservation. The terms that I have used merely designate abstract aspects of the mind, not concrete faculties; they indicate theoretical distinctions, not sharp or clear-cut subdivisions. The individual mind is a single whole; and the independence of its various functions is a relative independence, never absolute.

1. INTELLECTUAL ASPECT

Let us begin with what I have called the intellectual aspect. The term intellectual I use in a somewhat broad and extended sense. By intellectual I understand all that de-

logists like Hughlings Jackson and Sherrington (cf. *The Integrative Action of the Nervous System*, p. 314 and refs.). For more recent versions of the doctrine see G. W. Allport, 1938, pp. 45, 139, and refs.

pends on cognitive as distinct from affective or conative processes. This will evidently include practical activities, such as those involving manual dexterity and co-ordination of hand and eye, as well as intellectual activities in the narrower sense, such as writing good English or calculating the answer to a sum.

Under this wide heading we have to assess in turn, first the individual's innate powers, and secondly his acquired attainments. If, for example, the physician is examining a possible case of mental deficiency, it will not be sufficient to test the child for reading, writing, arithmetic, and handwork. Attainments in these subjects are acquired attainments. They are influenced as much by opportunity and industry as by sheer native wits. A child may be deplorably backward in every subject of the curriculum without being mentally deficient. Inborn capacity, therefore, must be tested as well as school knowledge: for if the child is defective in inborn capacity, it will be useless to expect the teacher to bring the child's attainments up to the normal.

A. Innate Capacities.

What, then, are the innate capacities of the mind? As I have already intimated, intellectual abilities are of two kinds: there is, first of all, a general factor pervading all kinds of intellectual work, and there is, secondly, a number of more specific factors limited to one particular type of work alone.

i. General Intelligence.

The idea of a general cognitive factor we owe to Galton. Roughly, it may be identified with what Spencer and his French disciples (Taine, Ribot, and Binet) called 'intelligence'. A number of researches indicate that this general factor is hereditary or at any rate inborn. We thus obtain a convenient definition for the term intelligence. Intelligence may be defined as inborn, general, intellectual capacity.[1] If we accept this definition, then intelligence

[1] It is important to note that in psychology the word intelligence is used in this technical and specialized sense. Current criticisms are apt to confuse this meaning with several others, e.g. with the actual measurements obtained

becomes one of the most vital of all the qualities that the psychologist can be called upon to test. Fortunately we have excellent tests for measuring it.

The testing of intelligence must unquestionably constitute an important part of the school medical officer's duty, and, indeed, of the duty of every physician whose business it is to diagnose and certify the mentally deficient. But in studying all forms of mental abnormality—the backward, the criminal, the neurotic, the insane, it is desirable to estimate the patient's intelligence. What methods, then, may be recommended for general use?

Intelligence tests are of four main kinds. According to the procedure, we may distinguish between individual tests and group tests; and, according to the material, between verbal and non-verbal tests.

With individual tests each patient is examined, privately and alone, in the course of a personal interview. Such a procedure is essential wherever a definite diagnosis is to be made of his particular mental state. With those who are very young or very dull, it is indispensable for almost every purpose. Its special advantage springs from the fact that it allows the examiner to adapt both the tests themselves and his method of approach to the idiosyncrasies of every person tested. Only by dealing with a single individual at a time can he make sure that his questions are understood, or follow up a given problem or a wrong reply, and so track down the special mental function that is weak or operating badly. The drawback of the method lies in the time consumed.

Group tests are tasks that can be carried out by a large number of individuals simultaneously, sitting together like children in a class. Usually, therefore, group tests are also written tests. Roneo'd sheets or printed booklets, containing questions to be worked, are handed round to the examinees; and the examinees are required to write or mark the answers in the spaces provided. The procedure is very similar to that of an ordinary school examination.

by our somewhat fallible intelligence-tests or with what is called intelligence in ordinary parlance.

Both with individual tests and with group tests, verbal or non-verbal material may be used.

(1) *Individual Verbal Tests.* An individual verbal test approximates to what is popularly known as an oral examination: both questions and answers are given by word of mouth. Of this type the most familiar instance is the Binet-Simon scale. In order to diagnose mental deficiency among Parisian school-children, Binet and his colleague drew up a set of graded problems. In the main they took over the traditional questions of the consulting-room, added a few simple laboratory tests, and compiled the whole series into a progressive scale. The merit of their system was that the questions to be asked were carefully thought out beforehand, and were further standardized by preliminary trial upon children known to be mentally defective and normal respectively.

The child is asked such apparently casual questions as these: 'What is your name?' 'How old are you?' 'Are you a little boy or a little girl?' If he gives his name and sex correctly, but fails to give his right age, Binet would infer that the child probably possesses a mental age of about four, since average children can give their name and their sex correctly at about the age of three, but cannot give their age correctly until they are about five. Thus, by means of the commonplaces of everyday conversation, before the examinee has realized that the doctor is making anything but the most natural inquiries, an estimate of his mental level can be reached.

But two or three questions are not sufficient. The scale in its entirety contains about sixty-five tests. They are arranged in steps of increasing difficulty, each step consisting of about five questions for each year, from the age of three to the age of sixteen. Supposing, therefore, that the child answers all the questions up to and including those for age 8, and then begins to fail, succeeding perhaps in only four of the five harder ones for the subsequent year, he scores a mental age of eight years and four-fifths.

For the general purposes of the medical psychologist, the Binet scale is by far the simplest and the most effective.

Several cautions, however, have to be borne in mind. To begin with, the scale was devised for French children. Hence for use in this country all the questions have first to be translated; and, instead of using French coins and French weights and measures, the nearest English equivalents have to be found. Slight as they may seem, such alterations appreciably affect the difficulty of each problem. Consequently, the whole scale has had to be standardized afresh for English children. With the aid of teachers, inspectors, and school medical officers, working in the schools of London and elsewhere, this restandardization has been thoroughly carried out. A full account of the modified method and materials may be found in the Memoranda on *Mental and Scholastic Tests*[1] published for the London County Council.

For the examination of dull and defective children these may be regarded as the regular routine tests. Nevertheless, the tests themselves assume some modicum of general knowledge, such as is picked up by almost every child reared in a normal home or school. If, however, the child has lacked an ordinary home and school life, then it is impossible to take a failure with the Binet tests as indicative of innate dullness. Children brought up in an institution, for example, may have seen no coins but a penny or a halfpenny. Children of gipsies and tramps, and those who have spent their lives in canal boats upon the waterways of England, may be devoid of the simple background of civilized culture that these tests assume. This was admirably demonstrated in a research carried out by Mr. Hugh Gordon, one of H.M. Inspectors of Schools, and a research-student of my own, Dr. Frances Gaw, at a school attended by canal-boat children. Here nearly 60 per cent. would have been diagnosed as mentally defective by the Binet-Simon scale,

---

[1] *Mental and Scholastic Tests*, by C. Burt, Memorandum I, 'The Binet-Simon Scale', summarized in *A Handbook of Tests for Use in Schools*: both obtainable from the Council's publishers, P. S. King & Son (now incorporated in Staples Press, Ltd.). This version of the scale has also been printed by Dr. Ballard in his book on *Mental Tests* (Hodder & Stoughton). [Age assignments for the later versions are included in the appendix added to the present edition.]

but only 7 per cent. by means of tests involving no special skill or information.

Again, for older and brighter children the scale is far from satisfactory. The harder tests are somewhat ineffective, and too few in number. To remedy this shortcoming, Professor Terman, of California University, has issued what is known as the Stanford Revision and Extension.[1]

Those who use this revision should note that Professor Terman's wording of the questions is often more appropriate to American children than to English. 'What's the thing to do if you are going some place and miss your car?'— such a question is hardly intelligible to the six-year-old Londoner. 'What's the thing for you to do when you notice on your way to school you are in danger of being tardy?' is equally unintelligible to the English eight-year-old. Nor is it sufficient for the doctor to modify the wording (as he usually does) and assume that the difficulty and age-level will remain unchanged. Terman himself, in discussing these particular tests, insists that 'the form of the question must not under any circumstances be altered'. The coins, of course, must be altered; but when English coins are substituted for American, the problems are made more difficult. Even where the wording and the test-materials are satisfactory, the American age-assignments cannot always be taken over as they stand: for English children of the ages specified, the scholastic problems are a little too easy, and the practical problems a little too hard.

With the permission of Professor Terman and his publishers, however, both his earlier and his later versions have been revised for use with English children. The detailed instructions have not yet been printed, but are in use at many child-guidance clinics. The age-assignments recommended for the Terman and the Binet tests will be found in an Appendix to this volume.[2]

[1] L. M. Terman, *The Measurement of Intelligence*, G. G. Harrap & Co.

[2] The list of age-assignments for the Terman version was originally drawn up for the Mental Deficiency Committee, and has already been published in its *Report* (Part IV, Appendix B, pp. 218-20). This standardization was also worked out in conjunction with London teachers (to whom I am especially indebted for the time and trouble spent), and was used as the basis of

In examining older and brighter children I myself prefer to employ tests of an entirely different type. Of these perhaps the most convenient for quick practical use is a series of short tests of logical reasoning.[1] For more exact results a written test, of the kind to be described below, is probably the most suitable with children of the secondary school class.

All the tests so far described consist chiefly of verbal problems. In the Binet scale two or three practical tests, such as comparing lines, pictures, and weights, are included; but the scale as a whole has a strong linguistic bias, and the majority of the problems are set and answered in words. Now verbal facility appears to be a somewhat specialized ability, more or less independent of general intelligence. Hence, with the scale in its original form, it is often a ready tongue that scores; and some allowance for this factor has at times to be made. The glib, plausible, sociable little girl may sometimes seem brighter than she is; while the mute, shy, sheepish boy, unused to the interchange of conversation, may fail to do himself justice.

(2) *Individual Non-Verbal Tests.* In such cases Binet's tests must be supplemented by tests of a non-verbal type. These are commonly described as 'performance' tests. The patient is required to copy certain complicated movements (such as tapping blocks in a definite order), to fit small cubes together to make one large block, to build up human faces or figures out of dissected fragments, to fit pictures together, like jigsaw puzzles, so as to complete a scene or illustrate a story. Tests such as these require attention, quick perception, power to grasp a scheme of thought and fill it in, and usually a prompt co-ordination of skilled movements; but the whole task is largely independent of education and

Dr. Lewis's survey for the Mental Deficiency Committee. The revision of the detailed instructions is not yet in its final form; but provisional copies, privately circulated, may be obtained from child-guidance clinics at which they are in use.

[1] A scale of reasoning-tests will be found in the *Handbook of Tests for Use in Schools*; it is reprinted in Dr. Ballard's book on *Mental Tests*. Dr. Ballard's own test of absurdities—itself a test of critical reasoning—may also be used with older children.

experience. The best-known series is the scale of performance-tests drawn up by Pintner and Paterson.[1] These have been modified and standardized for use in this country by Dr. Frances Gaw and by Dr. F. M. Earle.[2] A more recent scale, in some ways more suited to English children, has been worked out in Scotland by Dr. Drever and Dr. Mary Collins.[3] For rough, quick tests in schools the Porteus Maze tests are perhaps the most convenient and suggestive of all.[4]

The defect of performance-tests is that success at them depends, as with most concrete puzzles, in a large degree upon luck. Hence a great many have to be used; and this consumes an appreciable amount of time. Further, most of them need special apparatus, usually cumbersome and often expensive. Nevertheless, in special cases such tests prove invaluable. They should be regularly employed, not only with those whose verbal facility is exceptionally poor or exceptionally good, but also with those who have an obvious defect either of speech or hearing, and, in particular, with those who are nervous and shy. When obliged to face an oral interview, the timid child is often thrown into a kind of examination paralysis: he becomes confused, monosyllabic, or altogether dumb. A performance-test does not require him to listen or to speak, or indeed to make any new personal contact, but merely to study simple concrete problems, of an interesting type, and to work them out, quietly by himself. The tests can be taken in the spirit of a game, and, to a large extent, are self-explanatory: frequently the child will complete the whole series spontaneously, without ever suspecting that he has undergone a psychological examination.

The performance-tests in current use are unsuited to

[1] Pintner and Paterson, *A Scale of Performance Tests* (Appleton & Co.). See also Bronner, Healy, Low, and Shinberg, *A Manual of Individual Mental Tests and Testing* (Little, Brown & Co., Boston).

[2] The methods and the results have been published by the Medical Research Council: Industrial Health Research Board's Reports on *Performance Tests of Intelligence*, by F. M. Gaw, and on *The Use of Performance Tests of Intelligence in Vocational Guidance*, by F. M. Earle, M. Milner, and others (Reports Nos. 31 and 53, H.M. Stationery Office).

[3] *Performance Tests of Intelligence* (Oliver & Boyd).

[4] The material for the Porteus test is given in the *Handbook of Tests for Use in Schools* (pp. 95–106).

children suffering from gross physical disabilities. For the
blind and deaf special scales have been worked out. Those
suffering from paralysis or motor inco-ordination have
mainly to be assessed by verbal tests. With children who
are too young or dull to respond either to the Binet tests or
to the commoner performance tests, the Merrill-Palmer
scale may be usefully employed;[1] and for those whose
mental age is below three, Gesell's norms of early development will be found particularly suggestive.[2]

(3) *Verbal Group Tests.* Group tests are chiefly helpful for
preliminary surveys. They are usually drawn up in the form
of printed booklets. Many such booklets have been published, particularly in America: they are, however, of varying value. With English children, the Terman, the Otis, and
the Simplex tests give better results than the National,
though this still seems the most widely known. For general
use I am inclined to recommend the Northumberland
Group Tests, 1925 Series.[3] These were compiled for work
in this country; norms, in the shape of averages for each age
with measures of the limits of normal variation, have been
obtained by careful trials with English children, and are
appended in the manual of instructions. The set includes
corresponding booklets for testing school attainments.

As I have already noted, with older and brighter children
a test of the group type often gives better results than tests
of an individual type: the intelligent adolescent is, as a rule,
far less disturbed by a written examination than by an oral.
It is, no doubt, only on exceptional occasions that the
doctor requires to test intelligence that is well above the
average. Yet, from time to time, he is bound to encounter
a neurotic or delinquent patient, of high, supernormal
ability, whose level cannot be adequately estimated by
the Binet scale. In such cases one of the harder group
tests should generally be employed: for supernormal persons over the age of fourteen—e.g. bright children at a

---

[1] See R. Stutsman, *Mental Measurement of Pre-School Children.*
[2] A. Gesell, *The Mental Growth of the Pre-School Child.* See also Ruth
Griffiths, *The Abilities of Babies* (1954).
[3] The University of London Press, Warwick Square, E.C. 4.

secondary school, or students at a university—a test known
as Group Test No. 33[1] may perhaps be recommended as
the most effective.

(4) *Non-Verbal Group Tests*. Nearly all such tests, however, presuppose a fair facility in reading and in the use of
the pencil or pen. With children below the level of Standard
II trustworthy results can hardly be expected. For these,
special group tests of a non-verbal type have been constructed; and have been occasionally used with some success.
The best are the Otis Group Intelligence Tests, Primary
Series.[2] This series was employed in the survey carried out
by the Mental Deficiency Committee: the modified version
adopted for this purpose is to be found in the Committee's
Report.[3]

Many medical officers prefer to work out and standardize
tests of their own devising. In this way the material
which they select for their own test-problems can be adapted
a little more closely to the special needs of their patients
than that of the better-known scales. This is particularly
true in dealing with children from somewhat exceptional
environments—from the remoter rural districts, for example,
or from less civilized colonies abroad. The problems chosen
should be chiefly such as will turn either upon power to
learn or upon power to grasp logical relations.

In judging younger or duller persons the more valuable
tests will be those that involve learning by experience; for
the young child's power to adjust himself to the needs of his
environment will depend largely on this capacity. With
older individuals and with higher grades, the most helpful
tests will be those that depend upon reasoning; for the
adult's capacity for rational adjustment will vary with his
power to reason logically. Now this does not necessarily
involve an explicit argument in words. Logical reasoning,
as recent psychology has shown, consists essentially in the
perception of relations. And although the most abstract

[1] Published by the National Institute of Industrial Psychology, Aldwych
House, Aldwych, W.C. 2.

[2] Obtainable from G. G. Harrap & Co., Parker Street, W.C. 2.

[3] Part IV, pp. 226–30; a copy of the test material is appended in the pocket
at the end of the report.

relations need words to express them, there are certain relations, more simple and more concrete, which can be conveyed through sensory or perceptual material—for example, through differences in weight, colour, spatial arrangement, or geometrical form. Hence, most of the current problems that appear and reappear in tests of a verbal type—problems depending on the perception of difference, of similarity, of opposites and contrasts, of orderly arrangement by serial analogy, and the like—can be presented in perceptual and therefore non-verbal form. Take, for example, verbal tests of the following familiar kinds:

(i) 'Say whether the second of the two words is similar to or different from the first:

Good   Bad?
False   Untrue?'

(ii) 'Number the following in order of size:
Baby, Youth, Child, Man.'

(iii) 'Add a fourth word having the same relation to the third as the second has to the first:
High *is to* Low
as Big *is to*. ... ?'

It is clear that, by substituting shapes or colours, exactly the same problems can be presented in non-verbal material. The child can be asked to say whether a given square is similar to or different from a triangle, a circle, and another square: to arrange a number of squares in order of size, or according to a given proportion: 'This square is to that as a third square is to . . . .? (Find the missing square).' Or again, given a particular shade of red, he can be required to say whether another shade is the same or different, or, given a series of shades, to arrange them in order of intensity, or, given two shapes of red, to find two analogous shapes of green, bearing the same relation as the red pair, and thus completing the square pattern. Moreover, the square pattern or 'matrix' can be enlarged to include nine or even sixteen related items, one or more being left to the examinee to find or fill in. If lines, dots, and simple geometrical figures are employed, there is hardly any limit to the material that can be systematically compiled for such purposes. On these principles the doctor can get together a number of supplementary tests for himself; he will find them in many ways easier to invent, easier to apply, and often more reliable in their results, than the verbal. Tests of this type, it may be noted, lend themselves quite readily to a group procedure, and are now in process of standardization for that purpose. In the near future they will come, no doubt, more and more into vogue.[1] The ideal group test will include both verbal and non-verbal tests.

With all these tests, verbal or non-verbal, individual or group, the final result is generally expressed in terms of a mental age. This is not the most scientific unit.[2] But other units are more technical, and presuppose some knowledge of elementary statistics: to the ordinary teacher, doctor, magistrate, or member of an education committee, they

[1] Perceptual tests of the 'matrix' type can be readily designed in accordance with the formal principles of matrix algebra and thus graded progressively in order of increasing complexity. [Since the above was written, Mr. Raven, with assistance from Dr. Penrose and myself, has standardized a serviceable series of 'progressive matrices', obtainable from Messrs. H. K. Lewis and Co., which has been very widely used. His work at the Royal Eastern Counties Institution has shown them to be especially suitable for testing abnormal patients. Cf. J. C. Raven, 'Perceptual Tests of Intelligence', M.Sc. Thesis, Univ. London Library, and *Brit. J. Med. Psychol.* xix, 1941, pp. 137–50.]

[2] For purposes of research the best unit is the 'standard deviation', or its equivalent—the 'percentile' rank. The term 'mental ratio' was proposed in my L.C.C. *Report on the Distribution of Educational Abilities* (1917). As was there pointed out, the relation between the standard deviation and chronological age is *approximately* linear (cf. loc. cit., fig. 5, p. 80). Hence for practical purposes a 'mental ratio' may conveniently be substituted. Mental ages and mental ratios, when obtained with different tests, are not strictly comparable. If, however, the results of each test are expressed in terms, not of the average for each age, but of the standard deviation, then all tests can be compared on an equivalent basis. Moreover, for brighter children at the older ages, neither mental ages nor mental ratios can be computed. If, for example, a child of 10 has a mental age of 15, his mental ratio will be 150. But what will be his mental age at the chronological age of 15? He ought to have a mental age of 150 per cent. of 15, i.e. 22·5 years; but no such mental age exists. The intelligence of such children, therefore, cannot be accurately measured except in terms of the standard deviation, though, by means of an arbitrary scale, it is possible to convert such measurements approximately into equivalent mental ratios when desired.

would hardly be intelligible. The idea of a mental age, on the other hand, can be understood by all.

A child's mental age, however, depends not only on the amount of his innate intelligence but also on the degree of his maturity. Hence it becomes desirable to eliminate the influence of chronological age or growth. For this purpose the mental ratio has been proposed. The mental ratio is the proportion of the child's mental age to his age by the calendar; in America it is more commonly known as his intelligence quotient or I.Q. The calculation is made by the simple equation:

$$\text{mental ratio} = \frac{\text{mental age}}{\text{chronological age}} \times 100$$

The great advantage of the I.Q. or mental ratio lies in this: by testing and re-testing the same children throughout their school life, it has been shown that the ratio of each individual remains approximately constant throughout the years of growth. We thus obtain a valuable guide towards a prognosis. Suppose, for example, a child is brought to the doctor at the early age of 5: the doctor tests him, and finds he has a mental age of 2—a mental ratio, therefore, of two-fifths, or 40 per cent. The mother inquires about the outlook for the future, and wonders whether the child will 'grow out of it'. In reply, the doctor, if his testing is sound and there are no obvious interfering factors, may venture on this rough prophecy, and that with a reasonable hope of fulfilment: the child's mental ratio of 40 per cent. will remain constant. Accordingly, at the age of 10 he will have a mental age of 40 per cent. of 10, that is 4; at the age of 15 he will have a mental age of 40 per cent. of 15, that is 6. And what will be his mental level when he is grown up?

That may be deduced from another unexpected result of psychological research. It appears that about the time of puberty the development of intelligence attains its limit. From 14 or 15 onwards the average child shows no appreciable increase in mental age. The dull and the defective come to an arrest a little earlier; the bright and the super-normal a few years later. The limit is a limit to spontaneous growth, not to intellectual progress. It does not mean that the child, after reaching adolescence, will learn no more. Up to that period his learning capacity has been steadily maturing; at that period it achieves its maximum, and ceases to expand; but it will remain at its maximum: and the child may continue to learn with that maximum capacity, though now the capacity itself will increase no farther. He may acquire more knowledge and more skill, but he will not develop greater intelligence. A practical corollary follows: the mental age which a child attains at puberty will roughly mark his mental limit for the rest of his life. Hence, in the case in question, we may safely hazard a guess that the boy, when grown up, will never possess an intelligence above that of the average child of 6.

In terms of the mental ratio it is possible to answer another practical question. How far do individuals vary among the normal population, and what are the limits of normality? Is their innate ability distributed like property or income, where those who have little are exceedingly numerous and those who have much are few and far between? Or is it distributed like physical characteristics— weight and stature, for example—where the average type is the commonest type and the dwarf and the giant are comparatively rare? In short, does Nature in scattering her gifts obey any discernible law?

Intelligence tests have now been applied on an extensive scale; and the results afford a convincing reply. In London, for instance, throughout a given year, every boy and girl of every age in every school of a representative borough was examined in this way—a survey covering more than 30,000 cases. More recently in Scotland the whole school population at the age of 10 has been subjected to a psychological test. And in several Civil Service examinations many thousands of adults have been similarly tested.

From all these surveys one remarkable fact emerges—the vast range of individual differences. In the London borough it was found that, in the elementary schools alone, the mental ratios varied from barely 50 per cent. to almost 150 per cent. Take, by way of illustration, all boys and girls aged 10: the brightest was found to have the mental level of an average child of nearly 15, the dullest that of an average child of little over 5.[1]

Teachers and doctors, whose experience is limited to one kind of school or one type of area, are apt to underestimate the wide variation that obtains among the normal population. The teacher, and still more the doctor, tend to accept, as marking a normal standard, those children with whom they are best acquainted within their own immediate circle. Not long ago a physician, reporting on a ten-year-old that he had referred to me, argued that the lad was manifestly defective, since he was unable to solve problems that his own son could answer at the age of $8\frac{1}{2}$. Such arguments are exceedingly common; but, in view of the facts I have just adduced, they are plainly misleading. The son of a professional man would probably inherit his father's high ability. Doubtless, therefore, the doctor's son at the age of $8\frac{1}{2}$ had a mental age of $10\frac{1}{2}$ or more. Hence it would be quite illogical to treat him as representing the average child, and adopt his performance as a standard of comparison.

Over the whole of this vast range it is found that individual variation is entirely continuous. No breaks, no gaps, mark off the defective from the normal, or the normal from the genius. Nowhere do we find discrete mental types, or well-marked classes abruptly separated and sharply defined. Subnormality, like abnormality, turns out to be a relative term. Most significant of all, the distribution itself conforms very closely with a well-known statistical law. Like height and weight, and sizes of bones or skulls, and, indeed, most anthropometric measurements, intelligence is distributed in accordance with what is termed the 'normal curve of error'. The average man is by far the commonest; those who deviate above or below are not so common: the more they deviate, the rarer they appear; and the fool is almost as infrequent as the genius. The form of such distributions can be computed from a single differential equa-

---

[1] The children with the lowest mental ratios, although in ordinary elementary schools, were actually mentally defective; and the majority of them were subsequently transferred to special schools.

tion; and tables have been compiled for the ordinates of the curve—that is, for the frequency of the measurements at each successive step. It is, in fact, the curve of chance—the distribution obeyed by all those variations that are due to an almost infinite number of almost infinitesimal factors. The curve itself is smooth and symmetrical, shaped like a bow or bell, conical, with one high peak in the middle, but flattened, or rather rounded, at the top, the whole suggestive of a heap of sand tipped from a bucket or dribbled gently from an hour-glass.

The significance of such facts is obvious; and the deductions may be of the greatest practical utility. If, for example, an education officer has to decide how many special schools, central schools, secondary schools, and the like, are to be provided for an area of a given size, he can calculate the requisite numbers with the same ease and accuracy with which an insurance company can foretell the number of deaths to be expected in a given year, or a gunner the scattering of shots from his gun.

For practical purposes, particularly for problems of educational and vocational guidance, it is convenient to divide the whole range into some eight or ten grades. In a large population it usually appears that about 2 per thousand have mental ratios above 150. Such persons are generally found either in the higher professions or in important administrative posts in business or the Civil Service: they are usually people of a good university honours type, though they may never actually have taken a university degree. Another 2 per cent. have mental ratios above 130. In London, at the time of my original surveys, a child of this high intelligence generally obtained a junior county scholarship and would proceed to a secondary school. Ten per cent. have mental ratios over 115; and were usually transferred to central schools. The majority of persons have mental ratios in the neighbourhood of 100, ranging from 115 down to 85. Within these limits fall 76 per cent. of the total population, approximately three-quarters. Since the distribution is symmetrical, much the same proportions are found for deviations below 100 as for the corresponding deviations above 100. Thus 10 per cent. of the population have mental ratios between 85 and 70; these, as we shall discover later on, are generally regarded as dull or backward. Persons with mental ratios below 70 and above 50 are during childhood generally regarded as feeble-minded, and incapable of profiting by instruction in the ordinary elementary school. Their actual number we shall have to investigate when we come to discuss the mentally defective; a rough estimate puts them at between 1 and 2 per cent. of the population. Those with mental ratios under 50 are usually regarded as ineducable defectives, fit only for a residential institution; they number about 1 or 2 per thousand.[1]

With these arbitrary but convenient lines of demarcation, then, the whole school population can be broadly graded according to the education each child is fit to receive. A similar grading can be drawn up for adults according to their profession or trade. The detailed classification can be found in works on vocational psychology.[2] The average mental ratio of the professional man, for example, is usually about 135, but exceptional individuals may rise to ratios of 160 or 180. The average mental ratio of the unskilled labourer usually works out at about 80 per cent. But these figures are averages only. Within any occupational class the range, as actually observed, varies enormously. It would not be safe to assume, because a man is a dock labourer, that his mental ratio must therefore fall below 100, nor, because a man is a teacher, doctor, or lawyer, that his mental ratio must

[1] In considering diagnostic borderlines, it must be remembered that errors in diagnosis may be of two kinds: (i) a 'normal' child may be wrongly certified as mentally defective; (ii) a mentally defective child may be wrongly passed as 'normal' and left in the ordinary class. The doctor usually regards (i) as less serious; the education committee usually regards (ii) as less serious. The correlation coefficient treats both as of *equal* moment. But in problems of practical selection this tacit assumption is often far from justifiable. Blackstone declares 'it is better that ten guilty persons escape than one innocent suffer' (*Commentaries on the Laws of England*, iv. 27). Hence the meaning of a particular correlation should always be expanded in the form of a bivariate frequency-table, and, if possible, a 'weight' or 'cost' explicitly specified for each type of decision.

[2] e.g. Medical Research Council, *Report of the Industrial Health Research Board*, no. 33, Table III, p. 13.

therefore soar well above the average. Nevertheless, the averages obtained in the different types of employment supply a useful criterion for vocational guidance. Such facts may at times prove suggestive to the examining physician, since, as we shall see later on, cases of delinquency or psycho-neurosis often occur in those whose mental level is not properly adjusted to the requirements of their occupations—whose intelligence, therefore, is, in one direction or another, unequal to the difficulties and responsibilities of their daily work.

The 'normal' distribution of individual differences is most clearly established for innate intelligence and for educational capacities. But there is reason to suppose that it holds good, more or less precisely, for all mental qualities, temperamental as well as intellectual, special as well as general. On this assumption rating-scales have been drawn up for qualities which cannot be directly measured by quantitative tests—for example, literary ability, drawing ability, moral character, emotional stability, and the strength of instinctive tendencies generally. In London the method has been introduced into the marking of character-qualities among candidates seeking to enter training colleges for teachers and of examination scripts for the teacher's certificate and diploma; the results show that interviewers' assessments and examiners' markings are thereby rendered far more trustworthy and precise.

ii. *Specific Abilities.*

We have seen that efficiency at work, whether in school subjects or in after-life, depends upon two intellectual factors: it is determined not only by the individual's general intelligence, but also by his special aptitudes. To do well in arithmetic, for example, a boy must have not only a high measure of intelligence, but also a specialized ability for perceiving numerical relations. Similarly, he may fail in arithmetic for one of two reasons: either because his intelligence is subnormal, or else because, with an intelligence perfectly normal, he possesses some peculiar, localized defect which prevents him from understanding or manipulating figures. This twofold principle appears to operate in every type of intellectual work.[1]

In theory, therefore, to make a complete study of any individual's mind, we ought to test not only his general intelligence but also his more specific intellectual capacities. Most researches reveal first a broad factor distinguishing the afferent or receptive type of mind from the efferent or executive—the intellectual from the practical, and secondly more specialized factors for different levels (sensory, perceptual, associative, and relational) and for different contents (verbal, numerical, visual, auditory, &c.). The lists put forward are admittedly tentative and incomplete: and, at first sight, they seem reminiscent of the old catalogues of mental 'faculties'—perception, memory, imagination, and the like. But between the two conceptions there lies an important distinction. An intellectual 'faculty' was supposed to be quite sufficient in itself to determine success or failure in its particular direction; the modern view insists that the specific aptitude is only one hypothetical component, so that efficiency in an actual piece of work requires the co-operation of the general factor, intelligence, as well. The old-fashioned faculties were pictured as completely independent entities, lodged in separate organs or areas of the brain; the specific factors of the modern psychologist are simply abstract constituents deduced by statistical analysis: it is conceivable that they have no more concrete existence than the north and south poles or the lines of latitude and longitude upon a map. In short, the so-called specific factor is nothing but a convenient name for a relatively general tendency that appears to underlie a limited group of mental activities, all correlated more or less closely together.[2]

[1] Medical writers usually attribute the distinction between 'general ability' and 'special aptitudes' to Spearman. It was in point of fact originally introduced by Galton. Spearman was highly sceptical of anything resembling 'special aptitudes', since they seemed to him to be reminiscent of the discredited doctrine of mental faculties.

[2] On the nature and number of the specific abilities see Burt, *The Measurement of Mental Capacities* (Oliver & Boyd, 1926) and 'The Structure of the Mind', *Brit. J. Educ. Psychol.*, xix, 1949, pp. 100–11, 176–99.

To test and measure these specific abilities nearly always requires a laboratory technique, and a statistical calculation to eliminate the influence of intelligence. New tests are constantly being devised. Of the older and more thoroughly standardized tests the best collection is that given in Whipple's *Manual of Mental and Physical Tests*. At child-guidance clinics and psychological institutions such tests are employed from time to time for special cases—largely for children suffering from limited disabilities in special subjects of the school curriculum, most frequently of all for vocational guidance. But the methods, the apparatus, and the computations required are hardly at the command of the practising physician.

B. Acquired Attainments

Having examined the child's innate capacities—both general and specific, the next step, in logical order, is to examine his acquired attainments. For this purpose tests of three main types are available: first, tests of educational accomplishments; secondly, tests of trade knowledge or skill; and, thirdly and less completely worked out, tests of general information and general culture. With these the psychologist can complete his survey of the intellectual side of the mind.

For the doctor the most useful of these further tests are the tests of school attainments; they are also the most thoroughly standardized and the easiest to apply. Such tests he may at times find helpful in assessing the general educational level of adults; but their chief use will lie in the preliminary examination of dull, backward, or mentally defective pupils. Until recently the school medical officer was wont to depend, for a note of each child's educational attainments, almost exclusively upon the teacher; now and then he might try a few improvised questions in reading or arithmetic, but these he usually standardized, if he standardized them at all, simply on the basis of personal impression or casual experience. To-day, almost every school medical officer is proficient in the use of scholastic tests; and, since a teacher's standard varies considerably from one school to another, it is essential that the examining doctor should be able to check the teacher's report by some more accurate procedure.

I have left the discussion of educational testing until last. In actual practice, however, it will generally save time to start with the educational tests, and then proceed to tests of intelligence and possibly of special ability, in those particular instances where the child's attainments are found to be definitely below the normal. Occasionally, for example, it will happen that a headmaster submits as many as a dozen cases of alleged deficiency for the doctor to examine in the same afternoon. In such circumstances the best plan will be to apply some simple educational test first—preferably a test of reading. This will occupy but two or three minutes. If the child's reading proves equal to the average for his age, the possibility of mental deficiency can forthwith be safely rejected—at any rate so far as intellectual capacity is concerned (a diagnosis of temperamental deficiency is still conceivable, but temperamental deficiency, as we shall find later on, is exceedingly rare). With this procedure the doctor may be able to dismiss almost at once a large number of the children put forward, and so be free to devote the remainder of his time to those that are genuinely backward.

There is a further advantage in this approach. Any child referred to the doctor for a mental examination is apt to arrive for the ordeal in a state of bewilderment and alarm. When he finds that the first thing he is asked to do is to read a passage of prose or a short list of words, he soon recovers confidence; and, by the time the doctor comes to the tests of intelligence, the child is more at his ease.

For almost every subjeċt of the elementary curriculum tests have been drawn up; and the average performance to be expected at each year of school life is accurately known. A systematized collection of such tests, with full instructions and norms, will be found in the London County Council's memoranda cited above.[1] In the complete version each test contains 10 words to be read at each age, or 10 words to be

---

[1] Loc. cit., Memorandum III. I have reprinted the more useful of these tests at the end of this volume (Appendix I, pp. 354-9).

spelt, or 10 sums to be worked, and so on. Hence a child's educational level can be computed in terms of mental years to an approximate decimal point, and his attainments in each subject in turn can be compared with his mental age for intelligence.

To save time, only one or two of these tests need be employed in most cases. If, as usually happens, the examination is oral, the reading test and the mental arithmetic test (one or two problems only for each mental age) will yield a fair estimate of the child's educational level. But if a number of pupils are to be examined at once, then a written test for spelling and a paper test in arithmetic will yield equally good results, except of course with those who are too young or dull to do any work with the pencil. In either case it is wise to add a drawing-test—the test of drawing a man, for example—as this may reveal some practical or manual ability in those who cannot do themselves justice in tasks involving figures or words: incidentally, a child's drawings will often throw light on other features in his mental make-up —his special interests, for example, and even his emotional stability. The drawings of the unstable child, particularly those of the hysteric, often possess distinctive features—a characteristic dash and eccentricity, with babyish and quasi-comic schematizations—which, with a little experience, may be easily recognized in such cases. But, with every test, the detailed result of the child's efforts, as well as his marks or mental age, should be noted. Often the most suggestive outcome of the testing lies not in the actual measurement, but in the child's method of approach, the faults he makes, the interest he shows, and in the innumerable sidelights cast upon his character and personality.

Where the child proves to be backward, without being mentally deficient, a more detailed examination of his educational capacities will be required. Occasionally the unevenness shown by the results, particularly in a child whose intelligence is normal, will indicate the need for a study of special disabilities. Such a study will be indispensable in those who suffer from some limited form of backwardness—in reading, for example (as in the so-called word-blind child), or in arithmetic, or perhaps in manual subjects, like handwriting and handwork. With adults an examination of scholastic attainments is usually unnecessary, and apt to prove disconcerting to the patient. At times, in a man who has had a regular education, a condition of extreme illiteracy may be suggestive of some deeper mental defect; and, where problems of vocational adjustment arise, systematic tests may be essential. But, as a rule, it is social rather than intellectual or industrial efficiency that forms the main question for the doctor.

I now turn to the most delicate part of every psychological examination. Hitherto we have been studying the patient's intellectual qualities, of which he is not usually ashamed; now we have to study his character, which he commonly prefers to keep private.

2. Temperamental Aspect

Character has been defined as the sum total of all those mental qualities which do not constitute, or are not pervaded by, intelligence. It is, however, well to avoid the moral implications that cling to the word character. Consequently, I prefer to substitute the old term temperament, and to redefine it according to the phrase just quoted. Yet a negative definition is not altogether satisfactory. What qualities actually fall under this heading must be determined by correlation. When this criterion is employed, a number of mental qualities are quickly discovered which have no correlation with intelligence, and yet disclose tolerably high correlations amongst themselves. These qualities are marked by affective and conative elements rather than by cognitive, by feeling rather than by knowledge, by will rather than by skill.

For the practical psychologist the temperamental aspect of the mind is of supreme importance, for here are to be sought the sources of all mental energy and the motives of all human action. Psychology in the past has been far too intellectualistic. It has assumed that man is primarily a rational animal: if the conduct of some particular individual was found to be irrational, then it was concluded that he must be either mentally defective or else insane. The recent study of insanity, however, and of borderline neuroses has brought into special prominence the affective and conative side of mental life, and has forced us to delve deeper into the ultimate bases of character. These, on close scrutiny, prove to be emotional rather than intellectual, unconscious rather than conscious. Popular parlance declares that when a man is mad he has lost his reason; modern psychology discovers that, as a rule, men only lose their reason when their emotions run away with it.

From the study of graver psychotic and neurotic conditions, however, the psychologist has been led back to the re-examination of the normal mind. There he discovers much the same tendencies at work, though in a milder degree and in a less eccentric form. And thus he has come to realize that no man's mental portrait is complete until this hidden aspect of his nature has been fully explored. Accordingly, in whatever case comes before him—in examining the dull, the backward, and the defective, quite as much as in examining the nervous or the delinquent— the doctor must always give at least a glance to the underlying emotional states. Often he will discover that, unless he carefully allows for them, these emotional influences may even upset his tests and estimates of intelligence. Constantly, too, he will find that what he took to be an instance of innate dullness or deficiency turns out to be the effect of temperamental abnormality; and, if he is on the watch for such conditions, he will find that in case after case the entire problem turns on the investigation of emotional rather than intellectual factors.

As in examining the intellectual aspect, so in assessing temperament and character, we need some systematic scheme to guide us. How is mind organized on the temperamental side? Here research has been less fruitful; and our reply must remain more doubtful. Nevertheless, there is already to hand a reasonable amount of evidence showing that the same distinctions that we have met with in dissecting intellectual characteristics are valid and appropriate in this newer sphere as well. Thus we may begin by distinguishing once again between the inborn elements and the acquired, and between specific and general tendencies.

A. Innate Elements.

Plainly, to discriminate those qualities of character that are innate and therefore permanent from those that have been acquired and are therefore perhaps removable would be a point of great practical assistance. To know whether a spiteful boy is inherently ill-tempered, or only venting some half-hidden grievance; to know whether an erring girl is constitutionally over-sexed, or merely putting into practice what she has picked up from corrupt companions; to distinguish a temporary nervous breakdown, due mainly to shock or strain, from chronic tendencies towards psychosis rooted in the patient's constitution and liable perhaps to issue in definite insanity; to separate the excitability that is but a brief and transitory episode of some pubertal crisis from an excitability that has been present from birth and will probably last a lifetime—these are problems that continually arise in examining the neurotic and the delinquent, and, when they can be satisfactorily answered, will make a world of difference to the outlook and the treatment.

The words 'temperament' and 'character' are sometimes used in a narrower sense to mark these separate levels, temperament being applied to those moral or emotional qualities that are supposed to be innate, and character to those that are presumed to be acquired. But the subdivision is abstract rather than real. A man's mind is not to be pictured as a building with two storeys, as though the later superstructure could be taken down and wholly rebuilt on the foundation of the old. To attempt such distinctions will be even more precarious in the realm of conduct than it was in the field of intellect. With adults it can rest on little more than guesswork. With the young a few suggestive hints may at times be gleaned from the family history, or from the early personal history of the child himself. One point, however, seems clear. Inheritance, or innate constitution, limits character far less rigidly than it limits intelligence. It is far more hopeful to try and improve the morally defective than the intellectually defective; and it will always be unsafe to infer that some particular temperamental quality must be beyond all cure because it seems inherited, or at any rate inborn.

i. *Specific Tendencies*.

With these reservations, therefore, let us consider what temperamental characteristics are generally supposed to be innate. We have seen that, on the intellectual side, there are certain capacities, presumably inborn, which are definite and specific: similarly, on the temperamental side, most psychologists recognize that we all inherit certain tendencies to action, equally specific, whose innate strength may vary from one individual to another. These specific tendencies are commonly termed instincts.

In the past an instinct has usually been regarded as a kind of compound reflex—a reflex which is excited by a complex object or situation rather than by a single, simple stimulus, and which involves an action of the body as a whole rather than the movement of a single limb or muscle-group. Such a description, no doubt, would still be accepted by the behaviourist school of psychology. Many present-day psychologists, however, certainly most in this country, would be inclined to argue that instinctive behaviour cannot be explained solely in terms of a physiological mechanism. It reveals a purposive character; it involves a release of energy which may act in the line of greatest resistance rather than in the line of least resistance; and it is conspicuously influenced by pleasure and pain.

In human beings, as distinct from animals, the overt bodily actions may themselves be suppressed. Movements entirely different may be substituted; or no outward action whatever may ensue; thoughts, images, complex states of feeling, or even an unconscious change of attitude may be the sole result. But the disturbance continues until some end is achieved. Hence, it is impossible to describe such tendencies in physiological terms; and we are tempted to speak of 'impulses' in this or that direction, or of the unwitting effort to fulfil this or that particular 'wish'. At the same time the arousal of such impulses or unconscious wishes may be attended by considerable physiological activity. The action of the skeletal muscles, being under the control of the voluntary nervous system, can be successfully inhibited; but the accompanying excitement of the viscera and glands are not so readily suppressed, since these organs are regulated, not by the voluntary, but the autonomic system. The frightened man may check the instinctive impulse to take to his heels and hide; but he cannot control the acceleration of his heart, the alteration in his breathing, the derangement of his stomach, and the secretion of his glands. Probably it is the obscure sensations caused by these glandular and visceral changes that we loosely call the emotion. At all events, with human beings, particularly with educated adults, the emotional reaction is more easily recognized than the instinctive. Actually, the two seem to go in pairs: to every instinct there is a corresponding emotion.

What precisely are the fundamental human instincts and emotions is a matter of controversy. Some psychologists admit but two or three; others distinguish as many as twenty or thirty; some think the term instinct altogether misleading.[1] For practical purposes the most convenient classification is that suggested by James, McDougall, Shand, and Drever. Except for minor variations their lists are the same. We may, therefore, provisionally recognize the following as probably innate: the emotion of joy, corresponding to the instincts of laughter and smiling; the emotion of sorrow, corresponding to the instinct of weeping; anger, corre-

---

[1] The view that man inherits instincts and emotional tendencies similar to those of the higher animals is due mainly to the British evolutionary school, notably Charles Darwin (*Descent of Man*, 1874, chaps. III and IV). Between the two wars it was vigorously challenged by American behaviourists and environ mentalists. It now (1953) seems almost universally accepted, though American writers generally prefer some different name—e.g., 'drives' (G. W. Allport and Holt), 'primary needs' (Murray and Mackinnon); 'primary tensions' (Lewin), 'primary urges' or 'ergs' (Cattell); 'prepotent reflexes' (F. W. Allport), 'unlearned motives' (Woodworth). As Woodworth himself observes, 'if we use the word "instinct", we become immediately involved in disputes over words' (*Psychology*, p. 371). However, the change of name implies no fundamental change of doctrine. This is admirably shown by Notcutt's comparative table of the 'basic motives' recognized by these different writers (*Psychology of Personality*, 1953, pp. 109–15 and 23 f.).

sponding to pugnacity; fear, corresponding to flight; sexual excitement, corresponding to the reproductive instinct; affection or tender emotion, corresponding to the protective or parental instinct; wonder or surprise, corresponding to the instinct of curiosity; disgust, corresponding to the instinct of rejection (the impulse to shrink from unwholesome smells and to disgorge unwholesome food); pride, corresponding to the self-assertive instinct (the instinct of self-display); humility, corresponding to the self-submissive instinct; and to these should perhaps be added a few vaguer tendencies that have no well-defined or clearly named emotional equivalent—such as gregariousness (the social or herd instinct), wandering, hunting, constructiveness, acquisitiveness, and the like.

These, it is maintained, constitute the innate bases of personality or character. If this view be approximately correct, then the first step towards understanding the temperament of any given individual would be to work through some such inventory of emotional tendencies, and assess, so far as is possible, the relative intensity of each in his particular constitution.

Common observation suggests that these emotional tendencies are specially correlated amongst themselves, so as to form two more or less antithetical groups; and this apparent correlation has been verified by statistical methods. We may distinguish first what may be termed the aggressive or sthenic group—joy, anger, self-assertiveness, curiosity, acquisitiveness, sex, and the like; and, secondly, what may be termed the inhibitive or asthenic group—grief, sorrow, fear, disgust, self-submissiveness, and possibly tenderness. If the former predominates, the result is an aggressive, or, as it is sometimes termed, an unrepressed temperament: such a temperament is especially common in those addicted to delinquency or crime. If the second group predominates, the result is a repressed or inhibited personality: it is a personality that is constantly found among the nervous or neurotic.[1]

---

[1] Admirable accounts of the two types as seen among children may be found in Leonard Guthrie's early volume on *Functional Nervous Disorders in Childhood*.

This opposition between the aggressive and inhibited, the explosive and obstructed, the demonstrative and reserved, the tough-minded and the tender, the classic and the romantic, crops up again and again in medical, psychological, and popular literature. The labels change, but the fundamental contrast appears again and again. At the moment the fashionable terms are 'extravert' and 'introvert'. The more salient examples are seen in psychotic cases; and the difference between patients suffering from manic-depressive states and dementia praecox gives the two pictures in magnified outline.

The new names and theories, however, are but a revival, with somewhat fuller evidence, of an ancient antithesis that is at least as old as Plutarch. The view that he expresses, revived by Shakespeare in his sketches of the 'lean' and the 'sleek' respectively, relates the contrast in disposition to a contrast in physique. It is immortalized in such portraits as those of Hamlet and Falstaff, or of Don Quixote and Sancho Panza. The sleek or plump are represented as typical extraverts—aggressive, unrestrained, and boisterous, varying from hilarious excitement to demonstrative grief, with interludes of easy-going amiability. The lean are depicted as typical introverts—inwardly sensitive but outwardly quiet, solitary, secretive, and engrossed in fantasy, self-controlled, self-centred, self-absorbed.

The traditional view, as embodied, for example, in the legend of Jack Spratt and his wife, connects the differences with dietetic habits. But, according to modern opinion, the differences, alike in physique and disposition, are attributable rather to a difference in bodily metabolism, although dietetic habits, as part of the temperamental preferences, may augment both physical and temperamental characteristics. An old-fashioned nomenclature, preserved in phrenological writings, emphasizes this further suggestion: for the two types are often termed the 'vital' or 'digestive' and the 'nervous' or 'mental' respectively. Three American physiologists, Bryant, Goldthwait, and Dunham, whose observations on this point are more careful than most, have proposed the terms 'herbivorous' and 'carnivorous', thus claiming a biological derivation, somewhat speculative it must be owned, for the supposed peculiarities in digestive habits and in general manner of life. Three Italian physiologists, Viola, Naccarati, and De Giovanni, have tried to show that the two tendencies can be demonstrated by physical measurement: they claim that the ratio of weight to height, or better of trunk to limbs, may be taken as a trustworthy index of the so-called 'morphological type'. They describe the two groups as microsplanchnic and macrosplanchnic respectively, that is, little-bellied and big-bellied; and declare that the difference is demonstrably associated with tested mental differences.

Of all such investigations the best known is that of Kretschmer. He has studied the two types as found among asylum populations. He finds that patients of a manic-depressive type tend to be short, thick-set, and obese, with broad face, sunken head, and thick, soft, rounded limbs; and that patients suffering from dementia praecox or allied conditions tend to be thin, lanky, and sparely built, with narrow face, long neck, and long and bony limbs. The two types he designates 'pyknic' and 'asthenic' respectively; and he believes that the diathesis is accompanied by a susceptibility to particular diseases. The asthenic often succumbs to tuberculosis; the pyknic is more liable to diabetes, arterio-sclerosis, and rheumatic conditions of every kind.[1]

For a view that has received so much popular and scientific

---

[1] The existence of body-types has been fully confirmed by factor analysis; but their relation to temperamental types still awaits verification by correlational techniques. The coefficients so far obtained are rather low—rarely over 0·30: (cf. Burt, *Brit. Ass. Rep.*, 1915, p. 695; 1923, p. 221). For a summary of the Italian work see Boldrini, *La Fertilità dei Biotipi*, 1931.

[In America a somewhat different approach has been adopted by W. H. Sheldon (*Physique and Temperament*, 1942). Of recent investigations in this country the most extensive has been the factor-analysis of body-measurements for 2,400 R.A.F. recruits (C. Burt and C. Banks, *Ann. Eugen.* xiii, 1947, pp. 238–56). For further investigations of temperamental factors among both normal and neurotic persons, see id., 'The Factorial Study of Temperamental Traits', *Brit. J. Psychol. Stat. Sect.*, i, 1948, pp. 178–203: this fully confirmed the previous factors, namely, (1) general emotionality, well marked in the neurotics, (2) extraversion *versus* introversion, (3) euphoria *versus* dysphoria].

support there is probably a good deal to be said. The whole theory, however, has still to be checked by the obvious method of correlation: (see p. 221). It will be remarked that the mental and physical peculiarities are reminiscent of the pictures frequently drawn of glandular and racial types: the slender, asthenic, microsplanchnic type is suggestive of hyperthyroidism, and of the tall, long-headed, active Nordic race; while the heavy, pyknic, macrosplanchnic type is similarly suggestive of hypothyroïdism, and of the short, round-headed, stolid Alpine race. More recent research, however, tends to connect such differences with peculiarities in the whole glandular equilibrium rather than with the functioning of one isolated gland, like the thyroid; and here, very possibly, may lie the root of all the associated characteristics. We still await the biochemist who may devise a series of delicate laboratory tests, and tell us, from the composition of the blood, to what temperamental type the owner of the specimen belongs.

ii. *General Emotionality.*

On a limited scale, the method of correlation has already been applied to the investigation of the relations between the emotional tendencies themselves. Besides confirming in some small degree the specific associations among the inhibitive emotions, on the one hand, and the aggressive emotions, on the other, it also reveals, with much greater clearness, the existence of a single all-pervading factor. Indeed, it is only when the influence of this general factor has been ruled out that the specific grouping appears. Thus the chief upshot of such statistical inquiries is this: they indicate that, as a general rule, though not of necessity in any single individual, an excessive liability to one emotion or instinct tends to be accompanied by a marked liability to most of the others. The correlation is plainer among children than among adults, and among delinquents than among the virtuous. The boy or girl who steals is nearly always secretive; often disposed to petty sexual faults; frequently a truant; usually rather quarrelsome and spiteful; and yet, incongruously enough, an arrant coward, an easy dupe, spasmodically generous, effusively affectionate, and prone to heart-broken tears of remorse.

As with intellectual capacities, so with emotional, one fundamental factor seems to pervade them all. The central factor underlying intellectual processes has been described as 'general intelligence': the central factor underlying instincts and emotions may be termed 'general emotionality'. These results are consistent with the hypothesis of a central fund of emotional energy, and with the facts suggesting that energy due to the excitement of one emotional tendency may be drafted off and enlisted vicariously in the service of a different impulse. The terms 'libido' and 'displacement of affect' have been sometimes used to explain these facts; and, though I do not wish to consider in detail the special implications of these phrases, the broad correspondence between the conclusions reached by statistical research and by psychoanalytic study is worthy of note.

If the account I have given can be provisionally accepted, then the attempt to classify an individual according to his temperament may conveniently proceed by two or three successive steps. Having roughly assessed his specific emotional tendencies, we note whether all or most of them deviate in strength above the average or below. Thus, the first and most important point is to consider whether the man's general emotionality is normal, deficient, or excessive.

In the normal man, we may presume, all the emotions and instincts would be developed to average strength: none should dominate, and none should be lacking; the aggressive and the inhibitive emotions should counterbalance each other, and no instinct should be too violent to be governed by whatever intelligence the man possesses. Such a temperament we may describe as well-balanced or *stable*: the impulses are not so much repressed as well-controlled.

In those who deviate from normal stability, the emotions may be either too feeble or too strong. Those in whom emotionality as a whole is peculiarly weak may be termed the unemotional or *apathetic*. They are indifferent, insensitive, and inert, slow to perceive and slow to move. And their slowness is due not to firm control or stern repression, but to a lack of ready energy, such as strong instincts and vigorous emotions would ordinarily supply.

The opposite picture is presented by the person whose general emotionality is excessive. He is excitable, passionate, and impulsive, as quick to feel as the apathetic is slow. All his instincts seem overdeveloped, or at any rate too strong for his intelligence to restrain. The feelings accompanying them may be violent enough while they last; but one impulse is quickly ousted by another, and the first mood may soon be followed by a different. Such a temperament may be called *unstable*.[1]

Having assessed the man's general emotionality, the next step is to consider the special groups of emotions, and to decide whether he belongs to one or other of the sub-groups named above—the introvert and inhibited or the extravert and uninhibited. The latter type is easily observed. Since the emotions are unrestrained, their nature promptly betrays itself in word or action, in tone of voice or change of facial expression. The inhibited are more difficult to detect. Inwardly sensitive, but outwardly repressed and wholly undemonstrative, they may often be mistaken for apathetic and unemotional individuals.

The third and final point is to consider whether any one instinct—fear, perhaps, or anger, joy or grief—may so predominate as to colour almost every mood and govern the man's whole behaviour.

It may be of interest to bring this rough classification into line with the fourfold classification of temperaments that has come down to us from Galen. Plainly the 'phlegmatic' temperament corresponds to what I have termed the unemotional or apathetic; the 'sanguine' corresponds to those who are merely unstable; the 'melancholic' corresponds to the inhibited or repressed sub-group; and the 'choleric' to the uninhibited and unrepressed. The normal, stable personality belongs to none of the four well-marked groups: it is commonly classed as a 'mixed' or 'balanced' temperament, to which, after all, the majority approximate.

Thus the grouping based on statistical investigation tallies

[1] Cf. Burt, C., 'The Unstable Child', *Child Study*, x, 1917, pp. 61–78.

to some extent with the ancient classification in its original form. In popular parlance, however, the old temperamental terms have acquired an additional implication, based on the most conspicuous emotion that seems to characterize each group. The most aggressive emotion is anger; hence 'choleric' has come to be synonymous with 'bad-tempered'. The most inhibiting emotions are grief and fear; hence 'melancholic' has come to be synonymous with 'sorrowful' or 'overanxious'. Brief emotional excitement of the instincts is pleasant rather than the reverse, and is thus apt to be accompanied by the emotion of joy: hence 'sanguine' has come to be synonymous with 'cheerful'. All through, it is plain, the popular love of antitheses—anger opposed to fear, joy opposed to sorrow—is largely responsible for this readjustment in meaning.

In recent scientific literature, temperament, and the classified types of temperaments, have acquired a signification that is still more narrowly restricted. Temperament is often defined to mean the manner in which all the emotions are aroused and tend to persist;[1] and this, it is supposed, is determined by the chemical or physiological responsiveness of nervous tissue, or by the effect on that tissue of chemical by-products floating in the blood-stream.[2] Hence two broad questions can be asked, and the alternative answers introduce a further distinction. Are the emotions quick to be aroused or slow to be aroused? Are they quick to subside or slow to subside? If they are quickly excited, but die down just as quickly, the man is classified as sanguine; if they are quickly aroused, but slow to die down, he is classified as choleric; if they are slow to be aroused and slow to die down, he is classified as melancholic; if they are slow to be aroused and die down again quickly before they have reached any appreciable degree of intensity, he is classified as phlegmatic. It will be observed that this yields an additional distinction between the sanguine and the choleric, which is commonly expressed by saying that the emotions of the sanguine are superficial and those of the choleric deep or profound.

[1] See Shand, *Foundations of Character*, pp. 129 et seq.
[2] See McDougall, *Social Psychology*, pp. 118 et seq.

These various analyses of temperament I have discussed in some detail, because the traditional terms so frequently appear in medical literature without any clear formulation of their meaning. Such broad distinctions may perhaps serve as a starting-point in observing each new personality; but, until more careful statistical studies have revealed how far the assumed correlations are justified by the facts, any attempt to pigeon-hole individuals in this way is to be made with the utmost caution. Generally speaking, a man should be described in terms of his actual behaviour rather than in terms of any hypothesis, however plausible; nevertheless, the hypotheses may serve to suggest tentative inferences and suggestive points for further exploration.

B. Acquired Characteristics.

Emotional tendencies, like cognitive tendencies, obey the ordinary laws of association. Just as ideas can be associated with each other, so instincts and emotions can be associated with ideas. In the baby, fear is excited only by one or two definite stimuli or situations, and tends to issue in definite forms of behaviour. But, owing to the effects of experience, fear may get attached to a totally new object, and may learn to vent itself in a totally new mode of action. Further, several emotions may become associated with one and the same object or idea. The result is to organize within the mind a number of complex emotional patterns, which tend more and more to regulate the growing child's daily conduct.

For these complex emotional patterns various names have been proposed. The patterns are of two kinds, according as the association is mainly unconscious and mechanical, or conscious and more or less logical. An emotional system which has been built up unconsciously, and is therefore apt to be illogical and even irrational, is commonly described as a 'complex';[1] the more rational and logical systems are called 'sentiments'. The difference is one of degree. The two

[1] I do not suggest that this is the strict psychoanalytic meaning of the term 'complex'. In this volume my endeavour has been to preserve a general and somewhat eclectic standpoint, and to sketch a rough basis, which (with some modification, no doubt) might be acceptable to all schools of psychology.

systems roughly answer to what in popular speech are some-times spoken of as moral habits and moral ideals respectively. To cover both perhaps the best generic name would be 'interests'.

Our oldest interests are interests in persons. At the very beginning of his life, a child's emotions inevitably become associated, first and foremost, with the one person who is constantly in his company—his mother or his nurse. Later, other members of the family become the objects of similar sentiments or complexes—his father, and his brothers and sisters. Later still, he begins to develop sentiments for concrete but inanimate things—his toys, his possessions, his home, or his school; and, when intelligence is more advanced, for abstract concepts—such as hobbies, school subjects, ideals of duty, and the like. But of all the child's sentiments or complexes, the most powerful is that con-cerned with himself. The 'ego-ideal' or 'self-regarding sentiment', as it has variously been termed—the notion, more or less idealized, that a child gradually acquires of himself, together with the associated emotions that the very thought of himself arouses—eventually forms the keystone of individual character. Any sentiment, it may be observed, can take the form either of love for its object or of hate for its object: complexes, being in their very nature illogical and inconsistent, generally include both love and hate, acting together in unstable combination.

To understand a given individual, therefore, and to appre-ciate his conscious or unconscious motives, we must first discover what leading emotional systems he has gradually built up. His chief sentiments, interests, and conscious ideals can be ascertained or guessed from tactful conversa-tion; his complexes, being unconscious, can only be un-ravelled by a special technique.

The Estimation of Temperament and Character. For qualities of temperament and character no simple tests are available such as are used for measuring intellectual capacities. Numerous experiments have been made in various directions—recording changes in pulse, respiration, muscular control, electrical conductivity, or the quickness of word-reactions. Some of the devices have yielded promising results, particularly in the study of neurotic conditions. But for the assessment of the character-qualities in the normal individual no trustworthy method as yet has been contrived. I shall, therefore, postpone the discussion of temperamental testing until we deal with the psychoneuroses. For more general purposes, we are forced to rely almost exclusively on methods of observation.

What points may be usefully noted I have indicated already. The first glimpse of a newcomer's physique and physiognomy may be suggestive. His behaviour and replies while under examination are still more enlightening. Particularly instructive is the way in which he reacts during the routine testing of his intelligence and of his intellectual abilities. But the most important of a man's emotional tendencies are those which relate to persons; and these are the easiest to elicit in a personal interview, just because all interviews are essentially personal.

In almost every instance, however, the psychologist should supplement what he himself is able to observe at first hand by the observations of others who have been in contact with the examinee over a long period of years. With children, parents' accounts of actual conduct are of first importance; the story of a child's early emotional development is always illuminating. Teachers are now trained in psychological observation and description; hence reports from schools may at times prove specially helpful. At a clinic, as we have seen, a preliminary account of the relevant facts can usually be obtained by a social worker who has been psychologically trained.

Such methods lead to no direct form of quantitative assessment. In the near future we shall probably have age-scales of typical emotional reactions for every year of child life, similar to the descriptive scales for the pre-school infant. Meanwhile, the best general method would seem to be to mark the strength of the various emotional tendencies in terms of some arbitrary rating-scale. Here figures or letters are allotted, usually in five grades: C may represent the average; B and D, qualities definitely above or below the average; and A and E, the extremes in either direction. In keeping with the principle described above,[1] it is generally assumed that each quality is distributed according to the normal curve; and each grade is then statistically defined in terms of the frequency with which it is found in a representative sample of the population. For purposes of research one of the schemes described in technical works upon the subject should be adopted; for practical purposes, however, each physician will probably prefer to work out his own.

I have now, in brief outline, described the structure of the normal mind, and the methods at our disposal for investigating the more normal characteristics. We shall find that most forms of mental subnormality turn out to be little else than exaggerated deviations in one or more of these characteristics. Certain symptoms and certain disorders are definitely pathological, and are found only in the mentally diseased; but these are comparatively rare. In the following chapters, therefore, I shall take up the various forms of mental subnormality in turn, beginning with those that affect the intellectual aspect of the mind and proceeding later to moral and temperamental disorders.

Notes and References. Individual psychology, that is, the study of the mental differences between individuals, was first placed on a scientific basis by Galton. Recognizing (as mentioned above) that the classification of individuals involves, not a sharp separation of clear-cut types, but a relative discrimination of overlapping groups distinguished by degree rather than by kind, Galton proposed to employ quantitative methods for measuring both the observable characteristics and the amount of their concomitant variation. For this purpose he introduced tests and rating scales, and emphasized the supreme need of statistical verification.

---

[1] See above, p. 37. I have given a more detailed account of the various methods, both observational and experimental, for assessing temperament in *The Young Delinquent*, pp. 400–19. The general pattern of a given individual's personality can be conveniently expressed by a 'psychogram' or 'profile'. To determine how far he approximates to a particular temperamental type the simplest device is that of 'correlating persons': for rough assessments it is sufficient to *rank* his emotional tendencies in order of strength and correlate the ranking with the theoretical order. The same procedure is extremely useful in assessing the amount of change due to growth, emotional experiences, and above all psychotherapeutic training or treatment: here what are correlated are rankings or ratings for the same person at different times.

The classification both of subjects (persons) and of their essential attributes (abilities and other traits) turns out to be hierarchical, involving progressive division and subdivision into genera (marked by 'generic factors'), and then into species, sub-species, and sub-sub-species, &c. (marked by specific factors—the broader being called 'group factors'). The statistical technique for verifying such factors is known as factor analysis and is due to Pearson's extension of Galton's correlation devices (1901). (See 'Factor Analysis in Psychological Medicine', *Brit. Med. Bull.* v, 1947–8, pp. 228 f.; and for an account of the hierarchical hypothesis, see E. M. Moursy, 'The Hierarchical Organization of Cognitive Levels', *Brit. J. Psychol. Stat. Sect.* v, 1952, pp. 151–80.)

The recognition of *both* 'general factors', entering into all forms of mental activity, *and* 'specific factors', influencing only particular groups of mental activity, is in keeping with what we know of cerebral activity. There, too, we have to recognize the twofold principles of mass-action and cerebral localization: certain functions are relatively specific and are associated with localized regions of the brain; yet at the same time in all normal mental processes the brain acts holistically. The central nervous system itself is roughly organized on a hierarchical plan (cf. C. S. Sherrington, *Integrative Action of the Nervous System*, pp. 314 f.).

On the 'cognitive' side the distinction between 'general ability' (or 'intelligence') and 'specific aptitudes' is due to Galton (*Hereditary Genius*, 1869, pp. 23 f.). For the more important cognitive abilities hitherto established see C. Burt, 'The Structure of the Mind', *Brit. J. Educ. Psychol.* xix, 1949, pp. 100–11, 176–99. For a summary of work on the inheritance of abilities and on psychogenetics generally, see Boring, Langfeld, and Weld, *Foundations of Psychology*, chaps. xviii, xix, and refs.

On the emotional side the evidence for the existence of a general factor which I termed 'emotionality' and for more specialized factors distinguishing 'sthenic' and 'asthenic' types was first put forward in my paper on 'The General and Specific Factors Underlying the Primary Emotions' (*Brit. Ass. Ann. Report*, lxxxiv, 1915, pp. 694 f.). Recent experimental work has revealed an innate general emotional factor and a similar distinction of types in infrahuman animals (cf. C. S. Hall, 'The Inheritance of Emotionality', *Sigma Xi Quarterly*, xxvi, 1938, pp. 17 f.; id., 'Temperament: A Survey of Animal Studies', *Psychol. Bull.* xxxviii, 1941, pp. 909–43).

On human instincts and innate and acquired emotional tendencies generally see W. McDougall, *Social Psychology*, 24th ed., 1942, and 'Symposium on Human Instincts', *Brit. J. Educ. Psychol.* xi, 1941, pp. 155–72; xiii, 1943, pp. 1–15. Of more recent publications dealing with the assessment of individual personality those most suited to the interests of the practical worker are the books by B. Notcutt on *The Psychology of Personality* (1953) and P. E. Vernon on *Personality Tests and Assessments* (1953).

For introductory textbooks on the normal mind and the development of child guidance in this country see references in Appendix V.

II

THE MENTALLY DEFICIENT

II

THE MENTALLY DEFICIENT

Definition. Mental deficiency is a legal rather than a psychological term; and, as defined by law, it embraces a number of widely differing conditions. From time to time the statutory definitions have been varied or revised; yet none of the formulae hitherto put forward is entirely satisfactory or self-consistent. It has taken centuries to establish a clear distinction between mental deficiency or *a-mentia*, on the one hand, and insanity or *de-mentia*, on the other— that is to say, between a mental subnormality that exists from childhood or birth and a mental subnormality that supervenes in later life. So long ago as the reign of Edward I a difference was drawn between the 'idiot', or 'born fool', and the 'lunatick', or person who 'at birth hath had understanding, but by disease, grief, or other accident, hath lost the use of his reason'. Yet the distinction was often forgotten; and even in the nineteenth century 'lunacy' was often held to include 'idiocy'. Later on various grades and types were distinguished: to 'idiocy' the milder conditions of 'imbecility' and 'feeble-mindedness' were eventually added; and 'moral deficiency' was appended as a further category.

The earlier Acts differed both in the criteria they adopted and in the degree of defect which they held to be necessary for certification. The criteria suggested in the Mental Deficiency Act turned mainly on social adaptability; those in the Education Act (1921) on educational capacity. For children, too, the borderline was higher than for adults. According to the definition incorporated in the Education Act, mentally defective children comprise all who, 'not being dull or backward, are . . . by reason of mental defect incapable of receiving proper benefit in the ordinary elementary schools'; the Mental Deficiency Act, which deals mainly with adults, restricts the term to cases of a more serious type, namely those who 'require care, supervision and control for their own protection or for that of others'. Thus many who were regarded as defective under the old Education Act would not be regarded as defective under the Mental Deficiency Act; and a few who would be regarded as defective under the Mental Deficiency Act—the morally defective, for example—would not have been regarded as defective under the Education Act.

By the Mental Deficiency Act of 1927 the term was extended to cover certain cases of acquired deficiency as well as those that are presumably inherited or inborn. Under the earlier Act of 1913 it was necessary to prove that the 'defectiveness' had existed 'from birth or from an early age'. According to the Act of 1927, 'mental defectiveness means a condition of arrested or incomplete development of mind existing before the age of 18 years, whether arising from inherent causes or induced by disease or injury'. Here it will be noted that, provided the condition supervenes before maturation is complete, mental subnormality induced by injury or disease is classed together with mental subnormality due to inherent causes. The latter—inherent or innate deficiency—is often described as primary amentia, and the former—acquired deficiency—as secondary amentia. A pure theorist might prefer to classify secondary deficiency, not as amentia at all, but as an early form of dementia—a kind of dementia praecox in a literal, but somewhat unusual, acceptation of that phrase. Certainly, if we adhere to simple etymology and to abstract distinctions, an ament should mean a patient born without a mind, and a dement one born with a mind which he has subsequently lost. No one, however, is born with a mind fully developed from the start; and evidently the legal view now is that any person with an arrested mental development is to be regarded as defective.

From the standpoint of practical treatment this is sound enough. In choosing a suitable school or institution it is far better to group all early cases of mental subnormality together than to place some of them among the insane. In young children, indeed, insanity as ordinarily understood is practically non-existent; and as regards major symptoms there is little difference between cases of secondary and cases of primary amentia. When the disorder arises before puberty, its manifestations resemble those of the born defective far more closely than those of the insane adult. If the mind of a child born normal is affected by disease or injury during childhood, the effect is almost inevitably to retard his intellectual development all round.

To define precisely when mental development commences or ends is, of course, impossible except in rough and arbitrary terms. According to the popular view it begins at birth. According to the physiologist it starts from conception; and some have even imagined that poisons circulating in the parent's blood before conception might cause mental deficiency in the offspring. The completion of mental development is popularly placed at 21. By the psychologist it is placed at 14 or 15. The existing clause in the statute is apparently based on the maxim: 'Call no one normal until he is 18', that is, until adolescence is over. Consequently, when the lines of division are bound to be vague, it would be foolish to substitute the abstract distinctions of the theorist for the rough but practical grouping which has been worked out in the light of actual needs.

The Intellectually Defective. The term mental deficiency, then, must not be taken to describe any well-defined clinical entity. It simply covers a group of individuals who, it may be from very different causes, are liable to be dealt with administratively under the various sections of the Acts. The practical criterion is apparently an ineradicable maladjustment to the social environment, whatever that may be—to the school in the case of a child, to the domestic, industrial, or civic world in the case of an adult. But social maladjustment is merely a symptom and an end-result; and the first step towards a scientific understanding of the problem must consist in an endeavour to classify the cases, if possible in terms of causes. This must be done on empirical lines: we must take a large group of defectives actually recognized as such, and discover how far they sort themselves into distinguishable types or subdivisions.

Social inefficiency may be due either to intellectual limitations or to moral and temperamental peculiarities. In many cases, it is true, both factors are actually found. But in the majority one cause or the other tends to predominate. As we have already seen, the correlation between intellectual qualities and temperamental is a low one; and, no doubt for this reason, the overlapping is less than might have been expected. The first broad classification, therefore, is into those whose defect is mainly intellectual and those whose defect is apparently moral.

Let us, then, consider first of all the group that may be called intellectually defective.[1] In these the salient feature is a relative lack of what the psychologist terms general intelligence. Other defects may be present as aggravating factors, but that is the central characteristic. Again, however, it must be remembered that a lack of intelligence may conceivably be due to a number of different underlying causes.

In speaking of this group as intellectually defective, I use the word 'intellectual' for want of a better adjective derived from the noun 'intelligence'. Intellectual, as I have already insisted, must be taken to include all disability due to defect on the cognitive rather than the emotional or conative side: it includes practical inefficiency, as well as intellectual inefficiency in the narrower sense. In the defective school-child intellectual deficiency in the narrower sense—inability to learn the essential subjects of the educational curriculum—is commoner and more conspicuous; but in the adult the defect may be betrayed chiefly by a failure of practical judgement.

In discussing the variations of intelligence among the general population I have pointed out that they approximate in their distribution very closely to the normal curve. Towards the lower extremity, however, the tail of the curve is slightly swollen. Its peculiar form, indeed, suggests that at this end there is a small admixture of anomalous cases, not part of the general distribution, arising from causes that

[1] The Education Act of 1921 provided for the certification of educable defectives deemed suitable for transference to special schools. By the Act of 1944 this provision is now abolished. See note on p. 112.

do not operate among the larger mass. This point, as I have urged in a previous work, is in itself an argument for supposing that intellectual deficiency must include at least two sub-groups. The larger simply represents the lower end of a perfectly normal distribution; the persons within this group, though labelled mentally deficient or subnormal, are, in point of fact, just as much a section of the normal population as those who are unquestionably above the nominal line of demarcation. Mingled with these, and indistinguishable from them so far as tested intelligence is concerned, is a second, smaller, and far more heterogeneous batch, comprising pathological cases whose intellectual inferiority must be ascribed to special intrusive factors.

Two questions will have to be answered, therefore, before we can lay down any general principles for diagnosis: first, where are we to draw the dividing line between normal and defective intelligence, and, secondly, what conditions are likely to bring an individual's intelligence down below this borderline? These are questions to which we must return after glancing at the other group.

The Morally Defective. The morally defective stand somewhat apart from the other three classes of defective persons enumerated in the Act. Here the underlying conception is still more difficult to define with precision, and demands a critical examination at greater length. It is popularly supposed that the morally defective must be far more numerous than the intellectually defective, on the principle, it might be supposed, that sinners are far commoner than fools. Actually, however, comparatively few cases have been certified under this heading; and the number has tended rapidly to decrease during recent years.

The point which the psychologist naturally puts first is this: in what particular mental function is the moral defective alleged to be deficient? The answer is to be obtained by tracing the history of the term. Early in the nineteenth century, it was realized that the traditional account of mental disorder, whether acquired or innate, was far too intellectualistic. Hence, side by side with 'insanity in the common sense, that is, disorder of the reason', it was proposed that we should recognize a complementary form, in which reason was unimpaired and moral behaviour alone affected, namely 'moral insanity'. When 'innate disorders' were finally separated from acquired, and given the special name of 'deficiency', it was natural to repeat the previous subdivision and distinguish 'moral deficiency' from other forms. Hence arose a fourfold classification: intellectual insanity and moral insanity, both acquired; and intellectual deficiency and moral deficiency, both innate.

It will be observed that this classification assumes that human faculties may be separated into two groups: the intellectual or rational on the one hand, and the moral on the other. This was the current teaching of the time. It was further maintained that the faculties themselves were implanted by nature. Older philosophers, indeed, like Hobbes and Locke, had contended that the mind possessed no innate ideas. In reaction to their 'materialistic views' a new school of thinkers arose during the earlier part of the eighteenth century—the 'intuitionists', as they were termed —who upheld the existence of certain inborn 'senses'. Of these the highest were the rational and the moral, which specifically distinguished man from the lower animals; other writers added an aesthetic sense, a religious sense, and even a sense of humour.

The favourite argument was this: just as colours are perceived by the sense of sight, and sounds by the sense of hearing, so there must be yet other senses which enable us to perceive the true, the good, the beautiful, and the comic or grotesque. The moral sense is thus depicted as a kind of inherited conscience. This doctrine was taken over by medical writers of the following century, many of whom postulated some quasi-phrenological organ for morality localized in the upper convolutions of the frontal lobe. If it existed, such a brain-centre for morality might conceivably be damaged or enfeebled from birth. Maudsley, for example, declared that 'just as there are persons who cannot distinguish certain colours, and others who, having no ear for music, cannot distinguish one tune from another, so there are some who are congenitally deprived of the moral sense'.[1] Guthrie contended that 'in some cases the normal development of the moral sense may be arrested by congenital cerebral lesion'.[2] Similarly, Tredgold explicitly adopts Hutcheson's doctrine of the 'four chief senses' which 'in varying proportions make up the mind of the average civilized man'—namely 'the logical or intellectual, the religious, the aesthetic, and the moral'. He declares that, of these, 'phylogenetically the moral sense is the latest to have been evolved and the latest to make its appearance in the individual'; hence it is the most liable to be disturbed. And the morally deficient he defines as those who are 'fundamentally lacking in this moral sense'.[3]

Now it is clear that the word 'sense' must be used by these writers as a term of analogy or metaphor. There is no sense-organ or sensory nerve by which we perceive ethical qualities or axioms. The actual sensory 'centres' within the brain subserve only those senses which have anatomical sense-organs: the rest of the brain consists essentially of association-paths, the majority of which are laid down during the individual's lifetime. All that we know of the brain and of its functions is entirely inconsistent with the hypothesis of some further sensory centre specifically set apart for moral perceptions and ideas. We have long given up the doctrine of an intellectual 'sense' or logical 'faculty' to explain our intellectual processes; and the notion of a moral sense has now become as old-fashioned and unscientific as that of a literal 'sense' of humour. Ethical perceptions, ethical judgements, ethical acts—these are complicated feats of the whole developed mind, processes whose slow evolution we can follow, step by step, in the race, in the nation, and in the child. To-day no psychologist would support so primitive and figurative a doctrine. Rather, he would be tempted to contend that, if the moral defective is to be defined as a person born without a moral sense, then we must all be moral imbeciles, for none of us

[1] Maudsley, *Responsibility in Mental Disease*, 1872; see especially pp. 31–65.

[2] *Functional Nervous Disorders in Children*, 1909, p. 102.

[3] *Mental Deficiency*, 2nd edition, 1914, pp. 314, 316, 326. It is only fair to add that Dr. Tredgold has in recent editions considerably revised his view; but his former theory is still occasionally quoted as authoritative.

is ever born with it. Morality, in short, is something which is acquired afresh by each individual from his own social environment, not a thing which is uniform all the world over and inherited as part of our common human nature.

By continental writers a slightly different picture has been put forward. Emphasis has been placed, not on the absence of a moral sense, but upon the absence of moral control. Writers of the schools of Kraepelin[1] and Lombroso[2] make use of a supposed analogy with epilepsy. In the epileptic a lesion of the higher centres is presumed (at any rate in certain forms) to release the check upon the lower centres; the result is an abnormal and convulsive over-activity. It is argued that the voluntary control of instinctive impulses forms the highest and most delicate function of all; and the real defect of the born criminal or moral defective must therefore consist in some congenital impairment of this power of inhibition. As a consequence, he suffers, not perhaps from physical convulsions of the limbs, but from spasms of violence, of wandering, or of theft. For Lombroso, indeed, the comparison was something more than an analogy, for he definitely regards the born criminal—*il reo nato*—as a special type of 'psychic epileptic'. A more plausible parallel is often drawn with the state of intoxication. Alcohol is said to 'paralyse the inhibitory centres'; and, as a result, the drunkard often behaves like a moral imbecile. A similar weakness of inhibition, it is concluded, may at times be constitutional.

The notion of an inhibitory centre, located in some definite area of the brain, is still met with in medical writings. But I believe no living physiologist or psychologist would accept it. Certainly, many instincts, such as disgust or fear, have what may be broadly termed an inhibitory effect. Pain, too, appears to inhibit the acquisition of new associations, just as pleasure seems to facilitate and fix them. But there is no one instinct of inhibition. Indeed, inhibition in the strict sense is now regarded, not as a positive function

[1] Cf. *Einführung in die psychiatrische Klinik* (1910).
[2] Cf. Ferrero, *Lombroso's Criminal Man* (1911), chap. ii, 'The Born Criminal and his Relation to Moral Insanity and Epilepsy'.

of some one particular centre, but a secondary and negative effect of any and all nervous activity. That is the teaching of almost every student's text-book. 'It is now conceded that inhibition is a general peculiarity of the interference of nervous and mental activities, which tend to modify each other by augmenting or repressing each other.'[1] 'Inhibition may be conceived as a drainage of nervous energy *from* the inhibited *to* the inhibiting system, owing to the latter becoming for the moment the path of least resistance:' if energy is diverted into a higher path, it is *ipso facto* drained away from the lower path.[2] 'Any one function can on occasion inhibit others. . . . No one centre of inhibition can, therefore, be expected to be discovered.'[3]

Here the analogy from the effects of intoxication becomes especially instructive. If we can trust the current view, what alcohol does is to depress the mechanisms of the central nervous system in the inverse order of their evolution, beginning first with those that are acquired, and leaving the inherited instincts and emotions for the time being unaffected. What are really 'paralysed' are not specific centres for inhibition, but all the higher organizations of the mind; directly or indirectly, these exert a controlling influence over the lower innate impulses, yet they are not themselves innate or centralized, but are built up by association during experience. Thus the effects of alcohol prove the exact opposite to the conclusion usually drawn: since, if there were indeed any innate inhibitory centre, we should expect it to be 'paralysed' later and not earlier than the acquired nervous mechanisms such as those for language.

On *a priori* grounds, therefore, the notion of an innate moral faculty, lodged in the brain, and of an innate moral

---

[1] Baldwin, *Dictionary of Psychology and Philosophy* (1909), vol. i, p. 541.

[2] McDougall, *Physiological Psychology*, p. 103. Cf. Sherrington, *Integrative Action of the Nervous System*, pp. 192, 202.

[3] Ladd and Woodworth, *Elements of Physiological Psychology* (1911), p. 274. Cf. also Sherrington *et al.*, *Reflex Activity of the Spinal Cord* (1932). [For more recent views on the existence of 'suppressor areas' in the cortex, see A. A. Ward and W. S. McCulloch, *J. Neurophysiol.* x, 1947, pp. 309–14, and G. von Bonin, *Essay on the Cerebral Cortex*, 1950. For a summary of recent work generally, see E. D. Adrian, 'General Principles of Nervous Activity' (Hughlings Jackson Lecture), *Brain*, lxx, 1947, pp. 1–27.]

deficiency, due to a 'congenital lesion' of this central organ, is evidently to be distrusted. Nor is there any empirical evidence in its support. No data whatever can be brought forward for the inheritance of morality or immorality as such. Elsewhere[1] I have analysed a series of cases where a diagnosis of moral deficiency had been made or suggested. A large number were simply feeble-minded persons of the ordinary type who had drifted into criminal or vicious ways. Over one-third were dull and backward individuals showing a high degree of emotional instability. Many were instances of a pubertal instability that quickly cleared up. A few were cases of organic neurosis or psychosis, traceable to some definite nervous or mental disease, supervening after birth or even after adolescence. The remainder owed their criminal habits to some kind of neurotic obsession or compulsion which often disappeared after proper treatment. I may add that, in a long investigation of the family histories of court offenders, it appeared that the delinquent with a pedigree of vicious or criminal relatives is the exception, not the rule.[2]

Of the cases where the misconduct is associated with some innate disorder, unamenable to treatment, the majority, it will be observed, are intellectually defective; and the rest suffer primarily from some simple innate emotional instability. This second and smaller sub-group forms the class with which we are here concerned. The nature of the innate components of temperament and character we have already discussed. In the main, we have found them to consist of certain specific instincts and emotions, together with certain wider, underlying factors, of which the most important was termed general emotionality. If a person inherits a high degree of general emotionality, then all his instincts and emotions may be too strong for his intelligence to control. That being so, he will inevitably behave in accordance with the traditional picture of the moral defective. But his misconduct is to be ascribed, not to the fact that his moral sense or his power of inhibition is

---

[1] *British Journal of Medical Psychology*, iii, 1923, pp. 168 f.

[2] Exact figures are given in the paper just cited and in my work on *The Young Delinquent*: see especially pp. 32 et seq.

deficient, but rather to the fact that his instinctive energy is excessive. Such cases are commonly described as emotionally unstable; and, if the innate instability is so extreme that the individual needs care, supervision, and control for his own protection and for that of others, then he may be legitimately certified as mentally defective on this ground.

There does not, however, seem to be any need for a special clause to cover these cases. Indeed, both the term morally defective and the definition offered are liable to mislead. Mind includes temperament as well as intelligence; hence the phrases 'mental deficiency' and 'feebleness of mind' may legitimately embrace those whose deficiency is due to temperamental peculiarities as well as those whose deficiency is due to intellectual disability.[1] In practice, therefore, the clause defining the feeble-minded should suffice. Actually, at any rate in London, it is now exceedingly rare for any individual to be certified as morally defective; nearly all cases are brought under one of the other clauses. If any special name were needed, it would be better to adopt the phrase 'temperamentally defective' instead of 'morally defective'. In any case, this form of deficiency seems comparatively infrequent, and its diagnosis a matter of much difficulty and doubt. There are so many other states which resemble that of the alleged moral defective that, with few exceptions, it will be unwise to certify any given individual on this one ground alone.[2]

[1] The main difficulty (which many psychiatrists, I fancy, do not sufficiently realize) is that our knowledge does not as yet enable us to diagnose irremediable emotional disabilities with the same confidence that we have in diagnosing intellectual disabilities; and to diagnose 'social disability' (or 'social inadequacy') as such is almost impossible. See below, pp. 92 and 112.

[2] *Note added* 1953. To avoid these criticisms the name 'psychopathic personality' has recently been introduced (D. K. Henderson, *Psychopathic States*, 1939). A wide variety of definitions have been offered. But the features most frequently mentioned are (i) that the outstanding symptom is 'recurrent disorder of conduct of an antisocial or a social nature', (ii) that this is 'not attributable to any other recognized condition, e.g., psychosis, intellectual deficiency, or neurological disease', (iii) that the tendency is congenital, or at least has existed from an early age and withstood all attempts at treatment, and (iv) (less frequently specified) that the patient shows a general emotional immaturity. Now, so far as the condition is supposed to be innate, it seems identifiable with the more extreme cases of what I have termed 'general

In point of fact, a small but positive correlation obtains between temperamental deficiency and intellectual deficiency or weakness. Most of those put forward for certification on the ground of moral deficiency prove to be dull in intelligence as well, even though their dullness does not bring them below the borderline ordinarily recognized as marking off certifiable cases. And if the general view that I have put forward be accepted, its practical consequence will be this: for those individuals who from birth or from an early age have been so unstable as to cause constant difficulties on the ground of misconduct, a higher intellectual borderline (say 85 I.Q. points) may be accepted for certification than would otherwise be adopted.

Causes. The next step in the classification will depend on the underlying causes. Without some view as to the probable cause both diagnosis and treatment are bound to be uncertain. Here opinion has differed widely, particularly in regard to the importance of innate and accidental factors.

Parents naturally prefer to attribute their child's undeveloped condition to some early misadventure rather than to some inherited weakness of mind; and in the past the medical man has often encouraged this consoling prejudice. If, therefore, the child's early history contains some plausible accident—an injury, for example, to the head either at birth or soon afterwards—then this accident is assigned as the probable cause of his deficiency. Hitherto there has been little or no effort to check such inferences by inquiring

emotional instability'. Dr. Stalker explicitly accepts this identification, and notes that the term covers what nineteenth-century writers called 'moral imbecility' (*Modern Trends in Psychological Medicine*, 1948, chap. ix). This again suggests that it corresponds with 'temperamental deficiency' as defined above (cf. *Report of Joint Committee*, Pt. IV, p. 49). Thus applied, however, the word 'psychopathic' is at once inappropriate and misleading. In its older and more correct sense it was used to cover 'any form of mental disease'; and in few of the cases cited is there evidence of 'disease'. As Dr. Stalker and others have observed, the phrase really designates a 'diagnostic lumber-heap in psychiatry', and Dr. Moodie observes that 'the term "psychopathic personality", like the diagnosis of "moral defect", is now being gradually given up' (*Modern Trends*, p. 191). Many could be dealt with as cases of 'mental illness'. But the majority of the highly unstable cases (including 'perverts') are out of place both in mental hospitals and in mental deficiency institutions. They really need separate legal provision.

into the frequency of such accidents among a control-group of normal children. My own records afford some indication on this point. Parallel sets of case-histories, taken from normal and feeble-minded children respectively, reveal quite clearly that milder accidents, of the kind so commonly cited, are as frequent among the normal as among the feeble-minded.[1] Among the lower grades—the imbeciles and idiots—injuries before, during, or soon after birth, usually of a serious type and due rather to disease than to accident, are commoner.

For the rest, the causes generally put forward are those that might naturally be supposed to impair the early development of the brain.[2] Only physical causes need be considered: in spite of an ancient superstition, the mental state of the mother can hardly affect the mental state of the child unless it first impairs the mother's physical health. Of conditions operating before birth the most important appears to be congenital syphilis. Among defective children attending London special schools congenital syphilis has been noted in about 6 per cent. of the cases;[3] in normal children of the

---

[1] Among 608 detectives a history of a fall or blow, usually affecting the head, was noted in 17 per cent. of the cases; of prolonged or difficult labour in 13 per cent. Among 200 normal children the proportions were 16 per cent. and 11 per cent. respectively.

[2] Most medical text-books devote much space to a discussion of the minute anatomy of the brain as examined *post mortem* in mentally defective persons. These histological studies have for the most part been carried out upon low-grade cases; and it is highly uncertain—in my view exceedingly doubtful—whether existing microscopical methods would reveal any characteristic peculiarities in the brains of the majority of mentally defective persons, for example in the large bulk of certified children attending special schools. The fact is that our knowledge of the correlation between intelligence, as accurately measured by psychological tests, and the minute structure of the cerebral cortex, as revealed by the microscope, is at present extremely meagre.

[3] In London mental hospitals the figures obtained are more than double the above—namely about 15 or 16 per cent. Here, however, the cases are of a lower grade, and the diagnosis is based on a Wassermann reaction. There is now an extensive literature on the Wassermann test as applied to mental defectives. With different investigators the percentage of cases yielding a positive reaction differs enormously: it ranges from less than 2 per cent. to over 55 per cent. The technique, at any rate until recently, has not been very well standardized; and it has been stated that the reports of two laboratories, examining the same specimens, may give a correlation as low as 0·3.

same social class, only in 0·4 per cent. Here, however, a more appropriate control-group would consist of normal children born of parents of the same degree of mental instability and dullness as the parents of the defectives. When that is attempted, the percentage rises to nearly the same high figure—namely 4·5 per cent.

Any cause that may produce miscarriage or abortion—for example, a poisoned, defective, or disturbed circulation of the blood—might conceivably affect the cerebral development of the foetus when not sufficient to cause its death.[1] Serious disease during pregnancy seems at times definitely responsible; and obscurer disorders of the mother's health, such as unrecognized disturbances of endocrine secretions, may very possibly be the decisive factor in certain instances. Tuberculosis, high fever, severe anaemia, jaundice, cardiac disease, lead poisoning, alcoholic intoxication, are the conditions most commonly suggested. But in these respects I find no difference that would be statistically significant between the defective groups and the control-group. There is, however, some slight evidence that mental deficiency is a little commoner in the first born and in the last born[2]: in the former case it is often associated with difficult birth and subsequent paralysis, in the latter with maternal ill health or exhaustion. Mongolian defectives in particular are frequently children of elderly mothers. Further, it should be remembered that of all the organs and tissues of the offspring the brain and nervous system are

[1] For a discussion of recent evidence see L. S. Penrose, *The Biology of Mental Defect*, 1949, pp. 79 f. Two unusual types of causation have of late aroused interest, chiefly because of their wider implications. Observations during the Australian epidemic of 1941 showed that, if the mother contracts German measles during the early months of pregnancy, the child may develop abnormalities such as cataract or deafness, with marked mental deficiency. Further, as a result of certain genetic differences between mother and foetus (for example, when a rhesus-negative woman has a child by a rhesus-positive man) the mother may become sensitized during pregnancy and form antibodies which pass into the foetal circulation and set up haemolysis of the infant's red cells: even if the child recovers from the ensuing anaemia or jaundice, it often shows grave mental retardation.

[2] The evidence is here statistically significant, because it is easier to obtain data from much larger groups, not because the difference between the percentages is itself much larger.

the most thoroughly protected. Contrary to popular notions, instead of being the most delicate and the most liable to impairment, they are, in many ways, the least likely to be injured. Offspring, therefore, born after an unhealthy pregnancy are more often weak in physical development than in mental development.

Of causes operative at or about the time of birth the most obvious are prolonged labour and difficult delivery. These seem genuinely responsible for some of the rarer paralytic or plegic types. Of the causes acting subsequently to birth, cerebral inflammation, most frequently diagnosed as meningitis or encephalitis lethargica, appears the commonest. The degree of the ensuing deficiency depends more on an early age of onset than on the severity of the initial attack. Direct injury to the brain, indeed, whether from accident or disease, rarely causes a *general* mental impairment unless it occurs before the end of the second or third year of life. A history of infantile convulsions, and still more of epilepsy, is common among defectives of a low grade; but usually the fits are to be regarded rather as parallel signs of an unstable nervous development. Epilepsy, in its various forms, is often followed by a marked and permanent deterioration, generally proportionate to the frequency of the fits; but its progress seems itself to be quite as much a symptom as a cause. The most usual sequence of events is first a gross cerebral lesion, secondly paralysis, thirdly epilepsy, fourthly a marked retardation of mental development, generally varying from month to month and even from day to day in its apparent manifestations and usually accompanied by emotional and moral disturbance.

Of all the causative factors acting in early life the most important would seem to be an inadequacy or overbalance in certain endocrine secretions. The earlier the condition arises, whether in post-natal or even in pre-natal life, the more probable is some consequent impairment of the child's mental constitution. Physical symptoms are usually found as well. The clearest instances are those resulting from derangement of the thyroid (producing the well-known picture of the cretin) and of the pituitary (associated with

Fröhlich's syndrome—an excessive and somewhat feminine distribution of fat, and a general and sexual infantilism). But such conditions are exceptional; and, even when present, may operate rather as aggravating factors than as sole causes. A few cases diagnosed as mentally deficient during later childhood are really instances of dementia praecox in the narrower sense. The child, often from an intelligent but unstable stock, can be shown to have possessed not only normal but sometimes brilliant ability up to the pre-pubertal period. Then, at 13 or somewhat later, he begins to lose interest alike in his work and in his play; he becomes unable to concentrate, and grows secretive and seclusive; presently, after a period of excessive day-dreaming, he seems to withdraw more and more within himself: his intelligence steadily deteriorates, until, when he is at last brought for examination, he presents to an uninformed observer the image of a typical defective.

The environmental factors so commonly cited—malnutrition and other effects of poverty—are of less importance than is popularly supposed. It must be remembered, however, that environmental conditions may at times be the deciding point in considering the certification of a particular child or adult. If the environment is good, he is less likely to be certified; if it is unfavourable, he is more likely to be certified. Hence, in studying cases actually recognized as mentally defective, we are studying a group where environmental factors, though neither the sole nor the most effective causes, may frequently have intervened to exacerbate the situation produced by heredity or disease. The more obvious of these influences, as we shall discover when we consider the dull and backward, seldom play more than a contributory part. They may perhaps turn a normal child into a dullard, with a superficial resemblance to a defective, and even drag a child who is inherently dull down below the borderline for certification. But with proper treatment and training, it is easy to show that such children may recover from their apparently defective state. Generally speaking, the most serious results of extrinsic conditions are found, paradoxically enough, where extrinsic conditions appear at first sight to be good. Where the environment as a whole is unfavourable, only the milder cases are found; and this is probably due rather to the duller stocks drifting to the slums than to the direct effect of slum surroundings.

There can, then, be little doubt that mental deficiency due solely to post-natal factors, or (to speak more precisely) to factors operating after, during, or just before conception, is comparatively rare. To these secondary cases the medical text-book devotes a misleading amount of space. For the pathologist, no doubt, they are the most instructive; but for the practitioner a knowledge of the prevailing forms is far more useful. He should, therefore, realize that secondary cases are comparatively infrequent—far more infrequent, indeed, than was formerly surmised. In private practice they may be met with a little more often than during inspections of elementary schools; but even here the child brought forward as a case of mental deficiency is more likely to be simply a child whose intelligence is relatively inferior to that of his fellows in the same superior social group.

In a survey of feeble-minded children attending London special schools I could find only 8 per cent. of a demonstrably secondary type; 63 per cent. seemed, so far as could be judged, almost certainly primary; 13 per cent. seemed attributable to a mixed causation, innate and external factors co-operating in various degrees; in the remaining 16 per cent. I could find no trustworthy data for any such classification. Indeed, to classify all cases as entirely secondary or entirely primary is to my mind distinctly precarious. Roughly speaking, secondary factors, whether acting as major or minor causes, are found among the feeble-minded in about 20 per cent. of the cases, among imbeciles in about 30 per cent., among idiots in about 50 per cent. or perhaps rather more; but it should be remembered that imbeciles, and still more idiots, are relatively rare.

In the majority of cases the chief factor, as a detailed study unquestionably shows, is heredity. But this conclusion is commonly mis-stated or at least misunderstood. It is usually supposed that inheritance implies that the majority of the mentally deficient are born of mentally defective parents. That is undoubtedly wrong. Let me take once again statistics from my cases in London schools. In barely 6 per cent. of the cases was the father or mother known to be mentally deficient. But in another 38 per cent. one parent was definitely dull—dull in the technical sense as defined above; some of them were also unstable. In another 12 per cent. the parent, though not intellectually subnormal, was more or less unstable—suffering perhaps from insanity, epilepsy, or (more frequently) temperamental weakness in some milder form. In the siblings—brothers or sisters of the child examined—mental deficiency was found nearly twice as often as among the parents, namely in 11 per cent. of the cases. If we extend the family history to the grandparents, uncles, aunts, and cousins, then some form of mental subnormality is traceable in nearly 80 per cent. All these cannot be claimed as necessarily examples of inherited defect; but it is clear that an intellectual sub-normality (sometimes, though not usually, amounting to actual deficiency) is the commonest antecedent of all, and that next in order of frequency comes what is loosely termed a neuropathic constitution.

In passing it may be observed that among the lowest grades—the imbeciles and idiots—hereditary factors appear to be far less common. In families where there is no sus-picion of intellectual subnormality—those, for example, of the professional classes, often eminent in social or intellectual life—a sporadic case of deficiency is by no means unusual. The case is generally severe—tending towards imbecility or even idiocy rather than mere feeble-mindedness, often of a definite clinical type, and explicable by injury, disease, or glandular disturbance dating from birth or from an early age. Even here, however, though there may be no history of intellectual weakness in the family, neurotic or emotional instability is exceedingly frequent in the parents or relatives.

Still more conclusive is a study of the offspring of parents known to be defective. In investigations into heredity the usual procedure is to start from the child and work back-wards: it would seem far more logical to start from the parent and work forwards. I have been able to keep in touch with nearly three hundred defectives, who were examined by me at schools from 1913 onwards, and who have since married and given birth to children. Through the kindness of school teachers I succeeded in getting information about another two hundred, known to have children, whether married or not. Among these children, the offspring of parents certified during childhood, 14 per cent. were mentally defective within the meaning of thê Education Act of 1921, and another 32 per cent. were dull and backward. Of those I was able to test personally, 87 per cent. had a mental ratio below 100. Among the children of unmarried defectives the proportions were much higher; among the children of defectives of lower grades (low enough to be certified under the Mental Deficiency Act) the proportions were distinctly smaller.

It is often said that the families from which the mentally defective are drawn tend to deteriorate progressively generation by generation: the first generation, for example, may suffer from psychosis or psychoneurosis supervening late in life; the second from early dementia or the graver forms of epilepsy; the third from amentia, present from birth; finally, 'a condition of gross idiocy appears, with complete sterility, and the family becomes extinct'.[1] In my experience such histories are exceptional and rare. Generally, as the above figures demonstrate, the offspring of the mentally defective appear to be more intelligent, not less intelligent, than the mentally defective parent: they seem to represent what Galton would have called a 'favourable regression', moving back towards the normal. Much depends upon the intelligence of the other parent; and, doubtless for this reason, the data vary considerably from district to district. In low-grade areas, for example, where the defective often marry those whose intelligence is almost as low as their own, the number of defective children is proportionately higher; in other areas and slightly better social classes, they often marry persons of normal intelligence; and here—and indeed in general, if my statistics can

[1] Tredgold, *Mental Deficiency*, p. 33; note, however, the reservations made, loc. cit., p. 34.

be trusted—the intelligence of the offspring roughly tends to strike an average between that of the two parents.

Far less, however, is known about the inheritance of mental defects than is commonly supposed. Methods employed in research upon heredity have during recent years made rapid advances; vague, unverified deductions based on semi-scientific observations can no longer be accepted. The application of a new experimental and statistical technique has gradually led towards an atomistic explanation of heredity. Wherever heredity has been indubitably established, the instances have been brought more and more clearly within the scope of Mendelian principles; and there is every reason to believe that heredity in man, including mental heredity as a special form, must ultimately be explained along similar lines.

In a few highly specific types of case it seems almost certain that a single gene may be the necessary condition for the appearance of the defect (which may, nevertheless, as in mongolism, be actually called forth by some environmental factor, e.g. the age of the mother). The clearest instances are those accompanied by other well-marked abnormalities—e.g. epiloia (due to a dominant gene), phenylketonuria and amaurotic idiocy (each due to a recessive gene), and microphthalmia (due to a recessive gene and sex-linked). But these forms are all exceptional. At one time, indeed, it was widely held that mental deficiency itself was a specific condition, inherited as a Mendelian recessive. Unfortunately, however, the majority of the early studies which seemed to point to such conclusions involved several fallacies. The most popular kind of inquiry has consisted in collecting family histories of the defective persons, and calculating the ratios of affected to unaffected individuals within the same fraternity. To find a mentally defective child with a mentally defective parent is, as we have seen, comparatively rare. If mental deficiency is a simple recessive, therefore, the calculator is forced to assume that in the majority of instances both parents, though outwardly normal, are carriers of the so-called 'simplex' type; for, if either of the parents were not of this type, we should expect all his children to be outwardly normal, though they might be carriers themselves. With the mating of two 'simplex' parents, we expect the ratio of defective children to normal to be 1 to 3. The investigator, therefore, examines the fraternities to which his case belongs; and discovers the defectives to number about 25 per cent. of the total.

Now we may take almost any characteristic, and if we select for our calculations only fraternities with affected members, we shall discover much the same proportion. For example, I have examined the fraternities of all the children on my case-sheets who have had the misfortune to break either an arm or a leg: I find that the proportion of injured to uninjured persons is almost exactly 1 to 3. The fact is that the average size of the family from which such cases are usually drawn amounts to about four children; by hypothesis, one of these four is affected, otherwise we should not be investigating the condition of his brothers and sisters: hence, if we take a sufficient number of cases, the proportion is bound to work out at approximately 25 per cent. It is true that the families from which the mentally defective are recruited are often somewhat larger than the average, particularly when the investigation is carried out among the elementary school population. But, so long as we start always with fraternities containing at least one defective child, the ratio cannot fall much below 1 in 4. If, therefore, mental deficiency was liable to inheritance, so that in the larger families of this type there was an increased likelihood of additional defectives, then the ratio would be brought back to the neighbourhood of 25 per cent. It is true that the more elaborate inquiries do not commit the fallacy I have illustrated in quite so crude a form as this. But even the best-known investigations—those of Goddard and Davenport, which medical and psychological writers still so constantly quote—will not stand scrutiny in the light of modern statistical requirements; and analyses of the type I have criticized are so common in recent medical reports and literature that it is worth while stressing their inconclusive character.

A second fallacy is still more damaging. Throughout

nearly all these studies mental deficiency is treated as a well-defined and isolated entity; whereas, we have seen, most mentally defective persons are simply an arbitrarily selected tail-end taken from a normally distributed group. Goddard's criterion for mental deficiency, in the cases he was able to test, was far above any borderline that would now be accepted in this country; and his methods for diagnosing deficiency in remoter ancestors must be far from convincing to biologists who work with first-hand material. His results certainly suggest that intellectual dullness, sometimes amounting to deficiency, is inheritable; but, from the very nature of the data, they could yield no sound evidence that 'feeble-mindedness is a unit character' and that 'normal intelligence is not only a unit character but dominant'.

At the same time, the fact that intelligence, like stature, varies continuously does not, as has sometimes been argued, exclude all possibility of Mendelian inheritance. On the contrary, both the form of the distribution-curves, and the correlations obtained between members of the same family, are very much what we should theoretically expect, were these graded and measurable characters—intelligence, height, and the like—determined by a large number of alternative genes, some dominant or recessive, some producing intermediate inheritance, some producing effects by addition or by interaction.

The careful study of particular pedigrees is more convincing than wholesale statistics. The results make it clear that mental deficiency as such can scarcely be regarded as a biological concept. It is not a single condition, but a collection of conditions; and the chain of causation between it and its genetic and environmental determinants must be far more intricate and variable than has generally been assumed. Man is a slow-breeding animal of low fertility, and his chromosomes are numerous. The facts, therefore, whatever they are, must be undoubtedly complex and hard to ascertain. Experiments in human genetics are all but impossible; and accurate observation on an extensive scale is difficult in the extreme.[1]

[1] For summaries of recent work on the problem see the volume by

These cautions have a practical bearing. Hasty deductions in individual instances are to be strongly deprecated. To begin with, it is clear that children may inherit deficiency without the parents themselves being defective: parents apparently normal may often be carriers. If my own observations can be trusted, the parents of defectives are far more likely to be dull than actually defective, and a little more likely to be normal than definitely dull; and it is particularly important to study the child's own brothers and sisters.

Moreover, since not the deficiency itself but some underlying factor or factors form the inherited characteristic, it is also desirable to search, not merely for deficiency as such, but for any form of mental subnormality. But even here we are in a dubious region. Fallacies, such as those I have described, equally beset the popular inferences about the inheritability of a general neuropathic diathesis. On theoretical grounds it is, of course, tempting to conjecture that some fundamental weakness of the brain or nervous system may produce the many manifestations that are designated as neuropathic, and that this weakness may be transmitted biologically. Those who accept this view for the most part incline to reject the applicability of Mendelian principles; they regard mental deficiency 'not as due to the absence or suppression of some specific germ determinant, but as resulting from a diminished germinal vitality, in consequence of which development tends to be incomplete. . . . The inheritance takes the form of a neuropathic diathesis, or an innate predisposition to neuronic weakness: the actual manifestation of this weakness—that is, the form it assumes —being often dependent on the nature of the environment.'[1]

It is, however, exceedingly difficult to decide what particular defects or diseases are to be comprised within so vague a concept. 'Insanity, epilepsy, hysteria, neurasthenia, asthma, chorea, deaf-mutism, criminality, intemperance or drughabits, and diseases such as syphilis and tuberculosis'—all

Penrose, cited above, and J. A. Fraser Roberts, *An Introduction to Medical Genetics*, 1940.

[1] Tredgold, *Mental Deficiency*, p. 25.

have been mentioned as 'indicating a neuropathic inheritance'.[1] Where are we to stop? For practical purposes all, no doubt, should be noted; but for purposes of immediate research what is needed is, not to lump together everything that can be regarded as a symptom of neuropathic disturbance, but to collect, on an extensive scale, pedigrees for separate and well-defined conditions, and then to apply stringent statistical tests.

One obvious point is too often overlooked. A man (or a woman) who is himself defective, or who has a skeleton in his family cupboard, is likely to be less particular about the mentality or the family history of the person he marries. Thus the mentally deficient are likely to associate with the duller specimens of the population, and to accept a wife or a husband who, though mentally normal, is in some way physically peculiar. The mere presence of an abnormality in oneself or in one's family is apt to make for an insensitive eugenic conscience. Karl Pearson, for example, noted that families marked by some patent anatomical malformation, such as a 'split hand', often contain a disproportionate number of persons peculiar in other ways. It would be rather rash to infer that the split hand is a sign of a neuropathic inheritance or a stigma of mental degeneracy, particularly as the associated defects appear almost as often in the wives and their relatives as in the blood-relations. Inevitably, therefore, this process of assortative mating will tend to accumulate many different kinds of physical and mental abnormalities into one and the same genealogical tree.

Above all, the investigation of control groups shows that the prevalence of so-called neuropathic conditions is much higher in the average pedigree than is currently assumed. In my own inquiries, for example, adopting, so far as possible, the same criteria in regard to symptoms and proximity of relation, I found among the case-histories for my normal groups as many as 37 per cent. of the families showing pre-

[1] Shrubsall and Williams, *Mental Deficiency Practice*, p. 30. Tredgold adds (besides migraine and one or two other mental conditions) 'a tendency to defects of anatomical structure, which are the well known stigmata indicative of an extensive germinal change' (loc. cit., sup., p. 33)—and usually appear, like the amentia, in the third generation.

sumptive signs of neuropathic inheritance. For all these reasons, therefore, it will be unwise to lay great stress upon an alleged hereditary taint. Too often the certifying physician, when he hears that an aunt is deaf and dumb, and an uncle has had epileptic fits, is tempted to conclude that the child before him must be the victim of an inherited infirmity, and to certify him mainly on this ground.

Diagnosis. The practical outcome of our discussion may be summed up as follows. Mental deficiency may show itself in two main directions not altogether mutually exclusive: first, what may be called intellectual deficiency, and secondly, what may be called temperamental deficiency, or, to use the commoner but inappropriate phrase, moral deficiency. Of the two the latter is exceedingly infrequent. Each type, according to its apparent cause, may be redivided into two sub-groups: first, that which is predominantly hereditary or at any rate inborn, and secondly, that which is chiefly due to injury or disease. Once more the second type is comparatively rare. It follows, therefore, that the commonest and most typical examples of mental deficiency consist in an innate deficiency in innate intellectual capacity, or, briefly, a defect of intelligence.

Intelligence, we have seen, is a technical term and has a clear and accepted definition. We have defined it as inborn, general, intellectual ability. By far the majority of mental defectives are instances of deficiency in intelligence as thus defined. In diagnosing the defective, therefore, the doctor has generally to be satisfied upon three main points.

First, the defect must be inborn and not acquired. Mere backwardness in school attainments, however severe, can no longer be accepted as in itself plain evidence of mental deficiency, since the backwardness may be due to accidental circumstances, such as absence from school or prolonged ill health. Secondly, the defect must be general and not specific. Ability to do work of a verbal, abstract, or numerical character depends in part upon a specific capacity; failure to do such work, therefore, may simply be the result of a specialized disability. Many have succeeded in practical life who have scarcely known how to spell their own names, or have been utterly incapable of solving the simplest sum. One form of mistaken diagnosis, by no means infrequent, is the assumption that a child must be mentally defective because he is unable to learn to read. In the past, cases of 'word-blindness' have been certified and sent to the special school on the ground that word-blindness, if not due to weak sight, must be a 'mental' defect. Such an argument ignores the fact that mental deficiency is a technical term, and has, like all such terms, a somewhat arbitrary definition. Otherwise the same inference might be drawn from lack of musical ability; for the capacity to recognize and reproduce a tune is a mental capacity, and consequently a defect in that capacity might legitimately be described as a mental defect. Disabilities that are specific, however, may be of little account in practical life, and to a large extent may be compensated for, provided the child shows all-round ability in other directions.

Thirdly, the defect must be demonstrably due to intellectual weakness rather than to weakness of temperament. Emotional instability, impulsive behaviour, want of moral self-control, lack of industry, conscientiousness, or zeal— any of these may lead to a state that simulates mental deficiency. Except in the extreme cases of temperamental deficiency, such conditions are usually amenable to treatment, and therefore should be ruled out before a diagnosis of intellectual deficiency is reached.

There are, then, these three alternatives to be considered and excluded. To this end, in the more doubtful instances, a thorough investigation along the lines described in the previous chapter may at times be indispensable. The family history should always be reviewed, because that, as we have seen, may indicate whether the subnormality is inherited: since general intelligence is a graded character, the most likely indication will be, not downright deficiency, but signs of general dullness in the relatives, most of all in the child's own fraternity. The child's personal history will be even more significant. Early injury or disease should, of course, be noted, particularly in cases suggestive of secondary amentia. The vital question, however, is whether anything indicating deficiency was noticed soon after birth or within the first few years of life. The younger the child, the more his capacities tend to be correlated. In the earlier stages all sides of mental development go hand in hand, and mental development itself runs closely parallel with physical. Hence, late walking, and still more late talking, when there is no other obvious explanation, may be a sign of general retardation. Delay in acquiring cleanly habits may mean that the child is slow in habit-formation generally, or that he lacks the necessary motives, or more probably that he suffers from some form of nervous instability. According to statistics obtained from the elementary school population in London, the normal child begins to walk at an average age of 1·05 years, and to talk at an average age of 1·09 years; bright children, particularly those coming from better social classes, begin to walk and talk a little earlier, the talking often appearing first. The feeble-minded child begins to walk at an average age of 1·93 years and to talk at an average age of 2·36 years, talking thus showing by far the greatest amount of delay. As regards cleanliness, bowel control is usually established in the average child by the age of 18 months, and bladder control by the age of 2. As a rule, boys are a little later than girls. In all these dates, however, the individual variation is exceedingly wide.

With older cases the personal history may after all reveal that, until the approach of puberty, the patient was apparently normal. Young adolescents often exhibit a marked degree of instability, which is at first taken as a sign of genuine deficiency. But if the report of the parents and of the school proves that mental development followed the ordinary lines up to the age of 14, then it may be inferred that in all probability the disorder is purely temporary.

Finally, a report should always be procured upon the conditions obtaining in the patient's environment. For children still at school the teachers can generally supply reliable information. This may at times be supplemented by particulars secured from the school attendance officers, and from the members or visitors of the school care committees. For those adults who are to be dealt with by local authorities working under the Mental Deficiency Act, the essential data will usually be collected by a social worker. But again I must emphasize that these social investigators should first have been trained both in the general principles of social work and in the special problems encountered in collecting psychological case-histories: reports submitted by untrained workers, without containing any definite inaccuracy, may, nevertheless, be quite misleading in their implications.

The private consultant may be forced to elicit the essential facts for himself, or to rely on information sent on by the family practitioner. In America consultants often employ social workers of their own. But in every case the inquiry should cover those special conditions in the environment which tend to retard intellectual development and progress: what these are I shall discuss in dealing with their influence on the backward child. In the case of the mentally defective, a further point of supreme importance is the manner in which the patient conducts himself in the ordinary activities of everyday life. With adults a hopeless inefficiency in practical affairs may often prove a deciding factor in the diagnosis.

The physical examination should be directed primarily to the detecting of any factors, removable or not, that may account for the child's apparent retardation. Uncorrected defects of vision or of hearing, for example, may produce a marked degree of backwardness, particularly in school subjects; adenoids may cause a general dullness not unlike the dullness of the innate defective. Any form of ill health may impede the child's progress; but disturbances of the nervous system and of the endocrine glands should receive special attention. Where physical retardation is accompanied by mental, the child's physique will often be well below that which is normal for his age. The detailed influence of such factors, however, I shall consider when we deal with the backward child.

To so-called stigmata of degeneracy—peculiarities in the size and shape of the skull, low, bossed, or bumpy foreheads, broad, depressed, or upturned noses, lobeless, projecting, or malformed ears, high, narrow, or V-shaped palates, fissured tongues, tiny, slanting eyes, lengthened or shortened arms, webbed fingers, port-wine stains—to all these anomalies little importance can be attached. Few normal individuals are without at least one such stigma; and when several coexist in the selfsame patient, the deficiency is usually so evident that there is no need to rely on stigmata for its diagnosis. In early days the severer clinical types—the mongol, the cretin, and the low-grade imbecile and idiot —were those most generally recognized; and these are frequently marked by anatomical malformations. This led to attempts at distinguishing other forms or types by similar outward and visible signs. In some cases it is fair to argue that the stigmata may be indications of a disordered development affecting the general physique as well as the brain; they may therefore, perhaps, be cited as pointing to a congenital origin. Actually, however, many of the stigmata are due to early disease—hydrocephalus, syphilis, rickets, nasopharyngeal obstruction by swollen adenoids or tonsils, and perhaps most frequently of all to disorders of the endocrine glands.

It has, therefore, become a maxim with the psychologist to diagnose mental disabilities by mental symptoms rather than by physical; and he is tempted to repeat the advice that Miss Mowcher gave to David Copperfield: 'Try not to associate bodily defects with mental, my good friend, except for a solid reason.' Intellectual disability thus has to be discovered by a direct examination of the patient's intellectual processes.

The commonest form of mental deficiency is, as we have seen, a deficiency in intelligence, in the technical sense of that term. We have also learnt that the variation of intelligence throughout the population is entirely continuous. Between the normal and the defective there is in nature no sharp line of cleavage. The defective merge into the dull, as the dull merge into the normal, and the normal into the bright. Hence our line of demarcation is bound to be arbitrary, based on educational and social requirements. The diagnosis of deficiency turns on a question of degree; and if we are to determine the degree of a patient's disability we must, if possible, measure it. In every borderline case the amount of mental retardation should be accurately assessed before the patient is classified as definitely defective or merely dull. Such measurements can be effected only by means of standardized tests of intelligence. Accordingly, the essential feature in the examination of the defective will be the psychological testing of each patient's intelligence.

With all these tests, as we have seen, intelligence is usually estimated in terms of a mental age. With adults the mental age can be taken as it stands for diagnostic purposes. Roughly speaking, a mental age of 8 marks the borderline for the feeble-minded, one of 6 the borderline for the imbecile, and one of 3 the borderline for the idiot. But clearly a child who is 5 years old could not be diagnosed as mentally deficient because he had not yet reached a mental age of 8. For children, therefore, the borderline is more usually expressed in terms of a mental ratio—the ratio of the child's mental age to his physical age by the calendar.[1] With children of school age the line of demarcation is generally put at a mental ratio of 70. With adults a mental age of 8 would correspond to a mental ratio of 55 to 60, and would cut off about 7 per 1,000.[2]

[1] The use of the mental ratio or intelligence quotient has recently been attacked on the ground that 'the concept of a rigidly constant I.Q. is contradicted by the facts' (Lancet, cclxv, 1953, pp. 869, 877 f., and refs.). But no psychologist has ever claimed that it is 'rigidly constant', since the relation between the standard deviation and chronological age is only *approximately* linear (as stated in the previous chapter). For the amount of fluctuation with defectives, cf. *Mental and Scholastic Tests*, pp. 152 f. Dr. Fraser Roberts has recently deduced a more exact equation to express the relation, and published a table for correcting I.Q.s obtained in the ordinary way (*Brit. J. Psychol. Stat. Sect.*, v, 1952, p. 65).

[2] The reasons for adopting a mental ratio in the neighbourhood of 70 per cent. are set out in my report on *Mental and Scholastic Tests*, pp. 167 et seq. It was shown that before mental testing was generally introduced there was a vast overlapping between the pupils of the special school and the pupils of the ordinary elementary departments. A simple calculation was suggested which would reduce the overlapping to a minimum; and in this way a more exact borderline of approximately 70 per cent. was deduced. But see p. 112.

For adults I suggest that, while accommodation is so limited, an average borderline of 55 I.Q. should be adopted. For them it is unwise to rely solely on intelligence tests, particularly if administered by a certifying officer who is not fully trained (at present his course of training lasts only three weeks); and of course only test scales standardized for a British population should be used.

With children such tests are invaluable. With adults they can be regarded as forming but a supplementary aid. Here the real diagnosis must be based on social behaviour—on the man's conduct and efficiency in everyday life. But even if such tests are not always reliable with the individual case, they nevertheless provide a uniform standard to which the doctor's judgement should on the average conform.

The value of the testing, however, is by no means confined to the quantitative mark—the mental age or mental ratio—which sums up the patient's performance. All such tests provide a simple standardized situation, familiar to the examiner who constantly uses it, wherein the patient's general reactions can be conveniently observed. Hence, with every test-problem, the significance of the result depends quite as much on the examinee's method of attack as on his ultimate achievement; and the examiner should always be on the alert to note the apparent causes of failure. Sometimes the cause is emotional. The patient may be careless or over-confident, unable to take thought beforehand, or too dashing and impulsive in the way he carries out his first ideas. Or, again, he may seem devoid of interest and effort, bored, inert, or quickly fatigued: he fails, not because he cannot grasp the problem or work out the answer, but because he has not the energy and perseverance to apply himself to the task. Or, again, the cause may be intellectual. The patient stands like 'those who have eyes but see not, ears but they hear not'. The slightest complexity confuses him; and his power of attention may be unable to take in all the details. Instead of thoughtfully planning a useful line of attack, he jumps at the thing blindly and at haphazard. He shows no power of self-correction, no power of profiting by experience, and so constantly repeats the same mistakes and sticks stupidly to the same routine. How far his attitude towards the test can be taken as indicating his attitude towards everyday problems in actual life may be a difficult point to decide; but, in many instances at least, such simple tasks offer a vivid insight into the man's peculiar limitations.

The foregoing, then, is the procedure to be followed in diagnosing mental deficiency. The diagnosis, it will be seen,

rests on a careful evaluation of data from half a dozen sources
—environmental, genealogical, developmental, physical,
psychological, and social. Throughout, the main points to
be established are whether the patient displays such inefficiency in his daily adjustments as to render him a case for
administrative action, and, if so, whether the inefficiency is
due, not directly to physical or environmental handicaps,
but to an incomplete development of mind.

Numbers. Before we discuss methods of dealing with those
who are thus diagnosed as mentally deficient, there are two
questions that call for consideration first of all: they have
a practical bearing both on the problems of diagnosis and
on the problems of treatment. Two inquiries are constantly
made, not only by those who have to handle the defective,
but also by those who profess a sincere concern for the
social welfare of the country: first, what is the proportion
of the mentally defective to the population as a whole; and,
secondly, is that proportion increasing?

The figures printed in official reports of the various public
authorities yield no reliable picture of the incidence of
mental deficiency throughout the population. In a few areas
the duty of ascertainment is rigorously carried out; in others
it remains almost entirely neglected. Even where it is attempted, the standards frequently vary with the individual
examiner, and sometimes there are no real standards at all.
By means of the test-methods I have described—methods
comparatively new to science—trustworthy surveys can now
be carried out; and, in London and several provincial
areas, investigations of this kind have already been successfully completed.

When I first took up my duties as psychologist to the
London County Council, my initial task was to make an
estimate of the number of defective persons to be expected
within the whole area. A kind of educational census was
attempted in the Council's schools; and the estimates were
based on standardized tests. With the borderline above
suggested (a mental ratio of 70) it was found that the proportion of defective children was almost exactly 1·5 per
cent. of each age-group—rather more among the boys,

rather less among the girls. Throughout the whole county the number of children of school age actually enumerated as mentally defective, and for the most part in attendance at special schools, was nearly 8,000—more than twice the number of the blind, deaf, and physically defective put together.[1]

On leaving school many of the defective children were virtually decertified. As pupils in a special school they were dealt with under the definition of the Education Act; as adults they were judged by the different definition embodied in the Mental Deficiency Act. Roughly speaking, it would appear that somewhat over one-third of the special school cases were educationally rather than socially defective; another third might broadly be described as in need of general supervision, though hardly defective enough to be recommended for transference to a residential institution; the lowest third of all were urgently in need of institutional accommodation or at least of the closest supervision or guardianship. Thus, of the adult population in London, I calculate that by psychological standards approximately 1 per cent. are mentally defective, but only about 0·5 per cent. by what I may call administrative standards.[2]

Do these proportions hold good all over the country? Similar surveys yield similar figures for most industrial towns. But it is popularly supposed that the country breeds a healthier stock. Accordingly, with the assistance of schoolmasters and others in one or two villages of Warwickshire, I made a rough survey of a small sample of the rural population by the same procedure. Here I found a figure of rather over 3 per cent. for children,[3] and just under 1 per cent. for

[1] The official reports describe these as forming about 11 per thousand of the children between the same age-limits. But at the earlier ages not all the defectives come under official notice.

[2] During school age or at the school-leaving period, the disposal of cases is generally based mainly on each child's intellectual ratio, supplemented by the teacher's report. In after years, as I have so repeatedly insisted, character-qualities should be regarded as a criterion of even greater importance. During the adolescent period, those removed to institutions are usually high-grade defectives whose intelligence may be near the borderline, but whose weak or unstable temperament prevents them altogether from making a satisfactory social adjustment in the world at large.

[3] My figures for the rural area included a few low-grade cases such as in London would be called ineducable. My figures for London omitted such

adults—proportions about twice as large as those obtaining in the towns.

More recently, a thorough and extensive investigation in a number of representative areas outside the metropolis has been planned by the Joint Committee on Mental Deficiency. The investigator, Dr. E. O. Lewis, conducted first-hand inquiries in six selected regions, each containing a population of approximately 100,000 persons. With the assistance of the local authorities for education, mental deficiency, and prisons, and of the various public bodies in each district, he endeavoured to enumerate all the mentally defective persons living within the area, whether at home or in residential institutions. Throughout the schools, which included private and preparatory establishments as well as all special and public elementary schools, the ascertainment was particularly thorough. The children were examined by group tests; probable cases were selected by the head teachers; and finally all who might conceivably be defective were personally examined by Dr. Lewis himself. As regards adults, Dr. Lewis took special pains to visit, and if possible to examine, not only the persons known to the public authorities as mentally defective, but also all the defectives discoverable in the district.

The results of his survey are briefly as follows. Among a population estimated at rather over 622,000 the number of defectives of both sexes, and of all ages and grades, amounted to about 5,300. This is a proportion of 8·6 per thousand population—or just under 1 per cent. The percentage, however, cannot be applied as it stands to the entire country, since it groups together children and adults, townsfolk and countryfolk, regardless of their relative numbers in different parts of the country. In the country as a whole the urban population is far bigger than the rural population, whereas in the particular areas investigated they were about equally divided. Hence percentages have

cases, since they are excluded from the special school: here the primary purpose of my inquiry was merely to determine the number requiring accommodation in such schools. (For details see Report to the L.C.C. on *Mental and Scholastic Tests*, especially pp. 163 et seq.)

first to be calculated for the chief constituent classes. For feeble-minded children Dr. Lewis's figures are, in towns, 1·5 per cent., and, in rural areas, 2·8 per cent., or, including imbeciles and idiots, 3·3 per cent.[1] These figures, it will be observed, tally closely with my own earlier and rougher estimates. It has sometimes been thought that figures and standards obtained in London can throw no light on conditions obtaining in other towns; accordingly, it is of special interest to find the two inquiries corroborating each other. For adults Dr. Lewis's figures are 3·2 per thousand for urban areas and 5·6 per thousand for rural areas. Here per thousand means per thousand total population, children and adults together; deducting the children from the denominator, the figures rise to 4·2 and 7·2—an estimate not very different from my own figures for London and for rural areas, which were computed on a strict age-basis.

Applying these several proportions to the totals for children and adults in urban and rural districts throughout the rest of the country, we may assess the total number of defectives in England and Wales as lying somewhere between 300,000 and 350,000. Thus, if all the mental defectives from England and Wales could be assembled into a single self-contained colony, a city as large as Dublin or Edinburgh would scarcely suffice to contain them.

The results of such surveys are something more than mere figures for the sake of figures. They possess a practical value. To begin with, they afford the certifying officer some notion of the numbers to be expected within his own special district. Out of those 300,000 how many are officially reported? Only 60,000 cases, barely one-fifth of the probable total. One area reports 3 per 100,000, another 466. It is, of course, preposterous to suppose that the proportion of defectives in the second district can be 155 times as great as the proportion in the first. The divergences

[1] [The figures on this page were based on *The Report of the Mental Deficiency Committee* 1929 (Table 12B, p. 184). Today (1953) about 59,000 are on the books of mental deficiency institutions, and of these rather more than 5,000 are out on licence; 82,000 are under voluntary or statutory supervision or guardianship, but of these nearly 10,000 are awaiting admission to hospitals.]

for mentally defective schoolchildren are almost equally surprising. According to the returns made by local education authorities to the Board of Education, the nominal incidence of mental deficiency varies from 0·73 per thousand in one area to 16·14 in another, with a complete range of intermediate figures for the remaining areas. Thus the reports by their own discrepancies show how incomplete and irregular the ascertainment actually is; and surveys like those of Dr. Lewis should be of great assistance by indicating the numbers to be anticipated in areas of a given type.

But the figures are of value for a second reason. They not only indicate how many defectives we have amongst us to-day; they also cast a lurid light on the position in the future. Is the number of defectives growing greater or getting less? For comparison we have the results of a similar survey carried out for the Royal Commission appointed in 1904. Could we accept their findings, it would seem that in the last generation the number of defectives was only 138,000, or roughly 4 per thousand. By 1929 the number had risen to over 300,000, or more than 7 per thousand. At first sight it might be concluded that, within barely twenty years, the amount of mental deficiency had almost doubled. Can these figures be true? At this rate, and with no counteracting factors, what must happen? Suppose for simplicity that doubling the proportion has brought the defectives up to nearly 1 per cent. during the last 20 years, then doubling it again would yield 2 per cent. after another 20 years; 4 per cent. in 40 years; 8 per cent. in 60 years. Continue multiplying the proportion by 2, and you will discover that in little over a century the mentally defective must actually outnumber the normal.

But, of course, to carry on a calculation in that simple way would be far too naïve. Such facile statistics are rather reminiscent of those Malthusian sums which prove that the progeny of one female plant-louse, at the normal speed of breeding, would literally cover the face of the earth within three years. The increase of a population does not depend solely on the rate of reproduction, nor can we assume that the rate of reproduction will itself undergo no change.

Many defectives die young; others fail to marry; others marry but remain sterile; in a few cases, they or their married partners are learning methods of birth control. On the other hand, the increasing care and protection that defectives receive to-day must be keeping a large number alive who twenty years ago might never have survived. Thus our figure for the rate of increase is itself a composite resultant; and we cannot suppose that all the factors that compose it will remain relatively constant.

A more serious source of error will occur to the critic. Can we assume that the two surveys were conducted on strictly comparable lines—with the same standards and the same margin of error? The earlier investigation unfortunately was made before the advent of psychological tests; and evidently the several investigators themselves had somewhat vague and varying notions of mental deficiency. In Lincolnshire, for example, one investigator discovered as many as 5·7 per thousand, while another investigator in Cork discovered only 1·1 per thousand. There seems to be no reason for assuming that there are fewer mental defectives in Ireland than in England. The second survey was carried out in all the areas alike by one and the same investigator, himself an expert in the diagnosis of mental deficiency. His standards were precisely defined in terms of mental age; and the mental ages were to be ascertained by scientific tests, supplemented by a first-hand examination. During the intervening period, the school authorities and the newer social services had become alive to the problem; and their knowledge of the individuals within their locality must have greatly facilitated his inquiries. At first sight, therefore, it would seem that the later survey must have been far more thorough and its ascertainment far more complete.

It is, however, chiefly in regard to higher-grade cases that standards have altered and that psychological testing has introduced greater uniformity and exactitude. Here, I fancy, the present standard is actually lower than it was twenty or thirty years ago. In those days, as we have seen, many of the merely dull and backward or socially inefficient were apt to be regarded as instances of definite deficiency. This seems confirmed by the descriptions given by the medical authorities of that date. Hence, if fewer of these higher-grade cases were discovered, the incompleteness, may, nevertheless have been counterbalanced, partly though not entirely, by the inclusion of other cases above the borderline adopted to-day.

Let us then inspect the way in which the numbers are distributed among the three categories in the first and second surveys respectively. The proportions are given in the tables below.[1] As we might anticipate, the analysis reveals the greatest proportional increase in the higher grades. This may be due in part to a more successful reduction in the mortality of the milder cases;[2] in part, perhaps, to some slight readjustment of standards; but in the main it must be due to more thorough ascertainment of defectives near the borderline—persons such as might easily pass muster as almost normal, unless examined by an expert investigator or by psychological tests.

TABLE I

Proportions of Defectives per 1,000 Population

	Idiots.	Imbeciles.	Feeble-minded.	Total.
First Survey, 1906				
Children	..	..	1·47	..
Adults	..	..	1·57	..
Total	0·25	0·73	3·04	4·02
Second Survey, 1926				
Children	..	..	3·36	..
Adults	..	..	3·34	..
Total	0·35	1·52	6·70	8·57

But the discrepancies are not so great as we might expect.

[1] The figures are taken from the *Report of the Joint Committee*, p. 174, and from Dr. Tredgold's summary, loc. cit., sup., p. 15. It has been suggested that the increased figures for the feeble-minded might be due to the inclusion of children educationally defective only and now in attendance at special schools; hence I give separate proportions for feeble-minded children and adults respectively. Dr. Tredgold does not give separate figures for children and adults in the two lower grades.

[2] Exact figures are not available for comparison. But this explanation is strongly suggested by the ratios given on p. 194 of the recent Report.

The earlier investigators discovered three times as many imbeciles as idiots, the later four; the earlier investigators discovered four times as many feeble-minded as imbeciles, the later about four and a half. The imbeciles, like the feeble-minded, have more than doubled in number (in number, that is, relative to the total size of the population); but even the idiots have increased by nearly one-half.

TABLE II

Proportions of Defectives per Single Idiot

	Idiots.	Imbeciles.	Feeble-minded.	Total.
First Survey, 1906				
Children	..	..	5·88	..
Adults	..	..	6·28	..
Total	1	2·92	12·16	16·08
Second Survey, 1926				
Children	..	..	9·60	..
Adults	..	..	9·54	..
Total	1	4·34	19·14	24·48

Making all allowances, therefore, for inadequate ascertainment and the like, I should estimate the number of defectives in 1906 as having been between 5 and 6 per thousand, whereas in 1926 it had risen to nearly 8 per thousand. This is an increase of at least 30 per cent. within a quarter of a century. I do not stress the precise amount of the increase: the important point is that an increase is definitely perceptible. The members of the Mental Deficiency Committee themselves have drawn a similar conclusion: they declare that 'it would be hard to believe that there has not been some increase in the incidence of mental deficiency during this period'. It is urgently to be desired that, before another quarter of a century has passed, a third survey, by the same intensive methods and with the same psychological standards, should be carried out, and that meanwhile some more detailed inquiry should be made into the causes of the apparent increase.

Causes of Increase. To what can this increase be attributed?

Our ignorance of human biology is so lamentable that we can do no more than make a few tentative guesses. One suggestion, put forward from time to time by various social writers, is that the main agency at work is the increasing unhealthiness of industrial life. Year by year, in larger and larger numbers, the bulk of the population has migrated from the country to the town; and there the insanitary conditions under which the newer generations are born and reared, together with the strain and stress of an urban existence, must—so at least it is argued—inevitably impair the mentality of the younger inhabitants.

To this explanation there are two obvious objections. First, it treats mental deficiency as an acquired rather than an inherited condition; and, secondly, it flies in the face of the actual statistics. It would imply that mental deficiency had been gaining only in the towns; but that is demonstrably untrue. In 1906 the proportions were 2·6 per thousand in the urban areas and 4·1 in the rural areas. In 1926 they had mounted to 6·7 and 10·5 respectively. It will be observed that both figures show an increase, and that the rate of increase is nearly the same in both areas: if anything, it is in the country that the numbers have grown more rapidly. Lured by the attractions of the town—the higher wages, the exciting life, the notion that the streets of the big cities are paved with gold—the brighter spirits from the country-side have been flocking to the towns for a century or more, and have left the duller elements behind. There is no evidence whatever that urban conditions as such have intensified the amount of mental deficiency, at any rate on any discernible scale.

Since the increase has occurred alike in town and in country, the reasons for it must be sought in some other direction. The most plausible explanation is the undoubted fact that mental defectives, and low-grade families generally, breed far more rapidly than the rest of the population. Among the more intelligent sections of the community the size of the family has been steadily diminishing; in the subnormal sections of the community it has remained comparatively large. It is from these less intelligent sections of the population that the mentally defective, as we have seen, are for the most part recruited—not solely, nor even mainly, from parents mentally defective themselves. In the London survey to which I have already alluded, the average number of offspring in families from which the supernormal children are drawn (the scholarship winners, central school children, and the like) was only 2·8; the number in those producing dullards or defectives was as many as 5·4—nearly double the size. One is tempted to express the facts as an arithmetical law: the smaller the brains, the larger the family. In rural areas no doubt in-breeding still further intensifies the result. In isolated villages the population may consist largely of a highly selected stock of subnormal individuals closely related, and between these families there is constant inter-marriage. In the village to which I have referred above, for example, the average mental ratio for the native population was 82 per cent.; and, as I noted in my Report, 'during preceding generations the brightest individuals in the village had emigrated to the neighbouring industrial towns, and the remainder had greatly intermarried'.[1] Every one, indeed, who has worked among the mentally defective would have been astonished had there not been some signs of augmentation in their numbers.

Measures proposed. Are we, then, to conclude that in the near future mental deficiency must become a serious social menace, and that the level of the population as a whole may even sink towards that of the feeble-minded? Such possibilities have certainly to be thought of. I fancy, however, that the alarmist's answer is based on too simple a deduction from the facts, and on tacit assumptions which modern biology would scarcely countenance.[2] As I have already insisted, we know little or nothing about the underlying mechanism of mental inheritance; yet, if we are to answer the question at all, some hypothesis must be adopted. The plainest and most plausible would seem to be that the commoner forms of

---

[1] *Mental and Scholastic Tests*, p. 171.

[2] For a review of the recent literature on this problem I may perhaps refer to my memorandum on *Intelligence and Fertility* (Cassell, 1952) prepared for the Royal Commission on Population.

inheritable deficiency depend on the combined action of a large number of genes. Now, a little mathematical analysis will show that any selective process must continue for a very lengthy period before it can bring about any considerable change in the distribution of a biological characteristic which is so determined. The idea, therefore, that the defective may soon swamp out the normal is hardly warranted by existing knowledge. Indeed, the problem is wrongly envisaged if we state it merely as a problem in the inheritance of deficiency: it is really a corollary to the much broader problem—the inheritance of intelligence generally and possibly of a so-called 'neuropathic diathesis'—or, as I should prefer to say, of a tendency to mental subnormality in any and every direction. Whether large or small, however, the danger is serious enough to warrant consideration; and there is an urgent case for investigating by the most accurate methods the genetic aspect of the question.

Meanwhile, on the practical side it is undeniable that the measures hitherto adopted are gravely inadequate. What proposals can we put forward in the light of present knowledge? And what part can preventive and social medicine play in alleviating the existing situation?

1. *Early Ascertainment.* The first step, and the most important, is that all defectives should be discovered and known. The discovery should be made at the earliest possible age. Here the new method of mental testing should save a vast amount of time, money, and uncertainty. Formerly, with the cruder means of diagnosis, the only thing to do with a doubtful child was to leave him in the ordinary school for a year or two's probation; and after that, all too frequently, he was forgotten or overlooked. Nowadays, with a test of intelligence, his condition can nearly always be diagnosed at the first short interview, and with rare exceptions a clear decision can be reached by the age of seven, if not before. With adolescents and adults a mental test is less conclusive: still there is no need to wait for an individual to fail and fail again before we can legitimately infer that he is devoid of all capacity for successful self-adjustment.

The medical officer, of course, cannot detect at first hand

every instance for himself. He must largely rely on the aid of teachers, school nurses, mental welfare workers, and the like. Year by year, an increasing number are being trained in psychological methods; and, as time goes on, their knowledge will greatly facilitate the medical side of the work. I do not suggest that either teacher or social worker is competent to make a diagnosis: but their training should lead them to note and bring forward the probable cases far more systematically than hitherto.

In the past, social workers and teachers have not been slow to indicate cases of supposed deficiency. But the difficulty has been that they have had no clear notion of what mental deficiency means. All through their years of training, most of them had never, to their certain knowledge, set eyes on a moron or an imbecile, and were forced to trust to home-made impressions. Accordingly, any child who was a nuisance in the classroom, any man or woman who seemed a danger to the community—the habitual thief, the incorrigible prostitute, the unbalanced adolescent—these were continually advanced as cases of mental deficiency, while the quiet and stable defective was too frequently passed by. To-day, having attended demonstrations of typical examples at the training college or at a child-guidance clinic, having witnessed and perhaps taken part in the psychological examination, they now possess a better picture of what certifiable deficiency really is, and of the criteria to be observed in diagnosing it.

2. *Early Provision and Training.* Early ascertainment, then, is the first essential. And the second is early provision —adequate accommodation and adequate training at schools or institutions. Once more, it is during childhood that the need is greatest. Special training was the main remedy put forward when attention was first drawn to the requirements of the defective. In those days the problem seemed comparatively simple. We had only to count up the number of defectives and provide the requisite number of special schools; and the majority would eventually emerge, fitted and equipped for the duties of after-life.

Further experience has revealed the error of these in-

genuous hopes. We now realize that no amount of training will 'cure deficiency'. The school may implant decent
habits and teach the elements of useful knowledge; but it
cannot convert a feeble-minded child into a normal adult.
The genuine defective is the outcome of a lack in nature
rather than of a lack in nurture; and, as Prospero laments
of Caliban, 'upon his nature nurture can never stick'.

The special schools have done magnificent work in the
past, and have their place to fill in the future. But they admit their limitations; and it is unlikely that their number
will expand much farther. In areas where the school population falls much below 8,000 or is very widely scattered, it
is hardly practicable to establish a day special school for the
defective alone, because so few would be able to attend.
On the other hand, a large proportion of the higher-grade
cases who are at present in attendance at special schools, and
for that purpose have first to be certified as mentally defective, cease to be so regarded when they leave the school;
and it seems, therefore, a gross injustice to brand these
borderline cases with a temporary stigma—for, in the eyes
of the public, a certificate of mental deficiency is a stigma—
even though the child benefits as a result.[1] These children
are not so much mentally defective as educationally defective; they should not be thrown among the low-grade feeble-
minded if it can possibly be avoided. However we define
them, the mentally defective cannot be regarded as a unique
little group standing apart by themselves. Wherever we
draw the line there will always be borderline cases: we shall
always have to recognize the existence of those who are
almost as defective as the legally defective, and yet are not
sufficiently defective to be certified or segregated.

For these various reasons the educational psychologist
has long pressed for a new attitude towards the whole problem, an attitude which has at length been explicitly adopted
by the Joint Committee of the Board of Education and
Board of Control in their *Report*. They recommend that
'all those children hitherto known as educable mentally

[1] This criticism has since been met by the abolition of certification (*Note
added* 1953).

defective children and all those known as dull and backward should be regarded as a single educational and administrative unit', and that the provision for both groups should be planned and carried out as an organized whole. If we make provision for the dull regardless of the particular degree of their dullness, we shall to a large extent be making provision for those higher-grade defectives who in so many areas are at present entirely ignored.

3. *Segregation.* For the low-grade cases, whether children or adults, a residential institution is undoubtedly the ideal plan. Permanent segregation on a larger scale is therefore the third remedy. This is not so costly as it sounds. At present these cases impose a heavy burden on their families and on the community in general. To place them in colonies where they might be trained to be in some small measure self-supporting would increase their own happiness and well-being and in the long run prove a measure of real economy. With cases of a higher grade the possibility of supervision and training *in the community* should always be considered first.

4. *Supervision.* To multiply the number of homes, colonies, and residential institutions, however, will be a slow and gradual process. A large proportion of the cases must still remain among the general community. For these, other measures—such as supervision and guardianship on a more effective scale—are urgently required. Dr. Lewis's survey gives us a first-hand picture. Of the mentally defective adults living at home, only 14 per cent. of the males and 5 per cent. of the females are earning enough to prevent them becoming a financial drag upon their relatives or upon the public funds. Nearly 90 per cent., therefore, are at present unable to support themselves. Half of them, it is true, are contributing in some small measure to their own maintenance; and of the remainder it is computed that, under supervision, a large majority might actually prove employable, if only at unskilled or mechanical tasks. The real need, then, is for better organization—some co-ordinated plan which will ensure that all who are capable shall be doing useful work, work which will keep them

happy and occupied, and at the same time partly self-supporting.

5. *Sterilization*. But if so many are still left at large in the community, will they not inevitably tend to perpetuate their kind? Mental deficiency, as we have seen, is mainly an innate and consequently an ineradicable condition; the fundamental problem, therefore, is one not of cure but of prevention. It will not be sufficient to maintain an army of regular defectives: we must also deal with the sources of supply.

Defectives of both sexes, it is urged, are liable to propagate deficiency, and that at a geometrically increasing rate. The most salient instances are those of the feeble-minded women that return again and again to hospitals to give birth to illegitimate children, who too often prove to be as feeble-minded as themselves. Accordingly, if we grant such persons their liberty, ought we not first of all to sterilize them, or at least to insist on some measure of birth control?

Sterilization is supposed to be a highly controversial proposal. But on the chief points at issue the answers are scarcely in dispute. It seems clear that sterilization, voluntary if not compulsory, might reasonably be sanctioned in certain definite cases; yet it seems equally plain that no measure of this kind can ever by itself solve the major problem. As I have several times insisted, the majority of mentally defective children are not the offspring of mentally defective parents, nor are the offspring of mentally defective parents necessarily defective. Accordingly, even could we introduce compulsory sterilization for all known defectives (a measure which nobody at the moment would consider to be practical politics), we should still fail to reduce the proportion of defectives by any very large amount. In addition, such proposals may bring with them incidental disadvantages of their own. First, there is the possibility that sterilization, if advocated as the main remedy, may hold back what might seem to be the more costly alternative—namely segregation. Secondly, the sterilized defective, if left at large, may remain as great a burden as before, and perhaps in some cases prove an added temptation and danger. No doubt these objections may easily be exaggerated. The prudent plan is to introduce such a measure on a limited scale by way of experiment; and then, if it proves successful and unattended by any serious risk, to enlarge its application step by step. At the moment, though the law is not altogether clear, it seems generally held that sterilization, except when requisite for health, is illegal. The first move will, therefore, be to legalize voluntary sterilization, so that those who are mentally defective, and, still more, those who are likely to transmit mental deficiency, may have a clear right to this protective measure.[1]

6. *Medical Treatment.* So far, the measures I have enumerated are mainly social, educational, or administrative; it remains to glance at those that are more definitely medical. There is little to be said. Curative measures are almost negligible in their results; but preventive efforts, directed to the protection of the infant before and after birth, may to some extent diminish mental as well as physical weakness.

Cure or amelioration by means of surgical operation on the brain or skull is a measure that is still often suggested. 'Where there is no morbid heredity', says Dr. Tredgold, 'and where there is clear evidence, or even a reasonable presumption, that the deficiency is due to fracture, splintering of the inner table, the pressure of a blood-clot, or other conditions causing increased cranial pressure, then not only is operation justifiable, but it is the duty of the physician to advise it at the earliest possible moment, and before changes have been induced which may be irreparable.'[2] Dr. Tredgold adds: 'I must confess, however, that I know of no statistics sufficiently extensive to show the results of operation in such cases, . . . and it may be said that to-day operations of this kind upon cases of primary amentia are absolutely unjustifiable.'

In view of the early success obtained with patients treated with thyroid extract, great hopes were at one time enter-

---

[1] While these pages are passing through the press, the *Report of the Departmental Committee on Sterilization* has been published (H.M. Stationery Office, 1934, 2s. net). It is to be hoped that its recommendations, both in regard to the legal position and the need for further research, may be speedily put into effect. [2] Loc. cit., p. 401.

tained that substances obtained from the endocrine glands might provide a possible method of cure. With thyroid the more remarkable results have been chiefly observed in conditions which, like juvenile myxoedema, are not congenital but only manifest themselves after early infancy. In the congenital cretin, the physical condition often shows a striking improvement, but in most cases mental development still lags far behind physical. A few patients suffering from dystrophy, attributable to some disorder of the pituitary gland, have shown physical and mental improvement after the administration of pituitary extract; but the benefit appears to be highly uncertain. With other cases, representing almost every type, combinations of thyroid, thymus, pituitary, suprarenal, and pineal extracts have been tried, but hitherto with little or no apparent success. With a congenital syphilitic the usual anti-syphilitic treatment often stops the progress of the disease, and so may conceivably arrest any further mental deterioration; but it seldom results in a positive mental improvement.

Nevertheless, though medical treatment cannot be expected to restore the damaged brain, it may effectually remove contributory causes of mental retardation. With those who are merely dull or backward, such measures, as we shall discover later, may influence intellectual progress to an appreciable degree; but the lower the child's mental grade, the smaller, as a rule, is the mental improvement. Educational and social assistance is nearly always the more important need. With the temperamentally defective, whose intelligence is nearly normal, more promising results may be looked for. High-grade cases of an unstable or a delinquent tendency have been much improved by the vocational instruction and the character-training received in small and specially selected institutions.

In a certain number, as we have seen, mental deficiency is caused or aggravated by adverse agencies, acting upon the child from without; and, though the damage cannot be cured once it has been inflicted, much may be done to prevent it by suitable precautions taken in advance. In this direction far more can be expected from an adequate medical approach. The care of the mother during pregnancy, and of the infant during early life, should do much to lessen those rarer cases where the innate factor is of minor influence. Anti-syphilitic treatment applied to the mother often seems to prevent the child acquiring a congenital form of the disease. Errors in the mother's diet and metabolism, and particularly glandular derangements, may be treated with some success; and the treatment may benefit not only the health of the mother but also the health and mental development of the child. More systematic ante-natal examination, together with improvements in midwifery, may help to prevent those injuries that attend prolonged labour and difficult delivery. Proper hygiene and diet during the first few months of life—the avoidance of serious infections, the supply of food containing the necessary vitamins, more sunshine and more fresh air—may save some of the poorer specimens from being dragged down below the borderline of mental deficiency.

But all these forms of treatment, preventive and curative alike, are relatively new; and research is needed quite as much upon the medical aspects of the subject as on the biological. Meanwhile, it remains obvious that no single plan of action will suffice to meet the whole difficulty. It must be attacked simultaneously along several lines of approach. Nor shall we ever successfully defeat it so long as we regard it as an isolated matter to be dealt with in and for itself. The real issue, as I have already urged, is not the limited one of mental deficiency but the larger one of mental inefficiency. Certifiable defectives form but the fringe of a much larger portion of the population—the portion which is sometimes termed the 'social problem class', and includes the dull, the backward, the unemployable, the habitually delinquent, in fact all who are subnormal in whatever direction. How to deal with this whole subnormal group forms a momentous question which almost every civilized society must face in the near future; and here lies perhaps one of the most perplexing tasks that social and preventive medicine can be called upon to undertake.

Notes and References. The standard textbook for many years has been A. F. Tredgold, *A Textbook of Mental Deficiency* (7th ed., 1947). For a discussion of the inheritance of mental deficiency see L. S. Penrose, *The Biology of Mental Defect*, 1949. The results of statistical surveys showing incidence, &c., will be found in the *Report of the Mental Deficiency Committee* (*Wood Report*, H.M. Stationery Office, 1929).

The evidence for and against the view that the average level of the national intelligence is threatened by decline is discussed in C. Burt, *Intelligence and Fertility* (2nd ed., Cassell, 1952, 2s. 6d.; a survey originally prepared at the request of the Royal Commission on Population).

Since the previous editions of this book were published, the Education Act of 1944 has abolished the provision contained in the earlier Act for certifying a child as mentally deficient before he can receive an education suited to his needs, and has thus done much to remove the stigma that formerly attached to attendance at a special school. The term 'educationally subnormal' is now used to cover both the dull and backward and those high-grade cases of mental deficiency who would formerly have been certified as fit for transference to such a school. A child of school age can only be dealt with under the Mental Deficiency Acts on the grounds (i) that he is incapable of receiving education at school, and (ii) that it is inexpedient that he should be educated in association with other children.

As noted in the text, for most practical purposes mental deficiency may be defined as an innate defect in general cognitive ability (i.e. in intelligence, as it is more conveniently called). To determine the degree of defect, the most useful scale of tests is that originally drawn up by Binet and Simon. But it is important to use a version standardized for British children. Since the last edition of this book was published, Terman and Merrill have brought out a modified version which has the advantage of including a larger number of practical tests (*Measuring Intelligence*, 1937). However, the American age-assignments may be slightly misleading if used as they stand with children in this country. A revised list of age-assignments for British children has accordingly been added to Appendix II below (pp. 364–7). To use and interpret all such tests accurately, a preliminary training is necessary.

Many of the newer definitions (e.g. 'social inadequacy', 'inability to conform to accepted standards of social behaviour', &c.) are far too loose for it to be possible, in the existing state of knowledge, to offer evidence for the conditions described that will be satisfactory from a diagnostic standpoint or cogent from a legal standpoint. Moreover, if systematically applied, they would entail the detention of far more patients than the available accommodation is ever likely to permit. Dr. Tizard has stated that already more than half the cases in mental hospitals (perhaps we should rather say in certain mental hospitals) have I.Q.'s over 70. Accordingly, owing to the difficulty of diagnosing higher grades, it would seem preferable to refer all doubtful or possibly curable cases to a classifying centre, e.g. under Sect. 5 of the Mental Treatment Act of 1930 (amplified if necessary): as a safeguard non-voluntary cases should be seen shortly after admission by visitors who for such purposes should be justices with appropriate training and experience.

The whole subject is now being reconsidered by the Royal Commission on Mental Illness and Mental Deficiency. A valuable summary of existing arrangements will be found in the *Minutes of Evidence: First Day* (H.M. Stationery Office, 1954).

III

THE DULL OR BACKWARD

III

THE DULL OR BACKWARD

The Problem of the Borderline Child. We have seen that the mentally deficient, viewed both as a social group and as a social problem, form only a fragment of a larger whole. Primarily they are the tail-end of a more numerous section of the community—the mentally dull. Every medical officer who has the duty of examining defectives soon becomes aware of borderline dullards whom he cannot conscientiously certify; and he quickly discovers that these marginal cases consist, not of a few problematic individuals, cropping up from time to time, but of an unexpectedly large proportion of the population. For every two or three that he can certify without hesitation, there are at least four or five to whom he must give the benefit of the doubt, and another half-dozen whom he knows to be well below the general level, and yet, beyond all question, impossible to deal with as mentally defective. That has long been an almost universal experience in examining both adults and children. But it is only during recent years that the difficulties involved have been explicitly recognized and faced.

The problem is plainest in the case of children. We have seen how the Education Act of 1921 described the mentally deficient as those who are 'incapable of receiving proper benefit from the instruction in the ordinary elementary school', and provided that such pupils should be educated in what were known as special schools. But the Act explicitly excluded from such schools any child who is 'merely dull or backward', and reserved them for children who owed their lack of progress to what it called 'mental defectiveness'. Unfortunately, it nowhere stated what degree of defectiveness brought such a child within the meaning of the Act. Hence the teacher, hearing the definition for the first time, was tempted to hand over to the doctor every boy or girl who seemed incapable of making normal progress in his own particular school. But schools vary enormously in the

standards of work which they exact; and a boy who seems
a hopeless failure in a good-class elementary school in the
suburbs might be welcomed as a brilliant pupil in a slum
school in the East End.

Fifty years ago, when the definition was first formulated,
and special provision was first attempted on a systematic
scale, it was hardly realized that mental deficiency was a
matter of degree. It was supposed that such persons constituted a species apart—a class sharply marked off from
the rest of the population, yet amenable to special training,
if not completely curable. Mental deficiency, in fact, was
conceived after the analogy of a physical defect. A man
either has or has not broken his thigh-bone; if he has,
then prompt attention may mend the fracture, though in
some instances the man may limp for the remainder of his
life. Similarly, it was argued, his brain is either normal or
definitely defective; intermediate states were thought to be
as impossible as a green-stick fracture in a full-grown man.
Nevertheless, even in the gravest cases, it was hoped that,
by adequate and early treatment, the deficiency could be
more or less remedied.

These simple views were quickly destroyed by the experience of the special schools themselves. It was soon found
that the two groups—the supposedly normal and the alleged
defectives—not only varied in intelligence widely amongst
themselves, but showed a large degree of overlapping.
Attention was turned to the borderline case; and it was
then that certifying officers began to observe how the
borderline cases were far more numerous than those whose
diagnosis was undoubted. Further, actual experience
showed that the undoubted cases were almost invariably
incurable. Once a defective, always a defective: that was
the final verdict of the teachers themselves.

When special schools were first started, a periodic re-
examination of the pupils was arranged. It was expected
that a large proportion of them might ultimately be sent
back to the ordinary school. In less than ten years that view
was completely reversed. Formerly, the education officer
congratulated the special school teacher on the number of

cases retransferred as normal; later he was more likely to blame the doctor for a mistaken diagnosis. The majority of the transfers proved to be children whose inborn intelligence is just above the line of certification, but whose acquired attainments were, at the time of the first examination, down to the level of the special school. Children such as these are not inherently defective; they are merely dull and educationally retarded. Their minds, though slow, are nevertheless sound; but their progress in the classroom lags two or three years behind the progress of their fellows. To group them with genuine defectives, who may be but little above the rank of imbeciles, seems grossly unfair; and to maintain them all in special schools would entail an unthinkable expense. It has therefore become increasingly urgent to know what is to be done with this huge intermediate group; and the attention of both psychologists and administrators has of late been largely diverted from the problem of the mentally deficient, and focused upon the problem of the backward and dull.

Definition of Backwardness. What educational provision can be made for such children? And what is their outlook in later life? Before we can answer such questions, it is imperative to define a little more exactly the type we have in mind. Our definition is bound to be somewhat arbitrary: as we have already seen, the defective merge into the dull, as the dull merge into the normal and bright, by insensible transitions and gradations. There is no dividing line in nature: its choice must depend on the educational and social adjustments which the various individuals are called upon to make.

In the past words like 'backward' and 'dull' have been used by teachers and medical officers in a rough and popular way. Any child who did not come up to the ordinary level of the school was apt to be dubbed backward or dull. Yet not all who fall below the average level for their age need special provision. Children who are but one year behindhand can be associated with younger pupils in a lower class without detriment or disorganization. It is the child that is still further retarded who occasions serious difficulties. Consider those older boys and girls who may be backward by as much as two or three years: unless they are to be faced with work that is wholly above their heads, the teacher must keep them down in one of the bottom standards; but hither will be promoted those brighter youngsters from the infants' school who are one or two years ahead. Clearly, such an assortment of big and little would be eminently unwise.

I have, therefore, proposed the following definition. By 'backward' I understand all those who, without being mentally defective, would, in the middle of their school career, be unable to do the work even of the class below that which is normal for their age.[1] The normal class can be approximately determined by the simple equation: Standard = Age−6. A boy of 10, for example, should be working in Standard IV. If he is fit only for Standard III, he can be kept down in this lower class; but if his level is that of Standard II or even of a good Standard I, some special arrangement becomes desirable. If it falls below that of Standard I, then, provided there is no extraneous cause to account for his backwardness, he may need transference to a special school, and in the past he would have been certified as mentally defective.

For the purpose of statistical surveys this general definition can be put into an exact numerical shape. If we translate these borderlines from 'standards' into mental ages or ratios, we shall discover that the two lines of demarcation work out as follows: using the words as technical terms in psychology, we may say that the upper borderline for the 'backward' is a mental ratio of 85 per cent., and for the so-called 'defective' a mental ratio of 70 per cent.[2] All those whose general educational attainments, measured in

---

[1] This definition has been accepted by the Board of Education's *Handbook for Teachers*, p. 34.

[2] Standard III corresponds with a mental age of (III+6) = 9; Standard II with a mental age of (II+6) = 8. The theoretical borderline between the two standards, therefore, is a mental age of 8·5. And a mental age of 8·5 at the chronological age of 10·0, implies a ratio $\frac{8·5}{10·0}$ = 85 per cent.

The 'standards' were levels of attainment prescribed in general terms by the 'code' formerly issued by the Board of Education. School classes are no longer labelled in this fashion. But many teachers still think in terms of these designations rather than of the equivalent 'educational ages'.

terms of a mental age, fall below 85 per cent. of their chronological age may be conveniently described as 'educationally subnormal'. And now a further distinction has to be made. Educational backwardness implies a retardation in educational attainments, and not necessarily a retardation in innate intelligence: that may be the underlying cause in many cases; it is certainly not so in all. But mental deficiency does of necessity imply that the retardation is innate. Hence we may distinguish between the innately dull and the merely backward. Dullness, like deficiency, will be defined in terms of *mental* ages or ratios; backwardness in terms of *educational* ages or ratios.[1] Accordingly, we may define a backward child as one who, without being defective, has an educational ratio of less than 85 per cent.

Frequency of Backwardness. Accepting, for the sake of a uniform standard, this somewhat arbitrary definition, we can now determine its frequency. How many cases are we likely to find in a typical educational area? From the surveys carried out in London I calculate that at least 10 per cent. of the school population are backward in the sense defined: in the elementary schools of the county there are over 40,000 backward boys and girls.[2]

Hitherto, so far as I am aware, only one other English educational authority has conducted a systematic survey by psychological methods. In 1920, at the request of the Education Committee at Birmingham, Dr. Lloyd and I carried out a census of backward children in that city. The inquiry was based primarily upon the method of sampling; typical districts and schools were selected; and from the results it was calculated that, in all the senior departments of the Birmingham schools, as many as 8,000 children were technically backward: that is, once more, a proportion of about 1 in 10.[3]

[1] By a mental age (without further qualification) is here meant a mental age for intelligence usually based on the Binet-Simon tests. By an educational age is meant a mental age for educational attainments, usually deduced from results obtained with standardized tests for reading, spelling, and arithmetic, the mental ages obtained from each separate test being averaged.

[2] L.C.C. Report on *Distribution of Educational Abilities* (1917), p. 36.

[3] *Report of an Investigation of Backward Children in Birmingham* (City of Birmingham Stationery Department, 1920), p. 5.

Much the same proportion, no doubt, holds good in nearly all the industrial areas of Great Britain. From time to time, in various parts of the country, the reports submitted by the school medical officers contain estimates under this head. For towns the returns apparently vary from 0·8 per cent. at Leeds to 14·6 per cent. at Sunderland; for rural areas the figures are vaguer and much higher. Owing to the lack of any uniform standard, the separate estimates are highly discrepant, and can have little value in themselves. The average, however, works out at about 10 or 11 per cent. for the towns, and is thus consistent with my figure.

For rural areas an estimate of the number of retarded children is more difficult to calculate. According to the figures of the Royal Commission of 1904, 'the incidence of mentally defective children is decidedly greater in the towns than in the country';[1] and it has sometimes been inferred that the same held good of the dull, though not perhaps of the backward. 'The rural child', it is said, 'is healthier, and therefore more vigorous in mind as in body: but educationally he is often ignorant or even illiterate.' As we have seen, however, more recent inquiries have shown that defective children are in point of fact far more numerous in the country, while dullness seems to vary even more widely from one rural district to another than it does from town to town. According to my own limited inquiries it would appear that, on an average, in the country villages the proportions both of mentally defective children and of dull and backward are roughly double the proportions obtaining in the larger towns. The percentages are highest in those parts where the exodus to industrial centres seems to have drained the adjacent countryside of its brightest families. They are lowest in those remoter districts which seem still unaffected by this emigration: among the Cotswolds, the Cheviots, the hills and dales of Yorkshire, the average rural population appears, if anything, to be rather above than below the level of the towns,

[1] For a discussion of this problem see Tredgold, *Mental Deficiency*, p. 160.

and the cases of genuine dullness would seem to be fewer. On the whole, I calculate that, if the same standards are preserved, the percentage of backward children in rural areas must average at least 20 per cent.[1] If these proportions are applied to the school population in rural and urban districts respectively, and certain reasonable allowances made, then I estimate that in the whole of England and Wales, between the ages of 7 and 14, there must be quite half a million who are so dull and backward as to need special educational provision.[2]

Quite recently, in 1932, an entire age-group was surveyed throughout the schools of Scotland. One hundred thousand boys and girls were examined by means of special psychological tests.[3] Adopting a mental ratio of 90 as the lower limit for the ordinary or 'average' child, the investigators conclude that about one-quarter of the school population, or rather less, fall below the 'average' as thus broadly defined. From the tables given, it is possible, with some further calculation, to compute the probable number who would fall within the limits of our own definition. It appears that in Scotland, taking rural and urban areas together, about 15 or 16 per cent. of the school children would be dull and backward in our sense. Could we assume that rural and industrial populations were roughly of equal size, the figure would tally almost exactly with that obtained by averaging the percentages for the two types of population in England. Actually, of course, the populations are not equal; and (owing perhaps in part to the fact that the exodus to the towns has not been so marked as in England) the rural

---

[1] I base this statement partly upon a small survey I carried out some time ago in certain villages of Warwickshire, and partly on the results of group-tests applied by teachers and others in different parts of the country.

[2] The *Report on Mental Deficiency* suggests a figure of 300,000. The difference depends on the standard adopted. The Report takes an upper borderline of 80 per cent. as being suitable to most parts of England, except the industrial towns. If my borderline of 85 per cent. were adopted, the number would rise to more than double this amount, probably to about 700,000. Since, as we shall see later, there are practical reasons for adopting the lower standard in the rural areas and the higher one in the towns, we may accept as a compromise a figure midway between the two.

[3] *The Intelligence of Scottish Children*, 1933.

population of Scotland appears to have a slightly higher average I.Q. than the rural population south of the Tweed. Nevertheless, the correspondence is close enough to show that the same tendencies hold good.

We may conclude that in most large areas the proportion of backward children will vary between 10 and 20 per cent. of the school population. About the size and the urgency of the problem, therefore, no doubt can arise: backward children are seven times as numerous as those formerly described as mentally defective.

Causes of Backwardness. Backwardness, however, is only a symptom. To rest content with palliating symptoms by superficial treatment—a little extra pressure here, a little extra coaching there—is as disastrous in the school as it would be in the hospital. It is like placing a feverish patient in a draught of cool air in order to bring down his temperature. With mental disability as with physical, we must find and fight not symptoms but causes.

Here the medical officer must play an important part. It will be his duty to discover in which cases the backwardness is an incidental effect of chronic ill health, of acute disease, or of congenital defects of physique, and to suggest the appropriate lines of treatment. What kind of conditions, then, are responsible for educational backwardness, and how far do they fall within the purview of the doctor?

Here let me turn to a second set of inquiries. In the hope of bringing to light the more immediate causes of backwardness and the precise manner in which they operate, I have taken 400 consecutive cases from London schools, and have made an intensive study of each one. But to enumerate the conditions found in a backward group alone would of itself prove little or nothing. In earlier researches this was all that was attempted. To learn that 30 per cent. of the cases are undernourished, or that 20 per cent. suffer from enlarged tonsils or adenoids, does not of itself suffice to demonstrate that malnutrition or glandular affections necessarily make a child backward in his lessons. There are many normal children, similarly handicapped, who show no serious ill effects either in their mental development or in their progress at school. A control group, therefore, is essential. We must institute a parallel investigation among the general mass of the school population. Double surveys on this plan have been carried out both in London and in Birmingham.

Let me summarize the results. They will serve to indicate not merely what causes should be looked for in studying the backward child, but also the frequency—that is the presumptive probability—of their occurrence.

I. Extrinsic Factors

Home Conditions. I shall begin with the environmental conditions first of all. In London a preliminary survey was made to discover the geographical incidence of educational backwardness throughout various divisions of the county. It was found that from one district to another the proportions vary enormously. Taking the same dividing line for the county as a whole, I discovered that in the better neighbourhoods, like Hampstead, Lewisham, and Dulwich, the backward numbered barely 1 per cent.; in the poorer neighbourhoods, such as Lambeth, Hoxton, and Poplar, they amounted to over 20 per cent. The figures for backwardness can be compared with figures for social conditions obtaining in the different districts; and, if plotted in the form of a map, they can be compared with a map of poverty, such as that published by Charles Booth towards the end of last century. On placing the two side by side, a remarkable correspondence leaps to the eye. Where Charles Booth blackened his streets to show the haunts of the criminal or tinted them blue to mark the hovels of the poor, there our map also displays the darker shades and reveals the largest numbers of backward boys and girls. Such a plan of the county shows at once where special provision is most urgently needed, and suggests a possible cause.

Evidently there is a close and local association between the economic handicaps of the child's own family and the educational backwardness of the child himself. Yet to conclude off-hand that poverty must invariably produce dullness or incompetence would be neither logical nor just.

A bare smattering of biography refutes that simple induction. Bunyan the tinker, Faraday the blacksmith's son, Burns, Cook, Giotto, all sons of peasants, D'Alembert, the foundling picked up one Christmas night on the steps of a Paris church—these and many like them have risen to the loftiest intellectual eminence from the lowliest social spheres. The slums of London contain many a youthful genius, some of whom win, more of whom merit but fail to win, scholarships to a secondary school or college. Stupidity, then, is not the inevitable result of poverty, though poverty is its commonest concomitant. Taking the economist's definition of the poverty-line,[1] I find that in London nearly 30 per cent. of the backward fall definitely below this standard. In the general school population only 7 per cent. fall below the poverty-line as so defined. Seven per cent., however, implies a large number when applied to the whole of the county. Fifty thousand boys and girls must be living in the most unfavourable surroundings, and yet be making perfectly normal progress in their work at school. This does not mean they would not do better if their handicaps were removed; but, poor as they are, they are not definitely backward.

So far as school progress is concerned, poverty operates in two main directions. It impairs health; and it limits general knowledge. By impoverishing the child's physical vitality it lowers his capacity to learn; and by restricting his mental horizon it deprives him of the preparatory background of worldly information and culture that most schools take for granted.

At the time of my survey, grave physical debility among school children, arising from sheer want of food, seemed decidedly exceptional.[2] The child in the poor home, when

---

[1] In this and other researches I have followed Mr. Seebohm Rowntree's definition, *Poverty* (1901), chap. iv, 'The Poverty Line'.

[2] The provision of school meals and school milk has done much to improve the nutrition of children from the poorer homes; and, thanks to the amelioration of the economic conditions of the working classes, poor homes are themselves much rarer. The facilities available under the National Health Scheme for medical treatment at home have also done much to diminish the incidence of debilitating illness.

he suffers in this direction, suffers more from improper food than from insufficient food. He may be dosed and even overdosed with bread, potatoes, and tea. Starchy foods are cheap; and the diet is apt to be ill-balanced rather than too scanty. Parents have still to be taught that a young child thrives, not by the quantity it eats, but on what it can digest and assimilate.

There is another handicap from which the poor child suffers—more prevalent, I fancy, and more easily overlooked. Among the weak and weary youngsters of the slums, inadequate sleep may be quite as responsible for their condition as inadequate meals. In one or two schools plans were actually made for sleeping the children on the school premises, not only during the afternoons but even during the nights. At the same time they were to be taught healthier habits in sleeping—better posture, sufficient but not excessive bed-clothes, proper ventilation, and the like. The War prevented the scheme from being fully carried out. But in one department a start was made, and the results were striking. At this school it was complained that the girls were exceptionally backward in arithmetic. The inspector blamed the teachers, and the teachers blamed the homes. The following experiment was accordingly arranged. The girls from certain classes were divided into two comparable groups, selected so as to be as equal as possible in physical condition and intelligence. One group was given extra coaching in arithmetic; and the other group, during the same period and for the same length of time, was put to sleep in deck-chairs. At the outset of the experiment the two batches were exactly level in arithmetical attainments, and their attainments were deplorably low. At the finish, both had made appreciable progress; but the group which showed by far the greater improvement was not the group that had been specially coached, but the group that had been put to sleep.

There are many other ways, equally apparent but less simple to remedy, in which bad home conditions may sap the child's vitality. The house may be damp and insanitary, and the rooms overcrowded; there may be no garden or yard for the children to play in; and, when they should be taking exercise in the park or recreation-ground, they are sent on errands, or kept indoors minding the baby or helping mother. Epidemics and minor infections spread like wild-fire from child to child, and from one family to another; and, when the children are ill, the parents may be unable to procure the proper treatment from the surgeon or the doctor. It is, too, usually the child from the poor home who takes employment out of school hours. But paid work outside the home is not the only form of work that may fatigue or exhaust the child. I can call to mind many a case where a backward little drudge, dull, drowsy, and listless, was no sooner relieved of domestic tasks at home—shopping, scrubbing, cooking the meals, and washing up the dishes— than she suddenly smartened up, and fully made good the progress she had lost.

The intellectual and emotional atmosphere of the home is even more important than the physical. Often both mothers and fathers have no intellectual interest outside their own special work, and neither time nor leisure—often neither the ability nor the will—to impart what little they know. If the parents are perpetually bickering, perpetually complaining, perpetually worrying how to make both ends meet, the child is bound to be affected: instead of giving his mind to the work of the classroom, he will be brooding over the misery at home. All this, of course, will be the concern of the teacher or the social worker rather than of the medical officer. Yet often the ultimate effects come within the doctor's province, since, if the mental conditions at home are antagonistic, the strain may ultimately issue in a definite nervous disorder or breakdown.

In the main, then, poverty acts indirectly. In no case is it sufficient merely to ascertain that a family is extremely poor. We must go on to inquire how precisely the stress of poverty is affecting each particular child.

School Conditions. I now turn from the environment at home to the environment at school. The first and most obvious cause of failure is simple non-attendance. If the child stays away from school, he cannot learn what is taught at school. In the London inquiry backwardness appeared attributable to inadequate attendance in 11 per cent. of the cases. The children had been admitted late, or had been absent on numerous occasions or for lengthy periods. Much of this was excusable—due to exclusion for ill health, infection, uncleanliness, and the like. But a good deal arose from sheer negligence, and from delays connected with migrations from one neighbourhood to another. In Birmingham frequent or prolonged absence from school was noted among nearly one-third of the backward pupils: no other single factor was encountered so often. Judged by the average percentage of attendance registered during the current year, while the normal child was present fifteen days out of sixteen, the backward child was present only six days out of seven; over one-fifth of the children made less than 80 per cent. of possible attendances.[1]

Roughly speaking, serious non-attendance is about three times as common among the backward as it is among the normal. But it is evident that backwardness causes non-attendance almost as much as non-attendance causes backwardness. A vicious circle is in fact set up. The backward child feels himself out of place in the ordinary classroom; he finds the work too difficult; his daily experience is one of failure, punishment, or reproof. No wonder, then, that he comes to hate his school, and tries to escape it.

I do not, however, urge that the measures taken to enforce attendance should be tightened up. In certain areas outside London the zeal of the attendance officers is so great that it sometimes does more harm than good. Here, I think, is an instance where the medical department might sometimes work in closer touch with the attendance branch. At times even teachers still seem to suppose that their prospects may depend on their keeping the schools well filled from day to day; and so, directly or indirectly, they put pressure on parents, and persuade them to send their children to school when the children's ill health requires rest at home and retention indoors. Naturally this happens only where the teacher is unaware that the particular child should not be exposed to physical or mental strain, or to change of

[1] *Report*, loc. cit., p. 26.

temperature; and it is nowadays much rarer than in the past. Yet most medical officers must have come across occurrences of this kind; and some simple method of promptly and effectively informing the teacher that the child should be excused attendance would do much to prevent such risks.

Where time has been lost through culpable non-attendance, many have urged that the child should be compelled to attend school beyond the normal school-leaving period. Compulsory measures of whatever nature are to be deprecated, and indeed are becoming rare. The best way of securing attendance is for the teacher to make the curriculum so attractive for the backward child that these youngsters will actually prefer lessons to truancy.

One plausible reason for backwardness, perpetually put forward, is sheer inefficiency of teaching. In the past the teacher has constantly been criticized if his pupils failed to reach the standards required by the official code. The result was a disposition to force these dull youngsters forward, so that they might at least make some fair showing at the end of the year when the inspector applied his tests. The annual inspections have long ago been discontinued. But their after-effects still linger in many departments. Certainly, by means of regular, intensive drill, it is possible to speed up the mechanical achievements of the dullest dunce; but the advance is made at the cost of any real intellectual interests the child might have, and often to the detriment of his physical and nervous health. Medical officers, therefore, should be prompt to discourage any form of over-pressure for the sake of merely scholastic ends.

In our surveys it was quite exceptional to find any instance of backwardness that could be ascribed to inefficiency of teaching. Where the teacher was to blame, it was rather for failing to discover the backward child than for failing to teach him. Even this, however, is becoming much rarer. By the use of educational and psychological tests, the teacher is now getting to know his backward pupils almost as soon as they enter his school, and is growing more and more alive to the fact that such children need special methods of instruction—that the curriculum, in fact, must be adapted to the child rather than the child to the curriculum.

But of all the conditions arising within school organization, the commonest were errors in promotion. A few children had been promoted too slowly; many had been promoted too swiftly; others, again, had been promoted from an infants' school run on the latest lines, with a maximum amount of liberty and play, to a senior department that still adhered to old-fashioned methods; and the sudden change from free activity to sedentary work, from an easy discipline to a rigid discipline, was producing something like a mild nervous breakdown.

In the past the examinations for junior county scholarships were often cited as an excuse for this over-pressure. The altered arrangements for allocating pupils at the age of eleven plus to the type of secondary school most suited to the needs of each have done much to diminish risks from this cause. But there is still the same eagerness to win places in the grammar school. Forgetting the wide differences that exist in innate ability, the teacher often argues that 'every child should have his chance'; the consequence is that all the pupils are pressed forward in the hope of bettering their chances. In former days the master who was eager to secure as many scholarships for his school as possible would pick out the most likely two or three and push them on into one of the higher standards. Now that the questions set for such examinations depend more on native intelligence than on acquired attainments in English and arithmetic, there is less need for such rapid promotion; but unfortunately in many schools there is still a good deal of coaching during the months before the final ordeal. Where schools have been reorganized on the lines of the recent Education Act, the primary school no longer contains any higher standards; and this often means that the general mass of the children in the lower standards are forced to do work that is really above the heads of all who are not of exceptional intelligence. The result is that the average children may do a little better than they should in the examinations for selection, but the dull child is penalized still further and suffers a greater strain. The system not only manufactures spurious grammar school candidates, but also spurious instances of mental backwardness and failure in the simpler subjects.

These flaws in school organization are matters primarily for the educationist and the teacher. But at most of the points the medical officer can render useful help, not only by discussing individual cases, but also by enlightening teachers, parents, social workers, and those who direct the educational policy of the area.

Physical Conditions. Having studied the child's environment, let us now pass to the child himself. Following the programme that I outlined in my opening chapter, we may examine his physical condition first of all, and leave his mental condition until later.

Here we come at once upon factors that directly concern the doctor. In the past, much stress has been laid, particularly by medical writers, on physical defect and bodily ill health as impediments to school progress. Too often it is forgotten how prevalent such infirmities always are in the very social classes from which the dull and backward are mainly drawn. At this point, therefore, more than anywhere else, the investigator must check his inferences by comparison with a control-group.

The data obtained both in London and in Birmingham are closely in accord. Among children whose school attainments are normal the average number suffering from physical defects amounts to about 38 per cent.; among those who are dull or backward it rises to about 45 per cent.; among the mentally defective, it is 52 per cent. The increase is steady, but not startling. Indeed, the striking feature of the two inquiries was the relatively small difference in bodily health disclosed between the retarded group, on the one hand, and the normal group, who came from much the same social surroundings, on the other. The conclusion seems clear. The presence of physical defects acts as a primary cause of backwardness in a small proportion of the cases only. Bodily weakness and bodily ill health are accessory factors, hardly ever fundamental causes. They may retard a child's ultimate development by the equivalent of six to twelve months' progress; but, unless a child's inborn capacity is subnormal to begin with, they cannot of themselves, except in rare instances, hamper his education so much that they convert a youngster of average intelligence into a downright dullard.[1]

We can, therefore, no longer hope that the removal of tonsils or teeth, the provision of spectacles or milk, or even generous arrangements for convalescent holidays in the country, will of themselves do much to lessen the numbers that are definitely backward. Not for one moment do I underrate the need and the value of medical or surgical treatment. For the backward child, indeed, such assistance is particularly pressing. Special efforts are required, not merely because he suffers from a larger number of defects, nor even because their relief may do something to disencumber his progress in the classroom, but still more because, in virtue of his own native dullness, and in virtue it may be of the dullness, poverty, and ignorance of his parents, he stands in greater need of competent external aid than those who are better off and more intelligent than he. Supplemented by suitable changes in the classroom, such treatment may improve the child's progress to a remarkable extent in isolated cases; but efforts along these lines cannot by themselves greatly alter the incidence of intellectual retardation.

With this reservation let us proceed to inquire what are the defects that occur most frequently, and in what directions they operate. The defects observed may be roughly grouped under two main heads: first, those that seem to lower the whole vitality of the body, clogging the child's development in every direction, and, secondly, those which manifest themselves in some more specific fashion and directly hinder the activities of the classroom.

Under the former heading there is a definite cycle of

[1] At Birmingham the medical side of the investigation was entrusted to Dr. B. R. Lloyd, who was associated with me in the inquiry and was specially appointed for the purpose. The results of this inquiry are of greater interest because from the outset Dr. Lloyd and I agreed that we should conduct our examinations in complete ignorance of each other's theories, methods, or results. Accordingly, when finally we met to co-ordinate our data, it was both striking and encouraging to discover that our independent conclusions were in close agreement on this point.

conditions that may be noted again and again among the backward. A large proportion of the children start life as the offspring of weakly or unhealthy parents, and seem to have been born with a low measure of physical vitality. Malnutrition in early infancy often ensues; and the tiny child, penalized by lack of proper food, fresh air, and sunshine, grows up with a weakened physique and a lowered resistance to infection of every kind. Occasionally he may even show signs of rickets, though during recent years this has become comparatively rare. There is a recurring tendency to catarrhal troubles and septic conditions of the tonsils and glands of the neck; and usually, as his medical record reveals, he succumbs to a quick succession of zymotic illnesses. These keep him from the infants' school at the very time he should be learning the first rudiments of reading and number. Later perhaps he is reported to be suffering from adenoids. And the final outcome is a feeble, stunted specimen, never perhaps seriously or dangerously ill, but constantly delicate and ailing.

One condition observed with especial frequency among the backward was that of recurrent or chronic catarrh. These catarrhal cases are apt to manifest symptoms and ailments that are often vaguely diagnosed as 'rheumatic'—sore throats, sore eyes, inflamed mucosae generally, headaches, pains in the limbs (often described by the parents as 'growing pains'), brief bouts of fever, and perhaps even affections of the heart or lungs. In the classroom they are known as fidgety little creatures, restless, inattentive, and impulsive —jerky in mind as well as in body. At times their spasmodic movements are so marked as to suggest a mild chorea. I may note that when sent to an ordinary open-air school such children often fail to improve: the sudden exposure to sharp changes of weather is apt to throw too great a strain upon their feeble circulation and body-metabolism. Where a more gradual regimen is attempted—first shielding the child from excessive exposure to cold and damp, and then carefully hardening him to it—I have found that he will often make steady progress.

Of nervous diseases the most frequent among the backward was undoubtedly chorea. Grave examples were comparatively rare; and among these the child's backwardness had been markedly increased by the long and frequent absences from school. In Birmingham, my sister Dr. Marion Burt investigated a group of such cases, and found that the average period of absence amounts to as much as 30 to 40 weeks in the course of a couple of years. In London slight cases are exceedingly common, and are nearly always associated with educational retardation. In my own backward groups the trouble was usually so mild that it was difficult to arrange for hospital treatment. The children were of a so-called rheumatic type, with mental and emotional symptoms often more marked than physical, such as might be diagnosed as 'quasi-choreic' or (to adopt a convenient phrase) as due to 'chorea minor'. In many the condition cleared up, more or less spontaneously, before the approach of adolescence.

With all these various defects short sharp remedies seldom seem to yield any lasting improvement. Great things, for example, were at one time anticipated from the removal of tonsils or adenoids; a careful study of the after-histories indicates that the operation by itself rarely has much beneficial effect on the child's educational progress, and may retard it by the shock. The immediate treatment, whatever it may be, always needs to be followed up for months if not for years. For all such cases a generous provision of modified open-air classes or schools, where the child can remain throughout the greater part of his school life, is a most urgent need.

Several writers have emphasized the importance of dental defects. Actually I found but little difference in this respect between the backward and the normal. A few cases were noted among those specifically backward in arithmetic. But in these instances the backwardness was usually temporary, though it was certainly relieved by proper treatment. Often the trouble had operated simply through the constant pain it had caused. Generally my impression was that the bad teeth were not so much a cause as a result of continued low vitality and poor health.

Of the more specific defects discovered at medical inspections, those that interfere most directly with school work are defects of sensation and movement. The most frequent of the sensory defects were defects of vision; hypermetropia and astigmatism proved far more important than myopia, and were far more frequently missed. Among younger children—just at the age when they are beginning to read and write—hypermetropia is exceedingly prevalent. The hypermetropic child is at a grave disadvantage in the close work of the classroom—in poring over reading-books and in shaping letters or figures on paper, as well as in the finer kinds of needlework. By an effort of focusing the child can overcome the difficulty, at all events for a few minutes, and so it passes unnoticed. Nevertheless, the child suffers from a continual strain; and the strain may quickly issue in aching eyes and an aching head, and a vague, unanalysed discomfort associated with every school subject that taxes his powers of vision.

Defects of hearing are rarer than defects of sight; but when they occur they impose a far greater obstacle to progress in school. Among boys and girls who gain scholarships, defects of sight are by no means infrequent; but to find a pupil who is partly deaf and yet keeps pace with his normal schoolfellows is altogether exceptional. Of the younger children put forward by teachers as cases of mental deficiency, quite a number prove, on due examination, to be merely deaf. It is amazing to discover how successfully the partly deaf can hide their defect. Among children as well as adults, there are plenty of individuals who fail to hear almost everything they should hear, and yet succeed in hearing quite well when not expected to. A single auditory test carried out at the medical inspection, often with a good deal of noise going on at the time, may easily miss nearly half the slight and intermittent cases; and the doctor is often forced to rely on the reports of the teachers.

In passing let me stress the importance of a peculiar form of deafness which seems almost wholly unrecognized. Just as colour-blind persons are blind to one end of the spectrum, so others may be deaf to one end of the tonal scale. Now the sounds of articulate speech differ mainly in virtue of their upper partials. Hence a person who is deaf to high notes may catch the general inflexions of the voice—the rise and fall of the deeper, fundamental tones, but completely fail to distinguish *ee* from *oo*, or *s* from *f* or *th*, and, in fact, confuse nearly all the consonants and vowels. An ill-adjusted loud-speaker that intensifies the bass and cuts out the treble conveys a rough impression of what these people hear and fail to hear. Children suffering from this type of partial deafness find the greatest difficulty in following speech, and as a result the youngest may never even learn to talk. Special methods have now been worked out for diagnosing and treating such cases; and they need no longer be put down as deaf-mute, dull, or aphasic.

It should be realized that the estimation of visual and auditory acuity is really a psychological problem, and involves a delicate technique. The quick and ready methods that the doctor employs for adults in his consulting-room are quite inadequate when dealing with the younger child. Here is one of the many instances where the school medical officer needs special psychological training for the work that he has to undertake. Here, too, is a task where the teacher might assist. From her special experience she is quick to see that, when the doctor thinks he is testing the sensory capacities of the small or backward youngster, he is really getting replies that depend on irrelevant factors, like lack of understanding or attention, ignorance of the names of letters or the pronunciation of sounds, and even general nervousness or fatigue.

Of motor defects the most important are stammering and left-handedness. Both these disorders may be the symptoms of a neurotic condition. The old notion that stammering was literally due to tongue-tie, to be cured by slitting the fraenum linguae, is, I imagine, nowadays held by no competent surgeon or physician; but it is still a favourite suggestion of the teacher. As regards left-handedness, there is a widespread notion that, since the brain-centre for speech is close to the centre for the right hand, therefore training a left-handed child to use its right hand is apt to induce a stutter. Stuttering undoubtedly may follow such efforts; but, when it occurs, it is nearly always traceable to the injudicious methods which the teacher has adopted in correcting the child's left-handed habits.[1]

Other physical defects, whose incidence is rarer and whose influence is less clear, I pass over. But from this brief survey one obvious conclusion stands out. The physical disabilities, found most frequently among backward children and tending to retard their progress in the classroom, do not consist of grave or acute disorders, but of slight and mild conditions such as may be easily missed or belittled as of no account. From the medical standpoint they may indeed be trivial; but in a child who is already slow or dull they may often have a most injurious effect upon his work at school.

The causes that we so far have considered sort themselves under three broad heads—bad health, bad homes, and bad arrangements in the school. These three categories comprise cases which are in the main restorable. If no deeper factor is co-operating, the backwardness may be removed by simply removing the external cause. A child may be half-way through its school career; yet we need not despair. Nature dearly loves an average; and just as the precocious occasionally fall off, so the backward frequently catch up. They are like neglected blades of grass, pressed, stunted, and whitened by some overlying board, which, when the shadow and the weight are lifted, presently spring up as tall and as green as any around them.

II. Intrinsic Factors

I come now to less hopeful cases—those where the backwardness is predominantly due to some hereditary or inborn mental cause.

Subnormal Intelligence. Since educational work is primarily intellectual work, it is natural to begin by searching for intellectual disabilities. As we saw in our preliminary analysis, the intellectual functions of the mind depend on

[1] For a fuller discussion of the treatment both of speech-defects and of lefthandedness, I may perhaps refer to the detailed chapters on the subject in *The Backward Child*, pp. 270 f., 360 f.

factors of two kinds: first, a single general factor entering into every form of intellectual work; and, secondly, a number of more specific factors, each limited to work of a particular type. The first question to determine, then, will be the influence of innate general ability—of 'intelligence', as it is popularly called.

In every case of educational backwardness, the fundamental point is to determine the child's inborn capacity. This will be done by means of intelligence-tests, such as those already described. Individual testing is essential, and usually the Binet scale will be employed. Where, however, the child's attendance at school has been irregular, or where some specific disability is suspected, verbal tests of the Binet type may at times give a misleading estimate. Their results should then be checked by applying tests of a non-verbal or performance type.

In the researches I have cited the intelligence of each backward pupil was systematically tested in this way; and it at once became obvious that the most important factor of all was here disclosed. With comparatively few exceptions, every child proved to be below the general average for innate capacity. The actual mental ratios varied from about 115 to 55. Children with mental ratios below 70 would ordinarily be classed as mentally defective; they were pupils that the teacher had missed in nominating cases for the statutory examination, and do not concern us here. They will, therefore, be excluded from our calculations. Children with mental ratios of 85 and upwards are suffering, if at all, from only a slight inferiority of intelligence, and should rank as 'merely backward' educationally. The vast majority, those with a mental ratio between 85 and 70, may be designated 'dull'—dull according to the technical definition of the term. Out of the whole series, excluding the defectives, as many as 60 per cent. were dull in this sense: that means that 3 out of every 5 were found to be suffering from a marked inferiority, apparently congenital and presumably permanent, in sheer intellectual ability.

Thus, of all the innate causes, by far the commonest is a weakness in general intelligence. The typical dullard is handicapped by much the same shortcoming that makes others mentally defective, only he is handicapped in a milder degree. It is a grave retardation in this fundamental capacity that produces the feeble-minded child; and it is a slighter retardation in the same capacity that produces the most intractable forms of backwardness. Since the capacity is inherited, or at any rate inborn, such cases will be backward for life.

Among about 15 per cent. of my backward groups no other contributory factor could be discerned: innate incapacity appeared to be the sole and sufficient cause. But in most instances the situation is more complex. Some extraneous influence, or set of influences—physical ill health, perhaps, or poverty at home, together with their attendant consequences—co-operate with some pre-existing weakness of the mind; and the joint resultant is that progress becomes doubly retarded. Such a combination of external and internal factors was found in more than one-half of the backward pupils that I examined: no doubt an investigation more prolonged and penetrating would have disclosed it in the majority.

For these reasons a child's educational age will nearly always fall below his mental age. In practice, however, where the usual standardized tests are applied, the medical officer may be surprised to find that, in a few sporadic cases, the child's educational age appears to rise above his mental age. The paradox is due to the inevitable limitations of the usual test-methods. In most instances the explanation is that the child has been conscientiously coached at the more mechanical subjects; as a result, in the simple exercises involved in the customary scholastic tests his achievements overestimate his actual level. Occasionally the child may possess some specific or limited aptitude that helps him at his school work: he may, for example, possess a good mechanical memory, and so be able to do well in the routine portions of his lessons; or he may possess a special knack for dealing with figures or words, and that in turn may produce a comparatively high mark in the elementary tests of reading, spelling, or arithmetic. At times it will be found that the

Binet tests underrate the child's real intelligence, and a performance-test will prove him to be a little brighter than was surmised.

Where backwardness is the result of innate dullness, the teacher should be warned that it is not only waste of time but positively harmful to press the child on in the hope of raising his attainments to the normal. Capacity must limit content; and if a child is born with a low measure of innate capacity, it will be as foolish for the teacher to try and instil into him a full amount of knowledge and skill as it would be to try and pour twelve ounces of medicine into an eight-ounce bottle.

Where the child's intelligence is nearly normal, the outlook is more promising. It is, therefore, imperative that the merely backward should not be confused with the genuinely dull. But optimistic predictions must be based on a careful testing of each individual case, not upon good-natured generalizations. It is a speech-day platitude that the most hopeless pupil may succeed in after-life. History is full of plausible examples—backward scholars who have made brilliant men. Newton and Darwin, Goldsmith and Sheridan, Watt and Stephenson, Wellington and Clive—the careers of these and many another celebrity testify how a dunce at school may prove a genius in disguise. But a closer study of biography reveals that the high intelligence was there from the start; and some extrinsic factor can nearly always be discovered which will account for the alleged stupidity at school. Such consoling examples are far less plentiful than popular opinion is apt to assume; and any suggestion that the genuinely dull may 'grow out of' their dullness is bound to be falsified.

Special Disabilities. It cannot, however, be denied that occasionally a child whom the teacher has marked down as dull proves, when tested, to be normal or bright. How, then, is the child's backwardness to be explained? If intelligence is equal to the average, if health, home circumstances, and classroom instruction are all that can be desired, then some further factor must be at work. What it is, only a closer inquiry can discover.

In most instances the next step will be to examine the child's special abilities. In theory we should test in turn all his intellectual functions—perception, both visual and auditory, memory, imagination, attention, reasoning, and the like. Standardized tests exist for this purpose; but, as we have seen, none but a psychological expert with laboratory facilities is in a position to apply them. A good deal can be inferred by noticing the way in which the child attacks the various tasks during the ordinary routine testing, and observing how far his successes and failures are scattered unevenly over the various processes involved. Often a child may succeed in every test that turns upon sheer reasoning, but fail with the easiest of the memory tests; or again, when his reading or spelling is tested, he will make recurrent errors that suggest some peculiar difficulty in analysing sounds or associating symbols.

The most frequent cases are those of special disability in some one subject of the curriculum. Specific backwardness in reading is common among the younger boys; specific backwardness in arithmetic among the older girls. If a child is seriously backward in reading, this will hamper his work at school on almost every side. Spelling and composition depend largely on understanding words in print; and hence the backward reader quickly drops behind in these subjects. Geography, history, and the like depend upon an ability to read the classroom text-books. Arithmetic is affected, because, at any rate in the upper classes, the pupil must grasp the wording of the problems before he can work them out. Indeed, it will often be found that, when a sum is put to such a child orally, he can do it quite well: the manipulation of the figures does not puzzle him in the least; yet the same sum written on the blackboard, or encountered in a manual of arithmetic, seems to defeat him utterly.

In other cases the situation is reversed. A child may be well up to the average in reading, spelling, and composition, but shows some special disability in dealing with numbers. In many schools pupils are still mainly promoted according to their attainments in arithmetic, for arithmetic is an easy subject for the teacher to grade and mark. Moreover, if a child is obviously unable to attack the arithmetic syllabus of an upper standard, the headmaster rightly argues that he will be a drag on the higher class, and, naturally, relegates him to a lower form. As a result, the child fails to make the progress of which he is capable in the remainder of the curriculum, and appears backward all round.

In all such cases a thorough study should be made of each child's peculiar difficulties. In the past it has been widely assumed that backwardness in reading, spelling, or arithmetic must be due to an innate defect in some specific faculty, expressly concerned with such work. For example, those who are exceptionally backward in reading have often been diagnosed as 'word-blind'. The argument is that, just as in adults some localized damage to the 'brain-centre for words' may leave behind it an acquired word-blindness, so an innate weakness in the same 'brain-centre' may cause a similar word-blindness of a congenital type.[1] At the suggestion of Sir Henry Head, several investigations have been carried out into alleged cases of this sort; and the main outcome of the research is to show that nearly all can be taught to read if suitable methods are employed. Indeed, it has proved exceedingly hard to find a single indisputable instance of congenital word-blindness.

An intensive study of such cases shows that specific disability in reading may spring from a variety of causes. In the great majority of instances the child has simply been absent from school at the stage when the elements of reading are usually taught. Between the ages of 5 and 7 infectious ailments are exceedingly common; hence, not infrequently, a child may be away from the infants' department for a period of several months. His convalescence is delayed; or somebody else in the family catches the complaint; and,

---

[1] Recently a renewed interest has been shown in alleged cases of 'congenital word deafness' and 'congenital auditory imperception' (cf. M. Barton Hall, *The Psychiatric Examination of the School Child*, 1947, pp. 109 f. and refs.). Several cases so diagnosed have been referred to me for examination; and the majority appear to have been suffering from high-note deafness. The theory that such conditions are caused by some congenital defect in a supposed cortical centre for the hearing of words is highly questionable.

when at last he is free to return to school, the time has arrived for him to be promoted to the senior department. There, in all probability, none of the teachers knows the special techniques for teaching the first rudiments of reading; so the child remains neglected. Never having made a start, he drops more and more behind the rest of his fellows. Presently his condition is noticed by the headmaster or inspector; at the age of 10 or 11 he is found incapable of recognizing a single word in print, and some one suggests word-blindness. The teacher protests that he cannot possibly graft a new word-centre on to the young child's brain; and so the child is left on the back bench, occupying himself with drawing or brushwork while the rest of the class bend over their books.

I have had numerous cases of this sort upon my records, though of late they have become increasingly rare. Periodical examinations with standardized group-tests pick them out at an early age; and teachers themselves have realized that, with a little private coaching day by day, many can be quickly brought up to the normal level.

But there are other cases where the root of the difficulty is more deep-seated. Reading depends on a long chain of mental processes; and if one link is weak, the whole mechanism may be thrown out of gear. Special tests will usually disclose where the weakness lies; but perhaps the most revealing procedure is to try various methods of teaching the child to read and to watch at what particular point he usually fails. Some, for example, have a special difficulty in auditory perception, others in visual: to split up the printed word or the sounded word into its elementary constituents is beyond their powers. Often they are at first supposed to be a little deaf, or to suffer from some defect of vision. A close examination, however, will demonstrate that the defect is not sensory, and arises from no fault in the peripheral organ: it is central and perceptual. For circumventing such difficulties several well-recognized devices have been worked out, and are usually successful; but, as a rule, the training must be carried out by a specialist at some psychological clinic.

In other cases the weakness lies, not in visual or auditory

perception, but in visual or auditory memory—in mental imagery, as it is technically termed. It can be detected by appropriate tests; but often it is apparent from the nature of the errors to which the child is prone. This can best be seen from a couple of contrasted cases.

A. B. is a boy of 12½ with a mental age of 11½. In mechanical arithmetic he is up to the work of Standard V, that is, of an average child of 11; in reading and spelling he is barely equal to an average child of 7. His mistakes show a frequent confusion between words similar in form but different in sound: he writes 'point' for 'paint', 'paint' for 'print', and 'beard' and 'bead' for 'bread'. To spell out the letters, or to hear the names of the sounds, does not aid him in the least. He seems to be guessing words from their dominant letters or from the shape of the word as a whole. With regular words like 'rapid' or 'habit' he often fails completely; but many irregular words like 'journey' and 'tongue' he can read correctly. He can even manage a few long polysyllables like 'autobiography' and 'encyclopaedia'. Further tests show that he is rather poor at auditory discrimination and exceedingly weak in auditory memory. He is, in fact, a visualizer, eye-minded rather than ear-minded.

This explains both his difficulties and his successes. The long words he evidently remembers as visible wholes: he says he has often seen them as titles on the backs of well-known books. With other words—'bicycle', for example—the alternation of tall letters and short letters sometimes make a picture that he can identify at a glance. 'Print' and 'paint' he confuses, because the visual form that they offer to the eye is almost identical; the pronunciation is utterly different.

Although he possessed a bad memory for sounds, this boy had been taught by the phonic method. Naturally the method failed. In other respects his mechanical memory was good; and by exploiting his power of recognizing and remembering word-forms, and by drilling him with a selected spelling-list, his teacher was able in the course of eighteen months to bring him nearly to the normal level.

C. D. is another boy of about the same age and intellectual

level. Long words like 'perambulating' and 'terminology' he can manage, provided their construction is regular; but he tends to spell them out syllable by syllable. He stumbles over words for 7-year-olds like 'journey'; 'tongue' he pronounces 'ton-gue'. In dictation he writes 'pickser' for 'picture' and 'plesent' for 'pleasant'; and, looking back over an old exercise-book that he had written three years before, I found a story that started 'I was hte god no hte tadle'.

This is an opposite case to the last. The sentence just quoted contains five reversals. The child had intended to write 'I saw the dog on the table'. The word 'god' does not look like 'dog': the general picture that it presents to the eye is quite different. But the component sounds are exactly the same. He remembered the sounds and the symbols for the sounds; but put them down in an incorrect order. Similarly, he confused *b* and *d*, which have practically the same shape differently turned. 'Pickser' he spelt almost exactly as in his own Cockney accent he pronounced it.

Here is a non-visualizer who had been taught by the look-and-say method. Give him a phonic method which will exploit his auditory imagery; and he will quickly surmount the difficulties.

In general, however, with those who are dull as well as backward, some form of the word-whole method proves more successful than a purely phonic procedure. Many of them grasp things best through movement—the movements of the lips as in muttered speech, or the movements of the hands as in writing; they are helped most of all by practical exercises, such as tracing the words in the air, or spelling them half aloud to themselves along old-fashioned alphabetic lines. But no short cut exists that can be applied automatically to all such cases. The methods must be adapted to each individual, and can only be discovered by repeated experiment and trial.

Of all the fundamental defects, perhaps the commonest is a weakness in what is technically called long-distance mechanical memory. Much of the regular classroom work demands a capacity to form mechanical associations between arbitrary or abstract symbols like numbers, letters, or sounds, and to retain them over a long period of time. Some children may seem to learn their tables quickly, and to remember them for the next lesson. Yet in a week what they once knew so well has faded like a photographic snapshot that has never been fixed. Education is a cumulative process; and it is essential that the child should retain whatever he has learnt, not for a few hours only, but for the rest of his school life. If he does not preserve the first foundations of each subject, it is impossible to build up any higher superstructure of knowledge. It is more particularly in the groundwork of the formal lessons—in reading, spelling, and arithmetic—that the effects of a poor memory are most commonly seen. Once the child has been helped over this stage, his backwardness may disappear.

One hint may be useful for practical diagnosis. If a child's short-distance memory is weak, his long-distance memory is nearly always weak as well; consequently, the tests of short-distance memory contained in the Binet scale—repeating numbers, repeating syllables, and the like—give a valuable clue to weaknesses in long-distance memory. The converse, however, does not hold true: a child may be quite good in tests of short-distance memory, and yet fail entirely where long-distance memory is required. Here, however, other test-questions from the scale may betray the defect—reciting the days of the week, the months of the year, or portions of the arithmetical tables. These and other incidental slips will often indicate where the child's inability lies.

No amount of practice can improve a child's power of mental retention. Repeated exercise may fix in his mind the particular facts that have been learnt; but it will not make his brain more retentive for other facts. Memory is not a muscle, to be strengthened by daily mental gymnastics. Many teachers still assume that hard lessons on subjects for which the child will have no further use, and in which he has no genuine interest, should nevertheless be retained in a syllabus for the backward class because of the general practice they afford. Keep the child learning, and his learning powers will gradually grow stronger: that is the popular maxim. Yet it rests upon a totally erroneous notion of the

working of the brain. A long series of psychological researches have conclusively disproved it.

On the other hand, though we cannot improve a child's
feeble memory, we can teach him to make better use of what
little memory he has. The teacher, therefore, should be referred to the innumerable devices invented for this purpose.
The best way is to begin by making the work to be memorized
at once more interesting and more intelligible. Some methods
make free use of various mnemonic tricks. The chief difference, however, between the pupil with a bad memory and
the pupil with a good memory is that the latter can get a
thing by heart after a small number of repetitions, and needs
to revise it only once a term, while the former requires two
or three times as many repetitions. Accordingly, the main
principle will be to introduce a good deal of extra drill upon
whatever has to be learned. The drill should not be tedious:
short, sharp, oft-repeated spells will be found the most
effective. There should be revision almost daily to begin
with; then the repetitions may be gradually spaced out. But
the teacher who has trouble with a pupil of this sort may
usefully study the chapters on memorization in any good
text-book of educational psychology.

Defective powers of reasoning make the younger children
backward in intelligent reading, and the older backward in
composition and above all in problem-work in arithmetic.
Backwardness in arithmetical reasoning is particularly common among older girls from the poorer social districts: in
this subject, however, an incidental cause is often irregular
attendance. The arithmetic syllabus is usually arranged in
logical order; and if a child has been absent while a certain
rule has been taught and practised, the consequent gap in
his skill and knowledge may hamper him in all his later work.
Reasoning itself is closely connected with intelligence; and a
large number of these cases seem to be due to an unusually
early arrest in the natural development of intelligence. Much
can be done by simplifying the steps in problem-work, and
teaching the logical process involved by numerous concrete
examples of an exceedingly simple kind, until the operation
becomes a habit rather than a mode of thought.

Temperamental Instability. The foregoing are the chief types of intellectual disability leading to backwardness in children otherwise intelligent: surveys show that such causes are somewhat rarer than might be supposed. Among those whose intelligence is normal, a far commoner source of backwardness is temperamental instability. In some the instability is obvious at the very first interview. The child is of the unrepressed type; and his high emotionality displays itself at once. These are the children who are commonly put forward as cases of inattention. Attention is popularly supposed to be an intellectual faculty; it would be truer to regard it as an emotional condition. It depends partly on temperamental stability and partly on interest. Often what seems to be a specific educational backwardness, or perhaps a peculiar disability in one special subject, springs really from lack of interest either in school work generally or in the particular subject in question.

This lack of interest may in turn have different causes. Sometimes it is due to the unattractive way in which the subject is being taught: the topics chosen may be well above the child's powers of comprehension, or they may be presented in such a style as to leave the child at once bored and bewildered. Sometimes it is due to the peculiar direction which the child's own energy has taken. He may have a passion for out-of-door pursuits, and chafe bitterly against sedentary or bookish tasks. Or again his emotions may be entirely absorbed by some inner personal conflict. As a result he spends all his hours worrying, brooding, day-dreaming, unable to concentrate on any objective task. In the extreme case he may be so inhibited and repressed, and his mental energy so locked up, as it were, in unconscious complexes, that he has no power left to apply to intellectual studies. Most frequently of all perhaps, the child has taken a rooted dislike to the subject because he once so heartily disliked the teacher who first attempted to teach it. Finally, in a few rare instances, the child may be innately apathetic. As we have seen, just as some are born with too much emotional energy, so others seem born with little or none.

With all these types the doctor, particularly if he has had

some psycho-analytic training, may be in a position to offer the most useful advice. With the excitable child the one fatal thing is to check and suppress his over-exuberant emotions, to stifle his natural instincts in the endeavour to control them. Rather the surplus energy should be re-directed by implanting more wholesome and more useful outlets—interests that may not only keep him from mis-chievous enterprises, but actually assist him at his work in the class-room. Such children cannot be expected to check their wandering thoughts by a sheer effort of will. Instead of urging the child to rise to the subject, the teacher must bring the subject down to the level of the child. By intro-ducing plenty of concrete illustration at the outset and supplying plenty of practical or manual tasks, the teacher can begin with a direct appeal to the child's own particular interests, primitive though they may seem, and then gradu-ally lead him onward to more abstract aspects of his work. Just because these children are so prompt in emotional ex-pression, their lack of solid intelligence is often unsuspected. They are bright in manner, but they may be far from bright in innate capacity. They are lively, high-spirited creatures, quickly responsive to personal appeals, sharp and smart in casual conversation. As a result, their true intellectual powers may easily be overestimated; they are given work of which they are really incapable, and then scolded for in-attention or wilful stupidity.

The repressed cases are more difficult to diagnose and deal with. Such children suffer from an excess in the in-hibiting rather than the aggressive instincts. Outwardly the child may seem quiet and slow, but inwardly he may be highly sensitive and unstable. Here the opposite error may be made; and the child may be set down as duller than he really is. A close study will reveal that the child is not so much dull in intelligence as dull in emotional response. Sometimes, rightly suspecting that the child has more ability than he puts into his lessons, the teacher brings him for-ward as a case of downright laziness. Laziness, however, shows itself in many different ways, and is due to many different causes. In itself it is not an explanation, but only a description—often a mistaken description at that. Very frequently the lazy child suffers from some mild neurosis which induces chronic anxiety or a special liability to fatigue; hence I shall postpone a fuller examination of such cases until I come to deal with the neurotic child as such.

Treatment. The treatment of the backward child I shall not discuss in any detail: it is a problem for the teacher rather than for the doctor. I have considered the various possibilities at greater length elsewhere;[1] and here, therefore, I need only recapitulate the more important principles.

Where a number of backward cases are found together, the obvious remedy is to organize a special school or class expressly for such cases. With junior children, i.e. those under 10, a special class is usually the better plan. With older children a complete remodelling of the curriculum is desirable; and this can best be done by instituting a separate school intermediate between the special schools for the mentally deficient and the ordinary elementary schools for the normal.

In a few cases removal to a backward class need be a temporary measure only. Where the child is not innately dull, but merely retarded educationally, individual attention to such matters as health, social conditions, school attendance, and teaching methods may result in progress being so accelerated that eventually the child can be retransferred to the ordinary class. Such cases will be comparatively infrequent, and will arise chiefly among the younger children.

In most instances those who are sent to an auxiliary class will need to remain there for the rest of their elementary school career. Accordingly, where children enter such classes several years before leaving school, more than one special class should, if possible, be established. In a large department the ideal plan would comprise a 'treble-track' system —a series of backward classes for slow children, a series of advanced classes for quick children, both parallel to the ordinary series of standards for children of average ability.

---

[1] Details will be found in my *Development Memorandum No. 1*, published by the London County Council, and since partly reprinted in the Board of Education's *Handbook of Suggestions*, Appendix A.

Each of these three types of pupil needs a different curriculum and different teaching-methods at every age and stage. But occasionally a pupil's rate of progress will profoundly change; hence cross-transference from one series to another should not be entirely excluded.

Where special classes or schools are impracticable, other expedients may be tried. The younger child may be retained in the infants' department for extra coaching in the rudiments of reading and number; the older child attending the senior department may sometimes be kept down in a lower class. Where the time-table is synchronized, children suffering from special disabilities in arithmetic or in reading may be relegated to a lower standard for that one subject alone. Often a teacher can arrange for special sets or sections within the same classroom. He can group his slowest pupils in a little batch by themselves. While the other children are doing written work he can then give attention to the backward; and while the backward are doing practical work he can devote himself to the rest.

Physical and social handicaps should, of course, be systematically dealt with so far as possible. Some cases may need a surgical operation or a spell of treatment at a hospital or clinic; but that by itself will seldom be sufficient. Such children almost always need continuous following up. With them it is as important to maintain health as to restore it. It is partly for this reason that such excellent results can be obtained in an open-air school or class.

Both the curriculum and the teaching-methods should be freely modified to meet the children's needs. The chief principle will be to abstain from aiming at too high a level in the more abstract subjects. The children should go more slowly, taking about twice the normal time over each phase of the curriculum. The exercises, particularly in arithmetic, should be simplified; the successive steps made more easy; and plenty of drill—interesting drill—should be given in the elementary work. Such children need never be taught to spell words that they are never likely to use They need never be taught to work out sums dealing with measures or processes that they are unlikely to require in after-life. For the older more particularly, much of the teaching should have a definitely utilitarian aim, and be specifically adapted to their probable employment.

But since backward children differ so much among themselves, individual attention and individual work is almost a necessity; and this means that the class should be small— 30 to 35 at the outside. All through, the education should be less academic and bookish; and more stress should be laid upon physical, manual, concrete, and practical aspects. Anything that makes for a constant sense of inferiority should be avoided; and self-confidence and self-reliance should be fostered by giving each child tasks that appeal to his special interests, and making them hard enough to require an earnest effort but never too hard to preclude eventual success. The depressing effects of perpetual failure, day after day and week after week, must be prevented at all costs. Discipline should be as free as possible; and character-training will be far more valuable than mere intellectual tuition.

The Backward Adult. Of dull and backward adults we know far less than we do of the mentally defective. From time to time psychologists have made small investigations of socially inefficient groups—the criminal, the pauper, the unemployable, and the unemployed. The results plainly show that among such groups the backward and the dull are far more numerous than the definitely feeble-minded. That, however, is largely explained by the fact that the milder degrees of intellectual inferiority are of necessity more frequent than the severer. But it would be unwise to stress such conclusions, or to infer that the dull or backward child necessarily grows up into an inefficient man or woman.

On the other hand, the popular belief that the child who is backward at lessons will nevertheless succeed in after-life is based on a misinterpretation of a few exceptional cases. Social efficiency, it is true, depends quite as much on qualities of temperament and character as on what the psychologist calls intelligence. Nevertheless, the lack of intelligence inevitably sets an upper limit to what is possible, and definitely precludes success in the more intellectual careers. On these grounds and from direct experience, I am inclined, so far as prediction is possible, to prophesy a poor measure of success in adult life for the child who makes poor progress at school.

But an important distinction must be borne in mind: a child in whom lack of educational progress is due to innate dullness will be far more severely handicapped later on than one in whom it is attributable to accidental factors. Those who are merely backward at school without being innately dull may rise to almost any walk of life to which their intelligence entitles them, except where academic knowledge is definitely required. They seldom enter clerical occupations, and practically never succeed in the professions; but in manual work, technical work, and work requiring a judgement of men, they are often unexpectedly efficient. On the other hand, the dunce whose backwardness is due to innate dullness seldom rises even to the ranks of skilled labour. Where planning, initiative, or thinking in advance is required, he is gravely at a loss, and seems incapable of giving satisfaction in any but the lowest forms of employment.

I have kept in touch with a large group belonging to this latter type—children who were tested at school and found to be dull in the technical sense. My records extend over ten or fifteen years of after-school life. When last heard of, as many as 21 per cent. were reported to be out of employment. Conditions vary, however, from trade to trade, from district to district, and from year to year; so that it is difficult to say how far the lack of employment was due to relative unemployability and how far to economic conditions. But in no case has a child within this group risen to, and permanently kept, any form of occupation demanding an intelligence above the general average. The boys who endeavoured to enter highly skilled trades never remained in their positions for more than 6 or 8 months. The girls who were sent to be trained as shorthand typists either never completed their course or never retained their jobs. Of the whole group, 38 per cent. were doing semi-skilled work in shops, offices, or factories. Another 16 per cent. were doing work which might be classified as skilled, but was of an exceedingly limited and wholly routine or mechanical order. The rest, so far as they had been engaged at all, had found nothing but unskilled work or coarse manual labour. During the first two or three years, the posts which they obtained did not differ very greatly from those obtained by the average youngster; but before they had reached the age of 21 there was a marked difference alike in the wages they were earning and in the satisfaction they were giving. A growing sense of disappointment leads easily to restlessness and crime; and as many as 6 per cent. had been charged with petty delinquencies. It seems clear, however, that, provided the child finds an employment suited to his simple talents, he may, in his own lowly sphere, make an efficient and a contented citizen.

Special aptitude and still more special gifts of character may do something to compensate for innate dullness. One investigator even claims that a dull intelligence is a positive asset for certain routine occupations: here it is the lively and the intelligent youngster who gives dissatisfaction and becomes dissatisfied himself. The least hopeful cases were found mainly among those who combined temperamental weakness with dull intelligence or else had accepted posts or occupations which were well beyond their capacities. It is from these dull, unstable individuals that the ranks of our criminals, our ne'er-do-weels, and permanent unemployables are so largely recruited. For reasons which are not difficult to guess they tend to gravitate towards, or congregate in, definite areas. The London map of backwardness, to which I have just referred, shows that these are, as a rule, particular neighbourhoods and particular streets in the poorest quarters of the county. This appears most clearly in inquiries into the incidence of mental defect. Dr. Lewis's surveys in the provinces,[1] and our own investigations in London, show that town and country alike are dotted with local centres of dullness and deficiency—what Dr. Lewis has called 'geographical foci'. But, when these foci are closely examined, mental deficiency proves to be only one of their many depressing features, and the problem of the

---

[1] See *Report of the Mental Deficiency Committee*, 1929, Part iv, pp. 74 f.

defective proves, as we have seen, to be but a special instance of the wider problem of mental subnormality generally.

Usually such centres coincide with what are popularly termed slums—slums in the cities and slums in the villages. The feeble-minded are found in greatest numbers among those sections of the population in which the general level is inferior throughout, inferior mentally, morally, and physically—in groups, that is to say, where there are not only numerous mental defectives, but numerous physical defectives, an excess of criminals, of chronic paupers, of dull, backward, and unstable persons of every undesirable type.

Is it the low-grade population that makes the slums or the slums that make the low-grade population? Both without a doubt: there is nearly always a vicious circle. Dr. Lewis observed that, in one of the areas that he investigated, a slum had actually been cleared of its population and the inhabitants moved to well-designed houses and hygienic surroundings in a better district; almost immediately it was found that the very conditions that it had been hoped to cure began to sprout up afresh, and the local authority had to intervene once more to stop the emergence of yet another slum. Indeed, it was in one of these newer areas that he found the highest proportion of mental deficiency observed throughout his inquiry.

Thus, closer investigation usually suggests that the foci are not so much local as personal. Transport the persons; and, if you keep them together in a batch, you create a new focus. The centres are family centres rather than geographical centres. We come back, therefore, to the conclusion we reached in the last chapter: mental deficiency forms but an extreme example of that general incapacity for adequate social adjustment which characterizes so many unfortunate families and stocks. Hitherto the doctor has concerned himself with mental deficiency alone; but he cannot understand this narrower problem unless he views it as one subordinate issue in a wider and a vaster task.

The entire question of intellectual subnormality must be considered as a whole. Even in dealing with the backward adult, the first and most promising steps will be those that can be taken at the outset of his life. Hence all that I have said about the improvement of physical conditions during infancy and the prenatal period applies with equal or even greater force when we turn from the defective to the dull: far more dullards than defectives are manufactured during those critical months that precede and follow birth. We are, however, beginning to recognize that, from the earliest days of infancy, mental influences count for quite as much as physical. During the school period the problem becomes simpler, partly because we know far more about conditions and needs, and partly because so much of the machinery is already available. Here again the key to the situation is to approach the entire retarded group as a single unit under a comprehensive administrative scheme. The measures I have just suggested—organizing special classes as well as special schools, instituting an active social service to cope with the innumerable difficulties that arise beyond the school walls— these are needed, not merely for the sake of the child, but also for the sake of the future adult. Provision for after-care is essential, and should extend at least to the end of the adolescent period; here vocational guidance along scientific lines will prove an invaluable help.

But once more the paramount need is for further study and research. Research is needed upon the more suitable methods of teaching and training during childhood; and as regards adults a co-operative investigation from a psychological standpoint into the whole problem of unemployment and unemployability is long overdue. Above all, public opinion has still to be awakened and educated, so that the wider bearings of the whole problem may be more fully understood.

Notes and References. The investigations upon backward children in London, referred to in this chapter, were undertaken in the course of my work for the London County Council. The results were described in reports submitted to that Authority, and a systematic survey of the whole subject was afterwards published by the University of London Press (*The Backward Child*, 1937). I am deeply indebted both to the Council and to the Manager of the Press for permission to summarize the data and the chief conclusions here. A brief and less technical review of the subject, with special reference to the treatment of the 'educationally subnormal', has since been issued by the same publishers with the title *The Causes and Treatment of Backwardness* (1953, 6s.).

As noted above, the Education Act of 1944 now proposes that special provision should be made for what it calls 'educationally subnormal' pupils. The term is in keeping with the classification and nomenclature adopted in this book, and is more precise than the plain word 'backward': indeed that is why I myself have used it, both here and in earlier writings. But it is liable to be misunderstood by the general public. The doctor, thinking chiefly of institutional cases, commonly describes mental defectives as 'suffering from an abnormality of the brain'; and to the ordinary parent 'subnormal' and abnormal' sound much the same. Subnormal, however, merely means falling below an approximately *average* standard (e.g. 'subnormal temperature'); abnormal means departing from a *healthy* standard—a much more alarming condition. In the broader sense both the 'dull and backward' and nearly all 'educable defectives' are merely instances of 'normal' biological variation: the main practical difference was that the former could be dealt with in special *classes*; the latter were transferred to special *schools*. And the fears of the parent are further aggravated by the fact that in many areas what were formerly known as 'special schools for the mentally defective' are now often referred to as 'E.S.N.' schools. Hence the label 'educationally subnormal' has come to possess almost as sinister a connotation as the older phrase; and the effort to wipe out the stigma that formerly attached to the one per cent. who were termed 'defective' has spread needless apprehension among the mothers of the ten per cent. who are now dubbed 'educationally subnormal'.

The official definition of the phrase will be found in the pamphlets on *Handicapped Pupils and Medical Services Regulations*, 1945, and *Special Educational Treatment*, 1946 (H.M. Stationery Office). Educationally subnormal children are there defined as 'pupils who, by reason of limited ability or other conditions resulting in educational retardation, require some specialized form of education, wholly or partly in substitution for that normally given in ordinary schools'. This category, we are told, is intended to include (1) 'children who in the past were certifiable under Sect. 55 of the Education Act of 1921' (these roughly correspond with the group usually described in medical textbooks as 'feebleminded children' or 'educable defectives'; in the Act they were described as 'incapable of benefit by instruction in ordinary elementary schools, but not incapable of benefit by instruction in Special Schools or Classes'). (2) 'Children who are retarded by reason of limited ability', but presumably less retarded than the former group: (they correspond with those previously described as 'the dull'). (3) 'Those who are backward in the basic subjects because of other conditions' (i.e. 'the merely backward'). The upper borderline, it is suggested, will be an educational age (and, for the dull, a mental age) of about 8 at the chronological age of 10, i.e., a 'quotient' of about 80 per cent. Those with a mental age of less than $5\frac{1}{2}$ at 10, i.e. an intelligence quotient of about 55 per cent. or less, should be regarded as 'ineducable'. Most medical and psychological investigators, however, still find it convenient to retain the intermediate borderline, namely, an I.Q. of 70 (in keeping with the practice in many other countries), and to describe those below this level as 'mentally defective', although they are no longer certifiable as such.

IV

THE DELINQUENT

THE DELINQUENT

Criminology as a Branch of Social Psychology. A man has been convicted of murder; and the record of his past career is put before the court. How often does it appear that the crime which may cost him his life is the last of a long series of offences, reaching back to his childish days! Again and again, in instances of this kind, the psychologist is asked whether something might not have been done, in childhood or at a later stage, to avert the tragic end. Is crime a form of moral deficiency, which nothing can eradicate because it is innate? Or is it perhaps a slowly developing malady, which may be successfully checked in its mild initial phases, but which, being neglected or ignored, continues its progress at an accelerated pace, and leads ultimately to a fatal close?

Turning, then, from the intellectual to the moral aspect of the mind, let us inquire what aid psychology can offer in those perplexing cases, in which intelligence is perfectly normal, but temperament and character seem warped or debased. It is natural to think of them first in their most flagrant forms. The murderer, the hardened thief, the kleptomaniac, the incorrigible criminal in whatever guise— here surely are problems of mental subnormality which call for scientific treatment, problems which to the popular mind are the most sensational of all that fall within the scope of social medicine.

Hitherto the psychologist has directed his attention chiefly to the more youthful and less startling examples. For this there are two cogent reasons: the juvenile criminal is far easier to study, and at the same time easier to reclaim. He is easier to study: for, when we are dealing with an offender of school age, it is a simple task to get full data for all those numerous points which, as we have seen so often, have to be scrutinized in every individual case. His family history, his early childhood, his physical development, his intellectual progress, his material and social surroundings—information on all these matters is nearly always accessible. Further, in childhood the mind is more easily explored; personality is less complex; motives are simpler to unravel. But, secondly, it is far more hopeful, and infinitely more urgent, to try to reform the incipient criminal while he is young. His habits are not yet fixed irrevocably. His character is still plastic. Society is more sympathetic towards him; and it is easier to control and superintend his actions. For all these reasons, the most successful investigations into the problems of crime and delinquency have been those carried out among younger persons.

The Investigation of Causes. In dealing with the individual delinquent, what is to be our approach? Here the psychologist's task and methods have often been compared to those of the modern scientific detective. But there is this difference. It is on the investigation, not of the offence, but of the offender that the psychologist's efforts are focused. In following up the misdeeds of younger boys and girls the main point to be discovered is not—who committed this crime? that is generally known; but—why was this particular child led to commit a crime at all? And, to reach the answer to this question, the psychologist will pursue the same lines of inquiry that we have laid down for other cases.

Contrary to popular opinion, there is, in essential principle, no difference between the examination of the criminal and the examination of the defective, the neurotic, or those who are backward at school. The psychologist's attitude towards a criminal is the same as the doctor's towards his patient, and departs widely from that of traditional justice. With questions of responsibility he is not concerned. To him the criminal is just another subnormal individual whose condition must be investigated, scientifically and sympathetically, and if possible treated and cured.

In assessing responsibility, the medical profession has always taken a standpoint very different from the legal. Yet there are signs that the law is now tending towards a humaner view. Curiously enough, it is not in connexion with the time-honoured question of the insane, but in dealing with the newer problems of the juvenile offender, that the law has been led to modify its point of view. In 1933 a new and important Act was placed upon the statute-book, dealing with the offences of young persons. There it is now set out, among the 'principles to be observed by all courts', that 'every court in dealing with a child or young person brought before it . . . shall have regard to the welfare of the child or young person'.[1] What a change from the days, which our grandfathers could remember, when children were sentenced to death for stealing articles worth only a few pence! And what a revolution if that phrase could be inscribed on the first page of the criminal code and engraved over the portico of every court of justice: 'Every court shall have regard, not to punishment or retribution for the crime, but to the welfare of the prisoner'!

Crime as a Natural Psychological Reaction. In the past, doctors and psychologists, it is true, have rather overstated their case, or perhaps I should say mis-stated it. Medical writers have sometimes claimed that all crime is a disease; and, with their materialistic leanings, they have usually implied that by disease they understand physical disease—disease in the literal sense. Were the word 'disease' used as a rhetorical metaphor only, there would be little to urge against it. If it merely meant that the criminal should be regarded primarily as a patient to be treated, rather than as a sinner to be chastised, every psychologist would allow the expression to pass. But usually it conveys to the public, if not to the medical man, some deeper connotation. It suggests that the regular offender is in some way pathological; that he suffers from a defect that is almost organic—from what the teacher and the social worker are so fond of calling a 'kink in the brain'.

More recently, several sociological writers have swung towards the opposite extreme. They propose to divide all criminals into two broad classes: those in whom the crime is a symptom of disease, and those who apart from their crimes are perfectly normal. And they argue that the psychologist is in no way concerned with the latter group; only

[1] *Children and Young Persons Act*, 1933.

with the former is his interference justified. If that were so, there would be little work, in the field of practical criminology, for the psychologist and the psychological clinic to do; for, as I shall show later, crime that results solely from disease or morbid weakness is the exception, not the rule. The analysis of a fair sample of cases will quickly indicate that conduct which society condemns as criminal, so far from being pathological, is, from a biological standpoint, as normal as yawning or shedding tears. Given certain conditions inside the individual and round about him, delinquency is a natural psychological reaction.

In any case, disease or no disease, crime certainly is nothing but an outward manifestation—a sign of some deeper and more complex cluster of causes. To scold or punish the criminal for his offence, and then do nothing further, is often worse than useless; it only complicates the situation, and adds a fresh factor calculated to antagonize the offender still more. Once again, it must be insisted, to treat the symptom alone is of little avail: we must search out and remove the underlying sources.

In endeavouring to discover the chief conditions that make for crime let us follow the same plan that we adopted in the case of the backward and the dull. Several scientific researches have now been made—a few upon adults, a larger number upon adolescents and young children. Here, very briefly, let me summarize the principal results.

In London I have taken 200 consecutive cases of juvenile delinquency, and have subjected each one to an intensive study.[1] As before, I have also carried out a parallel investigation among an equal number of normal, law-abiding children, selected to serve as a control group. A control group is indispensable. Nearly all the inquiries with which I am acquainted offer figures for delinquent groups alone. But, unless the investigator is dealing with an individual rather than with a group, it is impossible for him to be sure that

[1] These inquiries, like the preceding, were carried out in the course of my work for the London County Council, and were fully described in a report upon the subject, since published as a separate volume (*The Young Delinquent*, University of London Press, 1925). I am grateful to the authorities and the publishers for permission to summarize the data and conclusions here.

he is tracing the actual operation of a genuine cause. Here as elsewhere it is rash to infer that, because a condition, apparently adverse, is found over and over again in a batch of subnormal persons, therefore it must be the essential factor responsible for their subnormal state.

Multiple Causation. Having studied the two series of cases, and having compared the features that stand out in one group or the other, what is the main result? What conditions mark off the delinquents from the remainder?

The reply at first sight seems baffling. No single cause is found. More than sixty special factors emerge as characteristic of, or as predominating in, the group of juvenile offenders; and, even when we turn from the group as a whole to single individuals, we still find that as many as a dozen different factors may be operative in each case.

That, however, is a common outcome of psychological inquiries. In dealing with bodily disorders it may be possible to decide on a single factor as the essential cause, and to demonstrate that factor again and again in similar situations. With psychological disorders uniform causation is the exception, not the rule. Plurality of causes—what Freud has called over-determination or multiple determination—is an almost invariable principle.

Crime, then, in the human individual is assignable to no single universal cause, nor yet to two or three. It springs from a wide variety, and usually from a multiplicity, of alternative and converging factors. They differ in different cases, and in every instance more than one is present. Accordingly, the psychologist of to-day, unlike the criminologist of the past, is no longer content to invoke one all-explaining reason—inheritance, poverty, epilepsy, or an inborn defect of the moral sense. Nearly always he finds, when he looks for them, not one explanation, but half a dozen explanations for a given act of crime. This is of supreme importance for treatment. It is never enough to deal with the most obvious factor: all the subversive factors must be discovered and removed. It is not the last straw but the accumulation of straws that breaks the camel's back; and if the camel is to be relieved, it is not sufficient to lift away just one single blade or wisp. They must be unloaded, all of them, one by one.

A. Inherited Conditions.

Let us, then, take each of the main factors in turn, and see how they operate and how frequently they are found. In accordance with our previous scheme, we may begin with the hereditary factors first. Once again we become embroiled in the ancient controversy. Heredity and environment, nature and nurture, one or the other of these two opposing influences has constantly been cited by this criminologist or that, and treated as the sole key to the problem.

There is one school of thought which attributes everything to heredity. The youthful criminal, it says, is a born criminal. Very often he is dubbed a moral imbecile. As you gather no grapes of thorns nor figs of thistles, so, it is argued, from criminal parents you can expect nothing but criminal children. The delinquent child is the foredoomed legatee of ancestral depravity and vice.

On the other hand, there is another school of thought which declares that criminals are not born but made; and the making of them is ascribed to their early environment. Clean up the slums, close the public houses, find better homes, and grant better wages; and the criminal will shortly become as extinct as the dodo.

Which of these two doctrines is right? Those who acknowledge that crime is generally the result, not of a single all-pervading factor but of a concurrence of causes all making for the same end, will be ready to accept the psychologist's answer: namely that not heredity alone, nor environment alone, is to blame, but that in nearly every instance the two are working together. Before you can have weeds you must have a suitable soil; and into that soil must be deposited the seeds or germs of danger.

Nevertheless, in different cases the two may contribute in differing proportions. Let us, therefore, examine the actual figures obtained from a series of case-histories. Within the whole of my delinquent group, there were only 11 per cent. whose relatives had been sentenced for crime, and only

19 per cent. whose relatives, whether sentenced or not, were known to have committed some gross offence. Four-fifths of the children could plead no history of crime among their parents or their kindred. Even where the child had been brought up by a vicious mother or father, there it could generally be argued that it was the upbringing rather than the child's hereditary endowment that was responsible for his wrongdoing.

But one important exception, or series of exceptions, were noted. Even among children who had been removed from vicious home influences at a very early age, there were a number of instances in which a boy or girl displayed later on much the same immoral tendencies as the parent. But these tendencies were usually of a limited and definable kind. Nearly always they could be explained as the direct result of some common human instinct, apparently inherited with excessive strength. The plainest cases were those of sex delinquency. Almost equally clear, but perhaps less frequent, were those of violent temper. A few—though here the explanation is more doubtful—were instances of irrepressible and restless wandering.

It seems clear, therefore, that crime is not inherited as such. Lombroso, it will be remembered, argued strongly for the hypothesis of the born offender, *il reo nato*—a degenerate specimen of mankind, a regression apparently to the barbarous savage, cropping up like an alien stock in the midst of civilized society, and definitely forming a species apart. This theory has had some vogue in this country. Its popularity is largely due to Mr. Havelock Ellis's well-known and delightfully written work on *The Criminal*.[1] As we have seen, it has found its way into an Act of Parliament, where the 'moral imbecile', or, as he is now called, the 'moral defective', appears as forming one of the four main classes of mentally defective persons. 'We must', says Mr. Havelock Ellis, 'regard the group of moral imbeciles as identical with the congenitally criminal.'

The term 'moral deficiency' is sometimes applied to those

---

[1] From the preface to recent editions it will be seen that Mr. Havelock Ellis has himself appreciably modified his views.

who are mentally defective in the ordinary sense, but in addition have acquired criminal or immoral habits. Honesty in a complex world demands a certain degree of intelligence; hence every mentally defective child, if left to himself, is apt to yield to vicious or unlawful temptations. Lack of intelligence is an inherited characteristic: consequently, here is an important predisposing factor. It is one which we shall have to examine in detail later on.

But this is not what moral deficiency means. To cover such cases no new clause would have been needed: they could be certified as feeble-minded or as imbecile according to the degree of their intellectual defect. Moral deficiency, as we have seen, was a phrase introduced to denote an innate defect in an innate moral faculty. This conception we have already examined. We found no evidence for it whatever. The phrase, in short, is wholly misleading, and should be dropped in favour of some other form of words, such as 'temperamental deficiency'. This would accurately describe a mental state which, though far rarer than so-called moral deficiency is assumed to be, un-doubtedly exists.[1] The temperamentally defective are not necessarily immoral, though they may easily become so. Hence, in certain cases, it may even be wise to certify them. When certified and sent to a specially organized institution, they often gain sufficient stability to be allowed out on licence, and may eventually prove capable of maintaining themselves satisfactorily by regular employment, and give no further ground for anxiety on account of bad conduct.

Experience, indeed, shows that, while intellectual defici-ency is almost impossible to cure, so-called moral deficiency —granted favourable conditions, and judicious treatment starting from an early age—can very often be remedied. Character is as amenable to training as intellectual disabilities

---

[1] A label which has recently acquired great popularity, particularly in the law courts, is the phrase 'psychopathic personality'. It appears to connote merely a condition of marked emotional instability, accompanied by much anti-social behaviour (which is the natural outcome of undisciplined emotion-ality). Neither characteristic forms evidence of anything pathological. Hence the termination '-pathic' is at once unjustified and misleading. (See above, p. 73.)

are resistant. That is a point which practical psychology continually verifies: a man's intelligence is limited from birth; his character is far more plastic, and can be developed for evil or for good. The innate presence of certain temperamental disabilities, like the innate lack of intelligence, may no doubt render that training far more difficult. But it should not lead us to abandon all hope of treatment, and imagine that the only course to take with such cases is to condemn them for ever to an institutional life.

There are, then, various predisposing factors that may bias a child towards a life of crime. Such predisposing factors may certainly be inherited; but crime as such is not hereditary. It is due to the further operation of post-natal causes upon a temperament more or less susceptible.

B. Environmental Conditions.

Accordingly, let us now turn from the hereditary factors to the environmental. For the convenience of investigation and analysis, environmental conditions may be divided into two broad groups: first, those obtaining within the home, and, secondly, those obtaining outside it, whether at school, in the streets of the locality, or in the place of business where the offender may be employed. In every case it is essential to make inquiries in these several directions.

In regard to children attending elementary schools the chief facts are usually known to the officials of the local education authority—the teachers, the attendance officers, or the care committee workers. Such information should always be placed at the disposal of the court. According to the provisions of the Act of 1933, wherever a child or young person is brought before a court of summary jurisdiction, notice is to be given to the local authority, and the local authority, on being notified, 'shall, except in cases which appear to them to be of a trivial nature, make such investigations and render available to the court such information as to the home surroundings, school record, health and character of the child or young person . . . as appear to them to be likely to assist the court'. At a psychological clinic the information is usually collected by a trained social worker.

In the past social workers have usually limited their inquiries to a visit to the school and the child's home; it is, however, essential that they should extend their surveys to all the external conditions of the delinquent's daily life.

(1) *Conditions within the Home.*

Let us look at the home circumstances first. Here again the investigator is apt to take too narrow a view. Too frequently the social worker's report merely covers those concrete economic details which can most easily be noted and specified—income, expenditure, sanitary conditions, and the like. In every juvenile case it is important that the inquiry should deal not only with the material conditions, but also with the domestic, the disciplinary, and the moral conditions of the household. We may glance at these four aspects in turn.

First, what are the economic conditions of those families from which delinquents are actually drawn? During the course of my work in London I have tried to make a map for juvenile delinquency similar to the map for educational backwardness described in the preceding chapter. From the geographical distribution of delinquency, it at once appears that the greater proportion of offenders are recruited from the poorest districts. The highest figures in my list are supplied by the region around Shoreditch, Finsbury, and Clerkenwell—the scene of Oliver Twist's many adventures with his villainous companions. The poorer quarters facing the City on the south side of the river—North Southwark and the adjacent districts stretching into Lambeth on the west and into Bermondsey in the east— are nearly but not quite so prolific in juvenile crime. And the slum areas around the larger railway termini, particularly behind Euston and King's Cross stations, form little hotbeds of vice.

Taking London as a whole, I find that more than half my cases come from homes that may be described as definitely poor. This seems a high percentage. Yet, when we turn to the general population, we find that over 30 per cent. of the children in London come from homes of much the same type. Of the delinquents, 16 per cent. belong to families living definitely below the poverty line, as formulated on a previous page;[1] of the general population, only 7 per cent. fall into this extreme category. Here the disproportion is greater. Yet more than 40 per cent. of the delinquents were living in comfortable circumstances, many of them coming from homes that were quite well-to-do.

I conclude that poverty has a positive, though not very decisive, connexion with delinquency. It forms but one factor, and seldom the sole factor, in the causation of juvenile crime. Nowadays, thanks to the provision made through the schools and in other ways, it is rare to find the poverty-stricken youngster stealing because he is hungry. As a rule, it is the deprivation of little luxuries—of sweets, or toys, or evenings at the cinema—rather than of positive necessities that drives such children to theft. With the older offender it may be different. But, broadly speaking, poverty appears to act more through indirect than through direct means—through the overcrowding, the narrow life, the constant worry and friction, that lack of money inevitably entails.

Other factors in the home environment, however, are quite as influential as its economic status, though they are, in general, more easily overlooked. An imperfect family circle is a common feature in the case-histories of young delinquents. Sometimes the child is illegitimate. More often he is an only child, pampered and spoilt. The father may be dead, deserted, or divorced. Still more frequently, the mother is dead or separated from her children. Sometimes the child feels herself to be a little Cinderella revolting against the tyranny of an unkind stepmother, or of her elder brothers and sisters. Usually the tyranny and unkindness are quite imaginary: the modern stepmother seldom lives up to her traditional reputation for cruelty or callous indifference. What generally happens in such a case is that the child has suspected, or suddenly discovered, that his supposed mother is not his real mother; and half unconsciously he begins to persuade himself that she has no right to control him.

The vicious home is not so frequent as might perhaps be

[1] See above, p. 124.

thought. Actual incitement, or training in crime, such as Dickens has so vividly portrayed, is nowadays exceedingly rare. I have come across six or seven cases where boys were deliberately taught to steal either by their parents or by a receiver of stolen goods; and about a dozen where girls were urged or encouraged into yet more sordid forms of misbehaviour. The consciousness of vice or criminality in one's parents, without any direct encouragement, is far more frequent. Naturally, the thief, the burglar, and the prostitute have children of their own, and these children attend the Council's schools; naturally, too, a high code of honesty is not to be expected of boys or girls brought up by parents whose dishonest practices can hardly escape the notice of their children. Hence, in any large survey of juvenile delinquency, such households are bound to be included. But, when the survey is broad enough, the criminal family proves to be definitely the exception, not the rule. Parental drunkenness was common enough in my delinquent series. But it was almost as common in many other homes where the children had never been known to do wrong. Where it prevails, the drunkenness itself, and the adverse consequences that so often follow—crime, brawling, bad language, irregular unions, often molestation and ill treatment of the child itself—may at times prove disastrous. When these conditions are part of the child's daily life, they may set up such an atmosphere of misery and friction that the child is tempted to respond by some aggressive act of crime, or to escape from the whole situation by running away from home and then seeking to support himself by stealing or irregular means.

The most serious factor of all is undoubtedly a defective home discipline. In some homes there is no discipline at all. In others the discipline is weak. In others, perhaps the more numerous, it is excessively strict and severe. Worst of all is the spasmodic, alternating, forcible-feeble type of treatment, where the child is first petted and cajoled, and then scolded and whipped.

Treatment. These, then, are the main conditions to be noted within the home itself—poverty, defective discipline, defective family relationships, and an unwholesome moral or emotional atmosphere. When these are the main or only factors, the proper course is clear. If the child or youth is to remain at home, then the harmful conditions—material, moral, or social—must be drastically changed. Sometimes the court may be persuaded to apply a little needful pressure by means of fines or recognizances taken from the parents. But, where improvement cannot be procured without such pressure, to apply it may in the long run only serve to make matters worse. A court can never force a parent to be sincerely sympathetic or co-operative. The parent may, indeed, comply with the letter of the magistrate's injunctions; but, consciously or unconsciously, he will probably evade the spirit of it, and end by making the situation more difficult for the child instead of less. Where there is no reasonable likelihood of the home conditions being improved, the only remedy is to remove the child. Formerly it was a popular maxim that a young offender should not be committed to an institution except as a last resort; but life in an industrial school, and even in a Borstal institution, is now very different from what it used to be, and is approximating more and more, within the inevitable limitations, to life in a public school. Often, however, it is feasible to transfer an older youth to some residential club or other foster-home, possibly as a voluntary case. Children too young for an industrial school may be boarded out or committed to the care of other fit persons. Nevertheless, the investigator should beware of inferring that, because a child's home circumstances seem prejudicial, they are therefore the sole and sufficient reason for his misdemeanours. In every case the conditions outside the home, and, above all, the physical and mental condition of the child himself, should first be reviewed before offering any final recommendation.

(2) *Conditions outside the Home.*

In regard to conditions outside the offender's home, there are three special fields to study: the conditions of his work, the conditions of his leisure, and the companionships that he forms at work or at play.

Work that is uncongenial may be as damaging to a youth's morale as failure to obtain work altogether. Hence, in older cases, vocational guidance will play an increasingly important part. With the delinquent, even more than the ordinary youth or young girl, it is essential that the choice of employment be based on a sound and scientific study of the offender's personal capacities. Organizations like the Institute of Industrial Psychology can here render valuable help to probation officers and those concerned with the welfare of these young people. The bright aspiring lad with a job too tediously mechanical for his smart wits and high ambitions, the slow and bungling dullard with a job too difficult for his weak mind—both are equally ready to try their hands at unlawful but more stimulating escapades. The transition from youth to manhood, from the discipline of the classroom to a relatively free and independent life, overtakes most children in the very midst of adolescence, that is to say, at the most unstable stage of mental and moral development. If, therefore, the nature and the difficulty of the work required are not adapted to the nature and level of the young worker's intellectual powers, or if his new associates are unsympathetic in their attitude or irregular in their moral code, then the risks of delinquency are doubled. With younger children an uncongenial school may have much the same disturbing influence as uncongenial employment with the older. Here, however, the problem is simpler. If open or secret friction has grown up between the child and his teacher or his fellows, it is usually easy to transfer the child to another school.

The conditions of leisure are even more important than the conditions of work. A statistical study of the days and times at which juvenile offences are committed is highly instructive. It shows at once that the majority occur during leisure hours—during the free and idle moments when school or business is over for the day, and during the vacant afternoons of Saturday or Sunday. Mischief and crime seem frequently to arise as a feeble substitute for a week-end outing or a half-holiday's sport.

This suggestion is confirmed by the geographical distribution of juvenile offences. As our map reveals, petty crime is particularly rife in areas where there is little or no provision for wholesome recreation—no playing-fields near at hand, no parks accessible by bus or tram, no clubs or social gatherings to fill an empty hour. But it is almost equally prevalent in those districts where facilities for amusement are excessive and highly advertised—for example around those West-end thoroughfares where nearly every building is a cinema, a theatre, a sweet-shop, or a restaurant.

The influence of the cinema is one of the most popular of all explanations for the mischievous exploits of the young. Fifty years ago it was fashionable to lay the blame at the door of the penny dreadful. But the notion that the young adventurer may be tempted to imitate any crime he sees upon the screen, or reads of in the daily papers or the cheap novelette, is seldom borne out by the actual facts. In the whole of my series I can find but six clear cases where a definite offence was directly inspired by something the child had witnessed on the films. More frequently the craze for the pictures leads to theft or embezzlement in a far simpler fashion: it provides the young cinema fan with a standing motive to steal money for admittance. But probably the most serious danger from the cinema lies in its more subtle and elusive influences. The usual picture-house programme presents to the child a grossly perverted view of human life, and false but cheaply fascinating ideals. Existence is depicted as an almost unceasing round of excitement, frivolity, and fun. Intrigue, flirtation, lawless enterprise, and adroit deceit are set before him, surrounded with a halo of fictitious glamour. The love-interest, generally in its most sensational form, dominates nearly every programme. Almost inevitably, the child acquires a precocious familiarity with sexual affairs, and becomes acquainted with distorted if not degraded standards of morality and conduct.

At the same time it is easy to exaggerate the harmful influence and overlook the good. The better type of cinema supplies not a provocative but an alternative to mischievous amusement. Every social observer can cite instances where the opening of a picture-palace has reduced hooliganism among boys, withdrawn the younger men from the public house, and supplied the girls with a safer substitute for lounging with their friends in the alleys or the parks.

But of all the influences arising outside the home, the most important are the companions with whom the child or youth associates. His chief acquaintances may be persons of the same age or older, of the same sex or of the opposite; and they may exert their harmful influence by open incitement to mischief, or, more usually, by the low or cynical code of moral opinion which they help to set up. The lad who comes under their sway, the young girl who is drawn into such a circle, may be early initiated into such habits as betting, gambling, drinking, drug-taking, and even sexual promiscuity. The facile youngster, led astray by corrupt associates, has always formed a favourite theme for the novelist and moralist; and, though the actual course of events is generally more intricate and subtle than the popular stories might suggest, this avenue is one of the commonest by which a boy or girl, just fresh from school, enters on a career of crime.

Treatment. In all such cases, where a mere change of school or of employment will hardly be sufficient, it may prove essential to change the residence of the child himself. Sometimes the family can be persuaded to move to another quarter; sometimes it may be necessary to take the youth away from his home and neighbourhood. If, however, he is left where he is and merely placed upon probation, much may still be done by the probation officer. Often he can help the lad to find a better place for wholesome recreation, or better companionship in some athletic club or troop of boy scouts. Such organizations not only inculcate, by example, code, and habit, a spirit of public service, but also make systematic provision for filling the child's vacant hours with wholesome and absorbing occupations. Always it is necessary that the plan of treatment should be, not merely negative or punitive, but positive and constructive. It will seldom be enough to require the young offender to drop his bad associates or give up his pernicious amusements: an effort must be made to discover what healthy and legitimate activities will appeal most closely to his natural interests, and then put him in touch with the proper facilities.

In the main, it will be observed, the whole investigation of environmental factors endorses the conclusion that I have already put forward: namely, delinquency arises, not simply out of the delinquent's own personality, but out of the total situation. It constitutes, therefore, not solely a psychological problem, much less a medical problem, in the narrower sense of the words: it is a problem in social readjustment.

C. Physical Conditions.

We have now reviewed the delinquent's heredity and environment; it is time to turn to the delinquent himself. Still following our usual scheme, we may commence with an examination of his physical state.

The need for a medical examination in all difficult cases has been urged again and again; but generally the examination proposed is conceived on too narrow lines. In most remand homes children are examined by the doctor; yet, as a rule, the examination comprises little more than an ascertainment of height, weight, vision, and the like, together with outstanding ailments or defects. Seldom is any provision made for obtaining a complete medical history; and only in the more exceptional circumstances is attention paid to the child's mental condition.

The physical factors to be observed may be broadly divided into two main categories—the developmental and the pathological. Directly or indirectly, some deviation in normal physical development is often connected with delinquent actions. Most offenders are undeveloped and undersized—a point remarked by nearly every investigator. Generally, the lack of growth is an effect of weak health or malnutrition; occasionally, however, the lad's small size and light weight are simply an innate characteristic. In himself he may be strong, healthy, full of vigour; yet in the labour market he is turned away because of his puny physique. And then, for the despised and rejected from whatever reason, the path lies straight and swift to dishonesty and crime.

Quite a number of my cases, however, deviate in the opposite direction: they are overgrown and overdeveloped, endowed with an excess of animal vitality. 'Puer robustus, puer malus', says the Latin proverb. And the possession of superfluous vigour and strength is responsible for many feats of mischief and adventure. In adolescents the upshot is often serious. Among boys and girls alike, but particularly among the latter, bursts of delinquency are apt to occur with considerable frequency in those who are suffering from some temporary disharmony in physical, emotional, or moral development consequent on puberty.

As regards pathological states, much the same conditions are found among delinquents as have already been noted among the dull and backward. Physical defects were found in nearly 70 per cent. of my delinquent cases, as compared with 54 per cent. of the non-delinquent control-group. Weak health means weakened self-control; and anything that causes physical irritation may cause emotional irritation as well, and thus make for thoughtless or impulsive action. The ailing youth, too, commonly feels disinclined for work: frequently he is genuinely incapable of it. And so, during illness or convalescence, he may develop indolent, careless, and even deceitful habits, which continue when he regains his normal strength.

Of specific disorders, the most definite in their effects are those that make for nervous instability—chorea, epilepsy, hyperthyroidism, encephalitis, and the like. These, however, occur in but a small proportion of the cases; and their importance has been somewhat overestimated by writers in the past.

When severe or conspicuous defects are present, their influence on character is often indirect rather than direct; it results from the emotional reactions caused by the thought of the defect rather than from the defect itself. The knowledge of the defect, or the way the defective is habitually treated, may in the end set up a morbid frame of mind—a recurrent mood of envy and resentment, of embarrassment, self-pity, and self-consciousness, with a secret hankering after sympathy and protection, or a brazen defiance with compensating self-assertion—all the various symptoms, in short, of what is termed an inferiority-complex. The disfigured and the deformed at times develop a persistent attitude of malice towards the world at large, as though the victim longed to vent his grudge against the universe for forcing him to suffer. History and fiction are full of such antisocial outcasts—the Black Dwarf, the Crippled Smith, the One-eyed Giant, the Hunchback King. In the young, milder defects of this nature—lameness, deafness, stammering, squinting, and the like—are liable to produce a similar reaction, particularly if the sufferer has been treated with too little or too much sympathy.

Wherever a delinquent is hampered by physical illness or defect, it is a sound principle to urge that the physical handicap should be dealt with first of all. Bodily conditions, it is true, generally form but a contributory factor; nevertheless, in many instances it is found that the mere removal of such drawbacks is followed by a lasting reform.

It should be remembered that delinquent children may easily miss the benefits of the regular medical inspection and treatment arranged by the school. Some of them have played truant when the inspections were in progress; others have obstinately resisted all medical or surgical measures—refusing to go to the hospital, declining to take their medicine, screaming and kicking when a tooth is to be extracted or tonsils to be excised. Frequently their parents, being of the same dull and unstable type, are careless in matters of general hygiene, or negligent in carrying out the doctor's injunctions. Moreover, the ailments themselves, in the eyes of those who are thinking solely of physical consequence, appear for the most part trivial and unworthy of attention. They are of that mild, vague, intermittent type which under ordinary circumstances would probably be ignored; yet, slight as it is, the weakness or the irritation they engender may prove the deciding factor in precipitating a childish burst of folly.

There is, therefore, an undoubted need for special medical examination in all serious cases of delinquency. 'Every child who is charged should be carefully examined by an experienced medical practitioner before being brought before the court':[1] that is one of the chief recommendations urged in a recent report on juvenile delinquency. As one of our own magistrates has pointed out, 'a great defect in the English courts as compared with the American is the absence of medical reports: without such a report and without the means of acting upon it, children's cases cannot be fully and efficiently dealt with'.[2] But the reference of a case for medical examination does not avoid the need for the services of a competent psychologist.

It is desirable that the expert appointed to aid the court should be some one who is specially skilled in the handling of such cases. If a psychological specialist is not available, then the doctor should himself possess some psychological qualification. A mere psychiatric training is not enough. He should be intimately acquainted with the mental effects of physical disease, and with mental as well as with physical subnormalities—with delinquency in its numerous forms, with psycho-neuroses, and with the milder defects and disturbances of the mind. In addition, he should have had a special training in the application of psychological tests; and, if he has to deal with juvenile cases, he should have had considerable experience of work among children. Above all, he should be a man with a spirit of research. Every case is a problem for scientific investigation; and the whole field stands in urgent need of intensive and systematic inquiry.

D. Psychological Conditions.

i. Intellectual Conditions.

After all, a crime is a conscious act. Hence its immediate cause, if not always its ulterior origin, must lie in some inner mental state. As I have continually insisted, environmental conditions and physical conditions act for the most part indirectly, through their influence on the sufferer's mind. The essential feature, therefore, of the whole investigation must always be a comprehensive study of the offender's psychological condition.

[1] Report of the Juvenile Organizations Committee of the Ministry of Education on *Juvenile Delinquency*, p. 40.
[2] Clark Hall, *The State and the Child*, p. 56.

The Dull. The intellectual aspect may be considered first. Of all the psychological causes of crime the commonest and the gravest is usually alleged to be some form of mental deficiency. In England Dr. Goring has concluded that 'the one vital mental constitutional factor in the etiology of crime is defective intelligence'.[1] Dr. Healy has maintained that 'mental deficiency forms the largest single cause of delinquency'.[2] The earlier American psychologists who first applied the Binet tests of intelligence issued figures for mental defect that were amazingly high. It was stated, for example, by a psychologist of New York that 'probably 80 per cent. of the children in the Juvenile Courts in Manhattan and Bronx are mentally defective'. 50 per cent., 60 per cent., and even 90 per cent.—these are the proportions published by different investigators, and still quoted from time to time. At the present day I doubt whether any competent psychologist would support such views. With better tests and more precise standards of deficiency, the estimates have been greatly reduced: something in the neighbourhood of 10 per cent. is now the usual figure. Moreover, it is not always realized that, unless an offender is approached with considerable sympathy and tact, an intelligence-test applied in a remand home or a prisoner's cell will fail to do justice to his true capacity. Among my own juvenile cases barely 8 per cent. were mentally defective, and rather fewer among the adolescent and adult. In the ordinary population, only $1\frac{1}{2}$ per cent. are mentally defective; so that mental deficiency still remains an appreciable factor in crime.

Most criminals, however, are not so much defective as dull. The commonest characteristic that distinguishes the delinquent from the non-delinquent is not a certifiable deficiency, but a retardation in mental development, sufficient to handicap him in every way, but not enough to enable him to be dealt with under the Mental Deficiency Act. Though his intelligence is subnormal, it still rises sufficiently above the accepted borderline. Four out of every five among my cases fall below the middle line of average

[1] *The English Convict*, p. 184.　　[2] *The Individual Delinquent*, p. 447.

ability. 28 per cent. were definitely dull, whereas, it will be remembered, among the general population only 10 per cent. come within this category. After all, crime is a senseless, sorry way of compassing one's ends; hence those who perpetrate crimes are usually simpletons. Most rogues are also fools.

Treatment. Let me insist on the importance of dealing with such cases at the earliest possible stage, before they have drifted into the hands of the police. I have already tried to show how the institution of special classes for the dull and backward, similar to the special schools for the mentally defective, would save many a child from a career of crime. Where no such provision exists, the dull youngster who shows delinquent propensities should be singled out for special observation and assistance. The main thing to forestall is the formation of a criminal habit. As for delinquents who are definitely feeble-minded, it is obvious that they should be dealt with primarily as defectives rather than as delinquents. Take the record of this feeble-minded boy. At the age of 10 he was brought before the court for 'theft'; the offence was trivial, and he was merely admonished. Three months later he appears for 'malicious mischief', and is again 'admonished'. After another two months he reappears for 'attempted house-breaking', and is admonished once again. Now, at the age of 10, he must have had the mentality of a child of only 5 or 6: what meaning could these admonitions have conveyed to his mind? Four months later he is charged with robbery: the court apparently begins to lose patience, for he is ordered to be birched—'8 strokes'. And so it goes on for the next three years—theft, housebreaking, theft, theft, housebreaking, and theft again. At last, after four years of crime, when he is 14 and about to leave school, it is officially recognized that he is mentally defective.

The Bright. In a few cases the intelligence of the young delinquent is not below normal but above it; and, paradoxically enough, that in itself may lead to his undoing. The commonest instance is that of the bright boy born in the midst of a dull and poverty-stricken family. The type is sufficiently puzzling and important to deserve illustration at some length. The case I shall choose is one I was required to examine some fifteen years ago, and on which I happen just recently to have received a final report.

When I first saw him, he was a bright, red-haired youngster of 15, a little undersized, but full of health and life. He was charged with stealing stamps from his employer's drawer. His mother complained that he had always been difficult to manage. She and her husband were dull but well-meaning workpeople, who failed utterly to understand their boy. When she was foolish enough to argue with him, he always got the best of the argument; and when she tried to control him, he was able to outwit her at every turn. At school he had an excellent record; but the schoolmaster summed up the situation by describing him as 'a swan reared in a nest of ducklings'.

He could only get employment as an errand-boy; and, after twelve months' steady service, was rebuffed when he asked for a rise. So he began to use his superfluous wits by experimenting with dubious but ingenious means of adding to his wages. Amongst other enterprises, he ran a private little auction of his own. On pay-day he would turn up with his pockets stuffed with various articles dear to the young boy's heart—a couple of old watches, half a dozen pocket-knives, a few cheap fountain pens, most of them pilfered; and then would set his fellow errand-boys bidding for each article. Even the auction itself was little else than a clever swindle. He would ask the boys to hand over a shilling first, then hand back sixpence, and then demand another half-crown; after ten minutes of this sort of interchange, he would run through the arithmetic with such confusing speed that the duller youngsters fancied they were getting something for nothing when really they were being fleeced right and left. Meanwhile, he was also endeavouring to overreach his employer in various ways. He started by systematically defrauding his firm first of its time, then of its stationery and stamps, and eventually of the takings locked up in a cashbox.

On the intervention of a generous friend, the employer

stated he did not wish to press the case; and the lad was dealt with very leniently. Soon afterwards, it proved possible to get the boy a more suitable job—a job which really interested him, and called forth the best of his abilities. In the evenings he was sent to a night school, and encouraged to take up more intellectual hobbies and amusements. From that time forward his pilfering ceased. I have since had regular reports, at first every month or so, and then at intervals of one or two years. He is now a young man, and recently, I learn, has been appointed to a post of high responsibility in a municipal office. No suspicion of dishonesty has attached to his name during all the intervening years.

Treatment. Tactfully and wisely handled, these intelligent offenders are among the most hopeful cases that the psychologist is called upon to study. Wrongly treated, they turn into criminals of the most dangerous and elusive type. When the incipient rogue is bright as well as bad, sure detection is far more convincing to his mind than the chances of uncertain punishment. At the same time, owing to his skill in covering up his tracks, detection forms the hardest part of the problem. Nevertheless, it is essential that his malpractices should, from the very outset, be promptly and unfailingly discovered, before his ingenious stratagems have settled down into habits. Often the best course is to give the lad as much free rope as possible—not that he may hang himself, but rather that he may be left to his own unaided wits to see for himself that in the long run honesty is always the best policy, and meanwhile be prevented from cultivating a resentful grudge against those who are duller than he and yet try clumsily to control him.

In every serious case of delinquency then, a test of intelligence should be applied. When nearly half the offenders brought before the courts are either dull or deficient, there is plainly a pressing need, if only on this one ground, for the assistance of a trained psychologist. But, quite apart from the diagnosis of those who are technically subnormal, we can neither understand the mental process behind any particular offence, nor say what measures are appropriate to any particular offender, until we have ascertained the degree of intelligence that the offender himself possesses. To lay down what is to be expected from a child, before we know how far we can trust his powers of understanding and co-operation, is indeed to work in the dark.

Special Aptitudes. So far, we have been discussing general innate capacity, or the lack of it; it is also wise in most instances to note any special abilities or disabilities, and the general level of the child's acquired attainments. Dull though they are in general intelligence, many yet possess some limited aptitude which, if left unutilized at school or at business, is liable to lead them on to mischievous exploits in order to exercise and display it. Some are verbalists—glib, facile, plausible talkers, who impose upon the public by their chatter; they go begging, swindling, or perpetrating frauds, and often by their smart conversation mislead the teacher or psychologist into supposing that they are brighter than they really are. Others have a special gift of manual dexterity; and their nimble fingers, unoccupied by handwork and handicraft at school, may be tempted to try their skill at feats as entertaining and as profitable as they are dishonest and daring—picking pockets, forcing locks, coaxing pennies from the gas-meter with twisted hairpins, or sweets out of slot machines with flattened discs of lead. Others again have a vivid fund of visual imagery: they are highly imaginative; and the things that they inwardly picture, or have seen on the films or read of in books, obsess their minds with the force almost of an hallucination, until at length they feel compelled to put their obsessions into practice.

But special aptitudes, like special intelligence, are not to be sought out merely because they may explain a somewhat exceptional form of crime. Their discovery may make a wide difference to the treatment recommended. In examining each offender we should seek to discover his strong points as well as his weak, his good characteristics as well as his bad. To find, therefore, that a particular youth is endowed with some unusual talent may indicate at once a hopeful source of interest, and a latent ambition to which we may profitably appeal.

Acquired Attainments. As regards acquired attainments, particularly attainments at school, most young delinquents prove to be even more backward than they are in native ability. Many, of course, play truant; and truancy is usually the first step on the downward stair to crime. Later on, the mere fact that these youths and girls leave school in a state of extreme illiteracy will prevent them from earning an honest livelihood, and so tempt them to use their simple wits in illicit but lucrative ways. Here then is one more illustration of the value of special classes for the backward. Such classes would catch within their meshes over 70 per cent. of our incipient criminals.

ii. *Temperamental Conditions.*

Finally, let us turn from the intellectual side of the offender's mind to the emotional, and study a little more fully what is plainly of far greater moment in dealing with the wrongdoer—his character or temperament.

Innate Instincts. If we make a catalogue of all the complaints and charges alleged against juvenile offenders, it will be seen that they fall into several well-marked categories. The most serious offences are those that the legal mind classifies under the heading of violence—violence to persons or violence to property: these are commoner among the boys. Among the girls the commonest of the more serious charges are those connected with sex. Actual sex offences are no doubt just as prevalent among the youths, but they are less frequently brought to official notice. Both types of misdemeanour are observable at an astonishingly early age. I have known a little murderer of 7; and children of 5 and 6 engaging in precocious sex-practices. For the frequency and the early emergence of such traits the most plausible explanation is to postulate an inherited instinct —an instinct of pugnacity or anger, in the one instance, and an instinct of sex, in the other. Stealing in the tiny child may similarly be explained by a strong acquisitive instinct. The older thief, it is true, steals things because he wants what he steals. But the tiny child and the ill-trained defective grab whatever attracts their attention: they will pick up a bright, pocketable coin from the table or the mantelshelf without any intention to spend it—impelled by the same mechanical reaction which drives a squirrel to collect nuts or a jackdaw to run off with a cardinal's ring. In the same way, the truancy, the running away, the wandering of small children are occasionally referable to a migratory instinct: it seems to overtake them at certain seasons of the year, like the migratory instincts of certain animals and birds.

Obviously, innate impulses such as these must have had a rough and ready value in the forest or the cave. A primeval savage who was born without them could never have survived. To-day, though we adopt more civilized modes of procedure, we still inherit the same underlying impulses. No change, so far as we can tell, has occurred in the innate constitution of man since first he emerged from barbarism. We are still tugged, every one of us, savage and civilized, sinner and saint, by the same simple strings; and each tiny child as he enters on his life has to be educated and trained afresh to suppress these crude re-actions—kicking, cuddling, snatching, hitting, biting, and running away—and taught to substitute for them better manners and more indirect methods of achieving his ends. Much juvenile delinquency, therefore, is simply an automatic outburst of some inherited mode of response—a form of conduct which had a biological value in prehistoric life, but is now frowned on by a civilized community as an indecency or a crime.

This explanation not only holds good of those who, as we saw on an earlier page, inherit such instincts with an excessive strength: it applies more or less to all of us, since every human being comes into the world equipped with this primitive outfit of instinctive impulses, as part of his human nature. Nevertheless, as we have already remarked, in delinquents the instinctive constituents of the mind are usually more vigorous than they are in the rest of us, and often stronger than their intellectual control. The majority are at once dull and unstable. Between 30 and 40 per cent., we have seen, are definitely dull, if not actually deficient; an even larger proportion—46 per cent. in my own series—are emotionally unstable. In a few the instability has proved to be a merely temporary phase—an incidental effect of adolescence; but in an appreciable number—nearly 10 per cent. of the whole batch—the instability was so extreme that it amounted to what I have described above as temperamental deficiency.

Among the boys the aggressive instincts were most marked; and the greater proportion of them belong to what I have termed the unrepressed type. Among the girls, however, the inhibitive instincts were often more strongly developed; and many were of a repressed type, suffering, in several instances, from some minor psycho-neurosis.

It is, then, helpful to realize that the final act which stamps the child as an offender is usually an instinctive or emotional act; only in the older and the more intelligent is it the outcome of deliberate calculation or of a reasoned and premeditated scheme. Planning may be required in the selection of means or devices; but the aim and the motive are usually supplied by some relatively primitive impulse, which is obeyed almost without reflection. This is true not only of the grave misdoings which bring the culprit into conflict with the law, but also of those minor transgressions which amount to no more than a breach of domestic or scholastic discipline. Crime or delinquency, in fact, is nothing but an extreme example of common childish naughtiness.

Treatment. What, then, is the remedy? To stamp out or annihilate these inherited propensities is plainly a hopeless task. Since they are inborn they can never be wholly eradicated. The attempt to repress them will only ram them in, and bottle them up, until the ultimate explosion is worse than the first trivial overflow. The proper measure is to find some safety-valve, some wholesome outlet for this instinctive energy, instead of forcing it to vent itself in dangerous or illicit escapades: keep the child well occupied at interesting work or recreation, and his animal spirits will thus be diverted into less reprehensible channels. Here lies the value of sport and games. There is scarcely a single instinct which has not been made the basis of some form of play: we play at hunting, at fighting, at roving and roaming, at frightening ourselves with dangerous adventures, at organizing ourselves into teams and clubs for passing or permanent enterprises. And along similar lines the adventurous excitement of the high-spirited youngster may be harmlessly worked off.

The doctrine of human instincts[1] does much to explain the particular forms of misconduct occurring spontaneously in young or unintelligent children. Mothers so often turn appealingly to the doctor to ask: 'Wherever can the child have learnt such practices? Never', they will add, 'has my boy been allowed to mix with bad companions.' The answer is that each child inherits an impulse to take what he wants, to fight when he is thwarted, to hide or lie when he is afraid, and even to indulge in sexual misbehaviour. Yet this account is by itself too simple to cover the older and more intelligent cases. To say that the pugnacious man commits an assault because he has an overdose of pugnacity, or that thieves break through and steal because they inherit the instinct of acquisition to an inordinate degree, is to echo the truism of Molière's quack doctor who ascribed the magic gift of sleep to the faculty for somnolence which every one possesses. The working of the human mind is more intricate than that. If we are to understand the complex motives of the older criminal, we must investigate not merely the innate basis of his actions— what I have loosely called his temperament—but also the newer incentives that he has acquired and built up during the course of his personal history—his habits, his interests,

[1] About thirty years ago a vigorous attack was directed against the doctrine of human instincts, chiefly by the behaviourist school in the United States. As a result many medical writers appear to suppose that the notion has become obsolete. But more recent work has led to the reintroduction of practically the same concept, though American writers now tend to substitute some more innocuous word—'needs', 'urges', or 'drives' (the last borrowed from the German word for 'instinct', *Trieb*). For a review of the position with special reference to child psychology and delinquency, see 'Symposium on Human Instincts', *Brit. J. Educ. Psychol.* xiii, pp. 1–13 and refs.

his ideals, his sentiments, his complexes—in a word, his moral character.

Acquired Motives. Interests and sentiments play a double part in the causation of delinquency. The presence of unwholesome interests may be a direct determinant of the crimes that are carried out; the absence of wholesome interests may mean a lack of all restraining influences. To give a list of all the undesirable interests that may animate a criminal mind is hardly possible. The earliest and the simplest are merely a development of the ordinary instinctive cravings. Anything that has the natural property of awakening some particular instinct may easily develop into a focus of systematic interest, at times almost amounting to an obsession. The young child may develop a passion for certain edibles—sweets, tarts, fruit, and similar delicacies—the mere sight of which he is unable to resist; and so, day after day, he goes raiding his mother's pantry, or stealing money to be spent at the confectioner's. The older youth may develop a craze for drink in some intoxicating form. Sexual stimuli may easily turn into a permanent topic of attention, and afford a supreme preoccupation for the ribald libertine.

In a civilized community, however, these specialized interests need not be related to instinctive impulses in any direct or obvious fashion, though doubtless in their ultimate origin they rest on an instinctive basis. The more complex and sophisticated interests require a certain degree of intelligence and knowledge of the world. The most notorious is the infatuation for betting or gambling in its numerous forms. But any kind of sport or amusement may become a thing of such absorbing fascination that its indulgence may override the ordinary restraints of honesty or circumspection. The schoolboy steals sixpences for the cinema; the office-boy neglects his work to attend the local football match; the bank-clerk defrauds his employers to take his lady friends to restaurants and music-halls; the servant girl appropriates her mistress's clothes and jewellery, or rifles her purse to buy trinkets, because she has an overweening passion for finery and dress or wants to cut a glittering figure when she joins her boy friend.

The absence of desirable interests may be almost as injurious as the presence of interests that are directly or indirectly harmful; and is far more likely to be overlooked. Often the easiest way to reform the youthful criminal is to find some hobby or recreation which will appeal to him even more strongly than his lawless adventures. Of all wholesome interests the most powerful are those that centre on particular persons. The affection for a steady friend or relative is one of the most effective inhibitors of vice and crime. The child who is deeply devoted to his mother, or has a profound admiration for his teacher, or a loyal enthusiasm for his school, is not likely to go drifting wildly into the grosser forms of mischief. Those who are without such attachments possess nothing to rein them back when face to face with temptation.

At times, however, these personal interests may wield a detrimental influence. Boys and girls of every age are prone to acquire a temporary craze for some hero or heroine, and their standards of choice are not always of the best. The model may be some older and daring delinquent who plays the ringleader in their own little set, or possibly some imaginary personage, built up during spells of fantasy and day-dreaming, and based on some fascinating lay figure met with in novels or seen upon the films. With the girl some glittering cinema star, with the youth some dashing but unscrupulous desperado, too often furnish the ideal which dazzles an infatuated fancy.

The most difficult sentiments to unravel and deal with are those which have at once a wholesome and a harmful aspect, and involve a two-sided inconsistent attitude. A child, for example, may be passionately fond of his teacher, and yet at the same time angry and annoyed with him because, instead of making a favourite of his young admirer, he checks and scolds him, or perhaps shows a warmer interest in some other pupil. Of these mingled attitudes the most important are those which the child has developed towards his own parents. Outwardly he may seem to love his father with the utmost sincerity; inwardly he may be moved by a spi   n towards him. One motive may come uppermost on one occasion, and the opposite motive on another, so that the child swings from obedience to disobedience, from affection to fear or hostility, like a weathercock veering with each gust of wind. Nor is the difference altogether one of times and seasons, or of outward and visible conduct as distinct from secret thoughts. More often than not, the child himself is unaware of his rebellious impulses, and would strenuously repudiate any suggestion that he was not devoted heart and soul to his parent.

Such conflicting attitudes may be unwittingly encouraged by the conduct of the parents themselves. If the father is left to do the scolding and the whipping, while the mother pets and even shields the child, the result is easy to foretell. The child's devotion to his mother and his hostility towards his father may be almost unconcealed. But if the same parent seems at one time tolerant and indulgent, and at another a stern disciplinarian, the effects may be more difficult to trace: for it is not so much the real justice of the parents' acts that counts; it is the interpretation the child puts on them, in his fanciful or resentful moods, and still more his unconscious reactions towards them.

The repressed or unconscious emotional attitudes that thus gradually develop are, as is well known, termed 'complexes'. And, among the older and more intelligent cases, some complex of this type, resting on a conflict in the child's feelings towards his parents, lies almost always at the root of the delinquency. How to unravel these deeper motives is a matter too lengthy to be dealt with here: I have already discussed it in another place.[1]

[1] See *The Young Delinquent*, pp. 538 et seq. The general study of the development of sentiments or interests, as distinct from that of complexes, has been unduly neglected. On the other hand, the study of emotional attitudes (a closely related topic) has proved both practicable and profitable. Attempts at more rigorous methods of research started with investigations on children's attitudes to lessons, teachers, parents, and recurrent ethical problems, and marked differences were found between delinquent and non-delinquent children. More recently, however, the centre of activity has shifted rather towards the study of social, religious, and political attitudes among adults, especially in connexion with class-differences. For references see Burt, C., *Contributions of Psychology to Social Problems* (Oxford University Press, 1953), pp. 27, 42 f., and 76.

Finally, let me insist upon the important part played in criminal behaviour by the mere process of habit. In man the primitive instincts at their first emergence have little of that fixed and insuperable fatality that stamps the inherited actions of the lowlier animals; else we should be, every one of us, predestined criminals, doomed to the gallows from our birth. Human instincts are pliant, half-formed tendencies, and need opportunity for exercise and practice before they become irreparably fixed as habits. Thus, alike in the making and in the unmaking of the criminal, habit-formation is almost always the crux. The genuine first offender, who is found out after committing only a single offence, can generally be reclaimed. The habitual offender, hardened in the ways of vice, and trailing behind him a long series of misdemeanours, undetected and uncorrected, is likely to offer a more desperate case. For this reason more than for any other, it is essential to tackle the budding criminal at the very earliest stage. From an analysis of the after-histories of my cases I find that over 70 per cent. of those dealt with before the age of 9 may now fairly be described as cured; of those dealt with between the ages of 9 and 14 only 57 per cent.; of those dealt with during adolescence, 62 per cent., but this is apparently due to the large proportion of adolescent first offenders; of adults no more than 32 per cent. About the value of preventive psychology or medicine in dealing with the adult criminal I am, indeed, pessimistic; over the treatment of the juvenile offender I am almost always hopeful, and the younger the case, the higher my hopes.

Treatment. In the vast majority of cases the treatment of the juvenile delinquent will consist, not so much of 'treatment' as the psychiatrist or physician is apt to understand the term, but rather in educative or re-educative efforts— the gradual control or sublimation of emotional impulses, the breaking of undesirable habits, the formation of desirable habits—in short, character-training in the widest sense. The superior efficacy of this latter mode of approach is amply demonstrated by a comparison of the after-histories of cases treated along different lines.[1]

[1] For statistical evidence see *The Young Delinquent*, pp. 608 f., and

A helpful plan with the child who is beginning to form a habit of crime is that of graded moral exercise. The first thing is to cut off all opportunities for whatever offence is threatening to grow into a habit. If the offence is theft, then money must be kept locked up. The exact amounts and no more must be handed out for shop errands, so that change can never be embezzled. The child's own occupation, where he is and what he is after, should be known at every minute of the day. This does not mean that the child should be suspiciously or fussily watched: the supervision, though efficient, should be as unostentatious as possible. If these precautions can be maintained, then, after a period varying in duration with the antiquity of the habit, the habit itself will probably die of inanition: it will atrophy through disuse.

But the treatment is not over. The next step is to build up a firm habit of self-control, until the child feels that he is unhesitatingly trusted, and, what is more, is able to trust himself. Presently, then, by slow degrees, the old opportunities should be allowed to reappear: but vigilance, though still unobtrusive, must for the moment be redoubled rather than relaxed. The child may first be sent on some small commission which may seem to afford a possible chance for theft. Actually, however, the situation must be arranged so that any theft will be unfailingly detected. To begin with, indeed, the child may be allowed to see that detection can scarcely be escaped. But each succeeding day the task should be made a little stiffer than the last—the tempting opportunity still greater, and detection, in appearance at any rate, still less inevitable—until honesty has grown into a habit and the child feels that he and all who know him can repose full confidence in his word. At last it will become his special pride to discover that when any mission of trust is wanted he is the one person to be chosen.

There is a well-recognized psychological law which states that pleasure tends to stamp in and pain to stamp out any action which they accompany. The most effective pleasures

'Symposium on Psychologists and Psychiatrists in the Child Guidance Service', *Brit. J. Educ. Psychol.* xxiii, 1953, pp. 24 f.

and pains, however, are not irrelevant bribes and arbitrary punishments, but the satisfaction or dissatisfaction that comes from the success or failure of the original impulse. To allow the child to succeed, therefore, in some clandestine misdemeanour is the best way to ensure that his misdeeds will be repeated. To see that it fails, or at least is found out —which, in a furtive enterprise, is tantamount to failure, is the most certain way of crippling the tendency for ever.

When some half-unconscious complex lies at the back of the habitual crime, the treatment will have to be more radical. Here something like a course of psycho-analytic therapy may probably be requisite. To win the child's confidence and to get him spontaneously to unburden his mind of his private grudges and grievances may perhaps be the first step in this direction; but too often the grudges and grievances are unknown even to the child himself, and hence a more elaborate technique will have to be adopted. What form this technique will take we can best discuss when we come to deal with functional disorders generally.

Notes and References. As noted above, the conclusions summarized in this chapter are based mainly on investigations carried out in London. The research methods adopted for these earlier inquiries have proved effective in dealing with many similar problems of this complex type, and are recommended for adoption in other fields of clinical research. The chief innovations were twofold. First, in addition to examining the delinquent group which formed the main problem, a parallel examination of a control-group of non-delinquent children was carried out on precisely similar lines. Secondly, the method of individual case-study was combined with a statistical comparison of the two groups. This renders it possible to procure convincing evidence confirming or refuting the various hypotheses put forward in regard to causes and their relative importance, and also to gain light on the way those causes operate in individual cases. For further references see Appendix V.

V
THE NEUROTIC

V

THE NEUROTIC[1]

The General Nature of Neurotic Disorders. No word, I imagine, in the whole vocabulary of medicine is used so loosely as the term 'neurotic'. Over the nature and origin of the many disorders that go by this name the gravest misconceptions still linger. Among specialists, however, certain broad characteristics are now, after years of discussion, almost universally agreed upon. It is, for example, acknowledged that neurotic disorders may have both physical and mental symptoms. At the same time, it is also recognized that they are to be distinguished first from what are usually called, in a somewhat limited sense, mental diseases, and secondly from those nervous diseases that have an obvious physical origin as well as conspicuous physical symptoms. The various points of difference are currently summed up as follows.

To begin with, the term 'mental disease' is now generally restricted to those serious and certifiable disorders that have been traditionally classed as instances of lunacy or insanity. It thus comprises what have come to be called psychoses—conditions such as dementia praecox, manic-depressive states, general paralysis of the insane, and the like. In this sense, therefore, mental diseases are marked off from neurotic diseases first and foremost by the fact that they are usually grave and progressive: they tend to involve the whole mind—intellect as well as character. The patient, sooner or later, may become totally incapacitated—unfit not merely for his daily work, but also for ordinary social life; and, as a rule, he has from the very outset but little insight into his condition. Neurotic disorders, on the other hand, primarily affect certain limited functions of the mind alone; the

[1] I am greatly indebted to my colleague, Dr. Susan Isaacs, for her kindness in reading this and the following chapters in proof, and for the suggestions and amendments she has been good enough to make.

patient never completely loses his grasp of reality, and thus, in most cases, remains painfully aware that his state is abnormal.

So far, however, the difference is one of degree rather than of kind. Apart from well-marked clinical types, the symptoms of the one merge into the symptoms of the other. And, indeed, as we shall see in a moment, neuroses have been defined, not altogether inappropriately, as minor psychoses. There is, however, a second broad distinction—more important, perhaps, for theory than for practice. Mental disease is usually accompanied, and presumably produced, by some gross pathological change in the brain. No such change is discoverable in the merely neurotic.

Since, in neurotic conditions, the mind as a whole does not appear to be deranged, many writers prefer to class such ailments with nervous diseases rather than with mental. They go on to add, however, that nervous diseases may be of two kinds, or, at any rate, that the phrase covers two clearly distinguishable disorders, originating in different ways. There are first those disorders which have a physical origin. Like mental disease as above defined, they seem attributable to some definite pathological change in the brain or nervous system, only now the change is of a limited and localized nature, and consequently mind and conduct as a whole are not primarily affected. To this category belong such diseases as hemiplegia, aphasia, locomotor ataxy, certain forms of epilepsy and chorea, and the like. There is, secondly, a further group of disorders in which the functions rather than the structures of the nervous system are impaired. A paralytic of the former type, for example, cannot move his arm or leg; a paralytic of the second type can, but does not. From this standpoint the former group are classified as organic nervous diseases; and by contrast neurotic disorders are defined as functional nervous diseases.

The Physical Conception of 'Functional Nervous Disease'. But what precisely is meant by the word 'functional'? For the general practitioner, it would seem, the term has merely a negative and non-committal sense: he takes it to imply that the disease cannot be accounted for by any recognizable defect in any known anatomical structure. If a man can move his arm, but doesn't, then, it is presumed, this is simply because he won't: 'the patient himself is preventing it'. The pathologist tries to go deeper: he declares that the difference is once more but a difference of degree. In both cases, he argues, the defects must in the last resort be structural. We call them 'organic' if the structural changes can be seen by the naked eye or by the microscope. We call them 'functional' if the changes are so delicate that they cannot be seen but only inferred. A paralysis, for example, following an apoplectic fit can be ascribed to a visible lesion —to a haemorrhage into a motor centre of the brain, such as can be viewed *post mortem*; a hysterical paralysis following shell-shock is supposed to be due to punctiform haemorrhages into the same centre—haemorrhages so minute that no existing technique can detect them.

All this, however, is sheer surmise. Nor does it, I fancy, represent the distinction originally intended. The primary distinction was a distinction between a fault in the structures as such, and a fault in the working of structures which themselves are perfectly sound—a distinction which is often made the basis of the differential definitions of anatomy and physiology. It is based not so much upon a materialistic as upon a mechanistic view of mental process. The nervous system is conceived to operate like a machine; and the difference is often illustrated by analogies from other machines. A motor-car, for example, may slow down and come gradually to a stop for one of two reasons: first, some defect may arise in the parts of the machine itself; secondly, the task to which the machine has been put may be a task for which this particular make is not primarily adapted. In the first case, owing perhaps to grit or gravel which has found its way into the works, the carburettor may have become choked, or a cog may have broken in the gear-box; and a breakdown occurs owing to damage to the structure. In the second case, the car has been set to climb a hill which was too steep for it: another car with a lower speed and gear might have taken the hill quite easily, had the driver made the proper adjustments; but this car, though the gear be changed and the spark retarded, is still unequal to achieving the ascent. The first car, therefore, is afflicted with a 'structural' disorder, the second with a 'functional'. This explanation is certainly more plausible than the preceding; but to a psychologist the fundamental assumption with which it starts will seem more misleading than helpful. The picture of the mind as nothing but a peculiarly intricate machine may serve at times to illustrate, but never to explain.

Try as we may to interpret the current definition, every word in the phrase 'functional nervous disease' turns out to be ill chosen. To begin with, neurotic disorders are not diseases at all in the ordinary medical sense. Since the days of Sydenham disease has commonly been defined in physical terms. A disease, we are told, 'is the effect of a harmful interaction between the *physical* organism and some injurious influence invading it from the *physical* environment—bacteria, wounds, poisons, and the like'. A neurotic disorder is the effect of a harmful interaction between the *mental* organism and the *mental* aspects of its environment—the personal and social influences that surround it. As one eminent authority has said: 'Neuroses are the outcome of a conflict between the individual and society, whereas diseases are the outcome of a conflict between man and nature.'[1]

Secondly, whether classified as diseases or not, neurotic disorders have nothing to do with those anatomical structures which alone deserve the title 'nerves': they are not nervous in any but a popular or pre-scientific sense. The adjective 'nervous' dates from those days when it was discovered that nerves existed, but it was not known what were their true nature and functions. Nor is the position mended by saying that the disturbance affects, not the nerves, but the nervous system. The expression still conveys the notion that the nerve-cells or the nerve-tissue are demonstrably impaired.

Such terms, no doubt, have been largely kept alive by the fact that most patients insist on some concrete explanation of their illnesses. Lay notions of medicine, as of science and philosophy, are usually those which the

---

[1] Ernest Jones, *Treatment of the Neuroses*, p. 8.

professions popularized a century ago but have long since given up. Hence the only account that will content a patient has still to be couched in some formula which he understands, or thinks he understands, but which medical men might hesitate to use amongst themselves. As a result, when a patient says he is 'suffering from nerves' and thinks he is quoting a term used by his doctor, his doctor has probably been echoing a phrase that he thinks may be acceptable to his patient. To-day, the general public, or at any rate its more educated members, realize that 'nerves' are normal structures with a normal function, and that the word 'nervous' is at best a metaphor. Moreover, the words have acquired somewhat derogatory associations. So they are now translated from Latin into Greek; and the patient is told that he is 'neurotic' or that his disease is 'neurasthenia'. In all likelihood, the doctor's private view will be that the patient himself is responsible for his symptoms, not his nervous system.[1]

Yet, even so, the doctor, when pressed, will probably contend that at bottom such disorders, however they originate, must be essentially physical, since all our thoughts and actions have a physical basis. No doubt, so long as we hold that the brain and nervous system are the sole organs of mental process and of conscious behaviour, it follows inevitably that any disorder in conduct or thinking may be correctly described as a nervous disorder. But the argument is fallacious. In the nineteenth century, when materialism was a growing scientific creed, the medical man may have been justified in assuming that mental processes were at bottom material. To-day he has no right to beg a profound metaphysical question in explaining what on the surface is a mental rather than a bodily disturbance. And in actual practice the use of the

[1] The non-medical reader must bear in mind that the terminology of the medical textbook is not based solely on scientific considerations. The textbook writer is also a hospital teacher. Going round the wards with his students, he may wish to convey his conclusions in language that will impress, rather than distress, the listening patient. For the students a phrase like 'purely functional' may bear some tacit implication—perhaps that the symptoms of which the patient makes so much appear devoid of discernible cause, and are therefore either imaginary, or inexplicable, or at least irrelevant for diagnosis and treatment.

term 'nervous' is exceedingly misleading both for diagnosis and for treatment. It gives a materialistic turn to the whole outlook of the physician. Such a bias, in virtue of his training and his inevitable preoccupation with bodily disease, he is all too prone to accept. In the past the outcome of this tendency has been to make him turn almost exclusively to physical remedies, and, when these fail or are not forthcoming, to dismiss the case as unreal. With equal justice we might argue that the brain was the essential organ of intellectual work, and that therefore the intellectual training of the child should be carried on not by intellectual exercises in the classroom, but solely by efforts to accelerate his physiological growth. It must be insisted that we know far more about the nature of mental processes than we do about nervous processes. It is, therefore, far more helpful to think of neurotic disorders in psychological and biological terms than in anatomical or neurological.

Thirdly, the addition of the word 'functional' does little to correct this attitude. It rather encourages the physician still further to renounce all effort at direct investigation and treatment; for the term seems to imply that there is nothing wrong with the physical structure of the nervous system, and that the disorder results solely from the way in which the physical structures are functioning. The inevitable effect of such an attitude is that every case is approached along purely physical lines. In general practice a diagnosis of hysteria or neurasthenia is nearly always reached by a negative argument—by the indirect method of exclusion. The doctor makes a thorough physical examination; he discovers no organic derangement; he therefore concludes that the trouble is merely functional. To him this usually means that there is no real trouble at all, since the only source of trouble that he recognizes is something that is grossly physical. All disorder is assumed to have a material cause; if no material cause can be found, then there can be no genuine disorder.

The Psychogenic Character of Neurotic Disorders. Such arguments and such procedures might have satisfied a psychologist of the old associationist school that was flourishing sixty years ago. Twenty years ago it would have satisfied the numerous psychologists who then declared themselves 'behaviourists'. To-day, however, and in this country at any rate, there is scarcely a single psychologist who would assent to such a standpoint. Many are now convinced that mental processes can never be entirely explained in terms of physical causation; nearly all would insist that, whether or not a complete physical causation will ultimately be discovered, nevertheless, in the present state of knowledge, we are often quite unable to get behind the mental factors. The practical corollary is obvious. If, after all, it is true that we understand the working of the mind better than we understand the working of the brain or nervous system, then for the present we must still look for, and be content with, explanations couched in purely mental terms.

This view has gradually gained a wide acceptance; and the psychic origin of neurotic disorders is now very generally admitted. As a consequence, the terms 'neurosis' and 'psychosis' are being interpreted in a paradoxical sense which is exceedingly perplexing to the young student of psychology. In his psychological textbook he usually meets these words for the first time in accounts of a doctrine popularized by Huxley. Huxley assumed that, in the normal mind, every conscious process has some nervous process parallel to it, and he introduced the two terms 'neurosis' and 'psychosis' to designate the physical states and the psychical states corresponding to one another. But later on the same student, when he comes to mental disorders, is surprised to discover that the meanings of the words have lately been almost completely reversed: a 'psychosis' now means a disorder which is assumed to have a definite physical basis, while a 'neurosis' means a disorder for which no physical basis is known and which is presumed to be purely psychical in its origin. It might be better to abolish the word 'neurosis' once and for all, and to emphasize, at any rate for descriptive purposes, the mental character of both. As we have seen, in practice no sharp line can be drawn between them; and, had the word 'psychosis' not gained so sinister a connotation, it would be more logical to speak simply of 'major' and 'minor psychoses'. Indeed, in my view, even in psychotic conditions the importance of inflammatory and toxic causes is greatly overestimated. I venture to suggest that, alike in mental hospitals and in out-patient departments, a sharper eye for psychological influences would greatly reduce the amount of supposedly incurable mental disease.

Since, however, the term 'neurosis' has become almost universally current, I shall retain it here. After all, we have preserved words like 'hysteria', 'hypochondria', and 'lunacy', regardless of their etymology and original implications: we have almost forgotten that the first meant a disorder ascribed to meanderings of the uterus, the second a disorder due to some trouble beneath the abdominal cartilages, and the third an intermittent loss of reason caused by the vagaries of the moon.[1]

In any case, the notion that hysteria, neurasthenia, and neurotic or functional disorders generally cover a mere negative residuum, with no positive characters of their own, can be finally discarded. Already the specialist has been forced to realize that such disorders are distinguished, not by the mere absence of physical causes, but by the presence of special mental characteristics. For the discovery of these mental peculiarities, as we have seen, a definite technique is now available. This technique should be imparted in the hospital and in the medical school. Just as the student is taught how to make a routine examination of the heart or nervous system, so he should be taught how to examine a defective or disordered mind. It is true that the examining physician will generally be wise to begin at the physical end and rule out physical causes first; but in theory he should be equally able to start from the mental end, rule out mental causes, and conclude that, since he can find no

[1] The word 'psychoneurosis' might overcome the ambiguity. But in the present state of knowledge, it is best reserved for the hysterical group of neuroses, in which the symptoms have a mental meaning and therefore a mental origin. The remainder—the 'actual neuroses', as they are conveniently called—appear to be due predominantly to physical conditions. But this view of their origin is that of a particular school of psychology, and, though I personally incline to accept it, it does not seem right to assume it as a basis for an initial classification. Further, the particular physical conditions discovered are somewhat different from those discussed above: they are not in themselves morbid or pathological in the ordinary sense.

mental source for the trouble, therefore its origin must be physical.

Neurosis as a Special Form of Mental Subnormality. Let me briefly sum up the outcome of this discussion. A neurotic trouble is a positive condition to be studied in and for itself. It is a mental rather than a physical condition, a disorder rather than a disease. For this reason a neurotic person is best described as subnormal rather than as abnormal: to tell him he is diseased may only make him worse. And I regard neurotic disorders—as I regard dullness, backwardness, delinquency, and the commoner forms of mental deficiency—as primarily a special form of mental subnormality, that is, a somewhat extreme example of tendencies found in all of us, but in varying degrees.

Let us then note how a neurotic disorder resembles, and how it differs from the other groups. It resembles backwardness and delinquency, and differs from dullness and deficiency, by being acquired rather than innate. On the other hand, it differs from backwardness, as well as from dullness and deficiency, in being characterized mainly by emotional symptoms and by an emotional origin. Thus the nearest parallel to a neurosis is a tendency to delinquency or crime: indeed, crime and delinquency are often the result of a neurosis, and a neurosis is often the result of an effort to avoid delinquency and crime. In the last chapter I argued that crime and delinquency, so far from being moral diseases, arise from the natural reactions of a particular temperament to certain difficulties in personal or social life. In the same way, neurotic disorders, instead of being due to physical disease, prove on analysis to have their origin in reactions, formed along perfectly natural lines though by a somewhat different temperament, to much the same difficulties in much the same sphere, namely the personal and social life of the patient. Both are essentially the result of personal maladjustment. The distinction between the two is largely superficial: it is simply that delinquency manifests itself most conspicuously by moral disorder, while a neurosis manifests itself most conspicuously by an emotional disorder. In both, the patient's attitude towards other persons and towards society is fundamentally disturbed; but in a neurosis the disturbance usually follows lines which society does not regard as illegal. What is affected is primarily the peace and efficiency of the patient, not the peace and property of other persons.

A distinction of the same type marks the real boundary between neurosis and psychosis. The insane are chiefly those whom society is forced to segregate in order to protect its own members; the neurotic are left at large. Here too, therefore, the distinction is social and legal rather than medical or psychological. Certainly neurotics, like delinquents and dangerous lunatics, often inflict acute distress on persons with whom they come into contact; but in such cases it is usually presumed that the delinquent is responsible for his actions while the neurotic and the insane are not. The medical man, however, is often as severe in his condemnation of the neurotic as he is of the delinquent. Hence words like 'neurotic' or 'hysterical' have turned almost into terms of reproach. In the early days of the first world war there was even a risk that a neurotic soldier who gave way to emotional strain might be handed over to be shot for cowardice. From such a fate hundreds were eventually saved by a diagnosis expressed in physical terms, such as 'disorderly action of the heart', or 'shell-shock'—by which was understood a physical shock literally conveyed to the nervous system by the explosion of a shell. The same difficulty is sometimes encountered in civil practice. If, owing to an accident, a neurotic person suffers a mental shock, it is easy to obtain compensation so long as the effects are described in physiological language—called, for example, railway spine or a traumatic neurosis; but if the consequences are depicted as purely mental, then it is popularly supposed that the patient should be able to control and cure himself. A mere mental disturbance would be considered not a disease but a disgrace.

Unconscious Factors. There is, however, one special reason why the origin of such disorders has been held to be nervous rather than mental, physical in nature rather than psychical. It springs from a puzzling feature which nearly all of them display, and which has only recently received an adequate solution. Take any typical case—that of a man struck dumb by shell-shock. The old suggestion was that the exploding force of the gases released from the shell caused, through sudden pressure or expansion, minute and invisible haemorrhages in the centre for speech. As a result, the man became aphasic, but the damage was so slight that in the course of time it cleared up spontaneously. Such a theory will not fit the innumerable cases in which the same symptoms supervene when the man merely hears the shell from a distance and the explosion is far too remote to have produced any physical effect. Nor will it account for those cases in which the aphasia vanishes as soon as the man is assured that he need not return to the trenches, or perhaps, still more dramatically, when he goes to the cinema and has a good laugh, or tumbles into the canal and calls out for help. The new explanation insists that the causes alike of the disorder and of the cure are mental. The noise of the exploding shell creates a momentary terror; the natural consequence of terror is to inhibit speech; the man realizes that so long as speech is impossible, he will be kept in the hospital, and so avoid the dangers of war. When he is told that in no circumstances will he be sent back to the front, then the dangers no longer worry him; the need for his peculiar disability ceases; and the disability itself comes to an end.

To this new line of explanation several objections may at first be raised. To begin with, it is argued that if this account were true, then the man should be treated as a malingerer. But in many cases malingering is out of the question; if the patient were told that he himself was producing his speechless condition, not only would he deny it, but his denial would be unhesitatingly accepted by all who were in touch with the case. Since, therefore, such a man seems genuinely unconscious of the reasons for his disability, how can it be claimed that those reasons are really mental, and that the origin of the trouble lies in the man's own mind? Does not this very feature demonstrate that the disturbance is physical?

The reply to this argument is now familiar. It consists

in pointing out that a mental process is not necessarily a conscious process. To the older psychologists and to the physicians of last century such a statement might have seemed a contradiction in terms: to the practical judge of human character it is a truism. In everyday life we all acknowledge that a large amount of a man's behaviour springs from causes to which he himself is altogether blind. In the past, however, academic psychology has been primarily concerned with the study of consciousness as such, and has consequently shown an intellectualistic bias. Only gradually has it come to recognize that the mind includes, not merely conscious contents, but also underlying mental forces which play upon those contents, yet are themselves unconscious.[1] This is especially true of those beliefs or actions that have their basis in instinct, habit, or emotional states. When a man loses his temper, or takes a fancy to a particular woman, when he is smitten with a passion for landscapes by Leader, or displays the irritating trick of twiddling his watch-chain, do his friends immediately insist that the man himself must know why he acts in such a way? Yet, in more serious situations, the law, the medical profession, and all the older textbooks on psychology have insisted on the tacit assumption that no man can ever be influenced by a motive of which he is totally unaware. The earlier explanations of nervous disease were based on the view that a man must understand everything that goes on in his mind, but knows little or nothing of what goes on in his body. Hence an unconscious cause was supposed to be a physical cause. Modern psychology, however, now admits that numerous mental mechanisms may operate, and

[1] Psychiatric writers, who seem more familiar with American psychology than with British, often state that the introduction of the concept of the unconscious, and of a dynamic standpoint generally, is due to Freud. That is perhaps true of American and Continental psychology. But in this country Ward, Stout, and above all McDougall had already convinced British psychologists of their importance. Indeed, the doctrine of unconscious processes played a considerable part in the psychology of Hamilton and in the mental physiology of Carpenter; and the dynamic standpoint is at least as old as Hume. In Britain indeed the early interest in psycho-analytic theories was due far more to the influence of academic psychologists like Rivers, McDougall, and Myers, than to that of their psychiatric contemporaries.

numerous mental processes exist, of which the owner is altogether ignorant.

As a matter of theory, we may, if we like, continue to conjecture that the ultimate basis of instincts, habits, and emotions must consist in certain organized nerve-paths in the brain and nervous system. But for practical purposes such a theory is of little help. We cannot refer to the nerve-paths by name; and we know nothing of the manner in which they are arranged. Hence we are obliged to indicate them in mental terms, and to describe them as those mechanisms or processes which *would* give rise to such and such feelings, wishes, or motives, *if* their owner became clearly conscious of them.

Emotional Character of Symptoms and Causes. I have discussed in general terms the chief ways in which a neurosis differs from other mental troubles. The distinctions brought forward, however, are vague and abstract; and the true nature of a neurosis will best be gathered if the reader rapidly reviews a few representative cases that would be almost universally diagnosed as neurotic. I shall describe such cases in a moment; and a comparison of them will immediately reveal that they all possess one universal and outstanding feature. Different as their symptoms are, they all share this point in common: in every case, both the manifestations and the causes are primarily emotional. Here, I fancy, is the key to all such conditions: neurotic disorders are emotional disorders. If, therefore, we were to drop the old, misleading names—'nervous' and 'neurotic'—and yet retain our fondness for translating our diagnostic appellations into hybrid Greek, our course would be easy: we could say that such patients suffer not from neuroses but from 'thymoses', and describe them not as neurotic but as 'thymotic'. But I for one have no special hankering to add yet another neologism to a branch of science already too much addicted to them.[1]

On a closer examination of concrete cases it will be found

[1] In Greek θυμός (passion) is the term usually contrasted with νοῦς (intellect). The root is familiar in psychiatric nomenclature from compounds like 'cyclothymic' and 'schizothymic'.

that the symptoms nearly always arise on a basis of general emotional excitability. They occur, as a rule, in those persons whom I have called temperamentally unstable. Such instability is sometimes constitutional, and not infrequently, it would seem, inherited. In a large proportion of my cases —62 per cent. of those that I have studied in greatest detail —there is a history of emotional instability in the patient's relatives. The precipitating cause is frequently some form of emotional stress—a broken love-affair, a sudden fright, a spell of worry, some drawn-out moral conflict, some agitating crisis in the patient's life to which he cannot readily adjust his feelings or behaviour.

The part played by these two factors—the internal and the external—varies in different cases. In one who is easily unbalanced the most trifling stimulus may suffice to start a nervous breakdown. But, since we are each of us born with emotional tendencies, a degree of stress can be imagined violent enough or prolonged enough to provoke a nervous disorder even in the most stable. We all have our price. If under internal factors we include, not merely the patient's innate constitution, but his inner mental condition at the time the neurosis starts, then there can be little doubt that they are usually the more important. The popular notion that a nervous breakdown is due solely to some external cause a—shock or a strain, a sudden grief or an overwhelming joy—is yet another relic of views once held by medical writers but now abandoned. In most instances the maladjustment arises because the individual's inner powers of resistance are unequal to the stress which the outer environment imposes, and breakdown ensues.

The Genesis of Neuroses in Emotional Conflicts. How then do these emotional causes operate? To begin with, let us remember that any emotion is apt to issue in an irrational, or at any rate a non-rational, action. Indeed, we may go farther, and say that if an action, due to emotion, appears to an onlooker reasonable in view of the circumstances that called it forth—appropriately adapted, that is, to the situation that aroused it, then this is not because the agent deliberately adopted that action after realizing how reasonable and expedient it was, but simply because Nature has arranged that our inborn impulses shall, on the whole, be crudely appropriate rather than the reverse. A child hears a loud yelp from a noisy animal; and, under the stress of fear, screams and dashes to his mother's side. In those wild parts where wolves still roam in freedom, the child's action is rational; in London, where wolves no longer exist except in iron cages, and where the only yelping animals at large are dogs, and for the most part harmless dogs, there the child's action, nine times out of ten, is irrational. But in neither case is there any suggestion that the child himself is deliberately acting in accordance with the conclusions of his reason. He behaves simply as his instincts and emotions dictate. And, allowing for the complexity of the older mind, the same holds true of all emotional action.

To this extent, every neurotic action, being irrational, is an emotional action: its irrationality is due to its emotional nature. But that is not all. Because all neurotic actions seem irrational, we cannot argue that all irrational actions are neurotic. The mere irrationality of an act does not prove it to be morbid. Some further element is necessary. This further factor comes to light when we trace the way in which neurotic acts are engendered. A study of their genesis reveals that what are ordinarily described as neurotic symptoms appear to be the result, not of a simple emotional reaction to an outer stimulus, but of a complex situation in which two or more emotions are aroused: it is, in short, the outcome of an emotional conflict. It arises as a solution to that conflict—usually an unintelligent and at first a somewhat hesitant solution. Gradually, because in some degree it serves its purpose and relieves the emotional tension, it becomes fixed.

Let me give an illustration. If a child shows an unusual fear of dogs or an unusual hostility towards his nurse, I do not regard the symptom as necessarily neurotic because the emotion is exceptionally strong. A brief study of the case might satisfy me that the child's fear or hostility had been provoked solely by some special circumstance: the child, for example, may have been bitten by a dog, or his nurse may have been demonstrably unjust and cruel. In such a case I should consider the child's subsequent behaviour not neurotic, but normal. I should regard his symptoms as neurotic only if the fear could not be entirely explained by the outer events of his life, but was mainly accounted for by some emotional conflict in the child's own mind.

The last case of this type that I had occasion to examine was that of a boy of four. Both his fear and his hostility were the expression of a guilty conscience. Five months before he had started certain improper tricks for which his nurse had constantly rebuked him. Once, when she was out of the house, he began his tricks afresh, imagining that now he would be uninterrupted. But at that moment a dog barked.[1] These and similar incidents showed clearly that his dislike of the nurse and his dislike of dogs had both been engendered by a confused dread that one or the other might try to punish him for his naughty actions. The conflict, it should be noted, is not really with the outer object or person, as might be supposed by a superficial observer. It is a conflict between two inconsistent impulses within the child himself—the impulse to satisfy the primitive temptation (in his case, of sex), and the restraining impulse of fear and submission. The discord and the stress that generate neurotic disorder may thus be described as endopsychic, due to forces coming from within.

Or, to take another type of case, suppose that a symptom or habit arises as a normal compensation, not as an over-compensation, for some physical or environmental draw-back: then, once more, I should not regard it as neurotic. A youth with a weak or delicate constitution may devote an exceptional amount of time to out-of-door sport or athletic exercise; yet this of itself does not prove that he must be

[1] I omit a number of complicating details, and give only the outstanding points in the child's history—which, as every psychologist who deals with young children will know, is typical of many. With children who actually have been bitten, there is always the possibility—I am tempted to say the probability—that such an event might quickly get linked up with conflicts or fantasies that happened to be engaging the child's mind about the same period of his life. Hence in practice it is not always easy to satisfy oneself that the external cause alone has been operative.

inwardly animated by some deep and morbid sense of inferiority. Only when his interest outstrips the reasonable requirements of his handicap, and when his effort is directed not merely towards overcoming that handicap, but towards achieving something far above it, should I begin to suspect that it indicates some quasi-pathological conflict. How far a sense of inferiority is abnormal or not can only be determined in practice by a detailed analysis of each particular case.

This comes to light most clearly in those cases where a neurosis appears abruptly and without any apparent cause. Occasionally a child, brought up under the most favourable circumstances, nevertheless suddenly develops a neurotic symptom. In such a case it will usually be found that some inner emotional conflict has been going forward and gaining strength over a considerable period. Hitherto, its only effects have been mild, unuttered suspicions, or secret fantasies and day-dreams. But gradually these have come to dominate the greater part of the child's unconscious or semi-conscious life. Then some little event occurs; this makes contact with the underground emotional constructions, and, as it were, electrifies them. At once an unbearable tension is produced. The result is a neurotic disorder manifest to all.

The Personal or Sexual Origin of Emotional Conflicts. If, then, emotional conflicts are so powerful, how do they originate? To ask such a question, however, is to misconceive the order of development. Stability is a later and final product. The stable individual is one whose personality has been gradually organized to form a harmonious, self-consistent whole. He acts as though his mind were a single unit. But no mind is perfectly unified; the mind of a child least of any. The personality of each of us is constituted out of a number of diverse elements—out of the inherited instincts and primitive emotions, which provide the energy for all our actions, and out of the acquired habits, interests, and sentiments built up on the basis of this primitive and heterogeneous endowment. To organize these into a unitary whole is a slow and difficult process; and the mental disorganization, which always underlies a neurotic state, is in some respects simply an extreme instance of the lack of organization to which an imperfectly evolved mind is inevitably prone.

We have seen that the primitive emotions which we all alike inherit are primarily adapted for uncivilized life in a prehistoric age. Naturally, in their innate form, these impulses are largely incompatible with the demands of civilized existence. Hence, as with delinquency so with neurosis, the true source of the trouble lies in the lack of adjustment between one or more of these primitive emotions and the conventions of modern society. In both delinquency and neurosis a process of repression results. Instead of reconciling his conflicting impulses in some more intelligent course of conduct that will in some measure satisfy both, the patient abruptly represses one impulse or the other. It must not be inferred, however, that repression is applied only to impulses that are forbidden. This may be largely true in neuroses; but in delinquency, it is the approved rather than the disapproved impulses that are commonly repressed. The inhibiting tendencies are themselves inhibited. These are by their very nature negative; and in the delinquent, who, as we have seen, is generally of an uninhibited temperament, they are relatively weak. Hence no severe tension may ensue. But when some powerful instinct of a more positive character is repressed, a state of strain is inevitably set up. Emotional energy, like all forms of energy, must find some outlet; and it is especially characteristic of conative energy that obstruction tends to heighten rather than destroy it. The neurotic symptom supplies the safety-valve.

In a society which insists on ignoring the sex-instinct, the emotions connected with sex may prove the commonest source of moral conflict; and the energy of the sex-instinct is potent enough to overthrow the balance of those who, from lack of guidance or intelligence, cannot hit upon some satisfying solution to the problem. But other emotions may operate in much the same way. Within the smaller circle of the family, the self-assertion of the child has continually to be restrained; in face of authority, the annoyance and pugnacity of the subordinate or the employee; and on the battle-field, fear. In every instance, the prolonged repression of these natural impulses may issue in a painful strain, until at last the tension reaches the breaking-point. Thus, any emotion, being in itself a source of energy and driving force, may appear either as a cause or as a symptom of neurotic disorder. Since, however, in civilized communities, it is the feelings aroused by persons that have to be held most constantly in check, it naturally follows that what may be called personal emotions are by far the commonest sources of neurotic stress.

It is this last fact which the Freudian school brings out by its use of the word 'sexual'. As Freudian writers themselves have so repeatedly insisted, they employ the word in a broad and somewhat unusual sense. It is used not merely in connexion with the sex-instinct as popularly and narrowly conceived—that is, the reproductive impulses stimulated in an adult by a person of the opposite sex; it is used to cover any emotion excited by persons, no matter what their sex may be, and regardless of the age or maturity of the person excited. Thus, if the emotions are aroused by a person of the same sex, they are called homosexual; if they are aroused by a person of the opposite sex, they are called heterosexual; if they are directed towards the person of the patient himself, they are called auto-erotic.

This extension of the term is not without some biological justification. Since in the animal world the most primitive form of society was a society of two—a male and a female temporarily associating for procreative ends, the instincts that we now regard as social or personal were in all probability first evolved to subserve procreative purposes. Thus, the impulse to self-display (to use McDougall's term for the self-assertive instinct) appears—among those animals that possess it, the peacock, the stallion, the baboon, for example—as an instinct primarily tending to attract the attention of the female. Whether the instinct of self-submission appeared primarily as an impulse to yield to the male, and the instinct of pugnacity as an impulse to subjugate the female, may perhaps be doubted; but certainly in the less ferocious species they are most frequently aroused in this relation.

To the lay public the Freudian terminology presents some difficulty. But, addressed to the medical reader, it possesses an intelligible advantage. It conveys three or four important implications. First, it suggests that all such emotions should be viewed from a biological rather than from a moral standpoint; and secondly that, viewed in this way, nearly all such emotions appear to have evolved as adjuncts to, or differentiations from, the older and simpler impulses to keep the species alive. Genetically, therefore, they are to be considered as offshoots from or components in the sex impulse; and, thus interpreted, their developments are more easily understood. Thirdly, this phraseology reminds us that the majority of the personal emotions—the child's affection for its mother, for example—are, in the earliest stage, evoked by physical stimuli (largely by sensations of contact) and express themselves in a physical fashion (by tendencies to cling or cuddle close). The excitement and the pleasure felt during such experiences possess a sensuous quality analogous to the quality of the sexual emotions in the narrower meaning of the term.

Since sex itself is one of the strongest of the human instincts (that, at any rate, is the popular view), and since it is certainly the most commonly suppressed, it is found as a vital ingredient in the history of almost every neurosis. This is a point that can be easily and empirically verified. Other emotions, no doubt, may complicate the picture: but, as a rule, they appear so closely fused with the sexual aspect that they tend to be strongly coloured by its peculiar nature. Thus, if anger or self-assertiveness enters into the chief manifestations, they are described by the psycho-analyst as sadistic; if sorrow or self-submission joins in, they are described as masochistic. One drawback of this phraseology can hardly be denied. To the ears of the non-medical, it carries with it just that suggestion of moral blame which the psychologist so earnestly deprecates. The words sound sensational, and attract excessive notice. As a result, Freud's insistence on the importance of other impulses—the so-called ego-impulses, for example—has been overlooked. It is tempting to say that it is not so much Freud, as his lay readers, who have unduly magnified the sexual aspect in his theory. But even had he been writing for a non-medical public, I doubt whether Freud would have mollified his phraseology. One of his chief aims, I take it, was deliberately to challenge attention to factors that public opinion tends to ignore; and in this he has been unquestionably successful.

The use of the word 'sexual', then, must not be taken to imply that the trouble necessarily has its origin in the patient's difficulty over dealing with persons of the opposite sex, or controlling his reproductive instinct. Widespread as it is, the notion that the sex-instinct emerges only at puberty, and occasions no special difficulties until the age of 14 or 15, is nevertheless misleading and erroneous. Every teacher in an infants' school is aware that, in crude and erratic forms, this instinct is manifest from the earliest years of childhood. Accordingly, it is not surprising to find that, even in the youngest cases of moral or nervous disorder, the sexual impulse, or group of impulses, often plays an essential part. But, since the word 'sexual' is still apt to suggest a narrower set of emotions than we actually find in operation, I find it convenient, at any rate in non-medical discussions, to substitute the word 'personal'.

Infantile Origin of Neurotic Disorders. It is during the earlier years of child-life that all these primitive instincts, sexual and non-sexual alike, first emerge and are manifested most strongly. During this period, too, the factors making for self-control are as yet comparatively weak. Above all, it is on the first emergence of a tendency that its subsequent direction is primarily determined. Here, as in all other forms of habit-formation, *ce n'est que le premier pas qui coûte.* When, therefore, the whole history of a nervous case is analysed and traced down to its ultimate roots, it very commonly appears that the real origin of the disorder, alike in adult and in younger patients, is to be found in the first two or three years of infancy.

During this period the persons with whom the tiny child comes chiefly into contact are first of all his mother or nurse, secondly his father, and thirdly, and at a slightly later stage, his brothers and sisters, if he has any. Hence, with hardly any exception, the situation that gives rise to the subsequent neurosis proves to be a situation in which the other members of the family were concerned—usually, in the first instance, the mother or father. This becomes obvious in analysing the troubles of the neurotic child; it is less apparent, but equally important, in the case of the neurotic adult. It might almost be said, therefore, that, in the original production of the disturbance, the emotions chiefly concerned are not merely personal emotions, but filial emotions—or, more accurately, a combination of emotions aroused in reference to the child's own parents.

Classification of Neuroses. Let us now turn from the general causes to the more superficial symptoms. As I have already said, almost any emotion may dominate the picture; but certain emotions appear more frequently than others. The practical investigator quickly discovers that, among children as among adults, particular symptomatic groups— fairly definite syndromes—appear and reappear with slight variations time after time; and statistical analysis seems to have demonstrated a limited number of recurrent types.[1] Let us first consider their general nature.

I shall start with examples encountered among school children, and illustrate the various forms chiefly from these. Typical cases, as found among adults, have been fully described in recent literature; but, although the disorders observed among adults are known to be due very largely to conditions obtaining during childhood, and even to consist in the continuance of childish attitudes, comparatively few

[1] In other branches of applied science, particularly where an experimental approach does not seem practicable, questions like those that still perplex and divide psychiatrists would be subjected to a systematic statistical study, in the hope of at least verifying or refuting some of the rival hypotheses. It is surprising to discover that what little statistical analysis has been made by modern methods of the available material is the work almost exclusively of non-medical psychologists. Medical writers seem to suppose that statistical methods can be applied only to graded assessments, not to qualitative. But factor analysis can be used with frequencies as well as with correlations, and matching coefficients with verbal descriptions as well as with measurable traits.

studies have been made at first hand of nervous disorder among children as such. Yet early instances are particularly instructive. They exhibit the typical disorders in their simplest and most essential features; and they show how each disturbance, arising at first on the basis of a few fundamental factors that are almost universal, tends to assume a more specialized shape. Among children, too, as I have already pointed out, the causative elements are generally simpler; the history is shorter and more readily obtained; and the whole course of the disorder can be watched from earlier manifestations right up to adolescent or even adult life. Finally, as I shall demonstrate in a moment, the distinction between conscious and unconscious processes is far less complete during earlier years; hence in children the deeper factors can be more easily and more quickly reached.

With the youngest of all no clear-cut classification is possible. Each case is mixed and varied. Often it amounts to little more than an aggravation of the natural emotionality so characteristic of the tiny child. The symptoms complained of by the parent are, for the most part, minor disturbances of normal functions, their nature bearing little or no uniform relation to the fundamental cause—bed-wetting, night terrors, thumb-sucking, nail-biting, masturbation, temper, shyness, cruelty, lisping, lalling, stammering, squinting, and the like. As the child grows older, however, the condition either tends to clear up altogether, or else settles down to a more or less definite type; and the types observable broadly correspond with those described in the case of adults.

We can distinguish first of all two main groups. In the one the inhibiting emotions—fear, sorrow, submission, and disgust—are generally predominant; in the other, the aggressive emotions come chiefly to the front—anger, self-assertion, curiosity, sex, and the like. Children of the former type are commonly reported by teachers as 'nervous', and of the latter type as 'naughty'. The doctor will label them 'neurasthenic' and 'hysterical' respectively, using these terms in a far wider sense than is customary in modern psychiatry. Since the two groups of emotions have often been called 'asthenic' and 'sthenic' respectively, we may apply these words to distinguish the two tendencies, and so preserve the older and more specific terms for their proper purpose.

The two types of neurotic disorder show several incidental differences. First of all, on analysing the mind of the patient, it appears that the symptoms of the sthenic group nearly always have an elaborate psychological history behind them. They are not mere symptoms: they are the last links in a long chain of mental processes; each has its meaning and its purpose. On the other hand, in the asthenic group, the symptoms admit less readily of a psychological interpretation. Secondly, and as a corollary, it appears that the causes of the neuroses of the sthenic group lie in the earliest stages of the patient's mental development: they have to be sought for among the events and experiences of his remoter childhood. In the asthenic group the causes are usually current conditions, operative here and now. Thirdly, while in the sthenic group the causes are essentially psychical, in the asthenic they seem largely physical, or at any rate profoundly affected by physical conditions.

Freud himself originally suggested that this last peculiarity marked the fundamental distinction between the two groups. The latter group, which he termed 'true' or 'actual neuroses', were of physical origin, and their causes were held to be of a toxic nature; the former, which he called 'psycho-neuroses', were of a purely mental origin. If, however, we exclude the secondary neuroses, it would seem that the biochemical factors in the asthenic group are not essentially 'toxic'; they are not poisons in the literal sense. The observable symptoms are perhaps suggestive of excessive or deficient internal secretions, in which case we might regard them as the effects of auto-intoxication or endocrine deprivation: but such theories are too speculative to be of any practical value.

His early theory has since undergone much modification; and I doubt whether any competent neurologist would now lay sole or exclusive stress on bodily factors in any of the functional disorders. Nevertheless, there can be no question that the asthenic group is markedly influenced, if it is not specifically caused, by bodily disturbances; and it is doubtful whether any deep cleavage can be made between primary and secondary neuroses. On tabulating my cases, I find that nearly 80 per cent. of the children suffering from asthenic disorders yield evidence of current or recent bodily ill health. On the other hand, the majority of those suffering from sthenic neuroses are from a physical standpoint exceptionally healthy, and their history is often quite free from any relevant organic disease. After all, it is but natural that the sthenic emotions should manifest themselves with excessive strength in those whose nervous and muscular functions are in robust and vigorous tone, and that the asthenic or depressing emotions should chiefly arise in those who are physically weak.[1]

In my own experience, however, the presence of physical factors appears a subsidiary matter. Hence I am disposed to regard *all* the disorders that I am describing as 'psycho-neuroses', that is, as essentially psychical in their source.

Under the heading of asthenic neuroses, the following are the conditions chiefly encountered—neurasthenia (in the narrower sense of the word), anxiety-states, definite anxiety-neuroses, and possibly that special form of anxiety-state which has sometimes been distinguished as hypochondria.[2] Under the heading of sthenic neuroses, I include compulsion-neuroses, conversion-hysteria, and a condition that is especially frequent in children which I term an anger-neurosis. Anxiety-hysteria, marked as it is by obsessive phobias, with their elaborate psychological history, belongs strictly to the

[1] Among adults correlations for body-measurements indicate a factor making for disproportionate longitudinal growth, and a second making for excessive circumferential growth; and these seem to have some correlation with the temperamental factors already mentioned. Thus I find a small negative correlation between height and unrepressed conditions, and between girth (and weight) and depressed conditions. This tallies with the views of Kretschmer and with the results of the Italian school (whose investigations appear far more worthy of attention than Kretschmer's: *v. sup.*, p. 51).

[2] I have found very few cases of true hypochondria in children. Even in adults it would seem to be rare. In my experience it is often a late development, generally showing many of the features of a phobia, but, in many instances if not in most, having the nature of a mild psychosis, and so falling beyond the limits of the present volume.

latter group: in its superficial symptoms it links on to the former, and so forms a condition midway between the two.

This classification is not to be taken as implying a series of entirely disconnected disorders. Among mental sub-normalities, as I have continually insisted, we do not find a set of sharply distinguishable conditions, each having its own specific cause and treatment, as we so often do in physical disease. Indeed, time after time disorders belonging to both groups are found coexisting in one and the same patient. An anxiety-hysteria will frequently develop out of an anxiety-neurosis or a generalized anxiety-state. A conversion-hysteria or an obsessional neurosis will frequently develop out of a neurasthenic condition. Thus the classification I have adopted is a classification of types; it is not to be regarded as a classification of distinct clinical entities. Nevertheless, for convenience I propose to take each type in isolation, and, one by one, to examine their aetiology and mode of treatment.

Notes and References. Various attempts have been made, chiefly on an impressionistic basis, to classify the neuroses; and most of the earlier writers treated them as a collection of distinct clinical entities. The varying nomenclature and the divergent classifications, however, are of themselves sufficient to show that we have to deal, not with specific diseases, like typhoid, measles, or diphtheria, but with more or less fluid patterns—complex reaction-types merging one into the other. For such conditions, factor analysis, as I ventured to point out in an early article (*Brit. J. Med. Psychol.* xvii, 1938, pp. 158 f.), provides the readiest means to reach an objective and verifiable classification, and the basic procedure will be, not the correlation of traits, but the correlation of persons, including the correlation of assessments for a single person: for a fuller discussion of these points, see Burt, 'The Assessment of Personality', XXVIth Maudsley Lecture, *J. Mental Science* (c, pp. 1–28).

As already noted, the first attempt to apply factorial methods to the study of emotional types (*Brit. Ass. Ann. Report*, lxxxv, 1915, pp. 694 f.) revealed a factor of general emotionality and a broad distinction between sthenic and asthenic types, which closely corresponds with Jung's later distinction between extraverts and introverts: a more detailed account will be found in 'The Factorial Study of Emotions' in *Feelings and Emotions* (edited by M. L. Reymert, McGraw-Hill, 1950). Later studies revealed similar classificatory factors in neurotic children, with supplementary factors, apparently peculiar to neurotic cases and not found in the normal. It is often objected that factorial procedures cannot be adopted for the classification of pathological conditions, because there the symptoms often turn on the presence or absence of certain characteristics, not on their degree. But, as stated above, factorial analysis (like the chi-squared procedure) can be applied to what Pearson described as 'characters not quantitatively measured' by using frequencies or association coefficients instead of the ordinary coefficients of correlation. The method of 'correlating persons' (including assessments for the same person assessed on different occasions) was freely criticized when I first suggested it; but has since been widely used. To compare syndromes, i.e. patterns of varying traits, it is obviously more natural to assess resemblances between persons than between tests or traits (the approach commonly employed in the study of cognitive abilities). And the correlation of assessments for the same individual at different stages of his life proves an excellent device for studying changes in a child's character which result from internal crises (such as adolescence) or external crises (such as sudden environmental shock or stress). For a fuller explanation of the various methods and results see *Brit. J. Psychol. Stat. Sect.* i, 1948, pp. 178–203 (which gives a diagrammatic representation of the main neurotic groups), and ibid. iii, 1951, pp. 179–91 (both papers being based on earlier L.C.C. *Reports*).

For a comprehensive survey of the problems from a clinical standpoint see C. M. Louttit, *Clinical Psychology: A Handbook of Children's Behaviour Problems* (1936), and other references in Appendix V.

VI

ASTHENIC NEUROSES

ASTHENIC NEUROSES

1. NEURASTHENIA

Definition. Of all the terms employed in the diagnosis of neurotic states, alike in adult and in childish cases, the one most frequently used, and most frequently misused, is the word 'neurasthenia'. 'Neurasthenia' is applied to almost any patient whose more obvious symptoms may be summed up as physical, intellectual, and moral weakness. Even the medical specialist often adopts it to cover all neuroses that are not conspicuously hysterical; and the phrase 'nervous debility' is generally taken to be a synonym.

By the most careful writers and diagnosticians, however, the term 'neurasthenia' is now nearly always employed in a comparatively narrow sense. It may be defined as meaning a primary fatigue-neurosis. It is a neurosis; that is to say, it is a functional nervous disorder, or, as I should prefer to say, a minor mental disorder. It is a primary neurosis; that is to say, it is a functional nervous disorder which is not merely an incidental after-effect of some previous illness, but is itself apparently fundamental. And, finally, its essential symptom is an unusual susceptibility to fatigue. This, indeed, is the central point. No form of nervous breakdown should be called neurasthenia, unless its most evident, painful, and conspicuous symptom is an extreme fatigability on the part of the patient.

Illustrative Case. Let me begin with a concrete example. Willie B. is 12 years of age. He looks thin and pale, but is not definitely anaemic: indeed, his physical health is reported as 'excellent'. Yet he shows dark rings beneath his eyes, and wears a puckered frown upon his brow. The wrinkling is not a frown of bad temper or anxiety. Indeed, his whole facial expression, though highly distinctive, is not easy to describe. His eyelids droop; his jaw hangs loose, though his lips are closed; about his nose and mouth there lingers the suspicion of an habitual sneer or pout, which seems to convey a mood of boredom and almost cynical indifference. All the muscles of his body, like those of his face, seem lax and flabby. He walks slowly up to the table, and stands there with a slack, one-sided posture. His arms are limp; and he speaks in a low, dull voice, devoid of any lively inflection. His teacher calls him 'weary Willie', and bids him take more exercise. His mother retorts that he 'seems too tired even to walk round the corner to the Park'.

He has had no serious illnesses. Three years ago he complained of headaches which lasted for half an hour or so and once or twice finished up with actual vomiting. At first this was ascribed to 'stomach trouble'; but the family doctor declared that the boy's 'digestion was as sound as a bell', and advised that he should be seen by an oculist, since, during these phases, the boy occasionally complained that he could not see to read 'because something got in the way'. He now wears glasses to correct a slight astigmatism; and the paroxysmal headaches appear to have vanished. But he is still liable to feelings of sickness when he travels by tube, train, or tram. In the family history there is little to note. The mother is somewhat highly strung; and one of the boy's maternal aunts has suffered since puberty with migraine. At hospitals and clinics he has been examined on five occasions, and with the utmost thoroughness and care. The reports are always to the same effect: 'Nothing wrong physically; condition purely neurotic.'

The teacher fancies that the boy's headaches have recently started afresh, because the boy so often rests his forehead on his hands. But the boy himself, when asked whether he feels any pain, replies: 'No, I don't think so. Sometimes my head feels a little heavy, and that is why I hold it up' (a phrase which, I imagine, he must have caught from his parents). His whole attitude and expression are those of one who is worn and weary. 'He seems to have been born tired', says the headmaster. In the classroom he tries hard at his lessons; yet, towards the end of the day, he appears thoroughly fagged out, 'ready to drop off to sleep'. He is not nervous in the popular sense: he is neither shy nor timid, nor even anxious or worried. He simply looks and acts as though every movement cost him a load of effort.

Tested with the Binet-Simon scale, his intelligence proves to be perfectly normal; and yet, though he seems to work twice as hard as the others in his class, he progresses twice as slowly. With memory-tests he varies; on the whole, his logical memory seems good, and his mechanical memory a little weak. In reading and composition his attainments are nearly up to the average for his age. But he is a bad speller, and deplorably backward in arithmetic. His writing is slovenly, and his manual work clumsy, careless, and ill-finished.

Symptoms. Such a picture is by no means unusual in a child who is recovering from some acute disease or is weakened by some chronic disorder—constant colds perhaps, or auto-intoxication from gastro-intestinal disturbance, or septic trouble in teeth or glands. Indeed, the symptoms of 'nervous debility' are exceedingly common after any prolonged or exhausting malady, particularly complaints like influenza or diphtheria; and they are continually diagnosed in children with catarrhal or rheumatic tendencies. In such instances the trouble may be due almost entirely to physical causes; and attention to the physical aspect of the case may be sufficient to produce a cure. In many, however, whose physical health is perfect, much the same symptoms are found. They are traceable to no definite physical cause; and physical treatment proves wholly unsuccessful. In a large number, perhaps the majority, both factors co-operate; or, at any rate, it is difficult to decide which factor is responsible—the physical or the mental. Nevertheless, the difference in treatment requires that we should discriminate, so far as possible, between the two types of disorder, and employ separate descriptions. For this reason most writers now distinguish a primary from a secondary neurosis. But it is to be remembered that in any given case the two may be found in combination; and a statistical survey of actual cases shows that a pure neurasthenia is comparatively infrequent. Contrary to the popular notion, alike in children and in adults, it appears to be not the commonest but the rarest of all the many forms of neurosis.

With children of school age it is encountered chiefly among the backward, and is usually an important factor in their educational retardation. At all ages it is far more prevalent in the male sex than in the female. Like Willie, neurasthenic children are seldom as dull as they appear. In the classroom they sit listless, irresponsive, and inert. But often they possess deep and genuine intellectual interests. They are sincerely eager to make headway in their school work; and repeated failure and fruitless effort afflict their sensitive minds with the most pitiable misery and distress. When an appropriate appeal is made, their spontaneous attention may for the moment be ready and intense. Hence, with brief conversational tests, such as those that make up the Binet-Simon scale, they generally do well. But where attention has to be voluntarily sustained for a long period, the results are very different. Any effort of will soon induces feelings of exhaustion, and is itself easily sapped by this sense of fatigue: as a consequence, all continued application seems to be beyond them. Lack of sustained concentration is thus their gravest and most evident failing in school; and they are constantly accused—and accused quite wrongly—of laziness and indolence.

Memory depends largely upon voluntary attention. Consequently, the inability to attend carries with it an inability to memorize and learn. Wherever school work requires a retentive memory—in getting by rote the multiplication table, in mastering the rules and irregularities of spelling or grammar—there the neurasthenic may remain for ever at a standstill. His liability to brain-fag, as it is familiarly called, betrays itself in seeming carelessness and in perpetual inaccuracy. His paper work is all scribbled, blotted, and erased; and any unusual strain or stress is likely to reduce him to silent tears.

Often the neurasthenic patient may be picked out at sight from his posture. His gait is generally slouching and even flat-footed; his stance limp and lop-sided, with the shoulders bending forward, the back curved and bent sideways, and the stomach laxly protruding. Visceroptosis, indeed, is a postural defect that frequently arises from a depressed mental state, and in turn reacts upon it: as has often been said, 'drooping spirits and a drooping body go together'. The general lack of muscular tonus is often noticeable at the very first glance. But it is revealed most clearly by the old-fashioned test which Dr. Warner brought into regular use during the early days of medical inspection in the London schools. The patient is asked to hold out both hands. With the hysterical and highly-strung the muscles of both hands and fingers, particularly the extensors, are often so violently contracted that the fingers are actually bent backwards at the metacarpal joints—a pose often observable in paintings and sculptures of elegant or affected women; with the neurasthenic, on the contrary, the whole hand flops limply down from the wrist, like the flappers of a seal.

Neurasthenia is generally attended by distinctive physical symptoms. Without any manifest illness being present, the patient seldom seems well. He is intolerant of cold, and often looks as chilly as he feels. His pale face and puffy eyes wear the expression of one who is thoroughly tired, downcast, and unhappy. His whole being seems wanting in physical and moral tone. His appetite is often capricious. He is liable to various digestive disturbances, particularly flatulence and constipation. So-called acidosis may at times be suspected, and prove a remediable factor. In the popular view, however, constipation is most commonly regarded as the primary cause. It is due presumably to lack of tonus in the intestinal muscles, and, no doubt, aggravates the trouble, and so sets up a vicious circle. But often it arises quite late in the course of the disorder.

At times the feelings of fatigue are localized in definite parts of the body. The child, when sympathetically questioned, may admit that he suffers from aches or 'tired feelings' over his forehead, down his back, or in his legs and arms. A sense of pressure round the skull is a common complaint. And another frequent feature, often associated with the last, is the so-called irritable eye: both the retina and the small and large muscles of the eye seem to become

quickly fatigued, though no error of refraction may be discoverable. The child prefers to work in a good light, and
yet suffers easily from glare: reading, writing, and needlework are carried on with obvious difficulty. Sleep fails
to dispel the sense of fatigue, and the patient may feel more
tired on rising than when he went to bed. He may require
the greater part of the day to get properly waked up, and
then at night is unable to fall asleep. Sleeplessness is by
no means infrequent; but sleep-walking, sleep-talking, and
nightmares are comparatively rare. Nor is the insomnia
severe. The child finds it difficult to get to sleep during the
first hours of the night, and often dozes on until late in the
morning. Bad sex habits are often reported or suspected,
and may perhaps be indirectly connected with the child's
mental state.

The essential condition may easily be detected by one of
the many so-called tests of fatigue. Such tests are seldom
required for individual cases, but are occasionally useful for
broad surveys and purposes of research. The simplest is
the Kraepelin addition test. Here the child adds pairs of
one-place figures printed in columns; the number correctly
added during each period of ten seconds is computed; and
the diminution in amount measures the susceptibility to
fatigue. Such a test may be applied quite readily as a group-
test to a number of pupils working together in class, and
may serve to pick out the neurasthenic in a rough and rapid
review. The curves obtained by plotting each child's output
during each period of ten seconds generally disclose typical
differences between the neurasthenic and the normal. The
normal child, as he warms to his work and reaps the benefit
of adaptation and practice, shows at first a discernible improvement. No signs of fatigue appear for several minutes—
the time, of course, varying considerably with the age and
ability of the examinee and with the special conditions of
the experiment. The neurasthenic, however, shows evidence
of oncoming exhaustion almost from the start. His output
begins immediately to decline. At first it falls far more
rapidly than the normal; then the child struggles to maintain his work, and keeps it at a moderate level, though with

great irregularity, for some time. But before the exercise is over, flurry, flushing, and patent confusion reveal the intensity of the emotional strain; and presently there may be a sudden collapse. Of course, I would not for a moment suggest that a diagnosis can be reached simply on the basis of a paper-and-pencil test carried out in the classroom; but such methods are occasionally useful for preliminary screening and frequently throw much light on the individual case.

Causation. The popular explanation of neurasthenia is that the mind or brain has been literally exhausted by intense intellectual activity, prolonged and carried to excess. The mind is supposed to act like a tank which holds only a limited supply of mental force; or the brain is pictured as a reservoir in which nervous energy is stored. While we are at work, this energy is steadily drawn off; hence, it is concluded, we are compelled to stop work at regular intervals, for rest or recreation, while a fresh supply is taken in.

Such an account may be roughly true of muscular energy and of physical work; but there is little to show that we keep a stock of psychical energy as well, which can be stored, consumed, and then replenished, like so many gallons of petrol. As regards the brain, it is hardly necessary to say that, if it is true to describe nervous energy as being expended during work, then there must be quite as much expenditure during recreation—particularly if the recreation consists in games and bodily exercise—as there is during what is popularly called 'brain-work'. The notion that the energy of the nervous system can be literally used up or depleted by intellectual activity alone, where practically none is expended on innervating the muscles, is plainly absurd.

The slight muscular activity involved in sitting at a desk and writing rapidly from dictation will raise metabolism about 50 per cent. above the basal level. The exertion required for a sharp walk will raise it by 200 per cent. Even strong emotion may raise it by 10 or 15 per cent. But hard intellectual activity of itself will add only 2 or 3 per cent. As Benedict has put it, 'the extra calories required for an hour of the most intense kind of mathematical calculation would be fully met by eating half a salted peanut'.

In the psychological laboratory a series of striking experiments have been carried out on the nature of mental fatigue; and almost all observers agree that anything like true mental exhaustion can never be detected. The mental energy, or—to drop a question-begging term—the mental activity of young children appears almost unlimited. In the schoolroom what commonly passes for mental fatigue is at bottom very largely physical fatigue. It arises from sitting in an ill-ventilated room, with a cramped posture, the abdomen doubled up, the muscles of the back in strained contraction, and the tiny muscles of the eyes and the fingers overactive in reading, writing, or the like. Such passing fatigue can be quickly dispelled by a little vigorous exercise in the fresh air; to whip up the circulation, to rouse the stagnant digestion, and to relieve the muscular strain by smart bodily movement, is usually sufficient to restore the child to a normal condition of alertness.

For the rest, mental fatigue in the classroom is principally due, not to loss of energy, but to loss of interest. It is a state, not of intellectual exhaustion, but of sheer boredom. The chief characteristic of such a state is that output does not slow down progressively and sink steadily towards a minimum—as is found in conditions of physical fatigue: the child keeps plodding with constant renewals of effort, until, not gradually but abruptly, he reaches the end of his patience, and flings the thing up in despair.

To what is this final effect due? Not to the continued consumption of energy until no more is left, but to some special and irresistible impulse which seems definitely implanted by nature to prevent us going on with tasks for which we have no interest, aptitude, or will. This impulse, I suggest, is closely related to the instinct of disgust. It is the function of disgust to inhibit or arrest some conscious action for which the organism is not at the moment fit. If we have been through a five-course dinner, and are then suddenly offered a plate of soup, the sight of it inspires a positive nausea, which effectively prevents us from swallowing any more. But disgust may be aroused not only through alimentary stimuli—uncongenial tastes or smells;

like other instincts, it can be induced by any situation which in its general nature is analogous to the primitive stimulus that originally excites it. Disgust will supervene whenever we set ourselves to a task for which our mood or mental condition is ill adjusted at the time. Thus, an unseasonable sexual appeal will provoke as violent a recoil as an inopportune stimulus to the palate or the nose. And, in a modified form, the same impulse may be aroused by moral or intellectual situations. This is shown by many current metaphors. When common parlance says that we are tired of a thing, colloquial slang says that we are 'sick of it' or 'fed up'. And the young child condemns what he dislikes as 'nasty', and exhibits his distaste by a typical grimace of disgust.

Boredom may thus be of two kinds—negative and positive. The first is due to the absence of all energizing emotion, aroused by the task itself and enabling us to keep at it; the second is due to the presence of a specific inhibitive emotion, compelling us to draw back or stop. The two phases may follow in succession. During the initial stage boredom remains merely negative, and comes from lack of interest or loss of keenness and enthusiasm. But, if prolonged, it quickly turns into a positive aversion, brought about by the intervention of this instinct of withdrawal. What I have called, therefore, an excessive liability to fatigue may be largely an excessive liability to positive boredom. The child is unable to exert himself, not because his will or his energy is exhausted, but because he is perpetually inhibited by this chronic mood of repulsion.

If this theory is correct—and many other minor facts might be adduced to support it—then primary neurasthenia should be regarded as at bottom a disgust neurosis. This view may incidentally explain the nausea, sick headaches, and 'hysterical vomiting' that occur so frequently, with no physical cause, in the neurasthenic child. The part played by disgust in neurotic states has, indeed, never been sufficiently investigated. As an inhibitor of action it is as powerful as the instinct of fear. In many neuroses where sexual factors can be traced, it often proves that the disorder is actually precipitated, not so much by the sex impulse itself, as by the disgust that is incidentally aroused by sexual ideas. Disgust also plays a vital part in producing a sense of guilt. And where the neurasthenic's condition is ascribed to excessive sexual practices or to frequent self-abuse, there I am inclined to suggest that the result is produced, not, as is popularly supposed, by direct physical exhaustion, but by the emotions of disgust and repugnance that so frequently supervene.

What little energy the neurasthenic possesses seems directed, not towards the work in hand, but towards overcoming these inhibitions. In the case of self-abuse, for example, what appears to wear out the patient is not sexual excitement itself (that may be slight and infrequent), but the preliminary struggle with his moral scruples. So, too, in the case of intellectual work, it is not so much the work as the effort to overcome his boredom or revulsion that leads so quickly to lassitude. In many, a contributing condition is a state of anxious strain, arising from some internal stress: the patient's energy appears so occupied with his inner emotional conflicts that he has little left over for the tasks of everyday life. Here, therefore, even in what is usually thought to be the simplest form of neurosis, mental disorganization and conflict seem nearly always present as a crucial factor.

This, then, so far as current psychology can interpret it, is the picture which the typical neurasthenic seems to present. Future research, of course, may ultimately prove that the mechanism underlying the condition of disgust and weariness is at bottom physical or physiological—that the constant stimulation of one set of glands, which may also be congenitally inadequate, may eventually limit or modify their secretions, or alter the secretions of another set, and so, through the remoter effects on the nervous, muscular, or vaso-motor systems, tend to produce the limp, atonic state so distinctive of the neurasthenic patient. It is tempting to suppose that an exhaustion of the adrenal glands in particular, together with the consequent loss of tone in the sympathetic system, may be directly responsible for those bodily symptoms that usually accompany neurasthenia. In secondary cases, and perhaps in advanced primary cases as well, this exhaustion may perhaps be ascribed to toxins variously produced. In many instances, however, the physical disorders that are supposed to cause the mental disorder are, in point of fact, its effects. In a large number of instances, a vicious circle is involved; the mental trouble aggravates the physical, and this in turn exacerbates the mental.

Treatment. The treatment of neurasthenia will follow a double line, physical and psychical, concentrating on one or the other, according to the factor that seems to preponderate in each individual case. Even where the original source seems purely mental, it is often easier to break the vicious circle by physical measures. If the mental trouble has produced dyspepsia or sleeplessness, for example, this may mark the simplest point towards which to direct the attack. And, indeed, in primary cases as in secondary, the first step will usually be to tone up the patient's bodily fitness. Attention to general health is often followed by a swift improvement.

In all cases an essential element in the treatment will be rest. Just as the hysterical child needs occupation and activity, the neurasthenic needs repose. In some cases, a week or two in bed may be usefully enjoined to begin with; and later the patient may be allowed to get up each day for gradually lengthened periods. Not infrequently it will be found that what is wearing out the child are the customs of the home and the ways of his parents and relatives. Hence, rest away from home, preferably in the country or by the sea, is often indispensable. When the child returns to school, the more abstract subjects, such as tax a weak attention—mathematics, grammar, foreign languages, all that involves drudgery and drill—should be reduced to a minimum. In the classroom the neurasthenic is too often looked upon as simply a lazy child. Where this is the teacher's attitude, it should be explained that the apparent laziness is a defence-mechanism—an automatic form of self-protection. Hence it may be dangerous to coerce the child into applying himself to intellectual tasks for which he feels no interest, and wiser to tolerate a little carelessness or inattention. The best course, however, is to modify the school's requirements, and to drop all work in which signs of undue fatigue are apt to appear.

The neurasthenic, as we have seen, suffers from insufficient energy—or, to speak more correctly, from insufficient interest and emotional stimulus. The obvious remedy, therefore, is to place him in situations, and to provide him with occupations, that will make a more natural appeal, and so avoid the wearing struggle against failing will-power and attention. Every endeavour should be made to discover the child's chief interests and special aptitudes, and to supply him with fresh activities, specially calculated to awaken them most directly. Here lies the benefit of a change of scene. Indoor and sedentary amusements should not be too freely encouraged: enlivening games in the fresh air are far more beneficial. But too often it is forgotten that bodily activity may tire the neurasthenic almost as much as mental.

Wherever bad sex practices are suspected, they should be tactfully dealt with. Indirect measures will usually be more successful than any direct approach; above all, it is essential to avoid an attitude that may heighten the child's sense of shame, or magnify his fears about the possible effect of the habits on his health. And, generally speaking, it will be desirable to remove, so far as possible, all sources of worry and undue excitement. Serious cases, needless to say, should be in the hands of a physician.

2. Generalized Anxiety-States

Symptoms. Among children reported or diagnosed as nervous, by far the commonest feature is some manifestation of fear. On the surface they seem to suffer from what it has become the fashion to call an anxiety-state. The first impression of the examiner is that the child is labouring under an extreme liability to feelings of alarm, and lives almost chronically in a mood of groundless apprehension. I am tempted, therefore, to call this second type a 'fear-neurosis'.

In most of these cases the superficial history is much the same. The mother, when questioned, first of all attributes the child's nervousness to some shock or sudden alarm that upset him at the age of about two or three. But, on inquiring more closely into the circumstances, it generally appears that the so-called shock was an incident that would have left the majority of children comparatively undismayed: at any rate, after their first little fright, they would have settled down quite happily again, without being flung into a permanent state of trepidation. Further questioning usually reveals that, long before the shock, the child was exceedingly timid. He would start, tremble, or scream at anything new or unfamiliar.

Of the more recent symptoms what is most frequently reported is the way the child jumps or flinches at sharp or unexpected noises. With all human beings a loud or a sudden sound is the commonest stimulus to arouse an emotion of fear. Hence, all through life the nervous person suffers from what is termed—not quite correctly—an 'auditory hyperaesthesia'. This heightened sensitivity, and the din and clatter that play upon it, are often supposed to be characteristics of post-war civilization—the age of gramophones and loud speakers, of motor traffic and pneumatic drills. Yet scientific observations and experiments, such as have been recently carried out, show that, after a little habituation, nearly all healthy persons can, as a matter of fact, continue their work in the midst of the most deafening uproar, without detriment to comfort, efficiency, or speed. Evidently the susceptibility to noise is a widely varying characteristic, differing greatly in different individuals and rising to a maximum in the neurotic. Nearly a century ago, Carlyle described its torment in vivid terms: 'the dog's harsh note, the cock's shrill clarion, the melody of wheel-barrows and wooden clogs upon the street, and that hollow triviality of the present age, the piano, will torture the ear and set the nerves on edge beyond all bearing.'

Since, in its primitive origin, the instinct of fear is essentially an impulse to fly and hide from the dangerous enemy, it is natural that the voice, and even the breathing, the sound of which might attract the enemy's attention, should be more or less inhibited in conditions of fear. As a result, the fear neuroses are apt to produce, among their commoner symptoms, considerable disturbance in speech.[1] The most obvious example is the frightened silence, or the whispered monosyllabic replies, of the shy and diffident youngster. But speech may be affected in more serious ways. Stammering, which is almost always a neurotic symptom, is exceedingly prevalent in anxiety cases; and the popular notion that a youth who preserves a lisp remains at heart excessively babyish, dependent on his mother's protection, includes more than a grain of truth. To deal with such symptoms in and for themselves, by means of speech-training, breathing-exercises, or constant correction in the classroom, may often be worse than useless. The underlying condition must be attacked.

The symptom, however, which in the end most frequently brings the patient to the doctor is some serious disturbance of sleep. This, indeed, is a true danger-signal. In almost every instance of an anxiety-state sleep is more or less deranged. The child cannot get to sleep until very late at night. Or he wakes up early, and remains worn out and miserable for the rest of the morning. Even when he dozes off at night, he remains restless and fidgety, tossing, turning, grinding his teeth, often talking and sometimes walking in his sleep. In case after case there are stories of nightmares and distressing dreams. All through, it will be observed, these symptoms are the natural expression of an emotion or mood of fear, which, for some reason or other, has become constant or recurrent.

Causation. If we believe that each instinct may be inherited in varying degrees of intensity, then the inheritance of an excessively strong instinct of fear might seem sufficient to explain the development of a fear-neurosis. Because of their small size, their physical weakness, their general inexperience, children are especially prone to the instinct of fear. But, however intense, what may be called rational fear,

---

[1] In passing, I should point out that psychologists, both professional and amateur, pay far too little attention to the diagnostic significance of the voice. The voice expresses emotion quite as much as the face; and the instinctive changes in both often provide a suggestive clue to character. In neurotic conditions, the dull, flat tones of the neurasthenic are as distinctive as the rapid, high-pitched, up-and-down inflections of the hysteric.

a fear that is reasonable in view of the child's own ignorance of the world, hardly suffices to constitute a neurotic disorder. And, in point of fact, the history and the facts in nearly every case turn out on close analysis far too complex to be explained along these simple lines. Usually the neurosis develops, not out of the simple instinct of fear, but out of the way this and other instincts have been previously organized—in short, out of what we have learnt to call a sentiment or complex. In nearly every early case the sentiment in question is the sentiment which has grown up in relation to the child's own parents—generally his mother. There thus arise two predisposing characteristics, according as the parental sentiment involves either an excessive love for the parent or an excessive fear of the parent. In the first case the anxiety will spring from an imagined loss of the parent's love for the child; in the second, it will spring from an expected punishment which the parent is thought to have threatened.

(a) The first type is the commoner. Since children are so weak and tiny, nature has arranged—and society has encouraged the arrangement—that they shall, during their tenderest years, enjoy protection and support from within their own family. It is the partial withdrawal of this support, after it has become habitual, that commonly generates neurotic symptoms. Thus signs of excessive fear may emerge not merely because the child is constitutionally timid, but because during the first few years of his life he had grown accustomed to an exceptional dependence upon his protecting parent. Such states very frequently occur in first-born children when a new addition to the family arrives. For the first year or two, the child was an only child —the centre of its mother's affections. When the new baby appears, the mother inevitably turns her attention to the second infant. The older child then feels neglected. His affections now go unsatisfied, or seem callously ignored or rebuffed. He thinks that his mother no longer loves him. In a youngster of aggressive disposition this feeling may show itself by open jealousy, by a violent bid for sympathy, or (most frequently of all) by a new spirit of self-assertion, anger, and cruelty, not necessarily directed against the new intruder. In the child who is by nature of a less aggressive temperament, or keeps back his aggressive impulses, a spell of restless anxiety is a common outcome.[1]

In many cases, there may be some additional factor contributing to the same result. Every child, just because he is a child, necessarily starts life with a sense of helplessness; but this inevitable feeling of inferiority is often magnified in two different ways. In the first place, the child himself may be afflicted with some physical or mental weakness. He may be small, ill-developed, or deformed; he may be deaf, short-sighted, or peculiar in speech; he may be plain, unsightly, or odd in appearance—hump-backed, bow-legged, snub-nosed, or red-haired. Any peculiarity whether of body or mind will tend to augment his dread of ultimate failure. Secondly, his sense of helplessness may be intensified by something exceptional, not in himself, but in his immediate environment. He may be an only child, a stepchild, an illegitimate child, the only boy in a large family and the youngest child at that, or, finally, a derelict orphan brought up in a home or institution. Even in a normal family he may be unduly pampered, unduly repressed, neglected or misunderstood in innumerable ways. When he goes to school, the sheer novelty of his surroundings may increase his sense of insecurity; and, if the school itself is uncongenial, the loneliness may become intolerable. Factors such as these are exceedingly common in anxiety-cases of the first type.

(b) In cases of the second type, the anxiety arises, not so much from a loss of the parent's love and protection, but from fear of the parent's punishment. This second line of causation may be rendered more intelligible by a concrete instance.

John was a bright little fellow of 6. When tested he had an intelligence equal to that of a child of 9. He was in the

[1] It will be remembered that the behaviourists have argued that in newborn children two stimuli alone seem to arouse the emotion of fear—loud or sudden noises, and the sudden withdrawal of physical support. Now it is a well-known principle that emotions, biologically evolved to be excited as reactions to certain physical situations, may in human beings get excited almost as easily by an analogous social situation. Thus it is hardly fanciful to urge that the withdrawal of moral support may come to operate like the withdrawal of physical support; and, among slightly older children, prove an adequate stimulus for fear—possibly one of the most potent.

top class of an infants' school, making excellent progress; but during the past two or three months he had seemed unnecessarily worried over his lessons. Hardly a day passed by, but he was caught weeping over his copybook or his sums. The doctor concluded that the boy's teacher was pushing him on too rapidly, and that the child ought not to have begun formal work on paper at so tender an age. At home, the mother said, he had become peevish and shy, and was sleeping badly. He had frequent nightmares, during which he would cry out: 'Oh, don't, don't, don't!' or 'I won't ever do it again'. She, too, had thought that the fault lay with the school: perhaps his teacher had scolded him or punished him for his mistakes; for the child came home crying about his 'bad spelling' and 'bad sums', as though he had 'committed a positive sin'.

At length, she called at the school; and the headmistress quickly disposed of these suspicions. Then a different explanation occurred to her mind. After all, the boy's nervousness was no new feature, though of late it had assumed a more disquieting form. She now recollected a shock he received two or three years before, and was inclined to date his nervousness from that. When about $3\frac{1}{2}$ he had been knocked over in the street by a large Newfoundland dog. Since then he had seemed singularly afraid of animals. One day, when his older sister placed the kitten in his arms, he had screamed out in terror at the sudden contact of the fur; and had 'kept worrying about cats and dogs for days'. But these fears over animals hardly amounted to a special obsession. He was equally afraid of strangers, big men, being left alone in the dark—in short, added his mother, 'I don't know what he *isn't* afraid of!'

It was some time before I was able to examine Johnny for myself. The boy was so timid that the mother was sure the visit would 'scare him to death'. Accordingly, she insisted on coming alone, to describe his symptoms and unfold her latest theory. At last she was persuaded to bring him with her for an interview. Naturally, I refrained from any direct approach to the subject of his fears. After half an hour's play with pictures and toys he started chattering spontaneously about his favourite games and pastimes; and the topic of cats was one of the first to crop up. Presently, in a confidential whisper, he was putting eager questions about the kitten at home—questions which seemed to ventilate a number of long-stifled perplexities at the back of his mind. 'Why does it scratch? . . . Will it bite when it is grown up? . . . Could it kill you like a lion? . . . Why did we have it? . . . Where did it come from? . . . Why does it lick its mother with its tongue? . . . Has kitty got a daddy like me?' Almost the whole of this catechism, as I afterwards learned, had already been propounded on more than one occasion at home.

It was not difficult to guess that these little conundrums really concerned the relations between the child himself and his own parents. When a child asks: 'Has kitty got a daddy like me?' it is clear that the existence of daddies in general is the real problem on which he desires more light, and that the answer to the general mystery is in turn required primarily for the help it may yield towards understanding his own daddy's attitude and actions. The analogy the boy was trying tacitly to draw became evident again and again from the turn of his remarks. For example, having stated that 'Kitty's mother often slaps and bites it: once she nearly bit off its tail, but, of course, she never really hurt it', he immediately went on to inquire: 'Daddy wouldn't really hurt me, would he? If he whipped me, would he use a stick? . . . Once he cut my nails with a scissors, and I thought he was going to cut my fingers off; but of course he didn't do it.'

It was not only in his constant chatter about cats that his secret worries were betrayed. Later in the afternoon, as other superficial fears were mentioned, his talk invariably pointed in the same direction, namely, towards his own guilty apprehensions, and his continual dread of punishment from his father. His mother, seen soon after this interview, at once admitted that the boy was certainly afraid of his father, who was 'such a big man, with a loud and hearty voice'. Her husband, she said, was 'always a little impatient', and 'often snapped at the child when he asked silly questions'. When pressed to give an instance of such questions, she replied that the boy had been 'asking where babies come from'. This inquiry he had evidently dropped; but, instead, he started asking, 'Where do kittens come from?'

There was another trouble for which his father had threatened him. The child very frequently wetted his bed; and the next morning, the mother added, the boy would be in an agony of fear because he expected to be thrashed. Once or twice, when he was much younger, she had caught him practising in bed what seemed like self-abuse. She told her husband; and her husband had said later on, in the hearing of the child: 'That lad has got to be stopped: he must have weakened himself by his tricks, and that's why he keeps wetting his bed.'

The case is typical, not only in its symptoms and causation, but also in showing how an anxiety, of the kind popularly attributed to 'overwork at school', often proves on investigation to be really due to unsuspected features in the situation at home. But I cite it here to show how, in this and many similar instances, the root of the anxiety consists, not so much in a fear that the parent's love has ceased, but rather in a fear that the parent's punishment is impending. It springs ultimately from a feeling of secret guilt; and, with peculiar frequency, the sense of guilt is traceable to threats about the child's sexual interests or sexual practices. Such interests are apt to evoke from the parent an exceptionally stern note of indignation and repugnance, which makes a deep impression on the small child's mind. At this tender age, it must be remembered, the parent is himself the main source of the child's moral code and conscience; hence, to the child, whatever horrifies the parent seems an unforgivable sin.

(c) To these two main types, a third should perhaps be appended. At a somewhat older age the fear often proves to be a fear of the social group in which the child is moving, and not simply of his own parents. And in later years the anxiety springs quite as much from worry over social adjustments as from worry over moral adjustments. Once more, almost any of the symptoms I have enumerated may appear as a result; but now the tendency to stammer is found with well-marked frequency. Some measure of apprehension is natural in almost every person as he enters a new social sphere. In the child it often assumes morbid proportions when he moves from the family circle to that of his first day-school, or from life at home to life at a boarding-school, or, later on, from school to business.

Here, then, are the two or three main lines of causation that may be discerned among younger children. In many cases, possibly in most, more than one factor may be operative. According to the factor which seems uppermost, one may perhaps speak of love-anxiety (fear due to supposed loss of parent's love), guilt-anxiety (fear originally of parent's punishment), and social anxiety (fear of social consequences). In no case is excess of fear in itself the sole foundation for the child's abnormal state. Excess of fear is a name for the symptoms rather than the true description of the fundamental cause. Other emotions, invariably of a personal type, always enter in, and give rise to the underlying conflict and mental disorganization: sexual excitement in one instance, affection in another instance, conflicting emotional attitudes towards parents (transferred in older children towards other representatives of social authority) in nearly every instance.

Treatment. To describe the various modes of treatment in full detail will scarcely be possible here. The investigation of each individual case, and of its probable causes, will often suggest the most appropriate steps. These, as a rule, will probably involve, first, correcting, so far as possible, anything that is harmful in the attitude of those about the child—whether parents, teachers, or schoolfellows, and, secondly, remedying the harm already done. When the underlying conflict is neither deep nor grave, it may be sufficient to assure the child, preferably through action rather than by words, that his parents still love him, that there is no dire penalty hanging over his head, or that he is, and will be, quite equal to the social problems that he is called upon to face. A formal, reasoned talk about such matters will be of small value in itself. The moral effect of the suggestion may be helpful, and contribute in some degree towards altering the child's despondent outlook. But what will convince him most will be the subsequent attitude of those around him.

In most instances, however, the problem is not one of intellectual conviction. So far as conscious knowledge is concerned, the child may already be fully persuaded that his fears are wholly groundless. Something more radical, therefore, will usually be needed. Every serious case should, if possible, be referred to a competent specialist for prolonged treatment at a medico-psychological clinic. Where this is out of the question, the family physician may have to content himself with general recommendations to those who have immediate charge of the young patient, and with regular interviews or re-examinations to watch the progress of the child. Often he will be able to correct many obvious errors in the handling of the child at home, and may have to expound to the parents those broad principles of management recognized by every expert as essential in dealing with difficult children.[1] For the rest, it may be sufficient to insist on general measures of physical and mental hygiene.

In many cases it is the parents who require treatment rather than the child. Not uncommonly the mother herself, as was evident in the case of John, is a victim of morbid anxiety—worried because the child is worried; and anything that allays her own apprehensions will alleviate those of the child. For example, if each night, when the child's agitation reaches its height, the mother herself becomes visibly perturbed as a consequence, the child in turn is bound to be affected. Half-unconsciously he may even exploit his own susceptibility to terror, in order to draw his mother to his bedside and hold her there. The proper course, therefore, is not for the mother to rush to the child so soon as she hears him scream, but first wait to see whether his scare may not die down spontaneously; and, if after all she goes to him to assure herself that there is no unsuspected

---

[1] Detailed suggestions will be found in Dr. Alice Hutchison's book on *Motives of Conduct in Children* (Jarrolds) and Dr. Susan Isaacs's little volume on *The Nursery Years* (Routledge).

cause, then she should do so calmly, placidly, and unobtrusively. Similarly, in all other situations that are creating difficulties or helping to keep them alive, the physician will have to rectify the unthinking emotional reactions of the parents, and strive by his advice to substitute a more intelligent attitude towards the child's peculiar problems.

3. ANXIETY-NEUROSIS

Development of Anxiety-States. In the tiny child by far the commonest neurotic troubles, as we have seen, consist in these vague, enduring states of diffuse and generalized anxiety, such as I have just described. But when the more persistent cases are kept under continued observation, it is often found that, as the child grows older and his intelligence more advanced, the symptoms progressively change. Little by little he comes to realize that his general fears are without foundation, that his misgivings are seldom justified and hardly ever fulfilled. As a result, the manifestations of his feelings get more restricted and localized, though often at the same time more peculiar and intense. The consequence is that he now finds existence less of a torture, but begins to display new symptoms that strike the watchful parent or teacher as more irrational and morbid than ever.

This gradual limitation may follow one or other of two main directions; and, according to its nature, gives rise to two somewhat divergent forms of neurosis. They may be called, following the accustomed terminology, anxiety-neurosis and anxiety-hysteria, respectively. For convenience, I shall treat each condition as separate and distinct; but, as I shall presently point out, it is by no means unusual to find symptoms characteristic of the one accompanied by symptoms characteristic of the other.

In the first group of cases—and these, if I may trust my own statistics, are somewhat commoner among the duller and the younger children—the physical symptoms become the more pronounced. The result is somewhat startling to the non-psychological observer; but admits of an easy explanation. Every student of psychology is familiar with the James-Lange theory of emotion. It is a doctrine that maintains that what we call an emotion is really an unanalysed consciousness of certain physiological reactions. The sensations of fear are nothing but the sensations caused by its bodily symptoms. 'We do not tremble or run away because we are frightened; we feel frightened because we feel ourselves trembling, and because we feel like running away.' And of these physical and semi-reflex reactions the external impulse to move the legs in flight is by no means the most important or persistent: there are inner reflexes as well. The circulation is upset; the skin grows cold and pale; a gentle sweat breaks out all over the body; the breathing is quickened or impeded; the heart starts knocking against the ribs; the saliva dries up; the tongue cleaves to the roof of the mouth; and each particular hair begins to stand on end.

These visceral and glandular reflexes are far less easy to control at will. Indeed, they often overtake us with a violence of their own that seems more like the invasion of a disease. We hardly realize that they have a mental origin; and fail to appreciate that the peculiar perturbations are directly due to an emotional stimulus. In the laboratory, if psychological students are asked to introspect and say what they feel when an experimenter deliberately startles them, one student will describe his experience in physical terms, and report the visceral and glandular changes, much as I have described them above; another will use not physiological but psychological language, and speak of a brief but all-pervading thrill of fear, or a momentary sense of panic, which apparently he can analyse no farther.

Symptoms. Now in certain nervous cases this physical component of the emotion may become so intense that it attracts the patient's sole attention. He may, for example, wake up from a nightmare in the middle of the night; immediately forget the nightmare; and, instead of saying that he feels horribly frightened, declare that he feels a weight upon his chest and can scarcely breathe, or that he has a heart attack and thinks he is in for a bad illness.

The bodily manifestations are largely paroxysmal. The most characteristic complaints are of palpitation or of tachycardia, often accompanied by a sense of faintness or even of imminent death. 'Disordered action of the heart' (to use a phrase that became current during the War) covers the commonest of the well-marked symptoms. Occasionally the patient may faint; or he may seem to lose consciousness without actually falling—a symptom that sometimes suggests *petit mal*. But disturbances of respiration are almost as frequent as disturbances of the heart. The patient is over-taken with an oppressive sense of suffocation, and begins gasping rapidly for breath. Often the attack is asthmatical. Perspiration may be profuse; and the whole body may shake, shiver, and tremble—as in a rigor that precedes influenza or pneumonia. Not infrequently there may be some gastro-intestinal disturbance, with incontinence or precipitate excretion.

Almost all these physical derangements, it will be noted, are exaggerations of the normal expression of the instinct of fear. At times, however, the reaction is so strictly localized, so largely confined to some particular organ or system, that the physician is apt to suspect an actual disease of heart or stomach or lung, according to the part that seems most affected.

Causation. In many cases it is quite easy to show that the immediate origin of the disturbance is mental. Not in-frequently the trouble first appears after some definite emotional shock that occurred during the preceding day; or perhaps the patient has been labouring under some lasting tension or strain—worrying, it may be, over an impending examination, or agitated by a protracted love-affair. As time goes on, the attacks recur more readily, and may be induced by any slight crisis or excitement. Between the acuter paroxysms a mood of nervous irritability and cause-less apprehension will sometimes persist, and in certain cases become chronic and unceasing.

The precipitating shock, however, is not necessarily a shock of terror. The abrupt introduction of a young boy or girl to sexual knowledge, particularly where some temptation is provoked to which the child does not give way; the sudden discovery that his supposed parents are not his real parents—these and other incidents, in no way terrifying in themselves, are often followed by similar neurotic manifestations.

But whatever the detailed causes may be, in nearly every case a close investigation discovers two conditions co-operating—first, an excessive degree of emotional stimulation, and secondly, an inadequate opportunity for relieving the emotional strain. Their mode of working may be illustrated by a few transparent examples.

George D., a boy of 10 at a well-known preparatory school, was almost invariably 'seized with a heart attack' during the first night of each new term. On the last day of the vacation, his mother would see him off on the railway platform; say farewell after many ardent embraces; and George, surrounded by a batch of schoolfellows travelling down by the same train, would forget his grief and filial affection, and laugh and joke for the rest of the journey. At night, while other home-sick youngsters were sobbing on their pillows, George would wake up panting and clutching at his chest. The school doctor reported that the boy was in perfect physical health; and the headmaster himself rightly diagnosed the trouble as 'an excess of maternal tenderness'. A little advice to the parents, which he passed on, and they were sensible enough to accept, remedied the situation.

Jane F., a student aged 19, falls violently in love during the Christmas vacation, and goes to two or three dances with her young lover. When he escorts her home, there is (to use her own phrase) 'always a good deal of kissing and spooning, but nothing really wrong'. In the end she has a series of attacks diagnosed as 'hysterical angina'.

Charles E., aged 15, and about to be confirmed, suddenly gives up his habit of masturbation. He has a series of nightmares, calling out in his sleep, and wakes up, with all the physical symptoms of an anxiety-neurosis.

Although the precipitating cause is mental, the actual mechanism, and possibly the predisposing condition, would seem, in part at any rate, to be physiological. In anxiety-states the sympathetic and endocrine systems usually show signs of instability, together with over-stimulation or ex-haustion. In particular, the thyroid or the adrenals appear to be inadequately functioning for most of the time, but liable to brief spasms of overactivity. At present hardly enough is known about these glandular conditions to enable us to speculate in terms of physiology on the endocrine differences between an anxiety-neurosis and a case of neur-asthenia. Generally speaking, anxiety-neuroses would seem, in some obscure way, to be bound up with unrelieved excitement of the sex-glands; neurasthenia would seem to occur more frequently where the sex-glands are continually relieved or discharged without normal preparatory excite-ment. It seems clear, however, that by sex-glands we must understand, not merely the sex-glands in the narrower sense, but the whole glandular system so far as it is concerned in emotional activity of a sexual or personal kind. But the pathogenesis is too dubious to be discussed in further detail here.

Treatment. If there is a long history of vague anxiety-states preceding the more definite neurosis, the disorder may prove somewhat obstinate and resistant. But the earlier and simpler cases, so far as my own experience goes, prove quite amenable to treatment. In many instances the neurosis seems to have a fairly well-defined commencement, and appears to be aroused by some current and continuing cause: as we have seen, this is usually twofold—a persistent source of excitement, together with a persistent deprivation of normal relief. Accordingly, in such instances the first steps should be directed towards ascertaining the actual nature of this disturbing situation, and then, so far as possible, easing it.

It is important that the diagnosis should be correctly made. Neurasthenia and anxiety-neuroses are constantly confused. But in many ways their causation, and conse-quently their treatment, are entirely opposed. In neur-asthenia emotional energy is deficient, and the calls upon it too great; in anxiety-neuroses emotional energy is excessive, and there is no direct outlet for its discharge. The neur-asthenic needs more stimulation (though not, of course, excessive stimulation) and less activity; the anxiety-neurotic needs less stimulation, but more outlets for activity.

The contrast, however, must not be pushed too far. As I have indicated, in anxiety-neuroses the emotional excitement is of a personal and often of a sexual nature. But in addition there may be contributing factors, sometimes arising out of the main situation, sometimes arising quite independently—fright, grief, and mental stress in various forms. Occasionally, when these alone are removed or disappear, the neurosis itself clears up, at any rate for a while. In the background, however, there may be a further predisposition, set up by incidents in the child's earlier life; and, until a fairly thorough analysis of the case has been attempted, it is often difficult to distinguish an anxiety-neurosis from anxiety-hysteria or from anxiety-states of a vaguer sort, or even to make any exact diagnosis. Such cases are more stubborn; and it is usually necessary to deal directly with these underlying tendencies by psychotherapeutic treatment—preferably along the lines to be described in a moment for dealing with the hysterical.

Where all such measures are impracticable, it may still be helpful to make simple subsidiary recommendations: for example, that the patient should not be confronted with tasks or situations likely to cause apprehension or worry, that he should avoid emotional excitement of whatever kind, that a change of scene or interests should be arranged, and generally that his physical and mental condition should be braced up. Any toxic factor that may hamper the functioning of the endocrine glands should be looked for; and occasionally its removal may be followed by a striking amendment.

In severe cases it may be advisable to attack the physical symptoms more directly. The disturbances of digestion, circulation, respiration, and the like, may be dealt with along the usual medical lines. Occasionally a sedative may be prescribed to relieve the attacks of anxiety or the spells of sleeplessness; but the latter is better dealt with in the first instance by more ordinary measures, employing drugs only as a last resort. Anything likely to set up what is loosely called mental fatigue should be deprecated; but physical fatigue, within reasonable limits, is often beneficial. The patient can be freely urged to enter vigorously into games, sport, and outdoor work; and whatever will conduce to continuous, healthy, active occupation may be safely and profitably encouraged.

4. ANXIETY-HYSTERIA

In cases of the foregoing type the child develops some mechanism whereby his excessive fear can vent itself directly in bodily reactions, without piling up that accumulated tension which gives rise to the more painful and more intimate experiences of conscious anxiety and dread. Other children, however—the older and the brighter most of all, perhaps—escape this perpetual state of apprehension by a somewhat different process. They scrupulously shun every object or situation that may conceivably produce a reaction of fright. The avoidance grows into a fixed and almost irrational habit. And thus certain specific fears or phobias are progressively evolved.

Like any other mood or emotion, a free, floating fund of anxiety is always apt to attach itself to some definite idea or object. Having found some point of fixation on which he can centre all his feelings of fear, the child then ceases to be generally timid, but he exhibits a morbid horror of a particular class of things. The following case may serve to illustrate the process.

Mary G. was a girl of 11. She was sent to me, not at the instance of her teacher, but at the request of her parents. In her school work her progress had been fairly steady. But during the past year her mother had become exceedingly worried because she feared the child was 'going insane'. The mother's own sister was already in an asylum; and the parents feared that Mary might have inherited the same tendency.

The first sign of 'queerness' which the mother reported was that Mary cried whenever she was expected to go to church—a peculiarity that was not, at first sight, a conclusive proof of insanity. The mother, however, explained that one morning 'during the psalms', about ten months ago, the child had complained of feeling faint; and it was after this attack that she began to evince the acutest misery at the thought of attending service. And further, about the same time or perhaps a little later, another curious aversion was observed. Each Saturday evening the family went regularly to one or other of the neighbouring cinemas. Mary suddenly refused to go. More recently still, she had begun to protest that she 'could not bear being penned up' in any room whatever. Even at home, instead of sitting quietly with the others in the kitchen or the parlour, she preferred to potter about in the backyard.

Always she had been thought a somewhat peculiar child. As a baby she had many little tricks which her mother considered odd—banging her head, chewing her clothes, following her mother from room to room, inventing imaginary playmates, and the like. Incontinence persisted, with intervals, from the age of five to eight. She had often been known to call out at night, and once or twice to walk in her sleep. For the last six months, however, she had been sleeping more soundly.

When I saw her, I found that she was in no way bashful, timid, or shy. Indeed, she was, if anything, of an aggressive rather than a repressed or inhibited disposition. And her general appearance and conversation were those of a child perfectly happy and well. She confessed, however, to one or two specialized dreads. For example, like many young children, she had a horror of the dark: this, too, she said, had come over her, or at any rate got very much worse, during the last twelve months.

The origin of these special fears was not difficult to trace. The first step was to inquire what events had been happening in the family circle about ten or twelve months before. Up to that time, it appeared, Mary's grandmother had been boarding with them. Mary had been her favourite. After a long and painful illness, which had kept the household in a perpetual flutter, the old lady suddenly died. That was almost exactly a year ago. Mary attended the funeral, and had been deeply distressed. Every Sunday after that, the mere fact of sitting in church would flood her mind with horrible and overwhelming thoughts of death and dying people. The dread of the cinema began after she had been taken to a new picture-palace where the music was supplied by a rather ecclesiastical organ. The horror of the dark was due to a secret fear of encountering her grandmother's ghost —a common source of terror with young children. Mary vividly related how, one afternoon, after her mother had scolded her, she found herself sitting alone, and wishing her grandmother was back again: 'Grannie would stick up for me', she thought; 'she'd go for mother.' She began to picture her Grannie coming into the room, and then to imagine her voice. 'And it seemed as though Grannie began to go for me instead!' In the end she burst into tears.

In this and similar cases one can often trace, by a little intensive analysis, how the child's peculiar phobias progressively arise and develop. In the initial stages the things he fears are usually those general objects or situations which normally excite alarm in all members of the human race— darkness, solitude, unaccustomed sounds, thunder and lightning, strange men, large and noisy animals—and even dangerous creatures seldom met with in a civilized city, such as savages, serpents, and bears. Whether the fear of such things is innate is of minor importance: they are the traditional objects of fear, and each child's dread of them may possibly be caught from his mother or nurse.

At a later age the mental process is much more involved. Many of the fears turn out to be based on unsatisfied impulses and emotions—on motives which in the first instance have nothing to do with danger or alarm. Sometimes the child's life is relatively bare of sensation and excitement, and he extracts from his fears a morbid thrill which he could not otherwise procure. Often, from one point of view, he is secretly wishing for the situation which from another point of view he has come to regard with terror. A student, who had a pathological fear of infectious disease, once observed: 'The funny thing is, when I really *am* ill, I rather like it: I don't have to work; I can stop in bed and read novels; and every one waits on me hand and foot. But then, if I really enjoy being ill because of the trouble I give other people, I ought to be jolly well punished for it by a thoroughly nasty disease.' At times the fears seem actually used as a weapon for tyrannizing over others—a device for getting one's own way. When Mary, for example, began to work herself up into a panic over going to church, her father would intervene with the remark: 'Well, it's no use making her ill over it.' So in the end she was allowed to stay at home. Even with the young, the underlying processes are at times so complex that nothing short of a small research would suffice to disentangle them; and it would be quite impossible in a single chapter to summarize the various factors that may often be found at work.

Among older individuals, in consequence of these increasing complications, the situations feared and avoided tend to differ considerably from case to case. In most instances they appear to be situations which, as the patient has learnt from personal experience, are most likely to precipitate an attack of anxiety. One child that I had under my care started by refusing to cross the road for fear she should be run over by a motor-car; soon she came to dread any wide or open space; and now she can scarcely be persuaded to go outside her own home: even if the door of a room is left open when she is sitting inside, she screams out in panic. Others develop the opposite fear: they cannot bear being left alone in a room; they will not sleep with the door shut; to travel by underground, or to enter a dark and crowded theatre, makes them turn giddy and faint, and perhaps even vomit.

Fears such as these often generate one another in a semi-logical sequence. The end-result may be either a state of mind that is generally calm, or a course of conduct that is visibly eccentric, or possibly both. The child seems to begin by noticing his own panics; and he grows anxious lest another panic should overtake him in some place where he cannot get relief—in a room where he is alone, in an open street or field where he is far from home, from his parents, or from any human assistance. He begins to be afraid of his own fear. But, in the end, because of these very precautions, he may be able to free himself from his mood of constant trepidation, since he scrupulously shuns all situations that might provoke it. If the alarming situation is almost unavoidable, a set of obsessive thoughts or actions may be built up. A girl of 14, forced to sleep in a room well away from that of her parents, developed attacks of palpitation in the middle of the night. She dreaded these attacks so much that at first she tried to keep awake. This failed. The attacks continued. She persuaded herself that she was peculiarly susceptible to sudden illness; and that in turn she decided must be due to continual infection. Thus she developed an unreasoning horror of germs and dirt. The fear of dirt in turn started a washing-mania. And, during the day, the girl kept washing her hands so constantly that her skin was always chapped and sore.

As a result of such processes, the final situation which seems to arouse the abnormal fear may really be far removed from the original source of it, associated with it perhaps in the most circuitous and accidental fashion. Hence, in extreme and advanced cases, the disproportion between the intensity of the child's terror and the cause which apparently precipitates it may be quite incomprehensible to her relatives or friends. The girl I have just described would sit calm and unmoved through an aerial bombardment, and yet suddenly fly into a paroxysm of fright because she had found a speck of soot upon the table, and weep till dawn for fear there might be similar smuts on her skin or on her bedclothes.

Such instances are no doubt exceptional. And, as a rule, the fixed fears of children appear less morbid and less irrational than those of adults. Generally, too, with children, even more than with adults, anxiety-hysteria and anxiety-neurosis tend to appear in combination. With them the distinction is largely theoretical.

Treatment. The treatment of anxiety-hysteria is more difficult than that of any of the other disorders we have discussed hitherto. With a pure anxiety-neurosis, simply to remove a current cause of conflict or an existing source of unrelieved excitement may frequently suffice, as many of my cases show, to abolish for a while most of the physical manifestations. Anxiety-hysteria, on the other hand, usually springs from deeper roots, reaching far back into the patient's early history. As with other nervous troubles, the disorder is constantly attributed to over-pressure at school; yet it needs but a brief examination to demonstrate that the actual trouble springs not from intellectual overwork, but from emotional conflict and strain; and the disturbing elements are nearly always to be looked for not at school but at home, and reside not in the present but in the past.

In many ways, the causation of anxiety-hysteria is similar to that of conversion-hysteria. Hence the treatment of the former should largely follow the lines that we shall consider when we come to cases of hysteria generally. There is, however, this difference. With anxiety-hysteria the anxiety itself has also to be dealt with; and the anxiety, unlike other hysterical symptoms, does not yield easily to suggestion.

The popular notion of managing a simple phobia is to 'try and reason the man out of it'. Curiously enough, the only logical argument relevant to such cases—namely, a prediction of risks based on statistical probability—is hardly ever attempted: if a youth of twenty develops a phobia for cancer, you may show him the published statistics which indicate that barely 1 per cent. of the deaths from cancer occur between the ages of 15 and 25, and you may argue that, even assuming that he is bound to die of malignant disease, the chances against his contracting it in his twentieth year are still 999 to 1. I have known a few transient fears apparently dispelled by reasoning along these lines. But the hysteric is more likely to come back a week later, and say that he now fully realizes that he is not suffering from cancer, but he has discovered that dementia praecox is appallingly prevalent at his time of life. In such cases the phobia is manifestly nothing but a superficial symptom; and the real cause is not want of information or lack of a logical intelligence, but some deep-seated emotional force, which operates below the level of consciousness, and is proof against all rational, and indeed all conscious, influence. As a rule, therefore, the only satisfactory method of coping with the anxiety is to drop any direct and frontal attack, and follow those somewhat roundabout and piecemeal lines of approach that I have already indicated in discussing anxiety-neurosis and anxiety-states in general.

It is important to realize that in dealing with phobias we are dealing with something more than simple fear. Indeed, anxiety-hysteria is by no means infrequent among those in whom the fear-instinct in itself does not seem abnormally strong. As we have already noted, some other emotion, wholly unsuspected, often lies at the bottom of the disorder. A horror of solitude, for example, may prove to be really a desire for an absent mother, who hitherto has always been present to protect or console the young patient. A horror of the dark may be based, as it was with Mary, upon an expectation of ghosts; and this in turn may prove to be the outcome of a secret hope or desire for the reappearance of some beloved relative now dead. Again, the fear of strange persons, and even of strange animals, is often associated with a hidden fear which the child has developed towards its own father; and this fear itself may be motivated by some half-realized jealousy, or by a guilty sense that some prohibition that the father once imposed has been furtively transgressed.

In a large proportion of cases the patient, so far from being of a timid temperament, is by nature stubborn, dogged, and rebellious. His history shows no past evidence of early anxiety or fear. Hence, it is tempting to suggest that this particular neurosis might be more appropriately considered as a borderline form, verging towards the sthenic or aggressive group.

To explain fear as a result of aggressiveness may seem at first sight paradoxical. But, as I have already argued, emotional energy is not to be regarded as flowing solely or separately from single independent instincts. Energy aroused by the excitation of one instinct—anger, curiosity, or sex—may find an outlet through some other instinct, and on the surface appear as worry or alarm. In many cases, quite easily analysed, the patient proves to be at bottom afraid of his own sexual or aggressive impulses.

In others the continual apprehension really represents an aggressive rather than a timorous attitude towards the menace that absorbs his thoughts. A man, for example, sees ahead of him a series of small financial catastrophes which he is powerless to prevent. If only he could have been induced to accept the future resignedly, his worry would long ago have disappeared. He knows the struggle is futile; yet inwardly he strives against each impending misfortune, and thus seems to have his troubles incessantly on his mind and to be a prey to useless vexation. When the worst has happened, he grows calm again. So, too, you may see a man, faced with an illness or an operation, with the death of a friend or the loss of his job, at last accept the inevitable; and, as he gives up fighting against fate, the strain and the anxiety vanish. No doubt, it is for this reason that, in all religions promising consolation and peace of mind, self-surrender is imposed as an indispensable prerequisite: as a mode of psychotherapy, the principle is sound—particularly where the dread is primarily kept alive by some current situation.

But in the vast majority of cases, with a pure anxiety-hysteria as distinct from an anxiety-neurosis, the prime cause is hardly ever a present situation, but some forgotten situation, or series of situations, lying far back in the past. With younger patients it may be comparatively easy to trace out such causal factors, since the events are more or less recent; with older patients they are forgotten, and their influence at the time has remained unnoticed. Hence, for a permanent cure, a prolonged preliminary exploration of the patient's mind and mental history is almost indispensable. Indeed, if I may trust my own experience, I am inclined to conclude that, for cases of anxiety-hysteria, expert investigation and treatment at a clinic are even more essential than for any of the neuroses we have so far reviewed.

Notes and References. From a scientific standpoint the chief defects of the psycho-analytic theories of neuroses are that they are too narrowly conceived and insufficiently validated by experimental or statistical research: (for recent efforts in these directions see R. R. Sears, 'Survey of Objective

Studies of Psychoanalytic Concepts': New York: *Social Science Research Council Bulletin*, No. 51, 1943). Freud himself held that 'the fundamental phenomenon of neurosis is anxiety'; and supposed this to arise from the repression of some primitive instinct (sex or aggression) by a socially conditioned fear of what may result from gratifying it. It is inferred that the cure should consist in helping the patient to free himself from his repressions. This view has tended to suggest that the real mission of the psycho-analyst is to save neurotics, not from their sins, but from their consciences. The fact that neuroses, similar to those observable in human beings, can be produced experimentally in animals indicates that many of the fundamental concepts in the Freudian explanation (censorship, symbolism, the superego, the Oedipus complex, and the like) are far too fanciful. Unfortunately, however, following the lead of Pawlow, most experimentalists have tended to reformulate both disorder and cure in terms of an automatic conditioning of reflexes (cf. J. H. Massermann, *Behaviour and Neurosis*, 1943). Such interpretations have all the defects of the old associationist psychology. Admittedly human character, whether faulty or efficient, is largely a product of learning; but learning proceeds, not by simple mechanical association, but by organization and integration (see W. McDougall, *Outline of Abnormal Psychology*, esp. pp. 54, 537 f.; cf. also below, pp. 311, 320–1).

During and since the war an increased attention has been paid to the nature and causation of anxiety-states; and it now seems generally agreed that instinctive fear may itself operate as a primary factor, i.e. that anxiety is by no means always a secondary consequence of repressed fear or repressed aggression. Some writers indeed appear so impressed with the menace of insecurity that they erect a state of security into 'an indispensable condition for all healthy mental growth'. Yet, provided it is neither too great nor too prolonged, most healthy individuals not only tolerate but even enjoy some measure of adventurous risk. And with suitably graded practice even the timid can learn to face danger, real as well as imaginary, with a fair degree of equanimity.

The view that the most important factor in the formation and in the treatment of emotional disorders is learning (in the psychologist's sense) was put forward in several early papers (e.g. 'The Training of Emotions in Children', *School Hygiene*, vii, 1916, pp. 1–14). For the superior efficacy of the psychologist's use of training as compared with other methods of treatment, see below, pp. 351–2. More recently an active group of American psychiatrists have advocated very similar views: cf. E. J. Shoben on 'Psychotherapy and the Learning Process', *ap*. O. H. Mowrer, *Psychotherapy: Theory and Research*, 1953, chap. v.

For the medical practitioner, perhaps, the best general textbook dealing with the subject of these chapters is C. M. Louttit's *Clinical Psychology*: see also references below, pp. 381–3.

VII
STHENIC NEUROSES

VII

STHENIC NEUROSES

WE have seen that anxiety-hysteria, unlike anxiety-neuroses, is by no means found predominantly in those who are of a timid or anxious disposition; and the discussion of anxiety-hysteria and of phobias thus brings us to those forms of neurosis that seem to arise chiefly in temperaments of an aggressive rather than of an inhibited type. It is not generally realized that these are instances of neurotic disorder quite as much as those that are marked by worry, depression, or fatigue. To the teacher and the parent children of this type may seem naughty rather than nervous. Unlike the former group, they usually look healthy, happy, and strong; and accordingly no suspicion of a morbid disturbance may ever be aroused. Further, whether adult or young, patients of this kind are less ready to complain about their emotional troubles or difficulties, or to admit their erratic impulses and feelings; and hence their peculiarities are continually overlooked.

Just as patients in the 'asthenic' group are loosely termed 'neurasthenic', so patients in the 'sthenic' group are often said to be suffering from 'hysteria'. Here perhaps the extension of the term is more legitimate. But many writers prefer to confine the word 'hysteria', used without qualification, to the last type of neurosis that I shall bring forward for discussion —namely conversion-hysteria.

I have described persons belonging to this second category as being generally of an unrepressed rather than a repressed disposition. But this description must not be taken to imply that repression plays no part in producing the disorder. Repression of some sort is nearly always found. But now what is repressed is not an emotional impulse as such, but rather the first and most natural mode of expressing it. Emotion is shown, and shown freely; impulses are followed, and followed with little or no restraint. But the forms they take are warped and distorted, so that in the end the child's behaviour may seem far more extravagant, and his excitement may be far more obtrusive and annoying than that of the quiet and nervous youngster.

As in all neurotic cases, it is the emotions most liable to repression in the child's own social circle that give him the greatest trouble. Accordingly, under the head of aggressive impulses I shall include not only those of anger and self-assertiveness, but also those of sex. Indeed, the majority of the children in this group appear to be, in a greater or lesser degree, of an over-sexed disposition.

5. ANGER-NEUROSIS

Of all the more aggressive emotions, anger shows the sthenic quality in its most conspicuous form. Anger is usually defined in psychological textbooks as the emotion that accompanies the fighting impulse—the instinct of pugnacity. It may manifest itself, however, in various ways. In some cases it leads to open attack; in others to a defensive attitude of sulky resentment or passive resistance. Among children any of these tendencies may assume a morbid and exaggerated form, particularly when it is the outcome of some underlying mental conflict. Accordingly, if we are classifying by superficial symptoms, it seems as legitimate to recognize an anger-neurosis as a fear-neurosis. Indeed, to judge from the number of cases brought to clinics and to school psychologists, it might at first sight be supposed that this kind of disturbance is, among children at any rate, far commoner than any other. If, however, a survey is carried out among a complete sample of the population, the proportion proves to be much smaller. Evidently, youngsters of this type cause a maximum amount of trouble in the classroom, and consequently their presence is forced upon the notice of the teacher: simply because of the nuisance they create, advice is more likely to be sought in this case than in the others.

Symptoms. The complaints may be roughly grouped under four heads: violence to persons, violence to property (i.e. destructiveness), active temper (i.e. mere violence of emotional display, without injury to persons or property), and passive temper (i.e. sullenness and obstinate resistance). In younger children a show of active temper is the most frequent manifestation: the child shrieks, shouts, throws himself on the ground, howling and kicking till he is scarlet in the face. Sometimes the child will bang his head on the floor or against the wall; and this in particular excites the consternation of the teacher or mother. As a mode of expressing intense emotion, however, it is by no means restricted to anger: children will sometimes carry out the same motion in a paroxysm of grief or fear. All such exhibitions are popularly termed 'temper tantrums'. Teachers like to describe them as 'brainstorms'—a phrase which at times is taken to imply a kind of epileptiform seizure due to some physical cause. Others again, noting the excessive emotionality which marks such demonstrations, refer to them as 'fits of hysterics'. These outbursts are commonest in the nursery and the infants' school, but may occur at any age from 6 months to 9 or 10 years. With boys they occur rather more frequently at the earlier ages; with girls at the later. It is continually alleged that such outbreaks have no apparent cause. But careful observation will disclose that some sort of thwarting or frustration, perhaps of the most trifling character, nearly always precedes the attack.

In others, temper may express itself by violence towards people—biting, kicking, hitting, scratching, and the like. These reactions are usually considered more normal, at any rate in the young. But older children—lads between 12 and 16—will often start similar displays, throwing dangerous articles at other persons, for example; and then the parent or schoolmaster becomes seriously alarmed. In most instances a little inquiry will show that no actual injury is ever done. For this reason, I include such cases among the neurotic rather than among the delinquent.

Among children who are smaller or weaker than their fellows, and among girls, particularly girls of riper years, personal animosity finds a subtler and a safer outlet than the sheer use of physical force. Injury and assault are rare. Their anger vents itself rather in the modified form of hostile speech or moral persecution. They wound through the feelings, not with the fist. Taunts, insults, false insinuations, profane or scurrilous abuse, all the vexatious calumnies that a hysterical fancy can suggest, serve as the weapons of defiance or revenge.

A still more indirect method is adopted when the child does violence, not to persons, but only to their property. According to the age, sex, size, and strength of the child, and the surroundings in which he finds himself, destructiveness may take different forms. The younger child is reported for pulling his garments to pieces, for tearing up his books or his bed-clothes, for snipping things up with scissors, for smashing his toys or those of other children and flinging them into the fire. The older child is reported for viciously breaking furniture, crockery, or window-panes, or setting fire to premises inside or outside his own home. Sometimes he will not venture to destroy the property, but only to deface or dirty it.

Incontinence is often to be regarded as a manifestation of this sort. I have known tiny children of 4 or 5 deliberately threaten to soil their clothes or their bedding by way of reprisal. Sometimes a wave of filthiness will sweep through an industrial school or residential institution: for hysterical neuroses, based as they are in part on suggestibility or on contra-suggestibility (which is simply suggestibility in another guise), will frequently infect whole groups like a veritable epidemic.

Finally, the child may express his annoyance or resentment by more passive methods of resistance. When thwarted or required to do something he dislikes, the tiny baby will go as rigid as a poker, and hold his breath until he nearly chokes. Older lads will show their stubbornness by sulkily indulging in every form of tacit disobedience or defiance.

Causation. The motivation in all cases of anger-neurosis is bound to be somewhat involved. This follows from the very nature of the underlying impulse. Other emotions have each their simple and specific stimulus: noise excites fear; pain causes weeping; a nauseous taste or smell arouses disgust; the sight of a person of the opposite sex stirs up the sex-instinct. But the instinct of rage is awakened by no

simple sense-perception of this sort. Except for the pro-
verbial red rag that is supposed to provoke the ferocity of
the bull, there is no specific object which acts as a direct
stimulus for anger. Anger implies a complex situation. It
is always secondary to some previous effort or impulse,
which has already been called into activity, and it comes into
play only when this pre-existing impulse is obstructed or
opposed.

Hence it is seldom correct to account for a genuine
anger-neurosis by simply assuming that the child is innately
bad-tempered—that he inherits an exceptional liability to
the instinct of anger. This may explain why his neurosis
manifests itself through symptoms of rage rather than by
anxiety or harmless obsessions; but it does not explain why
a neurosis as such has arisen. To discover the underlying
cause a special analysis may be required; and, when
successful, generally brings to light a situation in which
two conflicting influences are involved. In many cases the
situation belongs to one of the familiar types already described. The child has been petted and pampered in earlier
years by an over-indulgent mother; and now proves resentful
or over-sensitive when at last she is obliged to correct him.
Or he has been hitherto the only child in the family—a little
despot in the home; and now resorts to these vindictive displays because a younger rival is ousting him from the centre
of the family circle. Jealousy, indeed, has been defined as
'anger at thwarted love', and the emotional conflict that it
involves is a common factor in childish neuroses.

A cause less frequently suspected is an inward state of
anxiety or apprehension. Worried people are often irritable;
and in a child of aggressive temperament a latent dread may
show itself, not by open fear, but by bold and daring acts
of defiance. Indeed, even in those whose temperament is
more prone to timidity than anger, an exaggerated display
of would-be aggressiveness may sometimes hide a sense of
inferiority and compensate for secret qualms.

Treatment. In treating such a case the first step is obvious.
We must search out the fundamental cause, and either
remove it or else induce the child to react in a more rational

way. Fits of temper can often be avoided by relaxing instead of tightening up the disciplinary control. At first, no doubt, the child may take advantage of the change, and even seek to exasperate his parent or teacher into making some kind of retaliation. But in the end it will be found that, on easing the situations that arouse the child's irritability, the irritability itself will often die down.

Unless some such method is adopted, there is a danger that the child's ill-tempered reactions will by sheer repetition get fixed as a habit. Yet in all such cases firmness is needed as well as tolerance and sympathy. Never should the child be allowed to grow up knowing that he can always gain his ends by a wild emotional display. Accordingly, if the mother is a weak disciplinarian, easily upset or intimidated, it will be best to remove the child from her charge altogether. At school, if the child's teacher is a woman, it may be wise to transfer him to masculine hands. In either case he needs to feel that there is a strong hand in the background, and that, though prohibitions and restrictions have been narrowed to a minimum, there are certain things which he will never be allowed to do, however much he flaunts his temper. For boys the tougher forms of game and sport provide at once an outlet and a discipline: best of all perhaps boxing with gloves, all rules being most scrupulously observed.

6. COMPULSION-NEUROSIS

In the whole of the sthenic group the most puzzling and peculiar cases are those marked by what are called 'compulsive actions'. The patient suffers from an uncontrollable urge to perform certain irrational movements—to touch lamp-posts or articles of furniture (like Dr. Johnson), to utter improper words or phrases on the most embarrassing occasions (like John Bunyan), to count everything he comes across (like Napoleon), or to execute a most elaborate ritual whenever he washes himself or retires to bed. The genius, it should be observed, is afflicted quite as often as the dullard. At times the impulse is a criminal one; and the few genuine instances of kleptomania, pyro-

mania, homicidal mania, and the like (if any genuine instances exist), should be classed as cases of a neurotic
obsession. They involve, or are believed to involve, an
involuntary compulsion to steal, to light bonfires or set a
match to hay-ricks, and sometimes even to wound and kill.

Such persons are often described as suffering from
'obsessional neuroses'. The phrase, however, covers a very
broad and miscellaneous group—disorders of a widely
diversified origin and requiring a very divergent treatment.
Obsessions are commonly divided into four main types:
sensory obsessions, such as recurrent hallucinations; motor
obsessions, which include compulsive actions such as I
have just described; emotional obsessions, which consist
chiefly, though not entirely, of doubt or fear; and, finally,
ideational obsessions—irrepressible thoughts or irresistible
thought-processes.

All these symptoms are met with among neurotic patients;
but most of them are comparatively rare among children,
and hardly concern us here. Further, the classification is
a little misleading. Hallucinations—true hallucinations, that
is—are produced by causes entirely different from those
that produce obsessions; and are hardly ever met with
before adolescence. Among children what are termed
hallucinations are, as a rule, nothing but mental images
that are peculiarly vivid. Most frequently, they are visual
images, eidetic in nature—usually memory-images of actual
persons, seen now with the mind's eye, but projected into
actual space; auditory images, generally voices of actual or
imaginary persons, are also occasionally found. These
pseudo-hallucinations are often associated with day-terrors
or night-terrors; they are sometimes based on a recollection
of people recently seen or heard; sometimes they are
imaginary mental pictures of some fanciful creature about
which the child has learnt from an unwise nurse or servant.
Dickens, for example, relates how his nurse used to tell him
ghoulish tales of Captain Murderer, and Chips the Carpenter, and of a huge spectral dog that he began to see
actually running after him—a great gigantic creature 'really
too large to bear': to this he even attributed the 'nervous

dyspepsia' to which he was a prey in early life. True hallucinations, when found among young people, nearly always
consist of patterns or objects that have no resemblance
to things seen in actual life. One child, for example, a
lad of 15, describes 'a large thing like a saw, all made of
light; it gets bigger and bigger, and it comes closer and
closer, and in the end it seems to saw down through my
head. . . . I can't read, because it gets in the way.' There
seemed little doubt that this child was tormented by a
peculiar form of migraine.[1] Genuine auditory hallucinations
—usually 'noises' rather than 'voices'—occur in epileptic
cases, and occasionally in children with aural or nasopharyngeal disease. All these, however, lie beyond our
present scope.

The phrase 'obsessive thoughts' covers two symptoms
which are commonly confused. First of all, ideas themselves
may tend to recur. They 'perseverate', as the technical expression puts it. The child complains that he cannot get some
catchy phrase or haunting doggerel out of his head, or that
he cannot help thinking of an accident that he has witnessed
in the street. As a rule, this again nearly always means
the persistence of a vivid mental image, visual or auditory,
though the child's descriptions occasionally lead parents or
teachers to talk of hallucinations. Blaise Pascal, the famous
philosopher and mathematician, was subject to an 'hallucination' of this kind. One day, while crossing the old bridge at
Neuilly, he and his coach were nearly flung into the Seine.
This was the starting-point of his religious conversion. Ever
afterwards he was apt to see 'a chasm at his left side ready
to engulf him'—an abyss which, he declared, was an appropriate symbol of those deep moral problems which terrify
all who attempt to fathom them.[2]

But, secondly, what obsesses the child may be not so

---

[1] Both true hallucinations and spurious or pseudo-hallucinations may be
found in the same neurotic patient. Dickens, who suffered from migraine
and hemianopia in after life, describes migrainous hallucinations—'long
minute filaments, which, spun together into ropes close to my eyes, occa-
sioned screaming' (*The Uncommercial Traveller*, ch. xxvi; cf. ch. xv).

[2] 'L'abîme de Pascal': the incident is described in Larousse, *Dictionnaire
Encyclopédique*, s.v.

much an idea as a mode of thinking, and the thoughts themselves are usually couched not in visual but in verbal terms.
The child does not see anything, or hear anything; but
he is compelled to follow some incessant train of thought,
to keep reiterating to himself some blasphemous oath or
indecent interjection, or, it may be, to imagine everything he
comes across as part of an infinite series. If he sees a house,
he wonders what is behind the house—a garden with a wall,
perhaps: and what is beyond the wall? Fields, and then the
sea, and after the sea the sky—and so on, till he reaches the
farthest limit of astronomical space; and then he is forced
to puzzle out what can come after that. Obsessive modes
of thinking, however, are really obsessive activities, not
obsessive ideas; and they seem due to mechanisms quite
different from those which underlie obsessive images.

A similar distinction has to be drawn in the case of so-
called emotional or affective obsessions. Usually what is
meant is an obsessive idea or thought which is coloured
by some strong emotion. This class again coincides with
the group already discussed, since, whenever an image or
idea acquires hallucinatory vividness, and particularly when
it recurs as an obsession, there is almost always a strong
emotion attached to it. Some patients may not mention the
emotion but only the ideas; others may not mention the
ideas but only the emotion. The clearest examples are
the phobias that we have already discussed. These might be
loosely termed obsessive fears. Strictly speaking, however,
the obsession is the alarming object rather than the feeling of
alarm. What justifies us in calling the condition obsessional
is not so much the reappearance of the fear itself (though
this may be the fundamental factor), but the attachment of
the fear persistently to one and the same object or situation.
Certain forms of sex-perversion—fetishism, for instance—
might also be classed under this heading; and the liability
to such aberrations might legitimately be described as a sex-
neurosis. But here again, it is to be noted, the feature that
makes the condition obsessive is not the recurrence of the
sex-instinct, but the preoccupation with one particular sex-
object.

Mere proneness to some particular kind of emotion alone should not be called an obsession. Certainly, it may be the cause of an obsession. But in itself it simply springs either from an inherited liability to that emotion in an intense and overpowering form, or from a repeated or intense excitement of that emotion in the past, until it has grown into a recurrent mood or habit. Thus, the mere fact that a timid child is exceedingly liable to fear, or that a bad-tempered child is exceedingly liable to bursts of anger, does not warrant us in pronouncing him a victim of an emotional obsession. An obsession, like all other neurotic symptoms, is based on a much more intricate process.

The remaining group—the cases where the child seems compelled to carry out certain definite actions—constitutes a separate and distinct condition. It is this condition that we have to examine here.

Symptoms. The obsessive impulses are generally semi-reflex or habitual tendencies that have become absurdly exaggerated. They range from simple, irritating, yet harmless mannerisms, such as biting the nails or making peculiar grimaces, up to more elaborate anti-social actions, such as apparently motiveless theft or destruction. Many of the simpler tricks are little more than an amplification of the antics of the normal child—like that of putting a foot into every frozen puddle, or stepping between the successive cracks of the pavement. Of this type are the peculiarities of gait, gesture, or speech that are so prevalent during the early school period. The child will suddenly take to walking with a step that includes a hop, a twirl, and a jump; he will echo every remark he hears, or mimic with his hands or face some oddity he has observed in his elders (echolalia and echokinesis);[1] or he will make little grunts, barks, ineffectual sniffs, or guttural noises suggestive of a pig or donkey. Usually such eccentricities will last for no more than a week

---

[1] These terms, like so many others that impart an air of mysterious profundity by translating simple statements into Greek, seem altogether superfluous. The specialist now rarely employs them; but others use them as though they were the names of specific diseases. The word 'echolalia' is nowadays chiefly applied to defectives who answer questions and the like by mechanically repeating the words they have not understood.

or two. And, as a rule, only one is present at a time. But, so soon as one disappears, another arises to fill its place.

Other instances are to be seen in the various tics and habit-spasms to which so many children are prone. They are not, however, always due to the same mechanism. The child, having been chafed by some article of clothing, or irritated by some transitory inflammation, still continues to make the movement which the irritation originally provoked. He blinks his eyes as though they were still sore; he twists his neck as though his collar still scratched him; he spasmodically shrugs one shoulder, even when undressed, as though his braces were too tight, or his woollen vest were tickling his skin.

A common compulsion, not ordinarily recognized as such, is the tendency to use the left hand for actions that should be performed with the right.[1] Stammering may also arise as a compulsive symptom, particularly in those persons in whom feelings of doubt and hesitation are unduly prominent. I have even known a transitory squint develop in this way. An instructive example is described by Dr. Inman, who has encountered many such cases in the course of his ophthalmological work. 'The association of squint with emotional states', he writes, 'is often noticed by lay-men. A school inspector told me that at one school she found a girl of fourteen who had not been sent to the cookery class, the explanation of the headmistress being that the girl was naughty and troublesome. The culprit on inspection seemed to be a nice amenable child, and the inspector remarked on this. "Yes", replied the headmistress, "but she is not squinting to-day." '[2]

The more elaborate compulsions—formerly called 'psychical tics' or 'Gilles de la Tourette's disease'—are rarer. The commonest is the tendency to repeat some obscene phrase or ejaculation (so-called coprolalia). Here, however, we see

---

[1] See *Mental and Scholastic Tests*, p. 311. I give further evidence for this view in my volume on *The Backward Child*, pp. 316–18. I do not, of course, claim that left-handedness is solely due to this mechanism, or may not appear without it; often it is inherited.

[2] See his chapter on eye-symptoms in Dr. Millais Culpin's volume on *The Nervous Patient* (chap. xvi, p. 230).

the motor type of obsession plainly passing into the mental type of obsession. The impulse to utter words is not very different from the impulse to think them. For example, what the girl says she cannot help thinking of, the boy says he cannot help blurting out. Both complain of a compulsion operating against their will; but in one the compulsion involves 'an act', in the other it merely involves 'an idea'. Socially there is a world of difference between the two; but psychologically the processes may be almost the same, since in many individuals thinking consists essentially of inner speech.

Naturally, a fully developed neurotic obsession, conforming to one or other of these various types, is comparatively rare in the very young. Indeed, it is usually said that even the simplest compulsive acts are not found until after the age of 4. It would, nevertheless, be easy to point to essentially similar modes of behaviour even in tiny infants.

The milder and the simpler forms, usually recognized as tics, are seen most frequently between the ages of 5 and 9. The more serious types occur mainly towards puberty —chiefly between the ages of 11 and 16. The more elaborate the compulsion, the older the child. All forms are far commoner in boys than in girls. To judge from my own limited statistics, compulsion-neuroses occur nearly three times as often in the male sex as in the female. As a rule, the patient's intelligence is well above the average; a few are feeble-minded. It would appear quite exceptional to find a well-marked instance of such a disorder in a person whose mental ratio is between 80 and 116.

Among cases seen at clinics, compulsion-neuroses are far less numerous than the disorders hitherto described; they are therefore supposed to be comparatively rare. This notion, however, is perhaps a consequence of the fallacy I have already pointed out. The isolated teacher or physician sees but few conspicuously neurotic cases among the many individuals who pass through his hands. Hence, when a flagrant case of compulsion comes before him, he singles it out as something exceedingly peculiar, standing quite apart from the rest of his experience, and is apt to overlook the milder manifestations. The psychologist, on the other hand, who goes searching for subnormal children among large groups of the population, quickly discovers almost every degree of mental eccentricity—from the so-called 'manias' that seem positively insane, down to petty tricks and idiosyncrasies that every one has observed but usually ignores as too trivial for attention. Certainly, therefore, if we took account of the minor examples, neurotic symptoms of a compulsive type, as of every other, would turn out to be far more widespread than we ordinarily suppose.

Causation. Compulsion-neuroses disclose much the same underlying mechanisms as are found in anxiety-hysteria. But the mechanisms are even more elaborate. And there are important differences. No form of neurosis illustrates so clearly the mental origin of these disorders. For this reason, and because the cases in themselves are at first sight so puzzling, I shall try to elucidate its nature at some length.

Unlike the worries of the anxiety-neurotic and the anxiety-hysteric, this form of obsession is seldom connected with specific or general fears; nor is there any persistent background of apprehension or alarm.[1] So far from being timid, dependent, or bashful, the patient is usually masterful and aggressive. As we have already seen, his strongest instincts seem to be those of anger and self-assertion rather than those of submissiveness, tenderness, or fear. This also distinguishes him from the ordinary hysterical patient; for the latter is usually suggestible, while the compulsion-neurotic is more often contra-suggestible and even negativistic; indeed, those who know him are not infrequently tempted to ascribe his peculiarities to 'sheer cussedness'.

On an average, too, children suffering from obsessive tendencies are older than those suffering from anxiety-states. Hence, it is not surprising to find that the origin of obsessional neuroses is more deep-seated, and their history is more prolonged. In most cases, a close inquiry will bring

[1] Except, of course, in those rarer patients where a phobia and a compulsion happen to coexist. It will be remembered, however, that many of the cases commonly classed as anxiety-hysteria do not show a markedly timorous or inhibited disposition.

to light a long series of slight or unsuspected peculiarities, existing years before the onset of the graver symptoms for which advice is sought.

When traced to its earlier sources, the development of an obsession is quite different from that of a phobia. When phobias change, they follow in quasi-logical sequence. The second phobia is a means of escaping the first. The woman who thinks sunlight makes her ill may have first been afraid of illness, then afraid of the sun, and then afraid of neither, because she always goes about with an umbrella up, except when it rains, and is now worrying ceaselessly about burglars, 'because' (she explains) 'they would certainly go off with my umbrella, as it's the most expensive article in the hall!'[1] On the other hand, when obsessions develop, and follow one another, the new obsession is simply a substitute for the old, or rather it is the old tendency in a new form—a means of fulfilling rather than avoiding the same fundamental impulse. As we shall see in a moment, the new association may be quite accidental; and the result, therefore, seems far more illogical than in the case of simple phobias.

The original impulse, very often at the outset nothing but a simple instinct, is first of all obstructed or checked, and then reinforced from elsewhere. As a consequence, the patient is obliged to carry out the thwarted action, or some obvious substitute for it, almost against his will. There is, in fact, a marked degree of mental disorganization—far more marked than in the forms of neurosis we have considered hitherto. The patient feels that the action is forced upon him from outside, imposed by some cause or condition beyond his control and beyond the limits of his conscious personality. This cause lies actually within his mind; but his mind is, as it were, dissociated, and divided against itself.

Let us note, first of all, that the instinct that underlies the obsessional act may, on the surface at any rate, be of very

---

[1] I owe this example to Dr. McDougall, who told me that the woman was at first treated by a psycho-analyst as a case of sexual repression—a treatment that met with little success—and then by himself as a case of repressed fear—a treatment that resulted in 'a perfect and permanent cure'.

different kinds. One child is impelled to keep touching things, and another to destroy things; one appropriates articles for which he has no use, another cannot resist the temptation to pry into every drawer or cupboard that he sees. The simpler forms of compulsion are thus in definite contrast to the simpler forms of phobia. In the latter, as we have seen, the obsessive state is always one and the same— an emotion of fear. In true obsessional neuroses various other emotional states seem to persist, or rather to recur— curiosity, anger, destructiveness, acquisitiveness, remorse, disgust, or the like. Further, while the obsessive idea or act varies from time to time, the animating impulse or emotion apparently remains the same in any given patient, though it differs from one patient to another. Ought we not, then, to distinguish as many types of neurosis as there are underlying impulses? I think not; and that for several definite reasons. The history of the case nearly always reveals that the underlying impulse is not of itself illogical or morbid, but natural and justifiable: the emotional state, in its first inception, arises as a reasonable and intelligible reaction, the working of a simple instinct. What is less rational is, first, the persistence of this impulse or emotion, and, secondly, the way in which fresh or irrelevant ideas and actions become subsequently attached to it.

Let us then consider, first of all, why the original impulse persists in this irrational fashion. Three reasons at least may be suggested. To begin with, it is a familiar fact that every mode of mental activity possesses a kind of inertia or momentum of its own. Whenever a mental process has been set in motion, it tends to continue in motion, even after the stimulus has been withdrawn: like a pebble kicked across the ice, a single impetus, once imparted, sends it sliding along until it reaches its goal. This tendency is commonly termed 'perseveration'—a word which probably covers a number of different and more or less complicated phenomena. Secondly, a mental process, just because it is mental, and therefore not merely conscious but conative, is intensified rather than arrested by encountering an obstruction. This view was originally put forward on purely theoretical grounds as the distinctive characteristic of all mental life. But it now rests on something more than mere deduction. Those who are acquainted with the recent work of the *Gestalt*-psychologists will know that there is clear experimental evidence which shows that any activity which is prematurely interrupted tends nearly always to persist, while a completed task may be forgotten as soon as it is over.[1] Thirdly, and particularly in pathological cases, there can be little doubt that at times this intensification of interrupted activities is reinforced still further from some deeper source—a source of which the agent himself is wholly unaware. Where does this unconscious reinforcement come from?

Patients who are able to retrace the hidden history of their own obsessive acts nearly always get back to one fundamental situation—a situation in which the original impulse was suppressed because it was forbidden. It is suggestive that such a patient usually describes his action, not merely as irrational or silly, but as definitely wrong. Yet at the same time he is tempted to justify it. He speaks of himself as having revolted against some code of morals or manners, some binding scruple, some puritanical restraint imposed by his conscience. These rebellions, of course, are rebellions of early childhood; and in the last resort a child's conscience is simply the opinion, or what he takes to be the opinion, of his parents. And so, in its first beginnings, the obsessive act is found to arise nearly always from a temptation to infringe some parental restriction. Relief is sought in defying that restriction; and this is effected, not necessarily by putting into execution the initial impulse in its original form, but by performing some other action which may be accepted as a convenient equivalent.

An example may make this clearer. A child of 4 was told by his mother 'never to touch a matchbox'. His mother, of course, meant that he should never take out a match and strike it. The child reacted in two ways. First of all, while

---

[1] K. Lewin, 'Vorsatz, Wille und Bedürfnis', *Psychologische Forschung*, 1926, vii, pp. 335 et seq. Cf. the series of experiments reported, ibid. ix, pp. 1–85; x, pp. 142–254; xi, pp. 302–79.

his mother was looking on, he would, with an audacious giggle, literally touch the matchbox with one outstretched forefinger, and do no more. Later, when the mother was absent, he would furtively amuse himself by pushing strips of paper into the grate and so lighting them, thus getting a joyful little blaze without actually touching a match. This surreptitious pastime continued for two or three years; and then, at the age of 6, the child was caught repeatedly lighting small bonfires in the classroom, and was referred for examination as 'an obsessional case' and even dubbed a pyromaniac.

Histories such as these reveal quite plainly the source from which the emotional reinforcement is derived. Anything that obstructs an instinct during its actual operation tends to call forth a supplementary instinct, which may be termed the instinct of self-assertion.[1] The effects of this further instinct, however, come into sharp conflict with another tendency, namely the instinct of self-submission. And, in the course of domestic discipline, the child's parents are continually arousing these two incompatible impulses.[2] The attitude of most small children towards

[1] It is possible that in describing this tendency as an 'instinct' I am (to use Freud's language) 'mistakenly hypostatizing into a special instinct what is in reality a universal and indispensable attribute of all instincts and impulses— their impulsive and dynamic character' (*Collected Papers*, iii, p. 281). As I have noted above, and as James has pointed out in a celebrated passage, it is a characteristic of all conative processes, as distinguished from the mechanical processes of the material world, that obstruction tends to heighten the tendency instead of bringing it to a standstill. Nevertheless, for reasons which for lack of space I cannot offer here, there seems to me to be something additional working in these particular cases. Freud himself (as he points out in a footnote added subsequently on the page just cited) now 'asserts the existence of an aggressive instinct', which he prefers to consider as primarily a 'destructive' instinct—an instinct to break down and destroy opposition.

[2] Actually, I believe, there is in nearly every concrete case a yet further complication: something more even than the impulses of self-assertion and self-submission is generally involved. They themselves are in turn reinforced by what many psychologists would call a sentiment. In early childhood these impulses are called out most commonly by the controlling parent, and so come to enter largely into his parental complex or sentiment. The child's attitude towards his controlling parent is thus an inconsistent combination of the submissive and the self-assertive tendencies. To put it in simple language, one part of him is willing to love and obey his parent; another part of him is tempted to defy and defeat the parent. The conflict may

their parents is mainly one of submission; and, though mutinous tendencies may secretly exist in nearly every one, they do not, as a rule, give rise to serious conflicts. In those, however, who are by nature of a masterful temperament, the self-assertive instinct gains the upper hand, and strengthens the inclination to revolt.

If this interpretation is correct, it now appears that the persistence of the impulse or emotion is really due to a special ingredient which turns out to be the same in almost every instance. It must be ascribed, not so much to the strength of the original impulse, as to the strong self-assertive impulse called out to reinforce it. Accordingly, we might almost class compulsion-neuroses as neuroses of self-assertion.

Such a description, however, lays stress on but one important factor in the disorder, and might seem to minimize the effect of other agencies. There is a second point to be explained—the apparent illogicality or irrelevance of the obsessive acts or ideas. These are usually due to a further mechanism: they arise, as we have seen, as substitutes for some earlier act or thought, which was more appropriate but at the same time seemed irreconcilable with the patient's moral code. To a large extent, the new impulses appear to be connected with the old by a simple process of association. Association is an accidental and mechanical process: it is therefore at once illogical and unconscious. It only becomes intelligible when we know the particular incident that has led a man to connect the two impulses.

A male student once told me that he could not sit in the same room with the matron[1] of his college without taking

become so intense that the parent is at once regarded as a beloved friend and a hated foe. As a result, the forbidden impulse is now revived, no longer for its own sake, but rather as an ever-present means of challenging, annoying, and outwitting his fancied enemy. Yet, to avoid converting his parent into a real enemy, the impulse has to be revived in a modified form: only in this way can the child successfully assert his own superiority to the authority of his parents.

It should be added that the rebellious tendency may also be directly evoked by the injudicious actions of the parent himself. Which is the more powerful factor—a temperament that is innately aggressive or a parent who is unduly provocative—is a question to be decided afresh in each individual case.

[1] I am compelled to alter the details a little to avoid recognition. I should

a fountain-pen out of his pocket and laying it on her table. After going over the events of his past life he was led to give this explanation, which at first entirely escaped him. The matron wore a dress which closely resembled that of his elder sister, who had looked after him when his mother had died. Being quick-tempered, he had once, during a violent quarrel, struck this sister with a table-knife. This had cowed her; and he felt he might be tempted to attack or threaten her with a similar weapon. In any dispute he would find himself fumbling in his pocket for his penknife, and 'to avoid accidents', as he said, 'or perhaps even to remind her', he would put it on the table. Eventually, he decided it would be safer not to carry a penknife at all. But 'from sheer habit' he still fumbled with whatever he had in his pocket—a pencil or a pen—and usually placed this on the table instead. To this extent, therefore, the obsessive act has the character of an associated habit; and, it will be noted, it has the form of a compromise—the knife or other article on the table reminds the sister of the danger, and it reminds the lad that he must not rashly use it as a weapon.

As I have already indicated, some of the simpler compulsive acts are constantly described as 'habit-spasms'; and habit-formation is, in point of fact, an important mechanism in the fixation of these tendencies. But a neurotic compulsion is, of course, much more than a mere habit. The fact that an action is repeated without reason, and seems to arise without any intelligible motive, does not of itself suffice to constitute a compulsion-neurosis. On this account very few recurrent delinquencies can be regarded as genuine 'manias' or compulsions. Of all the cases of so-called kleptomania and the like, the vast majority are simply the result of the normal laws of habituation. We have already traced the usual course of events. On the first occasion the anti-social act is so successful, and brings the child so much emotional pleasure, that the tendency to do the same act again is at once stamped in by the ordinary process of habit-

add that there were other and older associations contributing, which I have not mentioned in the text. This first and most superficial interpretation is sufficient to illustrate this element in the process.

formation. The act is thus repeated time after time, until eventually the most trivial stimulus is sufficient to set it going. In such a process there is nothing morbid or neurotic. Yet the new observer, ignorant of the child's past history and of the general laws of the mind, is tempted to declare that the action is 'motiveless', and hence infers that the child is not responsible for his actions.

A similar process plays a part in the formation of a true obsession; but it is by no means the sole essential factor. Something more is needed before the action can be regarded as really pathological. In the pathological case, as we have seen, investigation nearly always discovers a mental conflict, more or less repressed, and so tending, like every repressed conflict, to issue in an irrational rather than a rational solution. Just because it is repressed, just because it is irreconcilable with the patient's general code, the impulse, it would seem, must be more or less modified and disguised before it can be carried into execution. Its ultimate form, therefore, resembles that of a superstitious or symbolic gesture. The association, therefore, is not entirely fortuitous: it may be based on similarity, rather than on the accidents of time or place.

Sometimes the symbolism is obvious: the new action represents the original impulse by a kind of analogy. Lady Macbeth, it will be remembered, when walking in her sleep, was repeatedly seen to be 'rubbing her hands': this, we are told, was 'an accustomed action with her, to seem thus washing her hands; I have known her continuing this a quarter of an hour'. Evidently the constant effort to wash away imaginary blood is depicted as symbolizing an unsuccessful effort to purify her guilty mind of the memory of her crime—as a kind of *Reinigungsneurose*, as the Germans would call it. Unlike the washing-mania in a case of phobia, it constitutes, for the matter-of-fact observer, an illogical ceremonial rather than a quasi-logical measure of precaution.

So curious, however, are these various substitutions that they deserve further illustration not from fiction but from fact. The cases of young children offer the most transparent examples. A small boy of 7 used to tease his mother every night with an interminable catechism about imaginary sins, as though he was boasting of his numerous victories over temptation, and weighing these undeniable merits against some offence to which he had actually given way. Before going to bed, he would start asking some such question as: 'I haven't broken anything to-day, have I, mummy?' and add: 'And if I had, you would forgive me, wouldn't you?' Often the question was plainly suggested by the misdeeds of other school children about which he had heard during the day: for example, when another boy had been caught stealing, he asked: 'I haven't taken any money to-day, have I, mummy? If I had, you would still love me, wouldn't you?' The questions themselves were piled up, one after the other, in a long-drawn litany, till the mother would rejoin: 'If you keep on like that, I *shan't* love you any longer.'

The mother, with some justice, imagined that one motive was to postpone bedtime; and she further noted that the child was inclined to practise self-abuse in bed, though she had never referred to this in speaking to him. It seemed, therefore, that the child's insistence on his own virtues amounted to a tacit challenge: 'You can't object to my bad habits, because I give you every chance to say you disapprove of me, if you really do: besides, I'm trying to put off the temptation by not going to bed.' His reiterated penitence had an intelligible cause: but his overt requests were substitutions for the one he scarcely dared to make. Once more the obsession wears the character of a compromise. A few months later, presumably as a result of the measures recommended, the child's sex-habits ceased; and the persistent questioning was dropped from about the same period.

The counting-manias, so common among small children, often arise from a similar process of substitution. The first case of this sort that I analysed was that of a child of 5. He was a talkative youngster, encouraged by his mother in earlier infancy to show off and command attention by his perpetual prattling: that at least was the father's account. Later, the boy's chatter 'became unendurable'; and he was 'told that he should be seen and not heard'. On going to school, he learnt to count; and, one day, on being scolded for talking in class, replied: 'I'm only counting, teacher.' A few days later his father observed 'an apparent mania for counting, usually under his breath, every person or object in the room'. The counting was audible enough to be annoying; and, if any one rebuked him, he would say, as he had said to his teacher: 'I'm only counting' or 'I *must* say my tables', though, of course, he was not yet old enough to know any 'tables'. Several incidents that the father related clearly showed that counting objects was often a substitute for talking about them. For example, when playing with his leaden soldiers, he would formerly pester the onlookers to observe every stage of the game; now he would merely keep counting his little army in rather provocative tones. He disliked the visits of his aunts, and used formerly to say so with disconcerting candour. He was rebuked; and, on their next visit, he at once started ostentatiously reckoning up the number of persons present.

This case illustrates a point of some interest—one, too, which is of some assistance in diagnosing the inner feelings of younger children. When the child was counting, and, indeed, all through his unwelcome conversation, the true gist of his thoughts was conveyed more by the tones of his voice than by the actual content of what he said. For example, when counting the persons in the room, he would manage to give to each number, as he called it out, an intonation which announced most clearly: 'I like *you*!' or 'I *don't* like you!' or 'I think you are rather funny!' Similarly, when counting his soldiers, he would sometimes look round and repeat a number: 'Twenty; twenty, TWENTY?'—the interrogative inflection showing quite plainly that the remark was intended as an appeal for interest from the bystanders. Thus, so far as the words uttered were concerned, the child could literally claim that he was not chattering, but merely counting; but, so far as vocal modulation was concerned, he was most definitely making statements, repeating inquiries, or even issuing peremptory commands.

One ingredient in the causation of his neurotic compulsion was manifest on the surface. Constant chattering had been forbidden; hence constant counting had become his favourite device for drawing continual attention to himself and to his immediate wants. The remedy was clear. The parents were persuaded to allow the child far more freedom to express his personal interests in the more natural way; and, when this outlet was provided, the counting-mania vanished.[1]

A different form of the same process is seen in the following case. An older child—an exceedingly bright boy of 6—had complained that he could not get to sleep so long as he could hear his parents moving about and talking. The mother suggested that he should 'not think about the noises, but count the sheep in Mr. Johnston's farm, and that would send him to sleep'. A fortnight later the child had become obsessed with a passion for counting all day long; and the mother in despair came complaining to the headmistress, who in turn referred the child for examination at a clinic. The boy himself volunteered the explanation: 'When I don't want to think about nasty things, I start counting instead.' One day he had been caught counting the mince-pies in the pantry: he confessed, quite spontaneously, that he had gone there to steal a mince-pie, but stopped himself by counting up the number. Among his catalogue of 'nasty things' he included, significantly enough, 'sleeping in a room all by myself' and 'Mummy and Daddy talking and all that, when they ought to be asleep'.[2]

---

[1] Two months later he developed a different compulsion—a peculiar blinking of the eyelids. It was therefore evident, as indeed had been obvious from the start, that other and more intricate causes were at work. With a longer treatment, these were successfully dealt with; at any rate, for five years the child has been free from neurotic peculiarities.

[2] Certain features in this case strongly suggested that the child's chief mental conflict related to sex-habits and sex-interests. The suspicion was, as a matter of fact, first brought forward by the teacher, who had seen the boy exhibiting himself in the playground to one or two tiny girls. The mother, however, declared that she had never found the boy indulging in improper practices at night; but it is possible that the temptation was there without any overt action. Owing to the family's removal, the case was not in my hands long enough to elucidate these underlying points.

More frequently it would seem that in these cases the early childish conflicts with the parents relate, not so much to sexual tendencies in the narrower sense, but rather to what I may term alimentary problems—problems of feeding and above all of excretion. A history of incontinence is exceedingly common in the more youthful cases; and it would sometimes seem that the young child's early aggressiveness shows itself for the first time in connexion

In nearly every case, when the history can be analysed far enough, the irrational habit proves in the end to be intelligibly associated with the original impulse which has been repressed, and for which it acts as a kind of substitute. The obsessive action thus takes the place of some more natural action of which the child's conscience disapproves. He refuses to satisfy his primitive instincts in a primitive fashion; he seems unable, from lack of ingenuity or experience, to satisfy them in a more legitimate and enlightened form, and so is driven to find relief in some alternative direction. In this way he does not merely compensate himself for the satisfaction of which he is deprived: he tends to over-compensate, and thus the obsessive act takes an unexpected and an exaggerated shape.

Often the child's aggressive propensities seem themselves to have started the initial conflict or complex. Perhaps his first act of aggression evoked some warning or threat; and the movements that the child now makes, or the actions that he now feels impelled to carry out, can be shown to have some associative connexion with the penalties he believes he is still deserving, or with some penance or reparation that he feels bound to perform. The anxiety-hysteric lives in a half-unconscious terror of impending punishment; the compulsion-hysteric carries out his own self-punishment, and thus forestalls retribution at the hands of others, and at the same time, as it were, defies it.

The explanation I have offered seems also to account for another feature, found especially in the older cases. In

with these matters of daily routine, which, no doubt, to the child must figure as momentous episodes in his early day-to-day life. They naturally form the points over which the child's nurse or mother has first and most frequently to correct him; and, in consequence, it is in these primitive situations that the child originally acquires those habits of defiance and secret antagonism towards the persons who appear so continually to be thwarting him. At all events, in actual analysis, this is the source to which the child's inconsistent attitude towards persons—the curious blend of submission and defiance, of love and anger—is so often traceable; and, allowing for subsequent repression and displacement, it may constitute the real origin of the double feeling of compulsion and doubt, of obstinate impulsiveness and obsessive hesitation, that is so characteristic of these cases. But here perhaps we are still in a region of controversy and speculation, which can only be cleared up by first-hand study of emotional development in the tiny child.

compulsion-neuroses—as, indeed, in many of the other disorders which we have already considered—the underlying
mental conflict is apt to manifest itself, not only in the
intermittent symptoms which attract attention because of
their eccentricity, but also in a constant state of doubt or
indecision. This feature is particularly marked in the
adolescent. With them it is often accompanied by a sense
that the outer world and its problems are unreal. Like most
hysterics, those who suffer from compulsion-neuroses are
usually addicted to day-dreaming and fantasy; and they
sometimes appear unable to decide whether they are living
and acting in the real world, or in a realm of their own
imagination. With these older cases, too, the obsessive act
seldom takes the form of aggression: it is a means of self-
protection rather than of self-assertion, a mode of defence
rather than of attack. No doubt, in the early origin of the
trouble, there was a struggle against restraint or repression;
but now, instead of insisting on his primitive desires, the
patient is very apt to reproach himself inwardly for entertaining them.

At times the recurring doubts may get attached to special
actions only. For example, one youth—a lad of 15—is
always late in coming to school because he has first to go
through a long ritual in washing and dressing (to make sure
that he is quite clean), and then can never remember whether
he has put the proper books in his satchel: as soon as he has
buckled it up, he has to undo it again and count over his
books one by one. If he then runs off to fetch his coat and
cap, he comes back and still cannot recollect whether he
verified the contents of his satchel. 'I know I *thought* about
looking in my satchel', he will say, 'but I thought about it so
much, that perhaps I only *thought* I did it when I didn't.'
Apparently his thinking absorbed so much more time and
energy than the simple action, that he recalls only the thinking and not the action. And so he has to look inside once
more. His father declares that he 'spins out the business
wilfully, because he has never liked this new school'. His
mother thinks he must be losing his memory, and so brings
him for a psychological examination. A little testing shows

that the boy's memory is perfectly normal: what is abnormal is the fact that he cannot bring himself to trust his memory.

We all know the householder who goes round last thing at night to fasten the windows and bolt the doors, and then, after he has been in bed for twenty minutes, starts wondering whether he really did so. He has a vivid picture of himself carrying out the act; but cannot decide whether this vivid picture is a genuine memory of the act itself, or whether he merely pictured himself doing it in order to think out the details first of all, and then never put them into execution. So he has to jump out, and go the round all over again.

This blend of hesitation with an underlying self-assertion often generates a singular inconsistency in the patient's daily behaviour. These are the cases that are often diagnosed as psychasthenia rather than neurasthenia, and are sometimes supposed to be suffering from weakness of will. The condition may be illustrated by a final example, typical in more ways than one.

A postgraduate student, in training to become a teacher in a secondary school, had caused much annoyance by constantly changing his mind over courses, examinations, participation in seminars, and the like. His regular excuse was 'illness at home'. Frequently he failed to turn up at lectures, or at the school where he was due to take a class; as a result, he was seriously jeopardizing his prospects. The terminal report described him as 'an able and ambitious student, one of the most promising of his year, of strong personality and character, not in the least nervy or neurotic, but very difficult to understand'. When sent to me, his first explanation was that he felt 'it is not fair to my parents to expect them to keep spending money on my education': he proposed to 'give up teaching and take a job in a shop or in an office'. In point of fact, his parents were exceptionally well to do; and he was likely to inherit enough money at his father's death to make him independent. But this was precisely what distressed him. He declared he was 'relying on his father's death': if he himself started to earn his living, his father 'might live a good many more years yet'.

His father had recently had a slight stroke: and the youth

could not get it out of his head that he was hastening his father's death 'by thinking about it and depending on it'. But these were by no means his only peculiarities. One complaint had been that, in the schoolroom, he would not face the class when speaking to it. For this he had an immediate if somewhat singular explanation: 'When I am doing anything important, I feel I must always turn to the east.'

In the past he had suffered from several obsessions of this type, which he described as 'superstitions'. In childhood he had been exceedingly religious; and he himself dated his troubles from the time that he became, after a spell of unhappy struggle, 'converted to atheism'. Indeed, his eccentric scruples and observances almost amounted to a religion in themselves. Perhaps, however, the most marked feature of his case, a characteristic continually met with in neurotic persons of this group, was the supreme potency that he attached to his own actions and ideas. Although an exceedingly intelligent youth with a first-class science degree, and, as he insisted, 'a complete materialist', he could not avoid the conviction that his very thoughts and deeds would, in some mysterious way, directly influence the course of events—for example, that any action of his such as would imply that he was hoping for his father's death would actually prejudice his father's health: on the other hand, if he behaved as though his father were likely to recover and live long, then his father's health would improve.

Of the illogicality of this attitude he was, of course, keenly aware; and his constant vacillation was in part the outcome of these conflicting tendencies. To avoid the over-scrupulous examination of the imaginary effects of his actions, he had adopted the plan of acting on the spur of the moment. 'If I feel like coming to College, I come; if I don't I stay away, and that saves hours of arguing with myself.' Or, as he put it on another occasion: 'I knew I was headlong and hasty by nature, so I tried to correct it by always thinking before I acted. . . . But this got me into such a state of hesitation that now I feel it is better to act before I think; as a result, I am more headlong and hasty than ever.'

Where these doubts and indecisions are a permanent

feature of the case, the picture presented may in many ways resemble that of anxiety-hysteria. Both types suffer from obsessions; and are therefore often classed together. But a detailed study of the symptoms, and of the mechanisms that underlie them, shows that the differences are more real than the resemblances. And the general demeanour in the two cases is, as we have seen, nearly always in sharp contrast. Where anxiety is a symptom the patient is usually recognized as being, in the familiar phrase, of a 'nervous type'; where the chief symptoms are compulsions the patient is, as a rule, not regarded as 'nervous', though occasionally he may be spoken of as 'highly strung'; and too often the neurotic elements in his behaviour pass entirely unperceived.

This leads me to one last point of importance, which all these cases so clearly bring out. A marked degree of nervous tension, or, as I should prefer to say, emotional tension, may exist, not only in those who appear nervous in the popular sense, but also in those who adopt an assertive, pushful, defiant attitude towards life. These are the persons who often are said to break down from overwork. Actually, the overwork is, as a rule, not so much a cause of the nervous tension as a symptom of it.

Treatment. When the condition is well advanced, an obsessional neurosis proves peculiarly resistant to treatment. Hence it is essential to try and cope with the situation before the obsession has become firmly ingrained as a habit. With younger cases, it is nearly always wise to get rid, so far as practicable, of any restrictions that call out the child's assertive tendencies, and at the same time to allow as much latitude as possible for self-expression along legitimate lines. Punishment, as in all neurotic cases, is to be avoided. Openly correcting the child for his mannerisms will only aggravate the tendency, since it focuses the child's attention more strongly upon them. Removing local irritations is occasionally an obvious measure; but it must be remembered that the tic or trick is not so much produced by the irritation, as suggested by it; and, in most instances, habits of this kind, once formed, are apt to outlast their causes.

To dispel an existing obsession is not difficult. Sometimes

it seems to vanish through mere suggestion. These patients attach themselves quickly to the psychologist, and at first prove unexpectedly amenable to his influence. In their hearts they often welcome him as an ally against parents or teachers; they submit to his authority because they hope that it will help them to resist that of their parent or teacher: this is natural, since the first recommendations of the psychologist are that the parent or teacher should give freer rein to the child. As a result, the chief symptom will often yield quickly to suggestion from the psychologist— whether given with or without hypnosis. But unfortunately a new symptom nearly always springs up as soon as the old has been dislodged. And presently it will be discovered that the child is far less accessible to suggestion than was supposed.

In the long run I find that with obsessional cases suggestion proves less effective than with any other form of neurosis. A more radical approach is essential. Sometimes a cure seems to have been achieved and will apparently last for several months. Then the trouble recurs in a slightly different guise. In such instances it often appears that there was a definite periodicity in the neurotic trouble before ever the patient was referred for examination. In a few of the older cases the periodicity has been so marked that a diagnosis of 'circular insanity' or 'manic-depressive insanity' has been recorded. At times the obsessions seem to be definitely associated with notions or feelings of persecution and the like: in fact, to have arisen as a defensive reaction against paranoiac anxieties. In such cases the first step is to deal with the underlying paranoia. Every serious case, therefore, will need prolonged investigation and treatment, preferably along psycho-analytic lines. There is a prevalent notion that psycho-analysis is a form of treatment suited solely for hysteria. In my experience it is far more necessary with obsessional cases, and may here claim its most striking successes.

7. CONVERSION-HYSTERIA

Typical hysteria, in the modern acceptation of the term, is seldom seen before puberty. Of younger children reported as suffering from this complaint, the majority are hysterical only in the popular sense: they are examples of general emotionality, carried to an excessive degree, cases of a constitutional liability to unrestrained excitement in every form and direction; they are, in short, better described not as hysterical children but as unstable children. But on this basis a true hysteria, in the stricter sense of the term, may certainly develop; and in a few the fits of excitement may be so intense, so convulsive, and so peculiar in their nature, that the child is mistakenly thought to be suffering from manic insanity or epilepsy. Women and girls suffer more frequently than men or boys; adolescents than younger children. But my school surveys indicate that the differences in regard to age and sex are much smaller than is popularly supposed: the younger cases and the male cases do not conform so closely to the traditional picture, and so are more readily missed.

The typical symptom of true hysteria is a bodily disturbance which has a purely emotional cause. In this way the functional symptoms of almost any organic disease may be produced. The commonest consist in the loss of movement or sensation—the paralysis of an arm or leg, the loss of speech, sight, hearing, or touch (over a portion of the skin), and, finally, and in some ways most characteristic of all, the loss of memory. A physical examination shows that there is no bodily trouble to account for these peculiarities; and a psychological examination usually succeeds in tracing them to some emotional source. The pent-up emotion, instead of venting itself through the ordinary channels of emotional expression, is, as it were, converted into a physical symptom, which indirectly and unintentionally secures much the same relief or gratification as the more normal expression of the emotion. At first sight the troublesome emotion may seem to have disappeared. The patient is no longer worried, annoyed, resentful, or depressed, but on the contrary happy and at ease. It might almost be imagined that the bodily complaint has taken the place of the mental disturbance: hence the name of substitution-neurosis or conversion-hysteria.

Illustrative Case. Helen, for example, is a girl of 15 who is said to be suffering from a functional paralysis of the right arm. She comes from a secondary school; but her intelligence appears a little below the average of the other girls. Her school attainments are distinctly uneven. She is backward in the more formal subjects—mathematics, Latin, and French; but in English she excels. She is widely read; writes highly imaginative compositions; and is exceptionally good at elocution and dramatic displays—'the best actress in the whole school', says the headmistress.

She is an only child. Her father died soon after her birth; and her mother had to leave the girl very largely in the care of a neighbour—an ex-hospital nurse. While Helen was still at the elementary school, there had been numerous complaints that the mother continually kept her away from her lessons for long periods on the ground of trivial ailments. Indeed, a lengthy correspondence arose between her former headmistress and the mother, because Helen had been absent owing, her mother said, to a broken arm. It turned out that the arm had not been fractured, but only a little twisted and sprained; and the girl was at first supposed to have deliberately told lies about it. The mother, however, excused the child by saying that Helen was 'one of those people who always made a fuss about illness, and it was always difficult to know how bad the child really was'. The headmistress rejoined, not without justice, that 'Helen positively *liked* being ill'. Such remarks are typical of the comments that the hysterical child's behaviour is apt to provoke.

Her school-fellows treated her as peculiar, and were full of fantastic tales. Helen, it seems, had tried to impress them by highly coloured romances about herself and her family— how an aunt had inherited a lot of money and had sent her a real diamond necklace for a birthday present; how an uncle had bought a motor-car and was taking her to Paris for the summer holidays; how she had been to the Derby and actually spoken to Prince George. In class she had become a regular centre of disturbance—constantly making the other girls laugh, subject to fits of uncontrollable giggling herself, varied by spells of motiveless weeping. 'She wants to be for ever in the limelight', said her teacher; 'and, if she cannot

get attention by good behaviour, she is sure to try and attract
it by bad.'

She was eventually referred to me by the school doctor,
who could find no cause for the paralysis from which she
seemed to be suffering. According to her mother, the girl
had woken up one morning, announcing that she thought
her arm had 'broken again': anyhow, she could not possibly
move it. Her own explanation was that one of the girls had
pushed her over in the classroom the day before, and that
the bones had 'come undone'. She had, however, been
groaning about this arm for some weeks past. Apparently it
used to hurt on Mondays, Wednesdays, and Fridays; but on
Sundays, Tuesdays, and Thursdays it was perfectly well;
and on Saturdays it was strong enough for her to take part in
games and hockey matches.

It turned out that on the dangerous days Helen had to go
for lessons in arithmetic and algebra to a mistress whom she
detested. For all forms of mathematics she professed a
hearty dislike; and the family doctor thought such subjects
were a strain for her. His suspicion was true. They were a
strain, not because of their intrinsic difficulty, but because
of the emotional agitation that this particular mistress,
through no fault of her own, unwittingly aroused.

A little inquiry showed that the distaste for mathematics
was of quite recent origin; and it became clear that she hated
the subject because of the mistress, not the mistress because
of the subject. Hence it became important to trace out the
source of this peculiar prejudice. The child could give no
rational explanation, bluntly complaining that she 'loathed
her at sight'.

Now this mistress was a Jewess, named Rebecca—a name
which the school children regularly used of her amongst
themselves. And it so chanced that Helen's nurse was also
a Jewess, with the same first name. The nurse was a gushing,
moody woman—running from extremes of affection to extremes of severity. When Helen was a baby and cried, she
used to soothe and fondle her in ways that were (to put it
very mildly) distinctly injudicious. When Helen sprained
her arm, she was again called in to look after the child; and

once more treated her, so long as she was sick, with a lavish display of affection. Directly the child was well and able to get about, she became harsh and frigid, snubbing the child's insistent claims for continued sympathy and notice. Helen ended by taking a vehement dislike to her; and, on the very first day that she encountered the mathematical mistress, she was irresistibly reminded of this nurse.

When all these details were pieced together from the statements of the mother and the girl herself, Helen's conduct became intelligible. In view of these and other facts, which I need not enter into here, certain adjustments both at home and school were recommended; and finally, as soon as it had been arranged that she might be excused from the mathematical lessons, the paralysis disappeared in a night.

Symptoms. Adult cases of this kind are familiar to every neurologist. They became the subject of frequent discussion and intensive study during the first world war;[1] and it is now generally recognized that, quite unconsciously, physical symptoms of almost any kind—paralysis, contractures, convulsions, anaesthesia, mutism, deafness, partial blindness or night-blindness, amnesia, and the like—may be produced, which will enable the patient to avoid some dreaded duty or to realize some secret wish. It must be emphasized that both the underlying purpose, and the devices by which it is achieved, may be nearly, if not quite, unconscious: the patient is not necessarily shamming or malingering. With children the distinction between conscious and unconscious simulation is harder to draw. Children, owing presumably to the immature organization of their minds, are never quite so conscious, nor yet so completely unconscious, of their deeper motives and desires as adults so often seem to be.

Terman, Guthrie, and most writers on nervous diseases during childhood, declare that such conditions are 'rarely met with in children' and that 'true hysteria does not often develop earlier than 15 to 18 years'.[2] Among the young, it would

---

[1] See, for example, the early volume on *Shell Shock* (1917) by Professors T. H. Pear and G. Elliot Smith.

[2] Cf. Terman, *The Hygiene of the School Child*, p. 303; Guthrie, *Functional Nervous Disorders of Childhood*, p. 257.

seem, these functional disabilities tend to clear up swiftly and spontaneously. As a result they seldom get recorded; and their frequency—which admittedly is not great—is apt to be underestimated. Every now and then, however, a case is sufficiently spectacular to attract official attention; and a number of well-authenticated examples are to be found buried in the reports of school medical officers and in continental journals. Dr. Kerr gives a series of eight short case-histories, from his own personal experience among London schools, in which blindness, tremors, contractures, apparent hemiplegia, alleged dislocation of the hips, inability to stand and inability to write, were miraculously cured by such simple measures as pressing the hand on the forehead or scalp, and assuring the little victim that he would immediately get well.[1] On the other hand, I have known what seemed a functional paralysis to be diagnosed as pure hysteria, and subsequently turn out to be the first symptom of incipient organic disease—tubercular in one case, cerebral in another.

In the very young, certainly, clear cases of true conversion-hysteria are difficult to substantiate. In tiny children such disorders as constipation and loss of appetite may often be easily explained, and successfully treated, as simple forms of conversion-hysteria. Of the more dramatic types the few that I have seen were nearly always associated with some preceding or concurrent disorder of physical or organic origin. I have had a dozen cases of this nature in my notes, most of them, significantly enough, occurring in first-born children. The history is much the same. For several years, as the only youngster in the family, the child has been spoilt and indulged; then he has become jealous of a newly-born brother or sister; later on, during illness or convalescence, he has recovered his original privileges as the chief focus of family interest and attention; and, when he gets better, he seeks to maintain this egocentric situation by prolonging his earlier infirmities and making aggressive bids for sympathy and affection.

In children slightly older, the predisposing complaint seems often to be an accident or injury rather than a disease

[1] *Fundamentals of School Health*, pp. 405 et seq.

—possibly because the shock is more likely to have emotional effects on the child or on his relatives. A child who has broken his thigh will often, when the fracture is quite healed and the leg quite strong, still insist that he is powerless to walk or stand. In one of my cases the boy was supposed to be suffering from hip-disease. He was eventually discharged from the hospital as cured. He showed several unexpected relapses, however; and, on the last occasion, it was found that the disability had unaccountably changed from the right to the left leg. As with Helen, the main symptom had, as its half-unconscious aim, the evasion of certain lessons: while his leg was bad, the boy was excused attendance at a hated class held on the top floor of the school building. Again, a child who has suffered from some ocular defect, and perhaps has had his eye shaded or bandaged for several days or weeks, may still, when the defect has been cured and the shade or bandage removed, complain that he cannot see clearly, or even that he cannot see at all, with the eye that was previously affected.

In my experience instances of this type occur chiefly among children of a somewhat dull intelligence. Taking the whole series of my cases, it would appear that the average mental ratio for hysterics is lower than that for any other neurotic group. This is contrary to the notion prevailing among teachers and many school medical officers; but, as we have seen, they often use the term 'hysteria' in a somewhat anomalous fashion. During the War it was noticed, both here and in America, that true hysterical symptoms occurred more frequently in the private soldier, and anxiety-neuroses in the officer.[1] The bright, imaginative, supernormal child is by no means necessarily exempt; but in her case the complaint generally assumes some more dramatic form and appears at a somewhat later age—most frequently at or just

[1] See, e.g., Rivers, *Instinct and the Unconscious*, pp. 132 and 207; Hollingworth, *The Psychology of the Functional Neuroses*, pp. 80 et seq. It seems almost to amount to a general rule that psychoneuroses, particularly those of a hysterical type, are commoner among those whose intelligence is distinctly below or distinctly above the average than among those who are approximately average. Possibly the bright as well as the dull feel themselves maladjusted to their social environment.

after adolescence. In secondary schools for girls and in training colleges for young women, especially where the strain
of examinations coincides with the crisis of puberty or the
trials of first love, typical hysteria is far more common. Pre-
monitory symptoms, of the same order but milder in degree,
are then often recalled by the relatives.

The typical hysteric seldom looks ill or unhappy. Often
she is plump, rosy-cheeked, with an ever-ready smile. The
woman afflicted with a genuine organic disorder is usually
worried and distressed by her symptoms: the hysteric is
bravely resigned to them, and curiously eager to exhibit them
with a courageous or ingratiating beam on her face. Her attitude towards the most alarming or disabling symptom has
well been called that of *une belle indifférence*. She is usually
of an excitable and demonstrative disposition, a little affected
in her speech and gesture, something of a *poseuse*, and an
arrant lover of the sensational; frequently, with a certain
bland *naïveté*, she conveys, even at the first glance, an impression of strong sexuality.

Her general demeanour is distinctly aggressive. She is,
as a rule, not pugnacious, stubborn, or ill-tempered—indeed,
rather the reverse; yet she yearns to thrust herself forward.
Whenever I hear that favourite description of the teacher—
'she loves to be in the limelight', I begin to suspect hysterical tendencies. Though outwardly self-assertive, the ordinary hysteric is not a personage of strong character. Unlike
the patients who suffer from compulsion-hysteria, the
victims of conversion-hysteria are weak-willed, easily influenced, and highly suggestible. Indeed, it might generally
be said that they are the prey of their own suggestions. At
the earlier stages the process of self-deception can often be
traced. Among children, as I have said, deliberate feigning
and unconscious feigning are not so sharply separated as
with the adult; and often a teacher rightly remarks, 'the girl
has acted her lie so often that she has ended by believing it
herself'. A child who begins with something that is near to
conscious simulation will not infrequently end with genuinely hysterical symptoms.

I may note that among the younger cases a disproportionate percentage are of an alien race or nationality. A number are Jewish, and several Irish. A histrionic disposition is frequent; and in London it is remarked that children belonging to the theatrical profession (and therefore subjected to a special medical examination) seem particularly prone to passing disabilities and symptoms of a purely functional type.

Causation. With all such cases, analysis reveals a predominantly psychical origin for the disorder. Most of them fall under the well-known formula that the symptom is the expression of a wish, or, to speak more accurately, of a conative tendency, that is more or less repressed. The physical disability, thus mentally produced, appears as a kind of unconscious self-defence.

How this comes about in each particular case can only be understood by investigating the past life of the individual patient. It is a familiar law in psychology that, if a complex stimulus provokes a complex reaction, then, on a future occasion, any trivial element which formed part of the original stimulus will be liable to precipitate the complex reaction as a whole. If, for example, a dog is shown a piece of raw meat and a bell is rung at the same time, then, later on, when the bell is rung without the meat being shown, the dog will bark, salivate, and display all the excitement and interest that was formerly aroused by the meat. A newcomer, unacquainted with the dog's previous history, would be puzzled to explain its singular behaviour; he might never even connect it with the bell, much less with the association set up between the bell and the feeding-impulses.

An ill-organized mind—as in the young, the dull, and the emotional—is especially prone to react in this undiscriminating fashion. The hysteric carries the same process to a further degree. He is a martyr to his own associations. He is far more influenced by the past than by the present, and his emotional attitudes are at once infantile and out of date. As a consequence his behaviour always seems ill adapted to current reality. What happens is that some little item or incident in his present life has revived complex conative tendencies dating from a remoter past. The mathematics mistress aroused in Helen an attitude which was more appropriate to her nurse, and could only be understood when the child's early history was recalled.

Now these old conative tendencies can no longer reach their natural fulfilment. They are, as a rule, wholly out of keeping with the child's actual situation. Accordingly, instead of gratifying them directly, he is forced to indulge them in fantasy and day-dreams. Often this unreal life becomes entirely divorced from his conscious life, and his whole mind is split up into separate systems, which function independently. The repressed or dissociated emotions continue their activity, as it were, underground; and sooner or later they rise to the surface again in a form which is more or less disguised. Helen in the end was able to recognize how her mind had been working. Her comments are typical of such processes. 'One day, I thought—"If my arm was bad again, she [the mathematics mistress] would be kind to me: and I don't care if it is bad; it does ache a bit." And then I felt it to see if it hurt, and it did hurt, and the more I thought about it the more it hurt. But then Auntie came in, and she saw what I was doing, and laughed at me. So I didn't think any more about it.'

But why does the repressed emotion eventually relieve itself by this or that particular symptom? What determines the ultimate choice of an outlet? The explanation, I fancy, is to be found in three features which appear in nearly all case-histories of the young.

First, as we have seen, the hysterical child is of a suggestible type. Whether the suggestibility is an innate component of his temperament, or whether it is due to injudicious management during early infancy, we need not discuss; possibly both factors are essential. Whatever its origin, it is one of his characteristic traits. Any idea that is put into his mind tends to be acted out as though it were real. He has only to hear of an ailment or to read of it in a book, and at once he begins to imagine that he himself has got it.

But, further, two additional agencies are nearly always discoverable in the child's social environment, which unwittingly encourage him to change the mental manifestations of his emotions into a physical manifestation, and at the same time determine what that physical manifestation shall be. To begin with, he must necessarily have heard of the physical symptom. Nearly always it turns out that the physical symptom which the child develops has recently been brought to his notice—usually under circumstances distinctly impressive. Sometimes there is a positive fashion in the particular ailment of which the child is complaining. In a residential school, if a boy has died from lockjaw or appendicitis, every matron will relate how half a dozen youngsters come fretting about tiny pains and aches, openly or secretly wondering whether they have not got appendicitis or lockjaw too. Under the influence of 'crowd suggestion', epidemics of imaginary diseases will sometimes spread through whole families or institutions; and when everybody around him seems afflicted in the same way, the thought of the illness naturally obtains a vivid hold upon the child's mind.

A striking example, observed in a London school, will be found recorded in the school medical officer's report. A girl attending Standard II in an East End school, whose left arm was disabled with an infantile palsy, broke the other arm. She was absent for a short period; but, within a few days of her return, three other girls in the same class lost the use of their left arms, and a fourth had such violent pains in her arm that she could do nothing except hold it against her side. The headmistress wrote to the head office asking what was to be done. The school medical officer visited the department, examined the children, and confirmed the obvious diagnosis. By simple suggestion he was able to get all of them to wave their arms freely and without discomfort; and there the matter ended. It was noted that one of the children was very dull and undeveloped in general intelligence; another was somewhat histrionic in speech and manner; and two of them were Poles.[1]

It is on record that a school in Vienna had to be shut for some weeks owing to an epidemic of hiccuping which affected more than half the pupils; another at Budapest was

[1] *Annual Report of the School Medical Officer for Education*, 1907, p. 32.

closed owing to a wave of hysterical coughing which prevented all work in the classrooms; at Wildbad 26 out of 74 pupils were suddenly affected with what appeared to be St. Vitus's dance. And does not every master know how, if one boy faints during church service or an assembly in the hall, half a dozen others may collapse on the floor, or else totter out looking limp and pale?

But if the imaginary complaint is to reach definite and disabling proportions, a third condition is usually requisite. Public opinion must regard the physical symptom as less reprehensible than the mental symptom. The disability produced must be one which is less likely to be scoffed at or disapproved of than the moral or emotional disturbance for which it is a substitute. For example, if a small, delicate, and timorous lad goes to his housemaster, and frankly says: 'Please may I be excused from compulsory games, because I am sure to get hurt if I play football with the bigger and stronger boys', he may become the laughing-stock of his school. If, however, he can say: 'Our doctor says I have a weak heart, like Jones Minor', then he feels he will probably receive not ridicule but sympathy, and perhaps be excused without question. Accordingly, a day or two before he goes back to school, he gets whipped up into a nervous state, and may ultimately succeed in convincing himself, his family, and the family doctor that he is really a victim of cardiac disease.

An incident that arose in the course of a different investigation exemplifies all three influences rather aptly. At a certain orphanage I happened to be studying a small group of four children, all members of the same family, who seemed to be examples of a hereditary albinism, and were afflicted, amongst other troubles, with partial night-blindness. Hearing of my interest in these cases, the headmaster commented on the fact that night-blindness was singularly prevalent among the children at his school. Two other boys, he said, had been officially diagnosed as such, and several other instances had just been reported to him. A few simple tests showed that they were obviously functional cases. In one it proved quite easy to guess what had been happening at the back of the child's mind. The boy had always been terrified of the dark; his fears, however, had been jeered at. A friend of his, another lad in the same school, related how one evening, as they crossed the playground in the twilight, this boy had stumbled and suddenly clutched his arm, calling out that he could not see. This was mentioned to one of the staff, who suggested that in future some one should accompany the lad. In the course of a few weeks the boy came to regard himself as permanently night-blind. Once he had been officially set down as a case of nyctalopia, nobody was tempted to chaff him for being frightened of the dark. The child thus obtained a sympathetic tolerance for his weakness; and, though a coward at heart, was enabled in some measure to preserve his self-respect.

These cases sufficiently illustrate the more obvious factors in hysteria. To discuss the deeper causes, and all the elaborate mechanisms that help to build up the specific symptoms, would be beyond the scope of this volume. It must be sufficient to say that, when thoroughly analysed, nearly every case reveals a lengthy mental history, going back, through years of fantasy and emotional reaction, to the earliest stages of infancy. Apart from temperamental tendencies, the original basis for the disorder seems generally to lie in the ill-adjusted emotional attitude that the patient has taken up, from the very outset of his life, towards the persons in his immediate environment—in the first instance, towards his mother and father and the other members of his family. Thus, more than any other form of neurosis, hysteria consists in a personal maladjustment.

Often the patient still exhibits a childish attitude in his behaviour towards other people. Sometimes this childish attitude lurks in the background and is only revealed after a little exploration of his inner thoughts and motives; sometimes it is so open and conspicuous, leading to constant inanities and puerilities, that he is either accused of literally 'playing the fool' and deliberately 'trying to be funny' or else supposed to be mentally defective. Dullness and imbecility are among the countless complaints that hysteria will sometimes simulate. In such cases the superficial motive is only too obvious: consciously or unconsciously, the patient wishes to be treated like a child.

Regression to an earlier stage of emotional development may thus be a marked characteristic of the hysteric, though, it would seem, the regression is neither so complete nor so influential as in the other sthenic neuroses—the compulsion-neuroses, for example. In conversion-hysteria repression would seem to be a more potent influence than regression: the condition consists essentially in a kind of imaginative gratification, under a more or less distorted guise, of pleasures that have been denied and of desires that have been stifled. Those that are inhibited most commonly are, as we have seen, sexual desires: if the word 'sexual' seems too violent, let us call them desires for personal affection.

Almost all who have investigated such cases thoroughly and at first hand, agree with Freud that what he calls the sexual impulses play a paramount part. Nevertheless, as the more cautious psycho-analysts have insisted, 'one must guard against giving the impression that according to psycho-analysis *all* the factors are sexual'.[1] In practice it is always discovered that these functional symptoms are the outcome, not of one unconscious or instinctive tendency, but of many. What the particular tendencies may be can only be determined by an intensive exploration of each individual case.

Treatment of Hysteria. The treatment of the hysteric is one of the vexed problems of medicine. Many different methods have been advocated in the past. Hardly any have proved satisfactory. Yet nearly all yield beneficial results in certain cases. Hence, as more thorough measures must for long remain beyond the hopes of the large majority of patients, it may be well to review very briefly the various alternatives, if only to point out their serious limitations.

(1) The simplest measure—and still a fairly prevalent one—consists in virtually refusing treatment altogether. The reasons for such a course are well-intentioned. It is argued that the patient, perhaps unwittingly, is trying to make himself ill, or to make himself out to be ill, for the sake of

---

[1] Ernest Jones, *Papers on Psycho-Analysis*, p. 427.

the treatment itself, together no doubt with its incidental advantages—release from work and special sympathy and notice. So long as he receives such treatment, therefore, he will never want to get well. Moreover, so it is said, there is nothing really wrong with him; hence his peculiarities do not call for the intervention of a doctor at all. This is a standpoint often adopted, not only by the physician himself, but also by the patient's relatives or friends. Parents or teachers, for example, will sometimes decline to put the child forward for a medical or psychological examination: such a step, they say, will encourage him to imagine he is ill and to think that his case is interesting; so the best plan is to ignore his eccentricities altogether.

These contentions are not entirely unsound; but they overlook a possible alternative. A child's peculiarities may be quietly studied by the teacher in the classroom without the child becoming aware that he is a centre of any special interest; a patient can even be examined by a psychologist without realizing that any examination has been carried out. And should he recognize the examination for what it is, nevertheless a little tact and experience on the part of the examiner will obviate the evils feared. The same holds good of active measures of treatment: with children at any rate these can generally be so arranged that the patient remains ignorant that any special steps have been undertaken on account of his own behaviour. The arguments, therefore, in favour of a negative attitude are no more convincing here than in other fields of medicine. Whether surgeon, physician, or quack, every inexpert adviser is liable to do more harm than good by actively interposing in a matter he does not understand; but that is no reason for a universal policy of *laissez-faire*.

The more positive therapeutic methods may be grouped under four or five main heads, according to the particular aspect towards which the attack is primarily directed. Some forms of treatment concentrate chiefly on the environmental conditions, others on the physical condition of the patient; others again make straight for the mental factors, but even here one mode of approach may deal mainly with the rational aspects, a second with the emotional, and a third with the moral.

(2) Let us first consider the value of physical treatment, since in the past this has been principally favoured by the medical profession. Of the physical methods many have been frankly adopted for the sake of their mental effects; and are therefore to be classed rather as a form of psychotherapy. For example, a sharp electrical current is applied to the 'paralysed' muscles, not, as the patient imagines, because 'electricity is good for the nerves', but because the dramatic or painful nature of the proceeding may work on the patient's emotions. More particularly, it is argued, if the hysteric is secretly keeping up his illness primarily for the sake of the treatment, then the treatment must be made disagreeable; if illness brings him more annoyance than pleasure, then it is assumed that he will acquire a strong motive for recovering. That such arguments contain at times a modicum of truth is shown by the success of an 'active technique' in psycho-analysis: but, here as elsewhere, the value of such an attitude in this or that particular case is a point to be determined by a study of the case itself. I have known instances where the patient's main incentive seemed a morbid desire for punishment: the more painful the treatment, the more eagerly he welcomed it.

Methods designed to act primarily on physical lines consist mainly in the mitigation of physical symptoms. If, for example, a patient is constipated, not from organic causes but simply in consequence of nervous disturbance, then aperients and similar measures may ease the constipation. But, however complete the success, what is abolished is only a symptom, not the underlying cause. Nevertheless, all effort to alleviate physical symptoms is not necessarily to be renounced. It may be unwise to give morphine for acute appendicitis, but that does not imply that anodynes are everywhere to be banned. Indeed, the temporary relief of bodily disorders may be urgently desirable in order to improve the patient's general health; and, in addition, the relief may itself have a wholesome mental effect.

(3) A commoner type of treatment is that which I have

called environmental. It is repeatedly said—not without justice—that no hysterical patient can properly be treated in his own home, since the presence of his relatives is nearly always deleterious. No doubt one reason for the success of the Weir Mitchell treatment, popular some years ago, was the necessary change in the *entourage* of the patient. The overfeeding, the rest in bed, the massage, the electrical applications, were minor adjuncts: the central feature was to isolate the patient from his ordinary social surroundings. On similar grounds a sea voyage, or a prolonged visit to the country, is often advocated, occasionally with much advantage to the patient. With children beneficial results are often attained by simply transferring the young patient from his family to a convalescent home. And many physicians prescribe such changes automatically in every instance.

Certainly, the first effect is nearly always salutary. What, however, is disappointing, is that patients so often relapse as soon as they go back to the old conditions. With the young, at any rate, the aim should be, not to transplant the child into an easy environment or even to readjust his present environment to suit his special needs, but rather to treat and train him, so that he can face his inevitable difficulties in a more rational way, and support them without losing his mental or moral balance.

Environmental measures, therefore, like physical measures, are to be regarded as accessories only. Hysteria is a psychological condition, and must be dealt with along psychological lines. The essential aim is to improve the mental attitude of the patient.

(4) This may be attempted in three ways. The most obvious is what may be called the intellectual approach. An effort is made to get the patient to see that his conduct is irrational, and to induce him to act for the future in a more reasonable fashion. Much of what is commonly termed *re-education* follows this line of procedure.

The most popular form of it is the method of persuasion. It is based upon the simple principle of appealing to the patients' reason. A successful cure, it is argued, can only result if the patient himself is urged to take an active share in modifying his own mental state. The favourite plan is to arrange a series of what are known as 'therapeutic talks'. Day by day the patient is encouraged to unburden himself of his worries, grudges, and grievances. Hitherto, he has probably kept them to himself, or even implicitly refused to face the fundamental problems in his actual situation. Accordingly, he is induced to focus his mind upon them, and to talk them over one by one with the physician. Together they inquire where precisely the man's difficulties lie, and work out a scheme of action along more intelligent lines. The patient perhaps may be engrossed with the dark and painful side of some particular circumstance; the physician, therefore, tries to paint this circumstance in more attractive colours and draws attention to its brighter features. The various symptoms and their underlying meaning he endeavours to make plain, showing how they have originated in the man's earlier history. He thus gets him to look at all his troubles in a new and clearer light, and, generally, seeks to reason him into a more healthy frame of mind.

Or, in other cases, he may adopt a somewhat different line. He may argue that the patient's difficulties loom too large in his daily thoughts, and may advise him rather to turn his mind away from them and occupy himself with something new. The hysteric is often self-centred and self-absorbed. It seems logical, therefore, to try and engage him in other things, and so broaden his whole outlook upon life. At a public school the morbid boy is urged to take part in games and sport; and at the psychological clinic the old-fashioned rest-cure has now largely given place to the new method of the work-cure. This general plan of side-tracking the patient's attention has been developed systematically with some success in America. A study is made of the patient's special interests and aptitudes; and he is encouraged to take up some congenial occupation—some hobby, some form of manual work, some branch of intellectual study, according to his needs.

Such an approach is only feasible with older and more intelligent patients. With the younger or the less intelligent a different path must be adopted. Efforts at rational persuasion are not likely to be effective. Accordingly, re-education is directed not so much towards the patient's thoughts, as towards his habits. It is recognized that much of the disorder arises from the fact that, owing to events in the patient's past life, certain ideas have become associated in his mind with painful emotions or undesirable impulses. By dint of regular training, it is sought to associate those same ideas with pleasanter emotions or with more rational reactions. The final aim is to substitute a wholesome habit for a morbid one.

The method resembles the process of de-conditioning, on which behaviourists have recently laid so much stress; and it is undoubtedly successful in early stages with the very young. A child of 4 who had been bitten by a dog had developed a morbid fear of dogs in general. By continually connecting dogs with pleasant ideas and experiences, it proved possible to change the child's whole attitude towards them. When, for example, the child was enjoying a meal, a quiet puppy was brought into the room, but first of all kept at a sufficient distance to prevent it from disturbing the child's blissful state. With appropriate modifications, this experiment was repeated day by day until the idea of the dog was automatically associated with pleasant feelings; after a fortnight, the child lifted the puppy on to his lap, and began spontaneously to play with it. I cite this example merely to illustrate the procedure, not to recommend it. Plausible as it sounds, such methods may succeed with a couple of cases, but fail with others of the same outward type. Where a genuine, deep-seated, hysterical complex underlies the morbid reaction, such devices, unless supplemented by other measures, may be worse than useless; but, when intensive therapy has produced a temporary success, a further spell of training may consolidate the results.

For all these various methods conflicting claims are made; and what has been done in the researches on the delinquent should also be attempted in the case of the neurotic. A statistical analysis of case-histories, classified according to cause, treatment, and results, might conclusively demon-

strate what casual experience and *a priori* argument can
never prove. The mere impressions of the specialist are of
little value: naturally he believes in his own method, and
tends to decry the rest.

Where failure has been observed, the reason seems much
the same. As a rule, success can hardly be expected if we
deal solely with superficial symptoms. To implant a new
habit does not necessarily imply that the old has been successfully uprooted. As an overt action the earlier habit may
eventually disappear; but there is no guarantee that the
inner tendency does not still survive. It is like snipping off
the heads of a weed and leaving a live stump in the ground.
Similarly, to divert the patient's attention from his secret
dissatisfaction does not mean that the source of the dissatisfaction has itself been dried up; it may burst out afresh
when he is least expecting it. To reason with him is even
more ineffective: while sitting in the consulting-room he
may see all too plainly the absurdity of his emotions and
fears; but the hysteric, like the vicious, may justly lament:
Video meliora proboque, deteriora sequor.

(5) Many psychologists have consequently suggested that,
since hysteria is a moral rather than an intellectual disorder,
moral rather than intellectual aid is what is really wanted.
This is sometimes taken to mean that the patient's will-
power rather than his power of reasoning requires to be
educated and trained. More frequently it is argued that,
since his own will-power is weak, it must be reinforced by
the will and the moral influence of some one else. Physicians
who have justly claimed outstanding success with this or that
method of treatment often owe their success not to the treatment as such but to the force of their own personality. Accordingly, it is urged that this factor should be more deliberately exploited. The term *suggestion* has come into current
use to describe such effects. Hence, suggestion, it is maintained, instead of being casual and often unintentional, should
be converted into a systematic form of treatment.

With suggestion applied under hypnosis many have obtained almost miraculous results. At the earlier stages it
succeeds better with hysteria than with any other form of

neurosis. Paralyses can be removed, mutism abolished, insomnia relieved. In fact, there is hardly a single physical symptom which will not in most hysterical cases yield quickly to the skill of an efficient hypnotist.

More recently it has been found that much the same therapeutic aims can be achieved with patients in a waking state; nowadays, indeed, it is comparatively rare to find any physician actually hypnotizing his subjects. To reduce a man first of all to a hypnotic trance is often a slow and lengthy procedure, and one that is attended with manifest disadvantages and risks both to the patient and to the physician. But at the same time, though I do not advocate its re-introduction on any extended scale, it seems clear that the hypnotic process itself, and its various effects on mind and body, merit further study and research.

To suggestion, whether applied under hypnosis or during the waking state, the great drawback is the transient nature of the results. In a few cases, it is true, the benefits derived have apparently been permanent. Nevertheless, in the experience of most physicians and psychologists, there is a marked tendency for those who have been treated in this way to relapse. That is only to be expected when the true nature of the process is understood.

The old explanation of hypnosis is too simple. Formerly it was supposed that merely to introduce an idea into the mind, when the mind was in an uncritical and drowsy state, was sufficient for that idea automatically to work itself out in action or belief. Suggestion, however, is in its essence an emotional process. The main factor is the *rapport* or emotional attachment which the patient develops, sometimes at first sight, sometimes as a gradual outcome of the weekly or daily contact, for the physician himself. It is, in fact, a special form of what Freud has termed 'transference'. By transference is meant the carrying over of emotion from one person to another. In its various guises it may prove an effective help in treatment, and also a most troublesome hindrance. The patient perhaps has already built up a sentiment or system of emotions about the thought of an ideal personality. During childhood this idealized person is naturally the child's own father or mother. As he grows older and more independent, however, he comes into constant collision with his parents' desires; they no longer seem so near to perfection; little by little he is made painfully aware of their foibles and shortcomings. Soon he begins unconsciously to yearn for a more adequate object for his love and admiration. If, therefore, a physician, a schoolmaster, or a priest, in virtue of his prestige and his sympathy, appears as a fit target for this sentiment, the sentiment may be projected on to him. For the time being, the patient's emotional life runs more smoothly; and his course of action seems more easy because it is determined by the supposed demands of the new ideal.

Such a transference may be observed in diverse forms and in various degrees. It may be noted, for example, that, quite apart from any explicit or authoritative suggestion, most neurotic patients feel better when some person for whom they have a genuine regard takes a deep and sympathetic interest in them, just as others improve when they fall happily in love, or have a child of their own on whom they can centre their thoughts and feelings. Too often, however, as the physician may discover to his cost, the apparent improvement of the patient simply means that he has substituted a fresh symptom for the previous ones, the attachment itself being in many cases nothing more than a hysterical manifestation.

It is said that Breuer, who originally collaborated with Freud discontinued his work on account of the embarrassment thus caused. One of his women patients, towards the end of a prolonged treatment, declared that she could not part from her physician because she had fallen violently in love with him. Breuer concluded that the new method was dangerous for the practitioner, and made it difficult for him to maintain a strictly professional attitude. The risk is certainly a real one, unless the physician himself has been psycho-analysed and so is able to cope with his own emotional situations.

It is important, therefore, to inquire when suggestibility or transference may be safely fostered as a step towards a permanent cure. In my own experience I have found it more efficacious in delinquent than in neurotic cases. But even here there is a distinction. Some delinquents—those that might popularly be described as of a selfish or narcissistic type—are so much in love with themselves that they are incapable of attaching themselves to any other person, and indeed have never done so. With these, suggestion is commonly useless. With neurotics or psychotics showing persecutory symptoms failure is almost inevitable: the explanation presumably is that such patients have sunk back to, or never advanced beyond, the early infantile stage in which their emotional satisfactions are sought solely in connexion with their own persons.

With hysterical and with obsessional cases a *rapport* is readily produced. But what is really needed is not so much a displacement or retransference of the patient's ruling sentiments, but a reorganization of them. If, therefore, the patient is intelligent and old enough for a thoroughgoing analysis of his motives, this should always be undertaken. Where this more radical method seems impracticable—as in the very young, the very dull, the definitely defective, and, it may be added, the aged and infirm—suggestion may be advisedly tried. Where, too, the neurotic manifestation is simply a temporary and minor complication of some serious physical malady, in which perhaps the patient's attitude of mind may play a critical part—for example, in short and painful fevers like that of pneumonia, or in diseases requiring an operation that may incidentally involve shock—there, too, suggestion, with or without hypnosis, may prove highly beneficial. But in the ordinary cases of psycho-neurosis, suggestion, like the other modes of treatment that I have mentioned, must be regarded as an incidental adjunct, not as a sole or self-sufficient method: the defect of all of them is that they deal merely with one subordinate aspect of the case.

(6) A more radical treatment, as I have already implied, is that which is now generally known as *psycho-analysis*. Here it will be impossible to discuss in detail the principles on which this form of therapy depends, or to weigh its

advantages and limitations. Briefly it may be said that it is based on the view that hysterical symptoms are the end-result of an elaborate mental structure which for the most part has been built up unconsciously. Like all mental structures that enter as ingredients into the formation of the personality, such a structure has its roots in the earliest years of childhood. It is not an intellectual structure: it does not consist of thoughts, beliefs, or consciously accepted ideals. It is rather a dynamic or emotional structure that has grown out of the primitive instincts which the patient, like every human being, has inherited. The patient has made an effort to adjust these emotional impulses to the conditions of his everyday life, but the effort has been un-satisfactory and the adjustment incomplete. The physician has to discover its special points of weakness, and then help the patient to substitute a new and better adjustment for the old misfit which has brought him to his present plight.

Generally speaking, the defects of the original adjustment are due to the fact that it has been a blind, unconscious product rather than a conscious and a rational product, and that the instinctive tendencies have been simply driven underground instead of being allowed an enlightened and intelligently modified outlet.

The method suggested by Freud for dealing with these difficulties has itself undergone several changes. In the original form the prime object was to work down to the repressed emotion, and permit the pent up-energy to escape. It was at first assumed that the hysterical symptom had its origin in some early emotional shock which itself had been forgotten, owing to the effect of the immediate repression. Under hypnosis it proved often possible to transport the patient back into the situation or the mental state in which the symptom first arose. If in this condition the patient was encouraged to talk out his emotional difficulties, then it was found that his attitude became more normal. Often, when these forgotten experiences were revived, the patient would at once react in a violently emotional fashion. The impression given was that he was in this way discharging the accumulated energy and thus at last relieving an abnormal mental tension. As a result, the hysterical symptoms seemed, for the time being at any rate, to disappear. The principle was not entirely new. The idea that the mind is eased by working off, and purging itself, as it were, of any unwholesome excitement is as old as Aristotle; and Aristotle's term has been adopted to designate this therapeutic process. It is commonly described as the 'cathartic method'.

Further experience, however, showed that in many cases the relief was only temporary. It was as though a superficial abscess had been lanced, while an internal focus of infection had been left unnoticed. A fuller study made it clear that the supposed emotional shock marked but one phase in the development of the neurotic symptom, sometimes indeed an imaginary one. The growth of the emotional complex proved to be due, not merely to one or two isolated external events, but to a long inward process involving conflict, brooding, fantasy, day-dreaming, gradual habit-formation, and unconscious readjustments of many different kinds. A more elaborate technique was therefore called for.

Accordingly, the attempt to get rapidly back to the original situation through hypnotic revival was abandoned. It was found more effective to work slowly down to causal tendencies by the method of free association. Instead of being hypnotized, therefore, the patient is merely required to recline in a passive, uncritical state, and allow his mind to play around the topics suggested by his symptoms. He is required to utter every idea that rises to his mind, just as it comes, however irrelevant, nonsensical, or distasteful it may seem. The starting-point may be either the obvious symptoms for which he is primarily seeking treatment, or some other manifestation of his unconscious mental processes, for example his dreams or some slight but typical example of his mental inefficiency—a slip of the tongue or a lapse of memory. The theory is that if symptom A is associated, more or less mechanically and more or less indirectly, with the emotional complex Z, then the train of associations should work backwards as well as forwards; and thus the patient, allowing his thoughts to ramble on mechanically, will probably be guided by the unconscious connexions in his mind to the powerful complex of emotions that is so largely governing his personal reactions.

But this is by no means a complete explanation of the process; for, in the course of such work, it becomes amply clear that the unconscious nature of the linkage is not entirely explained by the fact that the linkage is mechanical. The psychologist often talks of unconscious mechanisms; but such mechanisms must not be regarded as purely mechanical in any literal sense. They consist not of passive machinery, but of active forces: they are more like insistent desires or wishes than lifeless pieces of clockwork. The patient's memories and motives are forgotten, not because a chain of associations is accidentally interrupted, but because they have been actively repressed; and they have been actively repressed because they are unpleasant in themselves, and wholly out of harmony with the aims and ideals of the man's main personality. The force which originally repressed these memories is still alive, and is continually experienced by the physician as a kind of resistance, preventing him from probing down to the painful tissue underneath.

The first effort of the therapeutic work, therefore, consists in seeking out and overcoming these resistances. Only when these have been overcome, one after the other, is it possible to explore the real nature of the older and deeper processes which have led to the neurotic disorder. It should be noted that the physician does not carry out the investigation by himself, and then present the patient with the results of his deductions. By a gradual and indirect approach, the patient himself must be led to understand the origin and meaning of his symptoms.

Psycho-analysis is thus not to be considered as a mere specific for certain kinds of disease. It is based on the sound scientific principle of discovering the cause before proceeding to the cure. And the special merit of psycho-analytic therapy is that, unlike all the preceding methods of treating nervous disorder, it lays bare the aetiology of each case.

Probably several factors play an important part in the cure. Transference and suggestion, no doubt, are operative, particularly at certain stages. Further, the fact that the patient himself becomes conscious of his secret motives and understands his deeper impulses makes it easier for him to deal with them unaided along more rational lines. Perhaps, too, the mere working off of pent-up emotion may itself have a wholesome effect. The main result, however, is to overcome the unconscious resistances and obstructions, and so to divert into useful and wholesome channels the misdirected energy which hitherto has found its only outlet in the production of hysterical symptoms.

Just because it is far-reaching in its aims, a psychoanalytic treatment is inevitably lengthy and expensive. Moreover, there are few physicians who are competent to carry it out along scientific lines. From what has already been said, it must be obvious that psycho-analysis is not a method to be lightly undertaken by the amateur, whether medically qualified or not. No one should attempt to apply it unless he has been analysed himself and has had at least two years' intensive study and practice under competent supervision. Since few persons will be able to take the double qualification—in general medicine and in the special psychological technique, there is much to be said for the plan of employing lay analysts, properly trained, who may work under proper psychiatric guidance. Even so, a full treatment will be available for but a small proportion of the cases. It may be added, however, that, where systematic treatment is out of the question, simple advice given by a physician versed in the principles of psycho-analysis may still be of the greatest practical benefit to a patient.

But, even in those cases that are sufficiently serious to require a radical form of treatment, the end is not accomplished when resistances have been overcome or fuller insight achieved. The graver the breakdown, the more essential it becomes to remould and rebuild the broken personality. This final step is too often neglected. I have found it instructive, in collecting after-histories of the pupils referred to this or that child-guidance clinic, to inquire why one case has apparently made a complete recovery while others have relapsed or degenerated still further. With the failures, I find, the treatment undertaken has, as a rule, been merely therapeutic (in the narrower sense): conflicts and obsessions may have been temporarily removed, but no firm habits imparted. With the successful cases there has almost always been a subsequent period of retraining, perhaps without any explicit recognition of the process as such on the part of the psychiatrist, the psychologist, or the parent. Often, when the physician has failed, the teacher, aided by his own professional knowledge of the needs of a growing personality and the best methods for guiding it, has proved unexpectedly successful. Thus, in the treatment of emotional or neurotic disorders of whatever type, as in the treatment of moral disturbances, by far the most essential measure is re-education. Both defects are at bottom defects of character; and character, whether good or bad, is made or remade by the processes of habit-formation. 'Our nervous system', says Carpenter, 'grows into the modes in which it has been exercised.'[1]

It is too frequently supposed that the education of the child is solely concerned with instructing his intellect, and that learning means consciously memorizing certain facts, ideas, and intellectual processes. Yet the special claim of English education at its best has been its emphasis on the education of character. British psychologists, from Hume to McDougall, have always insisted that emotions can be trained as well as abilities. Character-training is itself a scientific process; and much has been done by psychological research to discover the most efficacious procedures. Here it would scarcely be possible even to summarize, let alone to explain, the various devices likely to prove effective with

[1] *Mental Physiology* (1874), p. 345: quoted by James in his famous sermon on habit-formation, who adds that the moral of Carpenter's 'law of neural habit' is 'to make the nervous system your ally, not your enemy' (*Principles of Psychology*, i, chap. iv). Carpenter himself (p. 352) rightly emphasizes that the greater part, and the most effective part, of all moral education, whether it be self-education or education externally imposed, is *unconscious* education: those who imagine that the importance of unconscious mental processes was first emphasized by Freud might well refer to Carpenter's whole discussion of the subject (op. cit., chap. xiii).

this or that type of personality, or how such methods should be selected and adapted according to the age, intelligence, temperament, and social background of the individual child. It must suffice to point out that the requisite procedures will not be just those which tradition or common sense might suggest; they call for special knowledge, special skill, and special experience.[1] During the earlier stages the training will be negative rather than positive: bad habits will have to be broken, before better habits can be implanted. But the ultimate aim will be to reconstruct a harmonious and fully integrated personality. 'The health of the soul', says Robert Louis Stevenson, 'demands unity of purpose, not the dismemberment of men; it requires that each shall live, not in the pursuit of broken ends or a continual see-saw of passion and regret, but by the gradual reconciliation of conflicting tendencies in some great and comprehensive purpose, resolving the disharmony like notes in a satisfying chord.'

Notes and References

For a detailed discussion of the conditions dealt with in this chapter see Ernest Jones, *Treatment of the Neuroses* (2nd ed., 1932). Since the best known works of Janet and Freud were concerned with hysterical states, the neuroses that first attracted attention were what I have called sthenic disorders: asthenic conditions occupy only about one-tenth of Jones's book.

During the First World War 'the great majority of war-neuroses were' (as he observes) 'cases of hysteria'; and it was chiefly this that turned the interest of British psychiatrists to psycho-analytic theories. During the Second War, however, it was rather cases of an anxiety type that called for study: and these after all are far commoner and more obvious. As a result, the sthenic type of neurosis has been of late unduly neglected; and a large number, particularly in schools, now tend to go undetected.

For reviews of more recent developments in these and related fields of work, see *Modern Trends in Psychiatric Medicine* (1948, edited by N. G. Harris). One important 'modern trend', however, appears to have been overlooked, namely, the increasing tendency to interpret and treat such conditions from a biological rather than a purely pathological standpoint. This is largely due to the influence of the disciples of Adolf Meyer and his eclectic

---

[1] I endeavoured to formulate the essential psychological principles in a paper on 'The Development and Training of Emotions in Children' (*School Hygiene*, vii, pp. 1–14). A more general account of the process will be found in Sir Percy Nunn's *Data and Principles of Education*—a work which is specially valuable for its annotated references at the end of each chapter.

school of 'psychobiology'. See A. Lief, *The Commonsense Psychiatry of Adolf Meyer* (1948), and Meyer's own papers, esp. 'The Scope and Teaching of Psychobiology', *J.Ass. Amer. Educ. Coll.* x, pp. 93f. Meyer himself traces the origin of the biological standpoint to earlier British psychologists: cf. his Maudsley Lecture on 'British Influences in Psychiatry', *J. Mental Science*, lxxix, pp. 435–63.

In addition to the works already cited the advanced student may profitably refer to O. Fenichel, *The Psychoanalytic Theory of Neurosis* (1945), McV. Hunt (ed.), *Personality and the Behaviour Disorders*, and R. I. Watson and I. N. Mensh, 'The Evaluation of the Effects of Psychotherapy', *J. Psychol.* xxii, pp. 259–91.

VIII

ASCERTAINMENT AND INCIDENCE

VIII

ASCERTAINMENT AND INCIDENCE

I HAVE now briefly reviewed the main directions in which psycho-neurotic disturbance manifests itself. It will be observed that, in this new field of medicine, we have to deal, not with a well-defined list of independent diseases, but with a number of disorders that melt and merge into one another, and may be encountered with almost every degree of intensity. At the same time, however, there is a marked disposition towards grouping. Certain characteristics go hand in hand and form classifiable types. And the grouping, no doubt, is due partly to the fundamental correlations between various mental processes, and partly to the tendency of the mind itself towards habitual self-consistency and internal self-organization.

Having surveyed the outstanding features in each of these broad types, we can now see what various symptoms should be looked for in diagnosing any particular case, and what is their probable import or significance. How are the symptoms to be detected? As in investigating other aspects of the individual mind, the physician may, in theory at any rate, follow two lines of approach: he may rely either on the method of observation, or else on the method of experiment, that is, of specialized tests. In discussing experimental work on the normal temperament, we learnt to be somewhat sceptical of tests for emotional characteristics. Accordingly, let us first of all consider how far systematic observation will carry us.

1. *Observational Methods.* To begin with let me repeat what I emphasized at the outset—that the study of any individual personality must be based on an adequate knowledge of the general structure of the mind. Hitherto the psychology of mental abnormality has developed in almost complete isolation from the psychology of normal mental processes. Perhaps the greatest defect in present-day psychiatry is the fact that, unlike other branches of medi-

cine, it rests on no generally agreed or scientifically established theory of the structures and functions with which it deals. Hence its procedures are little more than plausible or fashionable improvisations based partly on personal experience and partly on the speculations of this or that particular school.

To be at once reliable and comprehensive our observations of the patient must systematically cover every aspect of his mental life. In practice they will comprise, first, what the patient himself has felt or observed, so far as he is able to communicate it to the physician; secondly, what has been noted by relatives, acquaintances, or social workers, and is embodied in their formal or informal reports; and finally, what the physician is able to observe at first hand, as he questions and studies the patient by the bedside or in the consulting-room.

Where possible, it is always desirable to check the patient's own account by reports from other observers. Sometimes a highly strung person will come full of extraordinary complaints of maltreatment; and these may be set down as symptoms of an unbalanced mind or a perverted judgement: later, inquiries from acquaintances will disclose that the man's statements were fully justified. In almost every case, as we have seen, a nervous disorder generally arises as a reaction to a personal or social situation; and frequently it is the situation that has to be diagnosed and treated, rather than the patient. Hence, in order to understand the causes, and still more in order to suggest the appropriate treatment, the social and personal factors will have to be explored, and the conditions at home or at business should, whenever practicable, be independently ascertained.

In diagnosing physical illness there used to be a common hospital maxim, quoted to the young student in the wards: 'Examine the patient for yourself, but do not listen to what the patient says.' In diagnosing nervous disorders, 'what the patient says', together with what his statements imply and what they significantly pass over, may be of the utmost importance. Paradoxically enough, patients of an inhibited type, once their confidence is gained, will usually unbosom themselves quite freely, and attempt a frank and detailed story of their mental troubles; on the other hand, those of a self-assertive type—patients suffering from obsessions and compulsions, for example—will often hold back the most relevant and crucial facts, and, after expounding their own notion of the case in assured and authoritative tones, close up like a sphinx when cross-questioned.

To base diagnoses on the results of an interview and on incidental observation may sound a precarious procedure. Two essentials are requisite for reliability and success. First, before he can judge whether the mental traits of a given individual amount to an indication of abnormality, the interviewer must have had a wide acquaintance with persons of varying types, both normal and abnormal. Secondly, he must himself possess those gifts of tact, sympathy, and imaginative insight which will enable him at once to win his patient's confidence and to guess when his patient is failing to confide. Many physicians will aver that it is impossible, in the space of half an hour's interview, to determine whether a man is suffering from a neurosis. The retort is easy: possibly the critics themselves never could. But there are others who have a singular knack of extracting from a stranger, in the course of the first few minutes, his most intimate thoughts and feelings. Personally I believe that both the requisites I have named can be developed by experience and instruction. I do not suggest that these will teach a man to decide the extent, the origin, or even the precise nature of a nervous malady from a single consultation. But certainly the trained expert seldom finds it difficult to determine whether or not the patient is neurotic—whether, that is to say, he shows symptoms sufficiently marked to warrant psychotherapeutic study and treatment.

In observing the patient himself, the points to be noted may be classified under two or three main heads. The general procedure I have already outlined in discussing the examination of temperament in normal persons. I assume that the physician has already listened to the patient's own story, has traced the superficial history of the case, and has made whatever physical examination he considers essential.

He will next review each of the several emotions and instincts in succession, seeking to determine whether any of them, or all of them, are exhibited in an irrational fashion or with an abnormal intensity or strength. In the laboratory or the playroom the psychologist can often stage-manage a series of lifelike situations which act as experimental stimuli to the more important emotions; but in the consulting-room a simpler procedure is generally desirable. It is the personal emotions—the patient's reaction to other human beings— that are of greatest moment. Now an interview with a doctor of itself involves just such a personal situation; it will, therefore, to a large extent reveal how the patient reacts to the remarks and the treatment of other people. For the rest, it is not difficult, in tactful conversation, to lead the patient, more or less systematically, through a set of hypothetical situations such as would arouse the symptoms most commonly encountered in neurotic persons.

All the time the physician will unobtrusively watch the outward and visible manifestations of each feeling as it is stimulated by his questions, criticisms, or sympathetic comments. Already he will have noted the man's habitual mood, so far as it reveals itself in the ordinary cast of his countenance. The patient who suffers from an anxiety-state often betrays it at first sight by the worried frown upon his brow.[1] The hysteric, on the other hand, as we have seen, is often characterized by *une belle indifférence*: she boasts of her physical troubles with a smile, and relates how her right hand is paralysed, or her left side becoming more and more insensitive, as though it was a most interesting pheno-menon, one which she is pleased to exhibit, but which does not ruffle her in the least—an attitude so different from that of a sufferer genuinely stricken with some organic disease.

Every emotion has its instinctive expression in outward movement: it produces facial changes, alterations in the voice, peculiarities of bodily posture and action. Hence a swift survey should be first directed towards these several

---

[1] In view of a common mistake, it is worth while noticing that a similar fixed corrugation often arises as a result of some long-standing defect of vision, and some experience is required to discriminate the two.

points. Are the man's facial reactions exaggerated and spasmodic, or are they automatically controlled and concealed by a strained and inexpressive mask? Is his voice peculiar—loud, high-pitched, marked by over-vivacious inflections? Or is it reduced to a flat inanimate monotone or a dull and husky whisper? Is his speech inordinately voluble, or curt and reluctant, confined to evasive or monosyllabic replies? Are his movements jerky, jumpy, or ill-controlled, so that his gait, his handshake, and his general demeanour all leave an impression of something eccentric? Are the organic accompaniments of emotion over-active— is he liable to excessive blushing, sudden pallor, a sweating of the brow or palms, an intermittent breathlessness, or an accelerated pulse?

Next, the physician will inquire into the inner working of the emotions as disclosed by the answers of the patient himself. Does he complain of being abnormally depressed and miserable, or, what is equally significant, does he profess an abnormal cheerfulness and optimism? Is he discontented with his work, and, if so, what conditions chiefly annoy him? Is he sociable or solitary? How does he get on with his superiors, with his equals, with his subordinates? Is he immoderately timid or shy? Is he thrown into a paroxysm of fear by some perfectly natural event in his everyday life—for instance, being called up for an interview by his chief? Does he suffer from disquieting nightmares? Does he start or tremble at unexpected sounds? Is he excessively irritable or bad-tempered, excessively assertive or excessively submissive? Is his sex-life normal?

Then again, how far are his various emotions built up into stable interests or sentiments? What are his relations with his parents, his wife, his children, and his friends? Has he any hobbies, favourite games, or petty vices? How does he occupy his leisure hours? And finally, what is the man's attitude towards himself—is he inordinately satisfied or dissatisfied with his character, his conduct, his achievements?

Emotions, however, show their influence not only by the

feelings that they immediately produce, not only by their outward physical expression, but also by the way in which they influence intellectual operations. Hence, having first of all gauged by intelligence-tests or other means how far the man is capable of rational thought and action, the psychologist proceeds to observe whether this capacity is thrown out of gear by the intrusion of emotional impulses. This may mean briefly exploring the man's views and judgements in nearly all the chief fields of everyday life. In particular, if the patient can be persuaded to relate in detail either his dreams or his daydreams, it will frequently be found that, without any further analysis, their content may suggest, not only the emotions to which he is specially prone, but also the conflicts and complexes from which he is predominantly suffering, and the topics or situations that form the active centre of disturbance.

Most of these preliminary points may be elicited in a kind of confidential chat. The inquiries will be thrown into a diplomatic shape, and the questioning will be indirect rather than blunt or point-blank. Generally the experienced interviewer contrives to introduce a series of stock questions that he has found to suit his own method of address and cover the ground most effectively.

The next step is to look for those definite symptoms which, though trivial in themselves, are known to be associated with certain morbid tendencies. Mental abnormality, as we have seen, is generally a matter of degree. Hence symptoms which in their most flagrant manifestations are distinctive of serious psychotic or neurotic disorders are found in slighter forms among the milder cases.

For example, one characteristic of the insane is the way in which they project their feelings out on to their environment. In a minor degree all of us tend to do that. With the neurotic and the psychopathic the tendency is so insistent that it colours all their remarks, and even their relatives and fellow workers begin to comment on it. A typist comes to work in an emotional state; her typescripts that day are full of errors; but this she attributes not to her own unstable wood but to some imaginary busybody who, she insists, must have been tampering with her machine. Or again, she complains that she 'can never understand her supervisor's instructions, because the supervisor is such an ignorant person', and that 'nobody in the office ever grasps what I say, because they are such a dunder-headed lot'. At first the examiner may feel that nothing short of a series of psychological tests applied to all concerned would show who was most lacking in intelligence—the typist or the other members of the staff. But when every little misadventure is ascribed to the stupidity, the spite, or the secret jealousy of those around her, never to her own shortcomings, the examiner begins to suspect a mental mechanism analogous to that which, in more serious cases, leads to a delusion of persecution; and he determines to probe the case more thoroughly.

Very often the symptoms will not be brought to light by direct, straightforward questioning, since the patient hardly recognizes them as abnormal; but she may casually mention them in discussing her habits of work or of domestic routine. It is a peculiarity of many highly strung persons that they cannot continue their work if there is the least noise in the room, or if another person is standing behind them, presumably watching them at their task. Some cannot bear to work alone; others again cannot work unless they are alone. The degree to which different people are put out by such circumstances varies considerably; and only prolonged experience will show where to draw a rough line between what is irrational and what is not.

A senior student of mine was examining in my presence a young journalist, who was obviously a neurotic subject. 'Are you ever haunted by thoughts which keep coming back to you?' the student asked. The reply was 'No'. 'Are you worried by doubts of any sort?' The answer was 'No, except in regard to religion when I was a lad of 16: but I soon got over that.' Later on the patient was asked whether he slept well. 'Oh yes, when I settle down: but that usually takes some time.' 'How do you mean?' 'Well, I can never remember whether I've raked out the fire and turned out the gas. Nearly every night I have to get out of bed three or four times to make quite sure.' Asked whether any complaints were ever made about his daily work, he replied: 'No, except once or twice for unpunctuality. Last week the editor said I could never send in my copy to time. You see, I get so engrossed in whatever I have on hand that I can never feel it is really finished. If I sent it in too hurriedly, I should have to ask for it back for final corrections.' Here is a man who would deny that he had any obsessions, compulsions, or morbid doubts; and yet, as he describes his life at home and at his office, it is clear that he presents a familiar example of mild psychoneurosis. One or two little idiosyncrasies such as I have just quoted might have but small significance; but in this case indirect inquiry gradually revealed half a dozen analogous incidents that had occurred in less than a fortnight.

Nothing short of a detailed and verbatim narrative of a hundred interviews along various lines could show how such symptoms may be elicited through tactful, patient cross-examination—through a process of slow and sympathetic questioning which gleans the necessary data by oblique approaches from countless different angles. But a few first-hand demonstrations would be worth more than a thousand pages of print. Is it too much to ask that every medical student should watch at least one patient being psychologically tested and at least one clinical study of a psychoneurotic case? It is commonly objected that, with nervous as distinct from physical ailments, it is impracticable to allow students to assist at the physician's examination. Elsewhere I have tried to show that this notion is altogether unfounded, and that, provided the cases are carefully selected and simple precautions observed, it is quite easy to demonstrate the method of approach, without distressing the patient or endangering the object of the interview. In any event, there is one demonstration that the instructing physician can always give: he can treat the student himself as a case; he can subject him to a series of clinical interviews, as though actually being treated for his own minor disabilities; and then explain the reason for this or that question or this or that mode of procedure. For the rest, I recommend the beginner to try his own hand by studying a single case or so in the fullest and minutest detail. Later, after he has spent a hundred hours exploring three or four different patients, he will discover how to reduce his examination to ten or twenty hours, and then, with further practice, perhaps to no more than one or two.

It must, however, be understood that, in briefly suggesting the foregoing method of approach, I have not sought to lay down a plan for investigating each individual case in all its particulars; I have merely tried to sketch a rough technique for the first exploratory interview. The detailed investigation can be carried out by none but the fully trained specialist. The preliminary consultation aims merely at discovering whether there is a case for further examination and psychotherapeutic assistance; and that will be a question which every general practitioner will from time to time be called upon to decide.

2. *Experimental Methods.* Yet even for these provisional and tentative diagnoses some more objective standard is badly wanted. The need is most evident in those inquiries that seek to make a census of neurotic complaints among various sections of the population; but for the private practitioner likewise some general guide is desirable: else how is he to tell what number or what gravity of symptoms will suffice to indicate that a particular patient requires special study and treatment? The specialist relies on his personal experience of a vast number of cases; but the non-specialist, particularly at the outset of his professional career, has seen only a few typical samples, and those no doubt in a highly advanced stage. We have learnt to appreciate the importance of standardization for intellectual defects. There, as we have noted, the mere observation of symptoms might serve to show whether or not a person is subnormal in intellectual capacity or attainment, but would never, except after long experience, suffice to establish whether the subnormality was severe enough to make special school provision advisable in the case of a child, or, in the case of an adult, to prevent the man from making a tolerable social and economic adjustment. If I am right in contending that neurosis is a matter of degree,

the same doubts must arise over temperamental troubles. How, then, are we to lay down borderlines for the various grades of gravity in neurotic disorders?

The obvious solution would be to supplement observational methods by experimental, and to base the standards or borderlines upon test-results. Unfortunately for the general examination of the normal temperament there is, as we have seen, hardly a single test simple enough and reliable enough to be used for practical work. On the other hand, with neurotic and psychotic cases a good deal of experimental research has recently been carried out; and certain somewhat novel tests, which show little significant variation within the normal range, nevertheless yield promising results when used for the more extreme abnormalities. It is conceivable that, in the near future, methods of a newer type may be devised which may claim at least the accuracy of the Binet-Simon scale during its earlier phases.

Even without formal testing a good deal may be done. With tiny children it is quite easy to arrange standard situations such as may call forth typical reactions. Gesell and others have shown how this procedure may be applied to secure norms for intelligence during the first three or four years of life; and investigations at present in progress prove that the same principle can be adapted to obtain standards for emotional reactions during the same and subsequent periods. Every child-guidance clinic has or should have a children's play-room; and here the toys, apparatus, and general conditions can usually be arranged so as to afford ample opportunities for quietly experimenting with the temperamental peculiarities of each young patient, without the patient being aware that he is undergoing any special examination or test. I do not mean that the experimenter should seek deliberately to provoke the child's passions or fears. Free play with suitable objects, if the objects are carefully selected and the mode of play recorded by the play-room workers, will often reveal his chief emotional tendencies and throw much light on his private fantasies.

Along these lines it should eventually be practicable to draw up a kind of age-scale of typical emotional reactions for every year of child life, similar to the descriptive norms drawn up for the intelligence of the pre-school child. To a large extent, the behaviour of the child who is temperamentally subnormal resembles that of a child who is considerably younger than himself. And thus, the notion of a temperamental age becomes of great assistance in formulating borderlines for diagnosis.

With older children pictures may be substituted for actual situations, and time and trouble saved. By this means a number of camouflaged tests can be devised, in which provocative scenes, jokes, or anecdotes are submitted to the subject and his responses noted. The child, for example, may be simply asked to arrange a set of pictures in a row in order of preference; and, if the pictures have been appropriately chosen, the results may be most illuminating.

With adults, still more abbreviated methods have been tried. The obvious plan is to describe each situation, and simply ask the subject how he would react. This leads to the familiar expedient of the questionnaire. All the different lines of interrogation that I have outlined above could easily be reduced to a series of systematic questions, and embodied in a printed list.[1] In point of fact, several questionnaires of this type have been drawn up and employed as written tests. One of the earliest and best known is that adopted for detecting neurotic tendencies among recruits during the war. Usually the examinee is required to reply, not in his own spontaneous phraseology, but simply by underlining alternative answers which are put down in the test-sheet. Sometimes he has merely to mark words which are connected in his mind with unpleasant thoughts or feelings—with some personal worry or dislike: of this latter type the Pressey X-O tests, as they are called, are probably the most widely used.

At best, however, such questionnaires are suitable only for a crude preliminary investigation of large numbers at

[1] As this is one of the most instructive of existing tests for the purpose —at once more trustworthy and more practicable than the so-called 'objective tests of personality' requiring special apparatus—and since it may prove suggestive to those who know little of the types of symptom to be sought for, I print a sample in the appendix (see pp. 369-76).

once. In the laboratory they have at times been found helpful for supplementary inquiries in researches upon other
problems and for the training of students engaged in
medical, social, or educational psychology. Carefully modified, so as to avoid suspicion or offence, they can even be
employed to make a rough census of neurotic cases in surveys
of schools, large factories, public offices, and the like, and
to pick out particular cases needing intensive examination
and treatment. But they suffer from the most patent disadvantages. And for private work they are to my mind of
little or no value. However skilfully the real trend of each
question may be veiled, the individual patient is apt to be
suspicious, reticent, or deliberately secretive. And in unscientific hands I have seen such interrogatories naïvely used
in the crudest and most ludicrous fashion.

Accordingly, instead of point-blank questions about
feelings and emotions, recent investigators have preferred
more indirect methods. Of these the most celebrated is the
old associative reaction. The procedure differs with different
investigators. The two chief forms are the 'continuous'
and the discontinuous or 'discrete'. With the 'discrete'
procedure a standardized list of words is called out, one
after the other, and the patient is required to reply, as
promptly as possible, with the first word that each suggests
to his mind. The time taken for the replies is usually
measured with a stop-watch. The standard list has already
been applied to hundreds of normal and abnormal persons:
hence the replies commonly given by persons of different
types are already known, and the average speed and the
mean variation of the times have been calculated. Now and
then a number of special stimulus-words are interpolated—
critical words which may not only stir up the commoner
complexes, but also possess some personal significance for
the patient who is tested. The particular points to review
are, first the speed with which the replies are given, especially
any instances where the patient seems to stick; secondly the
general nature of his associations—whether they are logical
or illogical, superficial or involved, natural, erratic, or wholly
incomprehensible; and finally the concrete interests or

ideals implied by the responses themselves. Emotional disturbance is usually indicated by such signs as the following: undue delay in the speed of response, failure to respond altogether, responses which consist merely in echoing the stimulus-word or some word already given, an interpretation of the stimulus-word in an unusual or a personal sense, replies determined rather by the sound of the stimulus-word than by its meaning, and finally a failure to remember the original reply when the whole list is worked through on a second occasion.

With the 'continuous' procedure the starting-point is generally not a prearranged list, but some topic or episode that seems to have a peculiar significance for the individual patient—most frequently of all, perhaps, an item from a recent dream. The patient is required to say what words or ideas are brought to mind by this topic, and to keep giving words, as they suggest each other, for as long as he can. As before, the value of the test lies partly in the specific thoughts thus expressed by the patient, still more in the slight emotional clues exhibited as each idea comes to the surface (blushing, hesitation, coughing, change of voice, unnecessary interjections, unconscious or involuntary movements, and all the little tell-tale signs of embarrassment or discomposure), but most of all perhaps in the special direction towards which the whole train of associated thoughts is tending and in particular the point at which the uttered thoughts come suddenly to a stop. The thought that should follow next, but is left unvoiced, is likely to be intimately bound up with some repressed emotional complex, which prevents it from coming to the surface.

As is well known, this test in various forms has been employed, with more or less success, by different schools of psycho-analysis. Of all the technical devices that have been tried, this is the one which I should chiefly recommend to the practising physician. It is simple to apply. It consumes but little time. It needs no elaborate apparatus or prolonged training for its use.[1]

[1] For an admirable discussion of the method, and its value and limitations, see the chapter on 'Word-Association in Psychopathology' in Ernest Jones's

In the foregoing test, and throughout the examination of each patient, it is assumed that the investigator is quick to note and to interpret the passing signs of emotion. Now, instead of trusting to the unaided eye to observe such hints, it might seem at once more certain and more scientific to detect or record them by means of special apparatus. As is well known, most of the outward accompaniments of emotion can be objectively measured in this way. The changes in pulse, in temperature, or in breathing, the extent or direction of the unconscious movements of the hands—all can be registered by means of simple instruments. Outside the laboratory, however, such methods have proved as disappointing as they are cumbersome and clumsy. Most of these physical measurements have so far revealed only small correlations with temperamental characteristics, and even in extreme cases of neurosis supply little that is definitely diagnostic.

One particular reaction has attracted less attention than it deserves—the so-called psychogalvanic reflex. Whenever an emotion is experienced, a change in the electrical conductivity of the body occurs, lasting for a few seconds only. If, therefore, the subject places his hands on a couple of electrodes, and the electrodes are wired to a battery and a galvanometer, these electrical changes can be observed and recorded. We seem here to have a method of measuring the emotionality of different persons and their susceptibility to exciting stimuli of various types.[1] But again too little is at

Papers on Psycho-analysis (1923, pp. 429–57), also the earlier reports by C. G. Jung and his colleagues, Studies in Word Association (transl. by M. D. Eder, 1918). A classic paper is that by Kent and Rosanoff in the American Journal of Psychology, lxvii (1910), pp. 317–77, 'A Study of Association in Insanity'. For suitable stimulus-words, see Appendix IV. [For more recent studies of this test see Rapaport, Diagnostic Personality Testing, 1945, ii, pp. 13–84, 460–5, and Vernon, Personality Tests and Assessments, 1953, pp. 172–7 and refs. As Vernon observes, this was 'the first projection test, being developed by Galton in 1879.' It was one of the three tests of personality chosen by Rapaport for intensive investigation with normal, neurotic, and psychotic persons.]

[1] So far as I am aware, the earliest experiments in which this reaction was used as a method of emotional diagnosis were those carried out by R. C. Moore and myself, with the help of Charles Sherrington, in his laboratory at Liverpool: cf., J. Exp. Pedagogy, i, 1912, pp. 379. Of these so-called

present known about the causes of the reaction for it to be applied on any wide scale as a serviceable test.

In all these latter experiments the emotional stimuli are usually words. Now words lead rapidly to emotional repression; whereas concrete or pictorial material appeals more directly to the primitive emotions and less easily to the higher feelings. Yet, even with the most vivid stimuli, the methods of expression—measuring pulse, breathing, blood-pressure, and the like—prove disappointing. On the other hand, the methods of impression—noting effects on memory, imagination, preference, and so on—may be highly suggestive. Far more than is commonly realized, our interpretation of what is presented to our eyes is influenced by our latent emotional tendencies. Polonius looks at a cloud, and sees now a whale and now a weasel. In one of Conan Doyle's stories, three wounded men gaze at a patch on the ceiling: the first sees a battleship, the second a girl, the third a man with a pistol. As the tale unfolds, the fancies they weave around the same discoloured blotch, 'like the visions of some clairvoyant crystal-gazer', are shown to be indicative of the secret fears or passions of each one. The psychologist calls such processes apperception: and tests of apperception reveal the most surprising individual differences.

Thus the pictures used will not explicitly depict the stimulus or situation; they should rather imply it indirectly or remotely, and thus suggest it only to those who are ready to perceive it. Hence the device of the 'ambiguous picture' which has countless suggestive uses. Both the form and the contents of the descriptions or replies can be systematically analysed with the aid of an appropriate schedule. If the principle be pushed still farther to its logical conclusion, it will mean that the picture to be shown need be no true picture at all, but simply a variegated blot or smudge,

physiological methods the first instance on record is that described by Galen, the physician of the emperor Marcus Aurelius. He kept his fingers on the pulse of a neurotic lady at the emperor's court, and referred in turn to the names of prominent courtiers of the day. As he spoke of a certain youthful actor, her pulse-rate increased so suddenly, that he was able forthwith to diagnose the cause of her malady.

specially selected because its pattern is capable of suggesting a countless diversity of alternative interpretations.[1]

This artifice is exploited in what is now known as the Rorschach ink-blot test. Binet and others had used blots to study emotional apperception. Hermann Rorschach seems to have been the first to adapt it for the purposes of clinical diagnosis. Rorschach himself, a young Swiss psychiatrist, died prematurely, before his method was fully worked out. But a number of researches have since been carried out with this procedure, chiefly in Switzerland, Germany, and America. In this country it is but little known; Miss Madeline Kerr, however, has used the test in London schools, and others at University College have made systematic studies of its reliability and diagnostic value.

The material consists of ten standard blots, some black, some grey, some coloured, each adopted after careful trial from a large collection. They are presented to the patient one by one; and he is asked to state what each particular blot suggests to him. His replies are subsequently tabulated and analysed according to a somewhat complicated scheme. Marks are allotted, first, according to the general way in which he apperceives the blot, secondly, according to the special determinants of his reply, and thirdly, according to the actual contents of his answer, particularly their trite or original character. The mental processes aroused are not unlike those set going by the ordinary associative reaction test with words; but the fact that words are dispensed with is a great advantage. The patient is almost bound to think about the blots: but to a verbal stimulus he can reply immediately and mechanically by means of his ingrained verbal

[1] These various apperception tests were devised and used, largely with the aid of William McDougall, in the investigations by Mr. Moore and myself, already cited (*J. Exp. Pedagogy*, i, 1912, pp. 379–84; cf. *The Young Delinquent*, pp. 404 f.).

[Owing largely to the work of Morgan and Murray (*Explorations in Personality*, 1938) the apperception of pictures has recently become one of the most popular tests; cf. Rapaport and Vernon, loc. cit. sup. and refs. For a history of this and similar procedures, with results indicating the superiority of scores based on content rather than form, see Sen, 'A Preliminary Study of the Thematic Apperception Test.' *Brit. J. Statist. Psychol.* vi, 1953, pp. 91–100.]

habits without any thought whatever. If scored for content rather than for formal categories, a kind of psychogram can be constructed, which will reveal, not only the abilities and interests of the patient, but his general emotional type and his chief emotional complexes.

The test has been used more frequently with psychotic than with neurotic patients; but in my own experience it is admirably adapted for the latter. The scoring is over-elaborate, but might easily be simplified and standardized; and the alleged diagnostic criteria still await verification by more exact statistical means. Rorschach himself has claimed that his ink-blots 'will distinguish with practical certainty between the well-adjusted, the neurotic, the schizophrenic, and the organic patient'. Dr. Vernon goes so far as to declare that he is 'unable to call to mind any other test of personality or temperamental traits which will tell me so much about my subjects in so short a time as does the Rorschach test'.[1]

One other method of estimating the personality as a whole deserves a mention. This consists in the so-called will-temperament tests of June Downey. The tests are founded on the idea that emotional disturbances affect not only modes of perception and thought, but also modes of movement, and that these will be more easy to detect and measure. Her particular theory is as follows. Temperamental differences are determined, first by the total amount of nervous or emotional energy at the disposal of each individual, and secondly by the tendency of this energy either to discharge immediately and as it were explosively into the centres for

[1] Cf. M. Kerr, *Brit. J. Psychol. Gen. Sect.* xxv, 1932, pp. 170 f.; P. E. Vernon, *Brit. J. Med. Psychol.* xiii, 1933, pp. 89 f. [More recently Miss Sen has demonstrated the superiority of scoring by content rather than by the somewhat speculative scheme proposed by Rorschach (*Brit. J. Psychol. Stat. Sect.* iii, 1950, pp. 40 f.). Since this volume was published, the inkblot test has become the most popular of all so-called 'projection techniques'. Nevertheless, as Vernon observes in his recent book, 'there is an unfortunate tendency for Rorschach testing to become a cult, like psychoanalysis, with the same tendency to dogmatism, jargon, and dissenting sects, and the same implication that it is immune from scientific standards of reliability and validity' (op. cit., p. 185). The term 'projection' has of late acquired a widespread popularity; but, as several writers have pointed out, the metaphor is at once highly ambiguous and decidedly misleading.]

muscular movement, or, on the other hand, to find a more devious channel owing to inhibition or repression. Such characteristics, she contends, are most clearly displayed in efforts at motor control; and for the purposes of measurement she selects the movements made in handwriting. The patient is required to write a chosen phrase at normal speed, at maximal speed, and then as slowly as he can, to disguise his ordinary handwriting, to imitate a model script, and to continue writing during slight and unexpected distractions.

For the most part her tests have been used only with normal children. She believes, however, that they would 'aid the physician in the diagnosis of temporary conditions of depression and irritability', and describes their application to one or two abnormal cases.[1] If, as she maintains, neurotic and psychotic conditions are mainly exaggerations of normal temperaments, then, in theory at any rate, her method should be valuable for the diagnosis of neurotic disorders. Unfortunately, the correlations empirically obtained by workers who have tried the tests in this country are not encouraging. It is, indeed, doubtful how far temperamental disturbances necessarily affect muscular movement as such, and to what extent handwriting may be treated as a typical example. That handwriting is influenced by emotional states, and by functional nervous disorders as well as by organic, can hardly be questioned; and tests of handwriting, along June Downey's lines, may at times be employed in practice, when more formal psychological testing would be difficult to apply. But our knowledge of the diagnostic criteria is neither detailed nor complete.

All the preceding tests aim primarily at getting a cross-section of the patient's mental attitude regarded as a whole. There are other tests that aim at measuring more precisely

---

[1] For details see June Downey, *The Will Temperament and its Testing*, 1923. Since the early investigations of Binet, the study of handwriting as a possible clue to personality has been singularly neglected by psychologists. For illustrative procedures see Burt, *The Measurement of Mental Capacities*, pp. 20 f. The professional graphologists unfortunately have little knowledge of scientific psychology or of the standard scientific procedures for testing the validity of their claims.

particular tendencies or qualities that are supposed to be well marked or characteristic in certain forms of neurosis.

Of these the tests intended to measure suggestibility are among the earliest and the most interesting. Here Binet was once more a pioneer. It will be remembered that he experimented with a number of devices for this purpose, and actually inserted one of them into his scale for assessing intelligence. With patients of a hysterical type such tests occasionally furnish illuminating results; but as a means of measuring a definite temperamental trait they have proved of little value. Indeed, it appears doubtful whether there is any such quality as general suggestibility.

More specialized series of tests have been worked out by Professor Spearman and his colleagues—Dr. Bernard Hart, Dr. Wynn Jones, Dr. Stephenson, and many others; and have been applied on an extensive scale to patients in mental hospitals. Of the various expedients employed, some of the most fruitful have been those originally designed to measure what has been termed 'perseveration'. The examinee is first set to carry out some simple task—for example, writing S's in the ordinary fashion; and then, when a temporary habit has been formed, he is suddenly required to change the task—for example, to write S's backwards or mirror-wise. With some examinees it is found that the tendency set up by the first task is apt to interfere and produce an abundance of errors in the second task, which for preference should be slightly harder. It was expected that such methods would measure what was supposed to be a kind of mental momentum or inertia, and so bring to light any marked liability to obsessions. Actually, however, this theory proved to be too simple; and the characteristic tested now seems to be a definite but somewhat specific factor for which the best name is an entirely non-committal term—the 'p-factor'. Recent data indicate that this factor is closely related to stability of temperament—the 'w-factor', as it is sometimes styled; and this stability in turn appears to be the most general of all the character-qualities that are disturbed in the commoner forms of mental or neurotic disorder. In the 'p-tests' a moderate amount of interference or 'persevera-

tion' proves to be quite normal: on that nearly all investigators are now agreed. It is among those who deviate to an
extreme in either one direction or the other that the neurotic
and the psychopathic subjects are chiefly found. According
to one investigator, an abnormally large amount of interference is betrayed by repressed and obstinate persons
(the 'perseverators', as they were formerly called), and an
abnormally small amount of interference by the excitable
and unstable (the 'non-perseverators'.).

A second group of tests are those originally intended to
measure quickness and fluency of ideas. Here, again, deviations towards either extreme are significant. It is claimed
that fluency, when tested in this way, is markedly reduced
both among those who suffer from anxiety-states and among
those who suffer from obsessional states; on the other
hand, in excitable patients with manic tendencies, it is
apparently increased. Experiments carried out at the
Maudsley Hospital and elsewhere[1] suggest that in experienced hands these tests already possess a diagnostic value.

The use of tests for fatigability—the Kraepelin addition
tests and the like—I have already discussed in dealing with
neurasthenia. But one test, employed on a large scale by
investigators under the Medical Research Council, has
proved unexpectedly suggestive. This is the so-called
dotting-machine test—a contrivance originally invented by
Professor McDougall for measuring the capacity of sustained voluntary attention. It yields a close correlation with
independent diagnoses of the presence or absence of neurotic
symptoms. Broadly speaking, it appears that, when the
influence of intelligence has been discounted, those who are
temperamentally normal vary only within fairly narrow

[1] This statement referred to researches at the Maudsley and Bethlem
Hospitals which were being carried out under the supervision of Professor
Spearman at the time I was preparing these chapters (*Brit. J. Med. Psychol.*
xiv, 1934, pp. 7–135). More recently, as a result of his work at the Maudsley
Hospital, Dr. Eysenck has been led to advocate the use of 'objective behaviour tests', which he considers far superior to the more popular projection tests and questionnaires. I am, however, inclined to share the view
expressed by Professor Vernon: such tests are either 'too simple and specific'
or else too dependent on subjective interpretation. Moreover, their reliability
proves to be exceedingly low.

limits. Extreme deviations on either one side or the other usually prove indicative of neurotic tendencies. As a rule, those with obsessional symptoms usually do inordinately well; those suffering from anxiety-states do excessively badly.

With all these tests, it should be possible to work out averages and limits of normal variation for persons of different ages, of different social classes, and of different levels of intelligence; the figures might then be used to furnish comparable standards. For scientific research the best procedure in my view is to express each individual personality by means of a 'psychogram' (or quantitative profile) and to supplement the numerical assessments by a systematic case-history. To construct the psychogram the most effective method is to use the technique of 'correlating persons', i.e. comparing the pattern of traits shown by the patient with that of ideal neurotic types and with his own previous patterns.[1]

What then are the practical results so far achieved? Three questions urgently need an answer: First, how far are neurotic disturbances prevalent among the general population? Secondly, is there any sign that their frequency, owing to the stress and hustle of modern civilized life, is on the increase? And thirdly, what is the relative efficacy of different methods of treatment?

Frequency of Neurotic Conditions among Children. As we have just seen, the tests at our disposal for such inquiries are as yet too recent and too ill-standardized to offer much assistance. In consequence, surveys for the incidence of neurosis, corresponding to the surveys already carried out for the incidence of mental deficiency, are bound to be somewhat unreliable. We have to trust largely to the subjective estimates of the individual psychologist and

---

[1] In my view tests are likely to be of most use for general standardization and as starting-points for a more personal study of each particular case. The best basis of comparison is an assessment of the primary emotions. These assessments can then be correlated (*a*) with previous assessments for the same child, to determine the progress of his condition, and (*b*) with theoretical assessments found by factor analysis to be distinctive of the various neurotic types—sthenic, asthenic, &c. For the construction of 'psychograms' see L.C.C. *Report* (1917), pp. 64 f., and *Factors of the Mind*, pp. 427 f.

physician—to observation rather than to experimental tests. Even with these rough and ready methods, however, comparatively few investigations have hitherto been made.

It might be thought that the medical inspections of school pupils would yield some broad reply. But since the nervous child, with rare exceptions, gives but little trouble in the classroom, less attention is paid to this form of subnormality than to any other. Moreover, as we have seen, neurotic troubles from their very nature are difficult to detect without an expert and intensive study of each individual. Hence astonishingly little is known about the frequency of neuroses during early years. Much is done for the physically defective child; almost as much for the dull, the mentally defective, and the delinquent; but the nervous child still remains almost wholly overlooked.

During a survey of subnormal children made in a sample borough in London, I kept notes of the nervous condition of every boy and girl examined. Since the numbers covered were so large, it was impossible to make a thorough examination of each child. Even so, however, the figures were striking. As many as 4 per cent. showed symptoms so well-marked as to point to an urgent need for special treatment. In another 13 per cent. the symptoms noted were sufficient to indicate at least the desirability of further investigation of the case.

These rough percentages are confirmed by estimates reported from other districts and countries. Dr. Lloyd, for example, in making a survey for the Birmingham Education Committee, found that 6 per cent. of the average children and 12 per cent. of the backward children were suffering from defective nervous conditions. Terman has estimated that at least 5 per cent. of the school children in the United States are definitely neurotic. It will be observed that, if these figures can be trusted, the number of children suffering from serious neurotic disorder is certainly far greater than the number of mentally defective children, and possibly as great as that of the dull and backward. Could we make an intensive attack on these cases in early life, through child-guidance clinics or similar means, we should, I am convinced, not only save countless individuals from definite breakdown in later life, but enormously diminish the amount of unhappiness, inefficiency, and social friction that such conditions eventually engender.

It might be of interest to inquire how the various types of neurotic disorder are distributed among children of either sex. Here it is still more difficult to procure reliable figures, since a correct classification of any given case is rarely possible until an intensive analysis has been carried out; and, even after this has been done, it is continually found that, among children in particular, various types of neurosis may coexist in the same individual. On the other hand, a classification according to symptoms or complaints is almost equally untrustworthy, since it is rare to find a single symptom dominating the whole picture: a boy, for example, may be referred for examination on account of a stutter, and inquiry may almost immediately reveal that he suffers from incontinence, nail-biting, bad temper, and possibly bad sex habits as well. It is the exception rather than the rule for one neurotic symptom to occur in isolation.

Nevertheless, I have attempted a broad classification of those cases which I have subjected to a more prolonged study. The percentages for the main types of disorders are shown in the table below.[1] The commonest troubles are, first of all, anxiety-states of various kinds, which, on the surface at any rate, seem far more frequent among girls than among boys; secondly, disorders manifesting themselves by displays of temper or rebellion, which seem far more frequent among boys; thirdly, disorders manifesting themselves by minor neurotic symptoms of various types, which probably have a different origin in different cases. Neurasthenia and typical hysteria, it will be seen, are rare, although

[1] An interesting inquiry into the incidence of neurotic difficulties among young children has been published by Dr. Susan Isaacs in the *British Journal of Educational Psychology*, vol. ii, pt. 2, 1932, p. 78. Here the figures are chiefly derived from letters sent by parents appealing for advice. The classification is based on the outstanding symptom or the type of problem mentioned; and no doubt further inquiry would have revealed a considerable amount of overlapping. But, allowing for the difference in age of the several groups of patients, Dr. Isaacs's figures seem closely to correspond with my own.

these are the disorders which figure chiefly in the current textbooks. Compulsion-neuroses seem far commoner than is usually supposed. The incidence of each type differs considerably according to the age of the children; but my figures are too few to permit tabulation by age-groups. Broadly speaking, it may be said that the disorders which

TABLE III. *Distribution of Neurotic Symptoms among Children of School Age.*

	Boys.	Girls.
	per cent.	per cent.
Neurasthenia (fatigue-neuroses):		
(i) Secondary	8·7	6·7
(ii) Apparently primary	3·6	1·4
Anxiety-states (various)	16·1	30·8
Anxiety-neurosis	4·5	5·3
Anxiety-hysteria	3·2	6·0
Compulsion-neurosis	7·0	4·6
Conversion-hysteria	2·8	5·0
Anger-neurosis (temper, destructiveness, &c.) .	10·6	6·5
Assertiveness (excessively resistant to authority, &c.)	13·9	8·3
Sex (masturbation, &c.)	6·3	11·2
Speech-habits (stammering, lisping, &c.) . .	8·7	4·9
Minor habits (incontinence, nail-biting, thumb-sucking, &c.)	14·6	9·3
	100·0	100·0

lend themselves to a definite classification occur chiefly at the later ages. Those showing themselves through vague anxiety, general ill temper, or minor neurotic habits are more frequent at the earlier ages. But, all through the series, a neurosis that exactly fits a definite diagnostic label is the exception rather than the rule.

Frequency of Neurotic Conditions among Adults. It would be extremely helpful to know whether the incidence of neurotic conditions increases or diminishes as children grow up into maturity, and how far the frequency of such disorders among the adult population is really similar to that observed among the young. But unfortunately efforts at estimating the incidence of neurotic disorders among adult men and women have rarely been undertaken. In this country by far the most thorough inquiry is that carried out under the auspices of the Medical Research Council by Dr. Millais Culpin and Dr. May Smith.[1]

Over 1,000 persons were investigated: the groups included factory workers, clerical workers in government departments and in commercial firms, men and women holding administrative posts, students preparing for the professions of teaching, architecture, and the theatre. No rigid questionnaire was used. But each person was interviewed more or less along the lines described above; and the results of the interview were independently checked by the 'dotting test' already mentioned. According to the symptoms observed, each person was graded in one of six categories. Class 0 showed no symptoms; classes 1 and 2 showed symptoms more or less slight; class 3 well-marked symptoms, though not (at any rate on the surface) numerous or severe; and classes 4 and 5 showed a number of severe symptoms, grave enough to require treatment.[2]

Tables were published to show the distribution of the various cases among the different groups. Interesting differences were found between the two sexes and between the various occupational classes. The group showing the highest percentage were the students: these, it will be remembered, were not students of every type, but those training more particularly for the artistic and educational professions. Among clerical workers the highest percentage was found in the women; among factory workers and students the highest percentage was found in the men. The whole series may be taken as roughly representative of the general population; and it would appear that approximately 40 per cent. showed no symptoms whatever—that is, none discoverable in a single interview or by a single test. Sixty per cent.,

[1] See *The Nervous Temperament*, by Millais Culpin and May Smith: Industrial Health Research Board, Report No. 61.

[2] Loc. cit., p. 9. In the tables, classes 4 and 5 are generally grouped together, and I understand from Dr. Culpin that both classes were considered to be in need of treatment. [His estimates appear to be confirmed by the figures obtained during the recent war; but there the methods of investigation and diagnosis were of necessity much more hasty, and the standards varied widely between different examiners: cf. Blacker, *Neurosis and the Mental Health Services*, 1946, pp. 159 f., 'Incidence of Neurosis and Psychosis'.]

therefore, exhibited some kind of neurotic symptom, slight or severe. Among these, 11 per cent. had symptoms definite enough at least to warrant further investigation, and 6 per cent. had symptoms serious enough to require treatment. The percentages tally remarkably well with those independently obtained from investigating the school population. The figures are, if anything, a little larger among the adults; but this might be accounted for by assuming that the symptoms and the number of cases tend to increase very slightly with increasing age.

To estimate the proportionate frequency of the various types among adults is by no means easy. Different investigators employ different classifications, and often use identical terms with a very divergent meaning. Broadly speaking, it would seem that anxiety-states are by far the commonest: in women these tend towards the form of a definite anxiety-hysteria, and in men of an anxiety-neurosis; but the figures for the sex-difference are seldom reliable. Minor functional symptoms of a hysterical type are almost as common; but— in this country at least—typical instances of conversion-hysteria are comparatively rare, particularly among men. Well-marked cases of compulsion-neurosis seem rarer still; and true cases of neurasthenia rarest of all. The term 'neurasthenia', however, is unfortunately used in a very lax sense, and frequently includes what should be more properly termed an anxiety-neurosis or an anxiety-hysteria. What I have termed anger-neuroses are hardly ever diagnosed as such among adults: possibly the states are not recognized as neurotic at all; more probably (as my own experience would suggest) their manifestations change with advancing years, and the cases get classified under some other rubric.

So far as such vague data can be trusted, it will be observed that the relative frequency of the different types, and their distribution between the two sexes, appear to be much the same among adults as they are among children. With adults, however, the symptoms may take more specific and more numerous forms: for example, a number of the familiar industrial disabilities—writer's cramp, telegraphist's cramp,

miner's nystagmus, and countless other occupation-neuroses
that have earned a technical name—prove in many instances
to be simply specialized examples of psycho-neurotic
reactions.

One of the most eminent of all authorities hazarded some
time ago the pronouncement that 'neuroses constitute perhaps the most widespread form of disease'. The investigations that I have just described, among children and adults
alike, fully confirm this prediction. They show that neurotic
disorders are far more widely spread than is usually supposed, and that the figures for their prevalence far outweigh
those for any other group of ailments. Further, in the course
of the investigations on adults it has become clear that such
disorders are directly responsible for an unsuspected amount
of unhappiness and inefficiency. The records of firms,
factories, and schools reveal that a great proportion of the
occasional absences is due to so-called nervous breakdown.
Among those who continue at work, the diminution or the
variation in output can often be definitely referred to nervous
trouble; and the relations of such workers to their fellows,
their superiors, their subordinates, and the members of
their family at home are nearly always gravely impaired.
Some trades and professions seem definitely to aggravate
neurotic tendencies, or, it may be, to attract persons of a
highly strung temperament—notably, it would seem, those
of acting and of teaching. Yet, in all the different occupations, only a small minority of the sufferers are totally
incapacitated.

Treatment. Finally, what are the most efficacious methods
of treatment? Here the available evidence is far more
meagre. Among adults no adequately controlled investigations appear to have been carried out; and, in spite of the
competing claims made by the different schools, there is
little to suggest that any one type of psychiatric treatment
is more successful than any other: success depends more
on the man than on the method. Among children it is
easier to secure comparable figures. Thus in London, of
the cases referred to the psychologist's department and
followed up for three or more years, 67 per cent. showed

marked improvement; of those referred to a psychiatrist, only 53 per cent.; of those which were left untreated, 47 per cent. spontaneously showed the same degree of improvement. There was little difference in the type of case included in the three groups: if anything, the first comprised the severest cases. A study of individual case-reports reveals four main reasons for the difference: (1) with the psychiatrist the *psychological* study of the child is usually narrower and more limited; (2) he pays less attention to *environmental* causes of maladjustment than the psychologist; (3) he makes far less use of methods of *child training*; and (4) he is less familiar with the problems and possibilities of the *education service*—particularly with the actual conditions in the schools from which his cases come and the varied help that can nowadays be given by the teacher and the social services.[1]

From all that I have said, three urgent corollaries seem to follow. First, both the medical profession and the general public require fuller instruction about the characteristics of these disabilities. Secondly, better facilities for diagnosis and treatment are imperatively needed, particularly during childhood. Thirdly, far more research, on lines scientifically planned in advance, must be undertaken upon the symptoms, origin, and incidence of these peculiar kinds of subnormality, and above all on the relative efficacy of different modes of treatment. In every such inquiry a sympathetic co-operation between psychiatrist and psychologist would prove invaluable.

Abnormal psychology, or, as I should prefer to term it,

[1] The figures above are based on data collected between 1920 and 1935. For more recent evidence in regard to the efficacy of different methods of treatment among children see Symposium on 'Psychologists and Psychiatrists in the Child Guidance Services', *Brit. J. Educ. Psychol.* xxiii, 1953, pp. 8–28, esp. Tables I and II. In regard to adults the chief evidence comes from America (cf. C. Landis, 'Statistical Evaluation of Psychotherapeutic Methods', *ap.* H. E. Hinsie, *Concepts and Problems of Psychotherapy*, 1938): a synopsis of the main results will be found in H. Eysenck, *The Scientific Study of Personality*, 1952, pp. 27 f. Eysenck's own conclusion is perhaps unduly pessimistic: 'there appears to be an inverse correlation between recovery and psychotherapy. . . . We are left in the position where any belief in psychotherapy depends on faith, not on scientifically demonstrated fact.' Cf. also Watson and Mensch, *loc. cit. sup.*, p. 322.

the psychology of the subnormal, thus offers a vast and fertile field for scientific investigation. In the interests not only of the individual, but also of society, it calls imperatively for further study. Intellectual disabilities, it is true, seem comparatively resistant to treatment and training; but disorders of temperament and character are among the most hopeful of the psychologist's problems. Curiously enough, we know far more about the first than we do about the second. In both cases, however, the immediate and most profitable line of advance still lies, not so much through the attempt to understand the detailed structure and functions of the brain and nervous system[1]—helpful as such attempts have already proved—but rather through an effort to understand the working of the mind in and for itself. But the two lines of approach can never be divorced. Man is a unitary organism. Physical and mental are reciprocally involved. The psychologist has as much to learn from the doctor and physiologist as they have to learn from the psychologist: and the one thing needed is intensive, co-operative research, attacking these many-sided problems from every aspect and angle.

[1] The best summary is that by Russell Brain and E. B. Strauss, *Recent Advances in Neurology and Neuropsychiatry* (6th edition in the press). See also the books by Wilkie and Grey Walter cited below, pp. 377, 381.

APPENDIX I

TESTS OF EDUCATIONAL ATTAINMENTS

THE scales in this appendix and the next are reprinted here to illustrate the method employed in grading tests of intellectual attainments and capacity. The general principle, it will be seen, is to draw up a series of problems which will enable the patient's abilities to be measured in terms of a mental age. Thus in the reading and the spelling tests there are ten words for each year; and each word successfully read or spelt counts as one-tenth of a mental year. In the arithmetic test I have retained only four problems for each year; here, therefore, each problem successfully solved counts as one quarter of a mental year.

GRADED READING TEST

The easiest test to apply is a vocabulary test for reading. The material is given on the two following pages. The words have been carefully selected and standardized by a long series of preliminary experiments, and are printed in a type conforming to the requirements of the British Association Committee on School Reading Books. To ask each child to try every word is unnecessary. The simplest procedure is for him to run down the first column until he begins to hesitate. He may then work backward until he succeeds with all the words in a single line, and work forward until he fails with all the words in a single line. The figures in the margin indicate how the mental age for reading is to be assigned. If, for example, the child reads the list correctly down to the last word for age 7 ('tongue'), and can manage only five additional words from the lines for age 8 or later, then his mental age for reading is 8·5 years.

It should be added that this is but one of the many possible tests for reading: other tests have been drawn up for measuring fluency, expression, and—what is most important of all—power to comprehend what is read.[1]

---

[1] A full set of tests and test-materials for this and other subjects of the ordinary school curriculum was issued in the L.C.C. Memoranda on *Mental and Scholastic Tests* (21s.) and reprinted in my smaller *Handbook of Tests for Use in Schools* (10s. 6d.), both now published by Staples Press.

Age					
4-	to	is	of	at	he
	my	up	or	no	an
5-	his	for	sun	big	day
	sad	pot	wet	one	now
6-	that	girl	went	boys	some
	just	told	love	water	things
7-	carry	village	nurse	quickly	return
	known	journey	terror	obtain	tongue

8- shelves scramble twisted beware commenced
scarcely belief steadiness labourers serious

9- projecting fringe luncheon nourishment overwhelmed
urge explorer trudging events motionless

10- economy formulate exhausted contemptuous renown
universal circumstances destiny glycerine atmosphere

11- perpetual emergency humanity perambulating ultimate
apprehend excessively domineer theory reputation

12- physician fatigue philosopher melodrama autobiography
constitutionally champagne encyclopedia hypocritical efficiency

13- melancholy exorbitant influential terminology palpable
mercenary contagion fallacious binocular microscopical

14- atrocious phlegmatic refrigerator unique alienate
eccentricity ingratiating subtlety poignancy phthisis

GRADED SPELLING TEST

Age.

5—

| a | it | cat | to | and |
| the | on | up | if | box |

6—

| run | bad | but | will | pin |
| cap | men | got | to-day | this |

7—

| table | even | fill | black | only |
| coming | sorry | done | lesson | smoke |

8—

| money | sugar | number | bright | ticket |
| speak | yellow | doctor | sometimes | already |

9—

| rough | raise | scrape | manner | publish |
| tough | feel | answer | several | towel |

10—

| surface | pleasant | saucer | whistle | razor |
| vegetable | improvement | succeed | beginning | accident |

11—

| decide | business | carriage | rogue | receive |
| usually | pigeon | practical | quantity | knuckle |

12—

| distinguish | experience | disease | sympathy | illegal |
| responsible | agriculture | intelligent | artificial | peculiar |

13—

| luxurious | conceited | leopard | barbarian | occasion |
| disappoint | necessary | treacherous | descendant | precipice |

14—

| virtuous | memoranda | glazier | circuit | precision |
| mosquito | promiscuous | assassinate | embarrassing | tyrannous |

GRADED ARITHMETIC TEST

Age 4—.

1. How many fingers do I hold up? (Showing 2.)
2. Let me hear how far you can count—one, two, three. (To pass, the child should recite the cardinal numbers to 10 at 4½ years, to 19 at 5½, to 21 or beyond at 6½ or above.)
3. If you had three pennies in this hand, and then I gave you one more, how many would you have altogether? (Hold out the child's hand that he may visualize the money.)
4. How many halfpennies would you want to buy a penny bun?

Age 5—.

1. If you had 5 nuts and gave 1 away, how many would be left for yourself?
2. Take 2 from 4. How many would be left?
3. Four boys have given me a halfpenny each. How many pennies is that worth?
4. I once had 4 pet mice in a cage. One died; one ran away; and one was eaten by the cat. How many were left?

Age 6—.

1. How many do 6 and 3 make?
2. How many ears are there on 3 donkeys?
3. Write down (in figures) 35.
4. I have 3 pockets and 3 apples in each. How many apples is that?

Age 7—.

1. How many $\frac{1}{2}d$. stamps can I buy for $9d.$?
2. I have $2s.$ to divide among 4 children. How much should each have if all are to have the same amount?
3. How many days are there in 6 weeks?
4. My brother is 4 ft. high. How many inches is that?

Age 8—.

1. A boy had 20 marbles. Afterwards he won 3 and lost 5. How many had he then?
2. How many penny stamps can I buy for $7s.$?
3. Mother gave me $2\frac{1}{2}d$. Father gave me twice as much. How much have I altogether?
4. Norton is 36 miles away. What would the fare be at $1d.$ a mile?

Age 9—.

1. I have been for a week's holiday. I spent $6d.$ a day while I was away. How much should I have left out of $4s.$?
2. How many ounces are there in $1\frac{3}{4}$ lb.?
3. My bookshelf is $3\frac{1}{2}$ ft. long. How many books will it hold if each is 1 inch thick?
4. Share $1s.$ $3d.$ equally among 10 boys.

Age 10—.

1. I get 6*d.* an hour; and I work 8 hours a day. How much can I earn in 5 days?
2. I must be at the station a quarter of an hour before my train starts. It starts at five-and-twenty to one. When should I be there?
3. My brother was born in 1899. How old will he be in 1950?
4. I posted a penny postcard every day in January. How much did the postage amount to?

Age 11—.

1. A servant earned £26 a year wages. How much was that a week?
2. How much is seven-tenths of half a crown?
3. A man walked 2 miles in 30 minutes. How many hours would 20 miles take him?
4. If 3 glasses cost 4½*d.*, how many can I get for 2*s.*?

Age 12—.

1. What fraction of £1 is a third of 1*s.*?
2. What would be the cost of 129 rackets at 5*s.* each?
3. Divide 3*s.* among 2 boys so that one has 8*d.* more than the other.
4. How many pieces of a foot and a quarter can I cut from 5 yds.?

Age 13—.

1. What is the average of 6 inches, 7 inches, 9 inches, and 1 foot?
2. A motor goes 3 times as fast as a horse. The horse goes 36 miles in 6 hours. How long will it take the motor?
3. 4½ ozs. at 2*s.* 8*d.* per lb.?
4. How many square yards of paper will just cover a table 6 ft. long and 3 ft. broad?

Age 14—.

1. How many labels 2½ in. by 2 in. are needed to cover a sheet 10 in. square?
2. If 6 men do a piece of work in 15 days, how many men must I employ to get it done in 10?
3. One-third of my stick is in the water; one-quarter is in the mud; 15 in. is above the water. How long is the stick?
4. If 2 hens lay 2 eggs in 2 days, how many eggs will 6 hens lay in 6 days?

SCALE OF INTELLIGENCE-TESTS

THE following list includes the tests in the well-known Binet-Simon scale, together with the additions suggested by Terman, and a few simpler tests for the earlier years. The age-assignments are based upon a standardization made by myself and several collaborators during a long series of investigations with English children. These assignments were adopted for the inquiry into mental deficiency carried out under the Joint Committee; but a few slight modifications have since been made, chiefly in the earlier and the later years.

The tests are arranged and numbered in order of increasing difficulty. For most of them detailed instructions will be found in my larger volume on *Mental and Scholastic Tests*; those who prefer to use the Terman version will note that his age-assignments and numbering are appended, for the sake of reference, in the last column. Some of the tests suggested by Terman as alternatives (marked 'alt.' in the last column) prove more trustworthy with English children than those in the main group for each age. Tests marked 'Binet' are taken from Binet's 1911 series: they were dropped by Terman, but their convenience and effectiveness appear to warrant their retention. For the tests assigned to ages I and II, Gesell's instructions may be followed.[1]

Binet's tests were originally standardized according to a principle which differs a little from that adopted for the preceding educational tests; and his method has been preserved in nearly all subsequent revisions. The child has to pass *all* the tests assigned to a given age-group before he can be credited with the specified mental age. Thus, if the child correctly answers every question down to the repeating of four numbers, and three of the five tests for the following year (age VI), he obtains a mental age of $5\frac{3}{5}$, i.e. 5·6 years. This point should be carefully noted, since the inexperienced examiner, unfamiliar with the scheme adopted by Binet and Terman, is apt to interpret such a result as equivalent to 6·6 years.

The full set gives a different number of tests for different mental ages. Calculations are simpler if only five are used for each age (or four, owing to paucity of tests, for ages above XIV). Accordingly, the remainder are classed as alternative tests, to be used when one or

[1] See Arnold Gesell, *The Mental Growth of the Pre-School Child*. The 'Terman version' referred to here is what is now sometimes known as the first Stanford Revision.

more of the better tests yield an ambiguous response or cannot be conveniently employed (owing to lack of apparatus, previous familiarity, &c.). Since intelligence develops but little after the age of 14, the later mental ages have only an arbitrary significance, and are inserted simply to enable the intelligence of older and brighter children to be expressed in units comparable with the rest.

1. STANFORD-BINET VERSION

Age.

AGE I.
1. Eyes follow bright moving object . . (4 months.)
2. Blinks at sharp sound . . . (4 months.)
3. Picks up spoon from table . . (6 months.)
4. Sits up . . . . . (9 months.)
5. Seizes and pulls dangling ring . . (12 months.)

AGE II.
1. Unwraps cube . . . . (15 months.)
2. Drops ball into box . . . (18 months.)
3. Scribbles spontaneously . . . (18 months.)
4. Tries to turn door-knob . . . (18 months.)
5. Points to objects in pictures . . (24 months.)

Terman's Assignment.

AGE III.
1. Points to nose, eyes, and mouth . . III. 1.
2. Knows sex . . . . III. 4.
3. Names knife, key, and penny . . III. 2.
4. Gives name and surname . . . III. 5.
5. Enumerates objects in a picture . . III. 3.

Alternatives.
1a. Repeats 2 numbers . . . (Binet, III.)
5a. Matches counters by colour . . (Additional.)

AGE IV.
1. Repeats sentence (6 to 8 syllables). . III. 6.
2. Repeats 3 numbers . . . III. 7. alt.
3. Counts 4 pennies . . . . IV. 3.
4. Compares lines . . . . IV. 1.
5. Compares faces . . . . V. 3.

Alternatives.
4a. Discriminates forms . . . IV. 2.

AGE V.
1. Copies square . . . . IV. 4.
2. Triple order . . . . V. 6.
3. Repeats sentence (12 syllables) . . IV. 7. alt.
4. Answers questions (Comprehension: 1st Series) . . . . . IV. 5.
5. Repeats 4 numbers (once out of 3 trials) . IV. 6.

Alternatives.
3a. Gives age . . . . V. 7. alt.
4a. Compares 2 weights . . . V. 1.
5a. Distinguishes morning and afternoon . VI. 7. alt.
5b. Names 4 colours . . . . V. 2.

AGE VI.
1. Counts 13 pennies . . . VI. 3.
2. Names 4 coins (½d., 1d., 6d., 1s.) . . VI. 5.
3. Copies diamond . . . VII. 6.
4. Distinguishes right and left . . VI. 1.
5. Repeats 5 numbers . . . VII. 3.

Alternatives.

1a. Knows number of fingers . . . VII. 1.
1b. Defines by use . . . . V. 4.
3a. Transcription . . . . (Binet, VII.)
3b. Names week-days (without check questions) (Binet, IX.)
3c. Joins divided card . . . V. 5.
4a. Repeats sentence (16 to 18 syllables) . VI. 6.
5a. Describes pictures . . . VII. 2.

AGE VII.
1. Answers questions (Comprehension: 2nd
   Series) . . . . . VI. 4.
2. Recognizes missing features . . VI. 2.
3. Adds 3 pennies and 3 halfpennies . . (Binet, VIII.)
4. Repeats 3 numbers backwards . . VII. 8. alt.
5. States differences (concrete objects) . VII. 5.

Alternatives.

3a. Ties bow-knot . . . . VII. 4.
3b. Names week-days (with check questions) . VII. 7. alt.

AGE VIII.
1. Counts backwards (20–1). . . VIII. 2.
2. Answers questions (Comprehension: 3rd
   Series) . . . . . VIII. 3.
3. Vocabulary (20 words) . . . VIII. 6.
4. Gives change (practical) . . . (Binet, IX.)
5. States similarities (2 things) . . VIII. 4.

Alternatives.

1a. Reading (recalls 2 items) . . . (Binet, VIII.)
2a. Definitions, superior to use (Terman's
   words) . . . . . VIII. 5.
5a. Gives date . . . . IX. 1.

AGE IX.
1. Names 6 coins (½d., 1d., 6d., 1s., 2s., 2s. 6d.) VIII. 7. alt.
2. Repeats 6 numbers: once out of two trials X. 7. alt.
3. Ball in field: inferior plan . . VIII. 1.
4. Names month (without check questions) . (Binet, IX.)
5. Healy-Fernald Puzzle . . . X. 9. alt.

Alternatives.

1a. Tells change (verbal: 2 out of 3 questions) IX. 3.
2a. Reading: recalls 6 items . . . (Binet, IX.)
3a. Counts stamps . . . . IX. 8. alt.
4a. Repeats 4 numbers backwards . . IX. 4.
5a. Tells time from watch . . . (Additional.)

AGE X.	1. Makes sentences with 3 words	.	.	IX. 5.
	2. Names months (with check questions)		.	IX. 7. alt.
	3. Arranges 5 weights	.	.	IX. 2.
	4. Draws from memory	.	.	X. 3.
	5. Vocabulary (30 words)	.	.	X. 1.

Alternatives.

	1a. Gives easy rhymes	.	.	IX. 6.
	4a. Reading: recalls 8 items	.	.	X. 4.

AGE XI.	1. Absurdities	.	.	.	X. 2.
	2. Answers questions (Comprehension: 4th Series)	.	.	.	X. 5.
	3. Gives 60 words in 3 minutes		.	.	X. 6.
	4. Repeats sentence (20 to 23 syllables)			.	X. 8. alt.
	5. Repeats 5 numbers backwards		.	.	XII. 6.

AGE XII.	1. States similarities (3 things)	.	.	XII. 8. alt.
	2. Rearranges mixed sentences	.	.	XII. 4.
	3. Vocabulary (40 words)	.	.	XII. 1.
	4. Ball in field: superior plan	.	.	XII. 3.
	5. Interprets pictures	.	.	XII. 7. alt.

AGE XIII.	1. Definitions (abstract words)	.	.	XII. 2.
	2. Interprets fables (2 correct or equivalent)	.		XII. 5.
	3. Repeats 7 numbers (once out of two trials)	.		XIV. 7. alt.
	4. Solves problem questions	.	.	XIV. 4.
	5. Reverses hands of clock	.	.	XIV. 6.

AGE XIV.	1. Induction test (folded paper)	.	.	XIV. 2.
	2. Arithmetical reasoning	.	.	XIV. 5.
	3. Vocabulary (50 words)	.	.	XIV. 1.
	4. Draws reverse triangle	.	.	(Binet, Adult.)

AGE XV.	1. Repeats 6 numbers backwards	.	.	XVI. 5.
	2. Paper cutting	.	.	XVIII. 2.
	3. Code test	.	.	XVI. 6.
	4. Gives number of enclosed boxes	.		XVI. 4.
	5. Interprets fables: 4 correct or equivalent	.		XVI. 2.

AGE XVI.	1. Vocabulary (60 words)	.	.	XVI. 1. (65 words.)
	2. Repeats sentence (26 to 29 syllables)		.	XVI. 7. alt.
	3. States differences: abstract	.	.	XVI. 3.

Alternatives.

	3a. States 3 differences between President and King	.	.	.	XIV. 3.

AGE XVII.	1. Repeats 8 numbers	.	.	XVIII. 3.
	2. Repeats 7 numbers backwards	.	.	XVIII. 5.
	3. Summarizes passages read	.	.	XVIII. 4.

AGE XVIII.	1. Ingenuity test	.	.	XVIII. 6.
	2. Comprehends physical relations	.	.	XVI. 8. alt.
	3. Vocabulary (70 words)		.	XVIII. 1. (75 words.)

The further revision of the Binet scale, planned by Terman and referred to in the first edition of this book, has since been published.[1] As before, however, the age-allocations drawn up for American children are not altogether suitable for use in this country. The following rearrangement is based on extensive investigations with English children, and appears to give more satisfactory results.

2. TERMAN-MERRILL VERSION[1]

AGE II

1. Identifying parts of the body (3 points).
2. Identifying objects by name (3 points).
3. Three-hole form-board (1 point).
4. Obeying instructions (2 points).
5. Block-building: tower.
6. Word combinations (alt. only).

AGE II½

1. Picture vocabulary (2 points).
2. Identifying parts of the body (4 points).
3. Rotated form-board (1 point).
4. Identifying objects by use (3 points).
5. Identifying objects by name (5 points).

AGE III

1. Naming objects.
2. Repeating 2 numbers.
3. Block-building: bridge.
4. Picture vocabulary (9 points).
5. Stringing beads.
6. Rotated form-board (2 points) (alt. only).

AGE III½

1. Comparing sticks.
2. Picture memories (alt. only).
3. Obeying instructions (3 points).
4. Picture vocabulary (12 points).
5. Copying a circle.

AGE IV

1. Repeating 3 numbers.
2. Copying a cross (alt. only).
3. Describing pictures.
4. Picture Vocabulary (15 points).
5. Discriminating forms.
6. Counting 4 objects.
7. Comparing faces.
8. Identifying objects by use (5 points).
9. Comprehension, I.

[1] *Measuring Intelligence.* By Lewis M. Terman and Maud A. Merrill (G. G. Harrap & Co., 1937).

AGE IV½
1. Picture Vocabulary (16 points).
2. Naming objects from memory.
3. Pictorial identification (3 points).
4. Picture completion (1 point).
5. Comprehension, II.
6. Repeating 11 syllables (alt. only).

AGE V
1. Copying a square.
2. Triple order.
3. Picture completion (2 points).
4. Pictorial identification (4 points).
5. Definitions.
6. Paper folding (triangle).
7. Repeating 12 syllables.
8. Repeating 4 numbers.

AGE VI
1. Vocabulary test (5 words).
2. Opposite analogies (2 points).
3. Materials.
4. Number concepts.
5. Copying a diamond.
6. Making a knot.
7. Copying a bead chain from memory.
8. Repeating 5 numbers.
9. Pictorial likenesses and differences (5 points).

AGE VII
1. Vocabulary (7 words).
2. Repeating 5 numbers.
3. Tracing a maze.
4. Repeating 16 syllables.
5. Picture absurdities, I.
6. Mutilated pictures.
7. Comprehension, III.
8. Repeating 3 numbers backwards.

AGE VIII
1. Vocabulary (9 words).
2. Opposite analogies (5 points).
3. Similarities between 2 things.
4. Memory for stories ('A Fall in the Mud').
5. Comprehension, IV.
6. Verbal Absurdities, I (3 points).

AGE IX
1. Vocabulary (11 words).
2. Giving change.
3. Repeating 6 numbers.
4. Similarities and differences.
5. Repeating 4 numbers backwards.
6. Memory for 2 designs (1 point).
7. Verbal absurdities, II (2 points).

AGE X

1. Vocabulary (13 words).
2. Paper cutting (1 point).
3. Naming words (28 points).
4. Restricted rhymes.
5. Picture absurdities ('Frontier Days').
6. Memory for 2 designs (1½ points).
7. Reading and report (10 points).
8. Repeating 20 syllables.

AGE XI

1. Vocabulary (15 words).
2. Verbal absurdities, III (2 points).
3. Finding reasons, I.
4. Abstract words, set I (3 points).
5. Sentence building with 3 words.
6. Repeating 5 numbers backwards.
7. Answering difficult questions (alt. only).

AGE XII

1. Vocabulary (17 words).
2. Mixed sentences.
3. Abstract words, set II (2 points).
4. Purse and field.
5. Memory for words.
6. Response to pictures, II.
7. Similarities between three things.
8. Picture absurdity ('The Shadow').

AGE XIII

1. Vocabulary (19 words).
2. Completing sentences (2 points).
3. Abstract words, set II (3 points).
4. Induction.
5. Copying a bead chain from memory, II.
6. Repeating 7 numbers.

AGE XIV

1. Vocabulary (21 words).
2. Paper cutting, I (2 points).
3. Orientation, I.
4. Problems of fact.
5. Ingenuity, I (1 point).

AVERAGE ADULT (AGE XV. 4)

1. Vocabulary (23 words).
2. Arithmetical reasoning.
3. Repeating 25 syllables.
4. Enclosed boxes.
5. Codes.
6. Essential similarities.
7. Repeating 6 numbers backwards.

SUPERIOR ADULT, I (AGE XVII. 4).
1. Vocabulary (27 words).
2. Differences between abstract words.
3. Proverbs, I.
4. Completing sentences (3 points).
5. Reconciling opposites (3 points).
6. Ingenuity, II (3 points).

SUPERIOR ADULT, II (AGE XIX. 10).
1. Vocabulary (32 words).
2. Reconciling opposites (5 points).
3. Summarizing passage: 'The Value of Life'.
4. Proverbs, II.
5. Orientation, II.
6. Paper cutting, II.
7. Repeating 8 numbers.

SUPERIOR ADULT, III (AGE XXII. 10).
1. Vocabulary (38 words).
2. Finding reasons, II.
3. Opposite analogies.
4. Reasoning.
5. Repeating 9 numbers.

For measuring adult intelligence, several scales and tests were developed at the National Institute of Industrial Psychology, and used in varying combinations during the war. For general purposes Group Test 33 (which I based on work for the Civil Service Commission with ex-service candidates) is perhaps the most useful; but it is purely verbal. For dull or backward adults, the most popular test with clinicians at the moment is the Wechsler-Bellevue Intelligence Scale (see references below). This is nominally based on Spearman's single factory theory, but includes tests for both verbal and non-verbal processes. The alleged theoretical basis is open to criticism, and Wechsler's discussion contains many statistical errors. But the empirical work appears to have been efficiently carried out. However, investigations undertaken at University College show that this, like most other American scales, requires considerable modification before it can be used satisfactorily in this country. It is unfortunate that clinical workers are so apt to overlook this limitation.

For methods of assessing intelligence during the first two or three years of life see Ruth Griffiths, *The Abilities of Babies* (1954). This includes an English adaptation of the well-known scales of tests devised by Gessell.

APPENDIX III

QUESTIONNAIRE ON NEUROTIC SYMPTOMS

THE following list of questions, compiled from various sources and the study of actual cases, was first of all devised for a preliminary investigation of possible neurotics among students, and employed during both wars for examining recruits.[1] The original series has been greatly modified, rearranged, and extended in the light of subsequent research. After each question the words 'Yes' and 'No' are usually printed; and the examinee is required to underline the answer which seems best to apply to his own case. A few supplementary instructions may be desirable, and require, as a rule, to be adapted to the intelligence and probable attitude of the persons to be tested. Some such suggestions as the following will often avoid misapprehension. 'If you are doubtful about an answer (e.g. if you have been troubled by one of the symptoms, but only once or twice, and then only when there was an obvious physical or external cause), it will usually be safer to reply "No" rather than "Yes"; but it would be helpful if by the side of such a question you could explain your answer with a word or two of comment. At the end, add any further remarks you wish on points that seem worth mentioning.

In my experience the questionnaire is of great value as a means of preliminary training—e.g. for students of medicine or psychology,

[1] Of the various standardized methods for assessing personality, the questionnaire appears to be on the whole the most reliable and the most valid. With younger children, however, it can be given only in oral form, and is not so effective as a free clinical interview. With them the best of the quantitative procedures involves 'observation in standardized natural situations' (e.g. while playing games with others in a play-room, planning a day in an imaginary child's life with a toy house and dolls, or— better still where practicable—during systematic samples of his daily activities at home and elsewhere).

For a comprehensive review of the comparative reliability and validity of the commoner methods of assessing personality (reports, interviews, observations, experimental tests, &c.), see 'The Assessment of Personality' (*Brit. J. Educ. Psychol.* xv, 1945, pp. 107–21). Since the first edition of this book was published, what have been called 'objective tests of personality' have come once again into vogue, and have proved popular with many psychiatrists both here and in America. Those most widely used are modifications of the old-fashioned 'apperception tests', now rechristened 'projection tests'—a label, as one critic remarks, 'based on sound principles of salesmanship but bad psychology'. But the published data on the reliability and validity of all 'personality tests' remain decidedly unconvincing; and each enthusiast tends to favour his own special devices.

for intending teachers, and for psychiatric social workers. After each student has applied it to himself, his answers are discussed with him in the laboratory or consulting-room.

On applying the questions as a group test, in a form considerably expurgated and abridged, I have found it give a fairly high correlation with neurotic tendencies as subsequently and independently diagnosed. I myself would strongly deprecate its employment as a supposed method of diagnosis. It may, however, prove highly suggestive as a starting-point; and accordingly I append it here in response to many requests for its publication. The 50 items that proved to have the highest correlation with neurotic tendencies are marked with an asterisk. For practical purposes this shortened version will commonly be sufficient.

*1. Do you often feel weak or unwell without being definitely ill?

2. Have you a good appetite?

3. Do you sleep well?

*4. Do you have nightmares?

*5. Do you ever walk in your sleep?

*6. Do you ever talk in your sleep?

7. Do you often have disturbing dreams about your work?

8. Do you have too many sexual dreams?

9. Do you find it difficult to get to sleep when you go to bed?

10. Do you wake up early in the morning and find it impossible to get to sleep again?

*11. Do you lie awake in the middle of the night feeling frightened or depressed?

12. Do you wake up in the night finding your heart beating rapidly, and perhaps trembling or shivering as though you were going to be ill, though, as a matter of fact, no illness follows?

13. Do thoughts often keep running in your head so that you cannot get to sleep?

*14. Does your heart sometimes seem to thump noisily so that it prevents you from going to sleep?

15. Do you usually feel thoroughly rested in the morning when you wake up?

16. Do you often have a sensation of falling when you are dropping off to sleep?

*17. Do you often have bad headaches?

18. Do you often get an ache on one side of the head?

19. Do you ever feel a heavy pressure on or around the head?

*20. Do you often have aches in your muscles, joints, or back?

21. Do you often have bad pains in any part of the body?

22. Do you have strange, unpleasant feelings in any part of the body?

23. Do you often feel a constant tickling or itching on the face or skin?

*24. Have you ever fainted?

25. Do you often faint?

26. Do you feel faint when you see another person faint in the same room?

*27. Have you ever been subject to dizzy or giddy feelings?

28. Do you often have a feeling of choking?

*29. Are you ever bothered by a throbbing or fluttering of the heart?

30. Have you ever had heart disease?

31. Have you ever had St. Vitus's dance?

32. Have you ever had convulsions?

33. Have you ever suffered from anaemia?

34. Have you often suffered from indigestion?

35. Have you ever had asthma or hay fever?

36. Have you ever had an arm or a leg paralysed?

*37. Do you consider yourself nervous or highly strung?

38. Have you ever had a nervous breakdown?

39. Have you ever been afraid of going mad?

*40. Have you ever been subject to stammering or stuttering?

41. Did you ever as a child suffer from a bad lisp?

*42. Have you ever had the trick of excessive blinking, or of twitching your face or neck or shoulders?

43. Are you left-handed?

44. Have you ever suffered from a squint?

45. Do you often feel sick without any cause?

*46. Do you often feel sick when you ride in buses, trams, or trains?

*47. Did you ever suffer from incontinence?

48. Do your eyes often pain you?

49. Have you ever been blind or partly blind for a time?

50. Do things ever seem to swim or get misty before your eyes?

51. Do you ever see queer zigzag patterns in front of your eyes?

52. Have you ever been completely deaf for a time?

53. Have you ever been completely dumb for a time?

*54. Are you bothered a good deal by blushing?

*55. Are you bothered a good deal by sweating?

56. Do you find that you have to wear an exceptional amount of clothes to protect yourself from the cold?

*57. Are you often troubled by a trembling of the hands?

58. Have you ever seen a ghost or other vision?
59. Have you ever heard voices of people who were nowhere near you, e.g. voices that you thought might be those of dead persons or of spirits?
60. Do you think too much tobacco-smoking has harmed you?
61. Do you think drinking alcohol has harmed you?
62. Does alcohol make you quarrelsome?
63. Have you harmed yourself by habits of self-abuse?
64. Do you think you have harmed yourself by too much sexual intercourse?
65. Did you ever think you had lost your sexual powers?
66. Have you ever had the habit of taking drugs?
67. Have any members of your family had a drug habit?
68. Have any members of your family been heavy drinkers?
69. Has any member of your family committed suicide?
70. Has any member of your family been insane, apoplectic, or feeble-minded?
71. Did you have a happy childhood?
72. Were you an only child for a large part of your early life?
*73. Did you lose your father or mother when you were young?
74. Were you considered a bad child?
75. Were you a cry-baby?
*76. Were you troubled with nightmares as a child?
77. Did you ever talk in your sleep as a child?
*78. Have you ever had the habit of biting your finger-nails?
79. As a child, did you have the habit of sucking your thumb?
*80. Did you like to play alone better than with other children?
81. Were you happy between the ages of 14 and 21?
82. Did you prefer the company of adults to that of children?
*83. Did you prefer to play with tiny children rather than with those of your own age?
84. Did other children let you play with them?
85. Were you shy with other boys (or girls if you are a girl)?
*86. Were you shy with girls (if you are a boy) or with boys (if you are a girl)?
87. Did your parents treat you fairly?
88. Did you strongly dislike your father, mother, brother, or sister?
89. Did the teachers in your school generally treat you fairly?
90. Did you ever run away from home?
91. Did you ever feel a strong wish to run away from home?
92. Did you ever make love to a girl (if you are a man) or to a man or boy (if you are a girl)?

93. Have you ever fallen in love with a person of the same sex as yourself?
*94. Do you make friends easily?
*95. Do people find fault with you more than you deserve?
96. Do you get used to new places quickly?
*97. Do you try to avoid going to a strange shop or speaking to a strange person?
*98. Do you hate sleeping away from home?
99. Do you find your way about easily?
*100. Do you have difficulties over walking in the dark?
101. Do you like your work?
102. Do you find it difficult to work if there is a noise in the room?
*103. Do you prefer working alone rather than working in the same room with other people?
104. Do you find it difficult to work if someone is watching you?
105. Do your employers treat you fairly?
106. Do you get on easily with your superiors or chief?
107. Do you get on easily with your equals (fellow workers, &c.)?
108. Do you get on easily with your subordinates?
109. Do you mind if your work is a little monotonous?
*110. Do you find it a strain to have a responsible task?
111. Do you feel unduly worked up if you are suddenly sent for by your employer or chief?
112. Do you find the general conditions of your work trying owing to the stuffiness of the room, the bad lighting, &c.?
*113. Do you find it difficult to put aside a task that is really finished, or do you feel compelled to keep going over it again and again?
114. Do you vary greatly from day to day in the amount of work that you can get through?
115. Have you ever suffered from writer's cramp in either a mild or serious form, e.g. finding it difficult to hold the pen after ten or fifteen minutes' writing and being compelled either to hold it differently or to change your style of writing or to give up altogether?
116. Have you ever suffered from any other nervous complaint which interfered with your regular work?
*117. Do you usually feel too tired to carry on with your work?
118. Do you continue worrying about your work after you have left your place of business?
*119. Do you find little everyday tasks an effort or a strain?
120. Do you get tired of your work quickly?

*121. Do you get tired of amusements quickly?

122. Do your interests change quickly?

123. Have you any hobby?

124. Do you like outdoor sports?

*125. Do you find yourself unduly worrying over the little jobs of the day?

126. Do you have a good deal of difficulty in coming to a decision or making up your mind?

127. Do you usually know just what you want to do next?

128. Do useless or annoying thoughts keep coming into your mind so as to bother you?

*129. Does your attention wander so badly that you lose the thread of what you are doing?

130. Have you ever lost your memory for a time?

131. Do you consider yourself a person of exceptionally strong will?

132. Do you consider yourself a person of exceptionally weak will?

133. Are you easily led in your beliefs or actions by other people?

134. Have you ever felt as though someone was hypnotizing you or in some way forcing you to act against your will?

135. Are you ever bothered by the feeling that other persons are reading your thoughts?

136. Do you jump or start unduly at sudden or loud noises?

137. Are you afraid of fire-arms?

138. Are you afraid of knives, swords, or daggers?

139. Are you worried by the fear of being crushed in a crowd?

140. Do you sometimes think that people are watching you or following you in the street?

141. Are you worried with the idea that somebody is following you when it is dark?

142. Are you afraid of fires?

143. Are you afraid of any particular illness or illnesses, e.g. of cancer or catching infectious diseases?

*144. Do you worry unduly about illnesses, frequently imagining you are going to be ill and then afterwards finding you are perfectly all right?

145. Are you continually worried by the thought of death?

146. Are you continually worrying for fear that your friends, parents, or other persons whom you love may die?

147. Do you feel uneasy if you have to go through a tunnel or travel in the tube?

*148. Do you feel uneasy if you have to sit alone in a small room with the door shut?

*149. Do you dislike having to cross an open square or a wide street?

150. Do you feel uneasy if you have to cross a bridge over a canal or river?

151. Do you feel giddy if you look down from a moderate height, e.g. down the well of a staircase from the top landing of a three-storeyed building?

152. Do you feel that you might perhaps throw yourself down from a height; e.g. if you are standing at the top landing or looking over the parapet of a bridge?

153. Have you ever felt a strong desire to go and set fire to something?

154. Have you ever felt a strong desire to steal things?

155. Are you unduly self-conscious?

156. Are you unduly sensitive about your own peculiarities?

*157. Do you feel shy or uncomfortable with strangers?

158. Can you stand slight pain easily?

159. Can you stand the sight of blood?

160. Can you stand unpleasant or disgusting smells?

161. Can you sit still without fidgeting?

162. Are you usually cheerful or happy?

*163. Are you usually depressed or low-spirited?

164. Have you ever had a strong wish to commit suicide?

165. Do you find yourself continually changing from a cheerful mood to a depressed mood, or from a depressed mood to a cheerful mood, without any reason?

166. Do you get tired of people quickly?

167. Is it easy to make you laugh?

168. Do you think you pity yourself too much?

169. Do you find that you have a strong demand for sympathy and are always longing to confide your worries to other people?

170. Do you always want someone to look after you or advise you?

171. Do you consider yourself obstinate in the sense that you tend to do exactly the opposite to what other people suggest?

172. Are you argumentative?

173. Do you tend to take the opposite side to other people regardless of your own real views?

*174. Do you easily get irritated?

175. Are you quarrelsome?

176. Do you sometimes get violent without any real cause?

177. Is it easy to make you sulky?

178. Do you consider yourself over-affectionate or sentimental?

179. Do you easily get jealous without a cause?

180. Are you unhappy in your married life?
181. Do you feel that you are much more stupid than the people around you?
182. Do you find it difficult to lend things (books, money, &c.) to other people?
183. Have you a good sense of humour?
184. Can you take a practical joke easily?
185. Do you find it easy to forgive other people when they have annoyed you, or do you find yourself worried by thoughts of revenge?
186. Do you usually put the blame on other people when really you know you yourself are to blame?
187. Are you sometimes haunted by a fear that you might do some bodily injury to other persons, e.g. those whom you live with or love?
188. When you were younger, did your acquaintances complain that you always wanted to attract the interest or attention of other persons?
189. Are you exceptionally talkative? Do you, for example, find it quite easy to talk in public?
*190. Are you exceptionally silent, finding it difficult to talk easily with casual acquaintances?
191. Do you consider yourself unusually reticent or reserved, finding it difficult to give your confidences even to your friends?
*192. Do you feel irresistible impulses to touch things for no reason at all?
193. Do you get worried by irresistible impulses to count things?
194. Are you unduly worried over money matters?
195. Are you unduly worried over some love affair that has turned out badly?
196. Have you ever been unduly worried because you have been disappointed in love?
*197. Do you worry much about your mistakes or sins?
198. Do you find it embarrassing to undress in front of other persons?
199. Would you find it difficult to pass water in the presence of others?
200. Do you think you are puritanical or prudish?
201. Are you ever bothered by obscene thoughts or words?
202. Are you religious?
203. Do you disbelieve in all forms of religion?
204. Are you a spiritualist?

205. Are you a vegetarian, an anti-vaccinationist, an anti-smoker?
206. Do you think you are tending to become more and more absent-minded, as distinct from being practical and on the spot?
207. Do you find yourself constantly wanting to make sure that you have done something that you meant to do, nearly always finding that, as a matter of fact, you did it (e.g. getting up once or twice in the middle of the night to make sure that you have turned out the gas, &c., &c.)?
*208. Are you given to day-dreaming—brooding over recent events or living largely in a world of fancy?
209. Do you think your character or capacities have changed for the worse during recent years?
210. Do you find it much more difficult to concentrate or pay attention than you used to do?
*211. Do you ever have a queer feeling as if you were not your old self?
*212. Are you ever bothered by a feeling that things are not real?
213. Do you envy the general sense of inner well-being—the *joie de vivre*—that younger people seem to show?
214. Are you sometimes worried by the thought that you are beginning to grow old?
215. Do you sometimes feel that your whole life has been a failure?

Those who experiment with the foregoing questionnaire will find it instructive to classify and cross-classify the several questions from various aspects. (1) The answers, for example, may first be grouped according to the light they throw upon (a) the physical, (b) the intellectual, and (c) the emotional characteristics of the patient, the emotional characteristics being in turn brought together according to some classified scheme of specific instincts and general tendencies or factors (introversion, extraversion, and prevailing moods and attitudes): the list given in Chapter I will be found convenient for most practical purposes. (2) Secondly, the symptoms may be regrouped according to the particular neurotic or psychotic disorders which, in however mild a degree, they may seem to indicate, e.g. (a) neurasthenia, (b) anxiety-neurosis, (c) anxiety-hysteria (phobias), (d) compulsion-hysteria (obsessions), (e) conversion-hysteria, (f) manic-depressive or (g) schizophrenic states, and the like. (3) Thirdly, with a view to further study or ameliorative treatment, it will often be instructive to arrange the questions (if necessary a little modified) according to the particular aspects of the patient's environment with which they are nominally concerned: e.g. (a) his relations with his parents and their attitude towards him, (b) his relations towards the opposite sex, (c) his relations to business and money matters, (d) to religious problems, (e) to school, and (f) social life generally, &c.

The information so obtained cannot, of course, be taken at its face value. Answers to such questions as 'Do your employers (and the like) treat you fairly?' may not necessarily indicate real fairness or unfairness on the part of the persons named, but rather the patient's own attitude towards such persons, or possibly (if the replies are uniformly affirmative or non-committal) his tendency to repress any recognition of difficulties which all of us occasionally feel. Thus, whether the questions are put verbally or answered in writing, they must be regarded not so much as methods for obtaining objective information, but as stimuli that will arouse certain trains of association in the patient's mind and so reveal incidentally the main direction of his thoughts and problems, and the particular situations which have caused him trouble or towards which he has found some difficulty in adjusting himself.

With a little experience it will quickly be discovered that some of the questions are much more fruitful than others. One of the most extensive sets of questions compiled in the U.S.A. is that of the Thurstones (L. L. and T. G. Thurstone, 'A Neurotic Inventory', *Journ. Soc. Psych.*, i, pp. 3–30); but, on using this list with Chicago students, it was found that a shorter series of 40 was almost as trustworthy for preliminary diagnosis as the entire set of 223. As they stand, the American questionnaires and the American results are applicable only to Americans; and it would seem that the most effective type of question differs considerably with different social groups and in the hands of different examiners. Hence, each examiner must select his own abbreviated questionnaire.

Those who desire further information regarding the use and value of these and similar methods will find detailed summaries of researches and publications in P. M. Symonds's *Diagnosing Personality and Conduct* (Century Co., 1932) and D. Rapaport's *Diagnostic Psychological Testing* (Year Book Publishers, Chicago, 1946).[1]

[1] A diagnostic procedure which has attracted increasing interest during recent years is the use of the electroencephalograph. We have made tentative investigations in our laboratory, and found, like others, indications of cerebral dysrhythmia in difficult, unstable, and aggressive children. But in my view both knowledge and techniques are still too immature for the method to be of much practical service, except for the diagnosis of organic conditions. The reader may refer to the papers by Denis Hill (e.g. *Proc. Roy. Soc. Med.* xxxvii, 1944, pp. 317 f.) and to Dr. Grey Walter's fascinating volume on *The Living Brain* (1953).

STIMULUS-WORDS FOR FREE ASSOCIATION TEST

THE psychologist is frequently asked to recommend a serviceable set of words for the test of free association, which has been revived and popularized by psycho-analysts for the purpose of exploring repressed emotional complexes. Accordingly I append a list of those which I have found most useful in clinical work with delinquent or neurotic patients. It is based on an early series drawn up and standardized by Mr. R. C. Moore and myself. Our starting-point was the well-known lists of Kent and Rosanoff and of Jung respectively (loc. cit. sup., p. 338); but we quickly found that neither was altogether suited for English children, and that for different types of case different sets are needed, while the standardization of 'normal' replies—as distinct from 'abnormal' or significant—often differs appreciably with different ages, sexes, and cultural groups. (See *Journ. Exp. Ped.* i, pp. 260 et seq.)

The list is to be used as a source rather than in its entirety. For general purposes I recommend the short selection of one hundred words, marked with an asterisk, which we have kept as a standard. The headings under which the words are classified are for convenience of reference only. Since most of the words convey more than one meaning, particularly in colloquial speech, many could be .placed under more than one heading. In actual testing the order and the context should be modified to suit the special purpose in view. For the method of applying the test, see above, pp. 337 f.

1. *Senses.*	hungry	luck	wound	*worry
see (sea)	*greedy	lucky	sore	coward
look	*sweet	*nice	bleed	brave
peep	banana	*like	knife	strong
spy	milk	want	cut	bully
hear	suck	wish	pin	*alone
*smell	swallow	deserve	prick	*dark
taste		get	burn	*night
*touch			headache	nightmare
*feel	3. *Joy.*		cruel	*ghost
*tickle	happy	4. *Grief.*	unkind	bogy
*hot	glad	*cry	lost	burglar
cold	pleased	*sorry	can't	mice
smart	*fun	sad		fire
	funny	*miserable		gas
	joke	pity	5. *Fear.*	thunder
2. *Appetite.*	*laugh	*disappointed	afraid	lightning
eat	giggle	hurt	*frightened	wind
drink	thrill	pain	nervous	*noise

click
loud
shout
bawl (ball)
big
little
start
hurry
chase
hide
get off
dash
run away
run over
street
stand
fall
tumble
toss
hole
*ill
faint
giddy
choke
die
*dead
hospital
*doctor
dentist

6. Anger.

*temper
*angry
*cross
bully
brute
*fight
quarrel
row
strike
*hit
poke
bite
pinch
*hate
*kill

7. Affection.

*love
lover

fond
fair
jealous
*friend
sweetheart
darling
doll
pet
make-up

8. Sex.

*boy
*girl
*kiss
embrace
cuddle
spoon
couple
marry
wedding

9. Disgust.

dirt
mud
smut
spots
*dirty
slimy
filthy
*sticky
stuck
fat
greasy
raw
rotten
yellow
brown
*nasty
horrid
rude
shock
insect
flea
toad
worm
snake
fur
slops
spit
*sick

medicine
poison
*blood
wet
*bed
sheet
wash
water
bath
rub
towel
sponge
paper
rag
pot
pail (pale)
mug

10. Shame.

*shy
ashamed
blush
naked
undress
shirt
trousers
handkerchief
untidy
decent
manners
behave

11. Vanity.

conceited
proud
*selfish
pretty
looking
glass
toilet
clothes
*dress
cloak-room
lace
scent (sent)
powder
show off

12. Guilt.

bad
*naughty
wicked
disobedient
deceitful
*wrong
fault
innocent
coming
*catch
caught
ask
confess
own
*punish
scold
slap
whip
stick
strict
unfair
mistake

13. Delin-
quencies.

*take
*steal (steel)
*thief
*money
copper
diamond
ring
watch
*penny
sixpence
shilling
stamp
rich
poor
*dear
cheap
letter
*pictures
race
cards
bet
gamble
*lies
*story

tales
break
spill
spoilt
shop
bag
purse
box
drawers
bottom
matches
park
*bush
wall
mischief
nuisance
trick
cheeky
slang
swear
curse
*policeman
cell (sell)
court

14. Family.

*mother
*father
*brother
*sister
*baby
*aunt
grannie
*home
neighbour

15. School.

*school
*teacher
class-room
cloak-room
desk
door
*lessons
play-ground
holiday
clever
*silly
fool

*lazy
careless
*learn
*forget
*play
*work
copy
*cheat
*speak
talk
whisper
late

16. *Religion.*

*church
chapel
service
clergyman
Heaven

Sunday
Bible
prayers
hymn (him)

17. *Parts of the body.*

*body
*face
*eyes
*ears
*nose
*mouth
*lips
tooth
gum
arm
*hand
*fingers

toes
thumb
nails
breast
*leg
tail
stomach
heart
nerves
skin
flesh
hair
skull
skeleton

18. *Miscellaneous.*

*man
*woman

gentlemen
ladies
*dog
*cat
kitten
donkey
ass
bear (bare)
monkey
bull
cock
chicken
*egg
bus
engine
train
boat
sailor
French
Jew

*old
young
*toy
fairy
*dream
stunt
regular
daily
week (weak)
monthly
nine
thirteen
*name
*child's own name

APPENDIX V
SELECTED REFERENCES

In addition to the more specialized books and papers cited at the end of each chapter, the following may be helpful to those who wish to carry their reading still further.

General Psychology. Readers who are unacquainted with the elementary facts and methods of modern psychology will find brief but non-technical surveys of the subject in the following introductory volumes.

C. Burt (editor), *How the Mind Works* (2nd ed., Allen & Unwin, 1945, 8s. 6d.), or W. McDougall, *Psychology: The Study of Behaviour* (Home University Library, 2nd ed., Oxford University Press, 1952, 6s.).

The best textbooks are: R. S. Woodworth and D. G. Marquis, *Psychology: A Study of Mental Life* (12th ed., Methuen, 1952, 18s.), intended for the elementary student, and E. G. Boring, H. S. Langfeld, and H. P. Weld, *Foundations of Psychology* (Chapman & Hall, 1948, 44s.), intended for the advanced student.

For medical readers, J. S. Wilkie, *The Science of Mind and Brain* (Hutchinson, 1953, 8s. 6d.), is both up-to-date and admirably condensed, but deals more with the brain than the mind.

Child Psychology. Undoubtedly the best textbook is L. Carmichael (editor), *Manual of Child Psychology* (Chapman & Hall, 1946, £3). For the general reader a sound introduction to the psychology of education will be found in Sir Percy Nunn's *Education: Its Data and First Principles* (3rd ed., Arnold, 1945, 7s. 6d.). For a review of psychological studies of the social environment, especially in reference to its influence on the individual child, see C. Burt, *Contributions of Psychology to Social Problems* (Oxford University Press, 1953, 5s.). For excellent examples of the method of making systematic observations of children's personalities, see D. E. M. Gardner, *Testing Results in the Infant School* (Methuen, 1942) and *Long Term Results of Infant School Methods* (Methuen, 1950).

Clinical Psychology. The best general textbook is perhaps C. M. Louttit, *Clinical Psychology* (Harper & Bros., 1936, 36s.). W. McDougall, *Outline of Abnormal Psychology* (6th ed., Methuen, 1952, 21s.), gives a sounder and more eclectic review on the psychological side. N. G. Harris (editor), *Modern Trends in Psychological Medicine* (Butterworth, 1948, 50s.), is suggestive, but often at fault on the psychological side. C. P. Blacker, *Neurosis and the Mental Health Services* (Oxford University Press, 1946, 20s.), is an admirable survey of the administrative problems. D. Brower and L. E. Abt (editors), *Progress in Clinical Psychology* (Grune & Stratton, 1952) contains a valuable survey of recent work (to be brought up to date every two or three years), but is mainly restricted to American contributions.

On child guidance in this country reference should be made to Gertrude Keir, 'A History of Child Guidance' (*Brit. J. Educ. Psychol.* xxii, 1952, pp. 5–29), and to the 'Symposium on Child Guidance' by Professor Alexander Kennedy, Dr. Moodie, and others (*Brit. J. Educ. Psychol.* xxi, 1951, pp. 167 f., and subsequent issues).

Tests and Methods of Examination. F. L. Goodenough, *Mental Testing* (Staples, 1950, 42s.); C. Burt, *Handbook of Tests for Use in Schools* (2nd ed., Staples, 1948, 10s. 6d.: most of the tests are obtainable separately on cards); M. Barton Hall, *Psychiatric Examination of the School Child* (Edward Arnold, 1947, 15s.); L. M. Terman and M. A. Merrill, *Measuring Intelligence* (Harrap, 1937, 12s. 6d.); D. Wechsler, *The Measurement of Adult Intelligence* (3rd ed., 1944, $2.40); C. Burt, *The Assessment of Personality* (Maudsley Lecture, *J. Mental Science*, c, 1954, pp. 1–28); P. E. Vernon, *Personality Tests and Assessments* (Methuen, 1953, 18s.).

Mental Deficiency. A. F. Tredgold, *A Textbook of Mental Deficiency* (8th ed., Baillière, Tindall, & Cox, 1952, 37s. 6d.). A more up-to-date but less comprehensive volume is L. S. Penrose, *The Biology of Mental Defect* (Sidgwick & Jackson, 1949, 21s.). For statistics and an authoritative statement of administrative problems, see the *Report of the Mental Deficiency Committee* (H.M. Stationery Office, 1929, 5s.) and *Royal Commission on Mental Illness and Mental Deficiency: Minutes of Evidence* (H.M.S.O. 1954, 3s.).

Backwardness. C. Burt, *The Backward Child* (3rd ed., University of London Press, 1950, 25s.); F. J. Schonell, *Backwardness in the Basic Subjects* (Oliver & Boyd, 1942, 18s.).

Delinquency. C. Burt, *The Young Delinquent* (4th ed., University of London Press, 1952, 25s.); S. Glueck and E. Glueck, *Unraveling Juvenile Delinquency* (Commonwealth Fund, 1950, £2); J. D. W. Pearce, *Juvenile Delinquency: A Short Textbook on the Medical Aspects* (Cassell, 1952, 25s.). A brief and popular account will be found in H. Edelston, *The Earliest Stages of Delinquency* (E. and S. Livingstone, 1952, 10s. 6d.).

Psychoneuroses. H. C. Cameron, *The Nervous Child* (5th ed.,

Oxford University Press, 1946, 12s. 6d.); Ernest Jones, *The Treat-
ment of the Neuroses* (Ballière, Tindall, & Cox, 1920, 10s. 6d.); R. G.
Gordon (editor), *A Survey of Child Psychiatry* (Oxford University
Press, 1939, 10s. 6d.); W. Moodie, *The Doctor and the Difficult Child*
(Oxford University Press, 1947, 12s. 6d.); C. R. Rogers, *The Clinical
Treatment of the Problem Child* (Allen & Unwin, 1939, 30s.).

Factor Analysis. During the last few years psychiatrists have
become increasingly interested in the possibility of adopting the
statistical procedures that have proved so fruitful in other branches
of individual psychology. For the objective study of both classification and causation, factor analysis is perhaps the most appropriate. The main results of such investigations are reviewed in
R. B. Cattell, *Description and Measurement of Personality* (Harrap,
1946, 25s.). H. J. Eysenck, *Dimensions of Personality* (Paul, Trench,
Trubner & Co., 1948, 25s.), describes a co-operative attempt,
carried out at the Maudsley Hospital, to apply factorial procedures to
the problems of normal and neurotic personalities. An earlier study of
adult patients will be found in T. V. Moore, 'The Essential Psychoses
and their Fundamental Syndromes', *Stud. Psychol. Psychiat., Cath.
Univ. Amer.* iii, 1933, pp. 1–128, and a more recent in J. R. Witten-
born, 'Symptom Patterns in a Group of Mental Hospital Patients',
J. Consult. Psychol. xv, 1951, pp. 290–302.

Vernon, after summarizing the chief conclusions reached (*Personality Tests and Assessments,* an admirable study which has appeared
while this note was being prepared for the press), condenses the
essential results into a single diagram in which the main 'dimensions'
are very similar to those described in this volume. He adds that he
'doubts the claim (of writers like Cattell) to determine "source traits"
by factor analysis'. However, both Vernon and the writers he quotes
have been mainly interested in data obtained from adults. With
children 'source traits' are easier to determine. But I should heartily
agree that factor analysis alone cannot determine such traits, though
many factorists write as if they could. Hypotheses in regard
to 'sources' (i.e. causal factors) must in general be derived from
other modes of investigation: as I have insisted above, factor analysis
is chiefly valuable as supplying the readiest and most rigorous method
for verifying such hypotheses, not for formulating them. It is, however, likely to remain one of the most fruitful methods for theoretical
research in this field, provided it is based on adequate clinical data,
both observational and experimental.

INDEX OF NAMES

INDEX OF SUBJECTS